AF608257

Historical Essay on the Neapolitan Revolution of 1799

Vincenzo Cuoco

Historical Essay on the Neapolitan Revolution of 1799

Edited and Introduced by
Bruce Haddock and Filippo Sabetti

Translated by David Gibbons

UNIVERSITY OF TORONTO PRESS
Toronto Buffalo London

Toronto Buffalo London
www.utppublishing.com

ISBN 978-1-4426-4945-3 (cloth)

The Lorenzo Da Ponte Italian Library

Library and Archives Canada Cataloguing in Publication

Cuoco, Vincenzo, 1770–1823
[Saggio storico sulla rivoluzione napoletana del 1799. English]
Historical essay on the Neapolitan Revolution of 1799 / Vincenzo Cuoco ; edited and introduced by Bruce Haddock and Filippo Sabetti ; translated by David Gibbons.

(The Lorenzo Da Ponte Italian library)
Translation of: Saggio storico sulla rivoluzione napoletana del 1799.
Includes bibliographical references and index.
ISBN 978-1-4426-4945-3 (bound)

1. Parthenopean Republic. 2. Naples (Kingdom) – History – 1735–1816. I. Sabetti, Filippo, editor II. Haddock, Bruce, 1948–, editor III. Gibbons, David, 1969–, translator IV. Title. V. Title: Saggio storico sulla rivoluzione napoletana del 1799. English VI. Series: Lorenzo Da Ponte Italian library

DG848.38.C8513 2014 945′.707 C2014-904294-9

This book has been published under the aegis and with financial assistance of Fondazione Cassamarca, Treviso; the National Italian-American Foundation; Ministero degli Affari Esteri, Direzione Generale per la Promozione e la Cooperazione Culturale; Ministero degli Affari Esteri, Direzione Generale per i Beni e le Attività Culturali, Direzione Generale per i Beni Librari e gli Istituti Culturali, Servizio per la Promozione del Libro e della Lettura.

University of Toronto Press acknowledges the financial assistance to its publishing program of the Canada Council for the Arts and the Ontario Arts Council, an agency of the Government of Ontario.

Canada Council for the Arts Conseil des Arts du Canada

University of Toronto Press acknowledges the financial support of the Government of Canada through the Canada Book Fund for its publishing activities.

Contents

Acknowledgments

We wish to thank Professors Luigi Ballerini and Massimo Ciavolella for including this volume in the series Lorenzo Da Ponte Italian Library. We thank the two anonymous readers for the thoroughness of their responses to our project. We have responded to their comments, incorporated their suggestions and added, in some instances, our own evolving reflections stimulated by the two readers. Translation is not an easy art, and we appreciate the good and patient work to this effect by David Gibbons and the careful scrutiny of the translation by the readers. The result is a better book.

Filippo Sabetti wishes to acknowledge the support of the Social Science and Humanities Research Council of Canada (SSHRC 410–2011–0698) for research over the years in the Neapolitan section of the Biblioteca Nazionale "Vittorio Emanuele III" di Napoli and in Biblioteca Provinciale di Foggia "La Magna Capitanata." It is a pleasure to record with thanks the countless librarians and archivists there who offered guidance and assistance. Filippo Sabetti likes to remember the warm welcome to Naples of Professor Giovanni Vitolo who gave generously of his long experience and practical insight. I owe a special debt to John Marino who introduced me to the international network of scholars working on Naples, and to Antonino De Francesco, Giuseppe Galasso, Antonio Gargano, Jack Goldstone, Alfio Mastropaolo, Paul Rahe, and Anna Maria Rao for generously responding to calls for help. In Montreal, I was able to draw on the research assistance of then McGill students Eric Merkley, Cristina Ruscio, and Mohamed Sesay.

Bruce Haddock thanks Filippo Sabetti for the initial invitation to be involved in this project. The collaboration has been a thoroughly positive experience, deepening understanding and suggesting fruitful lines of enquiry. Bruce Haddock is, as ever, mindful that without the support of his wife, Sheila, and wider family, he would hardly be able to engage in sustained work of this kind.

Special thanks to Richard Ratzlaff at the University of Toronto Press for his help and encouragement throughout, to Anne Laughlin for overseeing the production of the book, to Beth McAuley and Barbara Kamienski for their copyediting, and to Judy Dunlop for the index. Vincenzo Cuoco was not always consistent in the use of names of people and places and Beth's and Barbara's sharp eyes minimized ambiguities in the text. Our original contact at the Press was Dr Ronald Martin Schoeffel. He died unexpectedly in July 2013. Ron Schoeffel was a superb editor and a gentleman and a scholar. In his long career as an editor at the University of Toronto Press, he founded the Collected Works of Erasmus project and was involved in many other projects that included the Collected Works of Northrop Frye, the Toronto Italian Studies Series, and the Collected Works of Bernard Lonergan. We especially like to remember Ron Schoeffel as an enthusiastic supporter and editor of the Da Ponte Italian Library, and dedicate this work to his memory.

Montreal, Quebec & Cardiff, Wales

Introduction: Vincenzo Cuoco and the Nature of Revolution and Constitutionalism

Bruce Haddock and Filippo Sabetti

Vincenzo Cuoco was born in the village of Civitacampomarano, near Campobasso, in 1770 to a professional family with deep roots in the Molise countryside. His origins gave little inkling of the place that he was later to occupy in the intellectual history of Naples and Italy and the study of revolutions and constitutionalism. He is one of the few Italian theorists of the French revolutionary and Napoleonic period to attain a European significance, as his work was almost immediately translated into French[1] and German. He has been hailed at various times by thinkers as diverse as Manzoni, de Sanctis, Croce, Gentile, and Gramsci; and his reformist sympathies, coupled with acute sensitivity to the decisive role of context and tradition in effective political argument, made him a key figure in the emergence of a liberal position in the Risorgimento (see Biscardi and De Francesco 2002).

Yet his role in the tradition of Italian political thought and practice only captures an aspect of his contribution to theory. Cuoco's life (1770–1823) spanned the period of revolution and reaction which was the crucible that formed the character of so much of the political thought and practice of the nineteenth century (Haddock 2005: 9–41). The contrast at the heart of his thinking is between positions that judged the adequacy of institutions in terms of the requirements of abstract theory and those that sought to understand the rationale of institutions in terms of their relations with popular attitudes, dispositions, and even prejudices; that is, the complex of mores and traditions, the habits of the heart and of the mind, that antedate a written constitution and serve as "its basis" (Cuoco *Fragments* 3 and 6, see appendix I) – what the Romans called *mos.*

1 The 1807 French edition translated by Bertrand Barère has recently been republished under the editorship of Anna Maria Rao and Maïté Bouyssy (2001) on behalf of the Istituto Italiano per gli Studi Filosofici of Naples. In their introduction, the editors explore at some length the relationship between Barère and Cuoco.

Cuoco's hostility to revolutionary and constitutional rationalism was grounded in basic assumptions about human beings and principles of organization that accepted human fallibility and the potential for error-correcting capabilities while rejecting perfectibility in human affairs and making a tabula rasa of the past. His views were influenced by the strictures of de Maistre and Burke (Burke 1967; De Maistre 1974; see also Losurdo 1989; Pocock 1982; Zapperi 1965), though he was a better historian than either of them and his theoretical reflections are accordingly more subtle. Crucially, from the perspective of the history of political ideas, he embraced the theoretical critique of political rationalism without endorsing either conservative or reactionary positions. His position, rooted in a suspicion of abstract construction, comes close to Hume and the authors of *The Federalist*, though it is doubtful that he knew of them. Cuoco deployed anti-rationalist arguments in defence of liberal constitutionalism; he saw the chief task of institutional arrangements not so much to prevent individuals from doing evil but to reacquaint them with the good even when advancing their self-interest (Cuoco *Fragment* 6, see appendix I; cf. *The Federalist* No. 55). For these reasons, while he was aware of the gulf that separated elite and popular views, he contended throughout his career that an effective political culture and resulting public spirit had necessarily to accommodate both perspectives.

The Making of a Theorist

Cuoco moved to Naples in 1787 to study law. It was an exciting time to be in Naples as relations between Enlightenment figures and the monarchy seemed to confirm Gaetano Filangieri's hope that, finally, philosophy was coming to the aid of government in moving society forward. But the self-description we have of Cuoco in his early years in Naples (Cuoco cited in Villani [1966] 2004: 6–7) and the less-than-flattering impression of his work habits by a standard bearer of Neapolitan Enlightenment, Giuseppe Maria Galanti (in De Francesco 1997: 9–13) suggest Cuoco was more interested in exploring the pleasures of life than in following public affairs in Naples and beyond. As late as 1792, Cuoco continued to practise law and did not take part in any clandestine activity or Jacobin club.

He found the vocation of political theorist forced upon him by circumstances. As he noted in a letter to a friend published in the preface of the first edition of the *Historical Essay* and reprinted in the second edition:

> Is it not strange how the world goes? The king of Naples declares war on the French, and is defeated. The French conquer his kingdom, and then abandon it. The king returns, and proclaims it a capital offense to have loved one's country in the time when it no longer belonged to him. All this happened without my having the slightest part in it, without even having predicted it. But all this also meant that I was exiled, that I came to Milan, where certainly, had my life followed its ordinary course, I was not destined to come, and where, as a result of having nothing else to do, I became an author. (11)

He turned to the study of the Neapolitan Revolution "to alleviate the leisure and tedium of exile."

Even a casual reading of the *Historical Essay* suggests that, by the early 1800s, he had read widely, with interests beyond the fields of history, political theory, and jurisprudence with which he is most closely associated (e.g., Battaglia 1925; Carpi 1992: 56–75; De Francesco 1997; and Tessitore [1970] 1995). Trained as a lawyer, he tended from the earliest years of his studies to focus on the detailed treatment of ideas in context, always with an eye on practical opportunities for reform and improvement. He put his professional expertise at the service of communities in their claim to common property resources on feudal land and in their support for reforestation projects, adding to his practical knowledge of the complexity of feudal land-holding and agricultural practices in the Kingdom of Naples. He felt closest to theorists such as Machiavelli and Vico, who in different ways set ideas and practices in a developmental frame of reference (see Di Maso 2005; Haddock 1986; Marshall 2010: 28–9).

His collected work[2] will take up seven volumes and more than two thousand pages. They show mature powers of observation and reflection covering a wide variety of topics from statistics and public administration to education and literature. There are now four different teams of researchers – one each in Campobasso, Milan, Naples, and Pisa – mining Cuoco's wide-ranging thought and insights (Tessitore 2008; see also Dainotto 2011; and Themelly 1990). A research centre in Campobasso is

2 A list of the principal editions of his work can be found in the References.

devoted to the study of Cuoco's life and thought and, since 2003, has been publishing an annual review, *Annali Cuochiani,* exploring Cuoco's ideas and times.

The movement of ideas that formed the Neapolitan Enlightenment and shaped Cuoco's repertoire of knowledge was far from being insular (Robertson 2005; Sabetti 2012). Leading French ideas were avidly discussed. Cuoco's preference, however, was always for theories that took historical context and tradition seriously. He preferred Montesquieu and De Lolme to Voltaire, Diderot, or Condorcet, and remained suspicious of elite-driven programs of reform, whether in the guise of enlightened despotism or republican theory. If he is sometimes portrayed as a critic of Enlightenment constitutionalism, we must remember that it is the rationalist and perfectionist strand that he has in mind (see Ferrone 2012: 153–75). Prospects for lasting improvement, he always argued, are best guaranteed through engagement with rich local cultures. His early work with Giuseppe Maria Galanti taught him to take seriously the value of detailed empirical research in any discussion of practical proposals. This experience would later become an article of faith in Cuoco's thinking and would shape his negative reactions to the republican constitutional design of 1799 presented in the *Fragments.* Wholesale reform imposed from a distant capital and based on assumptions of human perfectibility, he predicted, would have incalculable negative consequences in local contexts, would generate counter-intentional results, and would inadvertently undermine the smooth functioning of public affairs and social and economic life.

Working as a young lawyer in Naples, he found himself associating with men whose ideas had been formed in the great reform movement of the eighteenth century. In Naples a generation of students like Galanti had been introduced to the practical ideas of the Enlightenment through the teaching and writing of Antonio Genovesi. Identification with the Enlightenment, of course, as we have noted above, could not be viewed as the adoption of a unitary position. What was shared, however, was the assumption that moral and political problems could be resolved if rigorous scientific methods were applied to the study of society. Such ideas informed the cult of enlightened despotism: ignorance and ill will were seen as the principal obstacles to reform, and these could be most readily overcome if a ruler used his considerable power of direction and persuasion to focus the intellectual resources of a society on the resolution of specific practical problems. In practice, monarchs would only follow the recommendations of reformers if their own interests could be most effectively advanced in this way. But, more importantly, monarchs themselves would find their own actions constrained by the entrenched privileges of the Church and the aristocracy.

As recently as 1701, the Neapolitan nobility had risen in open rebellion against the Crown in defense of inherited position; and the Church had shown little or no inclination to slacken its hold on the structure of society. Pietro Giannone had estimated in 1723, in his classic *Istoria civile del regno di Napoli,* that the Church owned four-fifths of the wealth of Naples (see Giannone 1978). Giannone had a particular axe to grind against the Church and did not work with the sources. Thus his estimates are not reliable. But when these limitations are duly taken into account, there is something to his argument. In 1786, of approximately 2,000 communities (*universitates*), 384 were Crown demesnes, with a population of slightly more than a million, while 1,616 were feudal demesnes, with more than 3 million inhabitants (data from Bianchini [1839] 1983, reported in Rao 2012b: 228; see also Colletta [1838] 1858: 1, 134–6). At the same time, modern historians are discovering that the populations in feudal dominions were far from being "sacks of potatoes" or hapless victims of circumstances. Local communities used multiple strategies, including "adversarial literacy" (Castiglione 2005) to minimize exposures to systems of rule and taxation rigged against them. Various forms of resistance emerged, which in time became ways of coping with the contingencies of life (e.g., Cerere 2011; Musi 2007a, 2007b). Like the Roman and Venetian countryside of roughly the same time (Castiglione 2005; Muir 2000), the Neapolitan countryside was often the site of contestation between, on one hand, great aristocratic families and the expanding administration of the kingdom and, on the other, marginalized villages using local oral tradition and local charters as well as ideas and texts exported from outside to defend themselves; often the same dynamics pitted neighbouring villages against one another (e.g., Astarita 1992, 1999; Cerere 2011; Dandalet and Marino 2007: 3–10; Marino 2007: 407–29; Spagnoletti 1994). John Marino has shown that "Naples had a strong tradition of decentralized, neighbor-based political organizations, both noble and popular, through the Middle Ages" and that the Neapolitans succeeded in constructing a civic identity in the face of Spanish domination in the sixteenth and seventeenth centuries (Marino 2011: 3; see also Villari 2012). Research on the governance of natural resources and local undertakings has brought to light a relatively high level of local self-governance in the kingdom until the eighteenth century (Bulgarelli 2011; see also Alianelli 1873: 12–17). Thus there was something in Cuoco's calling up the practice of local parliaments as a way of thinking about another way of doing constitutional choice in Naples, one that drew on the practical experience extending from the bottom up rather than imposed by force or without consent from the top down and modelled on the French constitution of Year III (22 August 1795) (Cuoco *Fragment* 1, see appendix I; see also Romano 1904: 67–8).

Still, in the 1790s, the Kingdom of Naples was a feudal society, with the nobility and the Church enjoying considerable rights, including exemption from taxation and veto powers in public affairs. It was extraordinarily difficult for one single set of national leaders or enlightened despots to affect large-scale positive changes. In the face of concerted opposition from entrenched interests, the plans of reformers could make little impact on society (with or without the support of the Crown). With their practical ambitions frustrated, reformers could see little hope for the future other than in a radical, wholesale renovation of the entire fabric of society. In these circumstances, the appeal of the French Revolution became irresistible, tending also to disassociate the love of country from the love of the king. A case in point is Pietro Colletta (1775–1831),[3] a Neapolitan general and historian, who took part in the campaign against the French in 1798; by 1799, his love of country led him to adhere to the republic (Colletta [1838] 1858: I, bk. III, chaps. 2 and 3; see also Rao 1986; Villani 1976: x; cf. Elliott 2012: 62–3).

Cuoco was acutely aware of the deadening effect of the feudal heritage on the political, economic, and social development of the Kingdom of Naples. But he could never view Jacobinism as other than an excessively abstract and alien ideology. In this, he was out of line with most of his fellow intellectuals. As early as 1792, we see Masonic lodges transformed into Jacobin clubs (e.g., Galasso 1989: 509–48; Giarrizzo 1994: chap. 14; Nicolini 1939; Petraccone 1984). With the advance of the French revolutionary armies through Italy in the later 1790s, hopes were raised for the formation of a republic on the French model (e.g., Davis 2006: 71–93; for a general overview, Cantimori 1956; De Felice 1990).

---

3 Colletta's life, complex character, and devotion to liberty are ably sketched by John Davis in his introduction to the 2009 reprint of Colletta's two-volume account of *The History of the Kingdom of Naples* (Davis 2009: ix–xxxiii).

What Kind of Revolution Was the Neapolitan Revolution?

Successive generations of scholars have clarified what events since the seventeenth century can be considered revolutions, why they happened, and what their outcomes have been. There is a general agreement in the literature that the defining feature of social and political revolutions in Europe and Asia is a sharp structural and ideological break from the previous regime. The disagreement is in identifying the causes. The particularities of each revolution have played a part in fostering different interpretations of why revolutions happen and with what results. Equally, variations in interpretation are also due to the particular frameworks of analysis that inform research. As a result, we now have many different explanatory currents that focus on the following: class-based conflict and subsequent modifications; the inability of state officials to meet societal demands (the classic modernization thesis); the imbalance between the institutions and the environment that cannot be overcome (demography); and, more recently still, on state modernization itself creating enough societal expectations as necessary steps leading to revolution (for a review of the literature, see Goldstone 2008; Pincus 2009; Skocpol 1979). The tendency to identify a single factor that explains the occurrence of revolution is difficult to resist. It often comes with the recognition that "the analytical language [of a particular researcher] has been used to disguise political preferences" (Pincus 2009: 32). Work on "dynamics of contention" has tended to reject any kind of single-factor theory of revolution to advance the argument that large-scale social outcomes are the result of the concatenation of a diverse range of mechanisms and processes as well as time and place contingencies (McAdam, Tarrow, and Tilly 2001).

The Neapolitan Revolution of 1799 and surrounding events have generated a sizeable literature, highlighting the concatenation of mechanisms and processes that led to the events of 1799. Even though the restored Bourbon king ordered the destruction of documentary evidence that sent many patriots to the scaffold, not all archival sources were destroyed and many others remain untouched (Palmieri 1998). The anniversary celebrations in 1899 and 1999 spurred new research. Working from different perspectives and pursuing different interests, historians have displayed considerable ingenuity in tapping these sources and reinterpreting earlier conclusions (e.g., Cestaro 2002; Pedio 1974, 1978). Historians like Anna Maria Rao and Pasquale Villani have dedicated a large portion of their professional lives to researching the background, context, personalities, and groups involved in the Neapolitan Revolution (e.g., Rao 1999, 2002; Rao and Villani 1995; see also Davis 2006). As a result, we now have more information on the events and the dynamics of the time than what was available to the leading participants themselves. This richness of documentation has lent more nuanced findings to the concatenation of events and interpretations of the revolution.

Cuoco's *Historical Essay* points to the richly complex chain of events that locked contrasting personalities in the making and unmaking of the revolution in 1799. Interspersed in the narrative of the first five chapters are sufficient details for the reader to gain an understanding of the domestic and international context.

The creation of the kingdom of Two Sicilies in 1734 marked a turning point in the history of the South. It signified the union of the Crowns of Naples and Sicily under an independent dynastic monarchy ruled by a branch of the Spanish Bourbon. It also generated considerable expectations about economic and political reform and progress. The monarchy's policies, including efforts to modernize and professionalize the army by ending the monopoly of the nobility over commissioned officers, were not free of opposition and the implementation was not without difficulty. But there was little doubt that a new era seems to have set in as succeeding rulers – Charles III, and Ferdinand IV and his Austrian queen Maria Carolina – seemed open to, and cautiously supportive of, Enlightenment and progress. The French Revolution, the deposition and trial of Louis XVI, the guillotine of the king and the queen (a sister of Maria Carolina of Naples), the increasingly aggressive gunboat diplomacy of the new French government in the Mediterranean, and the various efforts to promote and spread Jacobin ideas among intellectuals and nobles in Naples – all combined to make the Neapolitan king and his queen fierce adversaries of the new political order in France. This hostility, fuelled by fear of Jacobin sympathy in Naples, led to several unwise government actions at home and abroad. The fate of the king and his court was sealed when the French army, which had already reached the Papal States, marched towards Naples in January 1799.

Cuoco recounts in vivid detail what happened with the fall of the monarchy in 1799. Three unique features make the Neapolitan Revolution stand out in a comparative perspective.

First, the creation of the republic in 1799 was possible only by the advance of foreign arms (see also De Francesco 2000; Pagden 1994: 139–40). It is generally accepted that the revolution owed less to popular initiative than to French military supremacy. Indeed, we have the paradoxical spectacle of a revolution that was designed to advance the lot of the common people being greeted by either indifference or outright hostility. Indifference or hostility stood in sharp contrast with the good intentions of the revolutionaries. In just a few months of rule, the revolutionaries legislated all sorts of positive changes aimed at transforming the entire face of the South. Cuoco captures well this rush to legislate, and one modern analyst who has examined the various parliamentary bills describes the work as "immense" (De Francesco 2011: 24). Much of the legislative program could not be implemented. Time was not on the side of the revolutionaries. The republic lasted only as long as the French were able to afford military protection: a mere five months.

Second, the armies of the revolution were defeated by popular resistance for the first time (e.g., Davis 1991, 2009: 2, 2006:119; see also chap. XXXV). The inchoate popular resistance was given organizational shape and direction through the efforts and leadership of Cardinal Fabrizio Ruffo. He landed in Calabria in February 1799 to organize the antirepublican movement, which became known by the pejorative name of *sanfedismo*. Cuoco and Colletta, like many other analysts since then, have tended to paint Cardinal Ruffo in the most negative of terms; they have downplayed the challenges and difficulties Ruffo faced in confronting organized resistance in the context of different and conflicting pressures coming from several sources. Ruffo's success was not automatic, and historian John Davis has recently drawn attention to Ruffo's predicament.

> [Ruffo] saw himself in the midst of two wars. One was being fought between the barons and *ceto medio*, whom the Republic had divided into opposing factions, or whose pre-existing factional alliances had regrouped along the division between royalists and republicans. The other was the war being fought by the people, and Ruffo agreed that they suffered intolerable burdens (*soverchi aggravi*). But these burdens could not be lessened without alienating the landowners and provoking a social war that could not be controlled. (Davis 2006: 119)

That Ruffo succeeded is a tribute to his skills.

By way of contrast, the creation of "the patriotic salons," discussed by Cuoco in chapter XL, was not enough to generate widespread public support for the revolutionary government. When the French army was forced to withdraw, the "patriots" were swept aside. A brutal reaction, led by leaders of the Church and nobility and abetted by British naval power, restored the Bourbon monarchy to the throne. The fierce traditionalism of the peasants and the *lazzaroni* of Naples had been exploited to rid the Kingdom of Naples of the only group that had shown any concern for improving the way of life of the lower orders of society (see Salvadori and Tranfaglia 1984; Davis 2006: 107–26). A generation of intellectuals was killed, imprisoned or exiled.[4]

Finally, this very failure and disaster made the Neapolitan Revolution stand out in other ways. One was suggested by Benedetto Croce. He acknowledged "the superficiality of the revolutionary patriots," "their innocent confidence in the redemptive powers of France," "their errors of judgment, the childishness of some of their actions, and the weaknesses of some of their leaders." But he put more emphasis on their "concrete accomplishments" and "their truly generous faith" this way:

> When I think of the exiles from Calabria, Abruzzo, Basilicata, Apulia, and Naples who discussed burning political problems in the newspapers, pamphlets, and flyers circulating in the Cisalpine Republic; who joined the newly formed Italian legions or signed up with the French or some local democratic government; when I read documents which testify to the friendships which they struck up with Lombards, Piedmontese, Ligurians, and Venetians, then I say to myself: "Here's the birth of modern Italy, the new Italy, our Italy." (Croce [1925] 1970: 201)

For Croce, the human tragedy and the political disaster of revolution were on the path of progress and human liberty.

The work of Cuoco on the revolution added light and instruction in another way. Despite his reservations about Jacobin ideas, he had participated in the revolution alongside the republicans. Following the reaction, he found himself briefly imprisoned and finally condemned to exile. Unexpected circumstances provided the conditions for Cuoco to distill the essential political lessons of the abortive revolution. Paul Rahe's recent reflections about political failure put Cuoco's lessons in a broad comparative context and are worth quoting at some length:

> There is not much to be said for political failure, but it does have one compensation. With some frequency, it provides not only occasion for reflection but the requisite time. Had he succeeded as a general, Thucydides would never have managed to compose his history of the Peloponnesian War. Had

4 A list of those who died on the scaffold can be found in appendix II.

> the Medici retained Niccolò Machiavelli in his post as secretary of the Second Chancery in Florence, he would never have written *The Prince* and his *Discourses on Livy*. Had civil war not broken out in England, Thomas Hobbes would not have produced his *Leviathan*. And had Alexis de Tocqueville's attempt to frame a practicable constitution for the Second Republic in France proven effectual and had its second President not mounted a coup against the regime Tocqueville served as Foreign Secretary, the latter would not have resigned his post, abandoned the political arena, and penned his *Ancien Régime and the Revolution*. In truth, had none of these disasters taken place, we, the intellectual heirs of these philosophical historians and political theorists, would have been much the poorer. (Rahe 2012: 1–2)

Cuoco's *Historical Essay* was first published in Milan in 1801, alongside the *Fragments*. He published a second edition in 1806, pruning rhetorical passages, reworking the narrative to make it more detached in light of subsequent events on the peninsula, thereby giving his account more credibility, persuasiveness, and staying power (see Parigi 1977; Tessitore cited in Villani [1966] 2004: 14–22). It was, in fact, the second edition that we publish that established the terms of reference through which a generation of theorists would interpret the revolution; but, more importantly, it introduced the Italian reading public to the wider issues that dominated political discussion in the post-revolutionary period (Haddock 2000: 11–49).[5]

Lessons

The influence of the *Saggio storico* extends far beyond Cuoco's generation or the problems they confronted. While his impact on the Risorgimento was pervasive, he continued to be widely read and admired in the twentieth century by theorists of widely differing political views. From Gentile on the right, through de Ruggiero and Croce, to Gramsci on the left, Cuoco has been seen as a seminal source of ideas. In general terms his appeal is undoubtedly in his acute awareness of a distinctively Italian political tradition, with roots in history and jurisprudence rather than

5 For quite some time, the first edition was unavailable or difficult to consult. This problem has been remedied through the efforts of Tessitore (1988) and De Francesco (1998), while acknowledging the importance that the revised 1806 edition occupies. De Francesco is now republishing an annotated version of the 1801 edition.

mathematics, logic, and the natural sciences. Yet, on certain crucial substantive issues, too, his ideas can be seen to have established the terms of reference for subsequent commentators. Croce, for example, in his influential *History of the Kingdom of Naples*, endorsed not only the broad lines of Cuoco's interpretation of the Neapolitan Revolution but used his contrast between the political culture of an intellectual elite and the traditional assumptions of popular culture as a key to the understanding of the lack of political, social, and economic development in the south (Croce [1925] 1970; Croce's view is challenged in Davis 2006).

Gramsci, too, went back to Cuoco for a distinction that has been widely used in recent interpretations of Italian political history. Cuoco described the events of the Neapolitan Revolution as a "passive revolution" (i.e., an attempt by an elite to impose a set of radical changes upon a society in the face of popular attachment to the status quo). Gramsci used a modified version of Cuoco's idea to explain the course of the Risorgimento, in particular, the view that moderates were able to exploit the lack of effective political leadership on the part of radicals in order to establish a unified state on terms that served their interests (Gramsci 1966). And the idea has been taken up to explain not only the implicitly authoritarian character of the liberal regime but also the specific direction of the so-called fascist revolution. Gramsci's stress on the importance of cultural hegemony in a revolutionary movement can be read as a response to the problems that Cuoco had seen as necessarily involved in any attempt to impose revolution from above.

Cuoco's *Historical Essay* is thus a seminal work that has suffered unjustified neglect, especially in the English-speaking world. Writing a widely read survey of modern Western political thought in the 1970s, Dante Germino observed that Cuoco "deserves to be rescued from the neglect he has suffered everywhere outside Italy" (1972: 232). Our concern with this translation of the text is to redress the balance, at least in a preliminary fashion. Students of revolution, constitutional politics, moderation, and democratic pragmatism can see for themselves the extent to which Cuoco's reflections and insights lend support, give historical and analytical depth to, and even extend their own inquiries (e.g., Aligica and Boettke 2009; Craiutu 2012; Knight and Johnson 2011; Pincus 2009; Rahe 2009; cf. V. Ostrom 2007).

The book opens with a declaration that sets the tone for the entire text. Cuoco declares that he has undertaken "to write the history of a revolution which intended to bring about the happiness of a nation, but in fact caused its ruin" (chap. I: 15). What we are presented with is not a sweeping condemnation of the ideas, ambitions, and motives of the revolutionaries (such as we find in Burke or de Maistre) but an analysis of the way noble ideals were undermined simply because they were formulated without regard for the constraints that established manners and customs imposed on the scope for political change. The mood is that of remorse or regret rather than contempt; and the intention is to glean such lessons from the disaster as would enable future plans for institutional reform to be set upon a secure foundation.

Cuoco's distance from Burke is especially evident in his treatment of the established Bourbon regime. Where Burke had been concerned to minimize the abuses of the ancien régime in order to heighten the absurdity of revolutionary ideas, Cuoco painted a picture of a Kingdom of Naples desperately in need of reform. Everything from the administrative apparatus of the kingdom, through the system of landholding, to the manners and habits of the leading classes, is found wanting. In the administration, for example, though everything was notionally centralized, there was no effective Council of State to coordinate the activities of the different ministries. What we have, in effect, is a system whereby ministers would be in competition with each other for the ear of the king or (as was more often the case in Naples at this time) the queen. The Crown had debilitated the public spirit of the nation by concentrating more and more functions at the centre; yet though everything depended on the government, the government in fact had neither the knowledge nor the resources to take effective action (see chap. VII).

In the financial field, too, the needs of the court had grown while the nation's ability to sustain a high level of taxation had diminished. From this vicious circle there seemed to be no escape. As the crisis deepened, the court had recourse to ever more desperate measures, culminating in the resort to worthless paper credit that simply served to undermine business confidence still further. The only group to do well out of the situation were lawyers, described by Cuoco as "wasps" living off the honest endeavours of ordinary citizens (chap. IX: 57). On top of these structural factors, we have the personalities of the king and queen themselves – the king weak and indolent, the queen a radical anti-Jacobin unable to distinguish her personal likes and dislikes from matters of state. In Cuoco's account, the queen and the English-born minister, Acton, are very much the villains of the piece. It was at their bidding that a *Giunta di Stato* (Commission of Inquiry) was established, charged with investigating such shocking crimes as discussing the political ideas emanating from France (chap. VI).

Cuoco describes the functioning of this political inquisition in some detail – the castles and prisons full of victims whose only crimes were the political opinions they were suspected of entertaining. "Almost all of them," he says, "emerged free as innocent men four years later" as if nothing had happened (chap. VI: 34). But the effect of the persecution took its toll on the political culture of the kingdom: "... people will never understand, and never follow philosophers. But if you persecute opinions, these turn into emotions. Emotions produce enthusiasm; and enthusiasm is communicated. Those who are persecuted become hostile, so too those who fear persecution, and the neutral man who condemns it. Ultimately, the persecuted opinion becomes widespread and triumphant" (chap. VI: 32).

The attempt to eradicate heterodox political ideas through persecution had thus proved to be counterproductive. The use of violence as a means of controlling ideas had merely served to mould a host of disparate opinions into a cohesive political movement. In taking this course of action, the Bourbons of Naples had repeated the mistake of the other royal houses of Europe. By attributing overriding importance to the ideas of revolutionaries, the sovereigns of Europe had exposed themselves to a ferment which (since it had its roots in opinion) would be satisfied by nothing less than the wholesale reconstruction of the political order. Cuoco also noted the prudent response shown at the time of the American Revolution. The ideas of the American revolutionaries had been very similar to those of the French; and yet the "court of Naples had publicly applauded" that revolution (chap. VII: 39). No one, it seems, "had been afraid that the Neapolitans might want to imitate the revolutionaries of Virginia" (chap. VII: 39). The danger to the sovereigns had simply grown in proportion to their fears, for "a revolution is defeated by the one who fears it least" (chap. VII: 43).Once the first steps had been taken in France in 1789, the revolution seemed to gather a momentum of its own. The inexorable progression from liberal, through democratic, to authoritarian forms of government in the years between 1789 and 1793 was interpreted, by both supporters and opponents of the regime alike, as a practical illustration of the implications of the ideas that had first inspired the events of 1789. But, says Cuoco, this is a misconception, and one which had fateful consequences for the political stability of Europe. "The French deluded themselves over the nature of their revolution, and believed that the effect of the political circumstances in which their nation found itself, was caused by philosophy itself" (chap. VII: 39).

France in the ancien régime had appeared to be an absolute monarchy, with the central power imposing order and coherence on the subordinate functions of government. In reality, however, French society was a tissue of abuses and contradictions, the most glaring example being the conflict between monarchy and aristocracy that had dominated political life for some 300 years. A plausible ideology had effectively bottled things up by presenting the society as if its various institutions and practices were so bound up with one another that amendment of one could not be undertaken without full consideration of the consequences for society as a whole. As abuses continued to grow in number and increase in range, so the principles that justified reform became more abstract. In trying to fashion an abstract ideology that would embrace a whole series of practical issues, the revolutionaries were simply responding in kind to royalist ideology. "The French," Cuoco writes, "were forced to deduce their principles from the most abstract metaphysics, and fell into the error to which men who follow abstract ideas are excessively prone – that is, to confuse their own ideas with the laws of nature. They believed that everything they had done or wanted to do was the duty and right of all men" (chap. VII: 41).

Here, in a nutshell, we have it. By divorcing ideas from the real needs of society, both royalists and revolutionaries had cut themselves off from any prospect of improving (or even understanding) the society they were trying to mould. And while it had become customary to pour scorn on the naïve rationalism of the Jacobins, Cuoco insists that the particular cast of revolutionary ideology was a natural product of the French political tradition.

Cuoco offers us a tantalizing sketch of what would later be described as "path-dependency" in political science. His focus is very much on the terms of reference that shape everyday engagement with the social and political world. Modern political theorists associate the view with Alexis de Tocqueville's influential *Ancien Régime and the French Revolution*, written in the 1850s, where the logic of centralized control and reform imposes a similar style of governance on both despots and revolutionaries, each bent on orchestrating their programs from the centre, often with little understanding of the consequences that might distort the impact of reforms in practice (Tocqueville 2008).

How and why centralized regimes emerged in early modern European history is a complex story in itself, triggered by security issues both domestically and internationally. A clear implication, however, in both Cuoco and Tocqueville, is that the conventional wisdom at the centre of political regimes represents a very narrow world of ideas. What is taken for enlightenment is very much elite driven, insensitive to context and tradition. Experience of centralized government engenders complex accommodation that may be more or less efficient. Where established governmental practice has been customarily more devolved, elite-driven reform may well become chronically dysfunctional at the local level, despite the best of intentions.

Cuoco presses the point further, focusing specifically on the cultural gulf that separates elites from the wider population. The French Revolution had been understood by only a few, fewer still actually approved of it, and hardly anyone wanted to see it imitated; but even if a revolution on the French model had been deemed desirable, it would still have been fruitless because "no revolution is possible without the people, and the people are not moved by ratiocination but by need" (chap. VII: 42). The needs of the Neapolitan people were so different from the French that the particular arguments advanced by the revolutionaries seemed abstruse, wild, and incomprehensible. As regards the intellectuals, Cuoco claims that "the majority of them would never have approved of the French revolutionaries' theories" (chap. VII: 42). The Italian tradition in moral and political thought had followed quite a different path (see also Sabetti 2011a). The trend had been to relate consideration of political ideas to close study of historical circumstances. A lead had been given by Machiavelli, Gravina, and Vico; and anyone who had profited from their works would find themselves estranged from both the theory and practice of the French revolutionaries (see chap. VII).

Given the striking divide between French and Italian political traditions, how could it come about that a generation of reformist intellectuals should transform themselves into Jacobin revolutionaries? Cuoco's answer is simple.

The first mistake had been to try to suppress ideas rather than to put them to the test of experience. Cuoco here recalled how an old diplomat, the marquis Gallo, responded when he saw the list of conspirators that had been drawn up. He suggested to the king that they be sent to France for he predicted, "if they are Jacobins, ... they will come back royalists" (chap. VII: 43). The second was to identify the fortune of the Bourbon rulers of Naples too directly with that of the ancien régime in France. The combined effect was that theoretical differences on specific points, or interest in particular practical proposals that had been advanced in France, would be interpreted as evidence of total rejection of Bourbon rule in Naples in the name of Jacobin principles. In truth,

Neapolitan intellectuals became "Jacobins" only because they recognized that little could be expected in the way of concrete reform from a timorous and obscurantist monarchy. When intellectuals welcomed the invading French army as the harbinger of political change, they had merely accepted the characterization of events that their own ruling house had foisted upon them.

The impact of the new Jacobin principles on the political life of the kingdom, however, was doubly unfortunate. In the first place, the ideas themselves had little to recommend them. A political theory that always appealed to abstract principles in the evaluation of institutions and practices could never be other than destructive (e.g., Klosko 2003). The view that wisdom could be acquired through experience was anathema to the man of "principle." He could not accept that political judgment was a matter of striking a fine balance between the theoretical desirability of certain reforms and the entrenched habits and customs that would inevitably modify whatever proposal a philosopher had dreamed up. In the last resort, the ideologist would lose patience with the world. If practical men refused to listen to the voice of "reason," then it would behoove men who could set things aright to compel them to come to their senses. The practical implication of an abstract political theory (as the French Revolution had illustrated so vividly) was terror.

These sinister implications did not have time to work themselves out in the Neapolitan Revolution. The fledgling republic, hampered as it was by the adoption of an untenable ideology, was further constrained by the alien origin of the newly dominant ideas. Access to French ideas had only ever been open to an intellectual elite. Instead of hailing the rejection of tyranny, the common people could only deplore the destruction of a distinctive way of life. The "patriots" had been relatively sanguine about their task: because their innovations had been designed to improve the lot of the common people, they had assumed that they would be greeted with enthusiasm. They found to their cost, however, that "to devise plans for a republican constitution is not the same thing as to establish a republic" (chap. XVI: 88). The idea that government should express the public will is itself noble; but in the Neapolitan context, where political life was still identified in the popular mind with royal discretion, the state of popular culture made talk of a "public will" purely fanciful. As Cuoco put the point, "the only way to promote freedom is by forming free men" (chap. XVI: 88; see also Romano 1904: 67–9). The principal obstacle to such an achievement was popular culture itself – the traditional picture of public life as an elaborate network of personal relationships, the customs and prejudices that supported the privileges of the nobility and clergy; and these obstacles to change would only be overcome if one had first taken the trouble to understand precisely how the different aspects of a culture were mutually supported in a complex way of life. To unlock the unused capacity of ordinary people calls for a revolution of the mind: "when a citizen no longer looks to earn his living from holding position; when serving one's country ceases to be equated with making one's fortune as is currently believed, you will have destroyed three-quarters of dangerous ambition" (Cuoco *Fragment* 6: 267–72, in appendix I). The abstract character of Jacobin thought, however, encouraged impatience. Traditional culture, in the Jacobin scheme of things, was simply a tissue of errors and superstitions. The only possible response to established institutions that failed to conform to the tenets of "reason" was to reject them. But in reacting in this rather crude way, the Jacobins had in effect cut themselves off from any real contact with the society they were striving to transform. Far from assisting the process of cultural transformation, they had merely accentuated the gulf that separated them from popular culture.

Here we come to the crux of the dilemma facing the Jacobins. Political leadership in the context of a spontaneous popular revolution would have been relatively straightforward. Enthusiasm would need to be harnessed, various initiatives would need to be coordinated, but the general objectives of the revolution would be shared by both the leaders and the led. No such cultural harmony existed at Naples. The success of the revolution depended upon the skill and efficiency with which a small elite could impose its will upon a scarcely comprehending populace. But the abstract philosophy that had sustained revolutionary ideology had little to say about purely tactical matters. The principal task in any "passive revolution," according to Cuoco, should always be the moulding of "popular opinion" (chap. XVI: 91). Yet in reality the differences between the "patriots" and the populace were so vast – in terms of ideas, customs, manners, and even languages – as to vitiate even the most basic communication. Publishing a newspaper in Neapolitan was not enough. The admiration for foreign ideas and customs, which had been such a marked feature of Neapolitan intellectual culture throughout the eighteenth century, could now be seen as "the greatest obstacle to the establishment of liberty" (chap. XVI: 91). In terms of everyday engagement, the Neapolitan nation was effectively divided into two peoples, separated by two centuries in terms of their levels of cultural development. The cultivated class had nurtured itself upon foreign models. Those who had remained faithful to Neapolitan traditions (the vast mass of the population) were entirely ignorant of modern culture. Thus we find that "the culture of the few had not benefited the nation as a whole," while the populace "virtually despised a culture that was not beneficial to it and which it did not understand" (chap. XVI: 91).

In Cuoco's interpretation, all the problems of the revolution can be traced back to this basic cultural divide. It was all very well to talk of a revolution in the interest of the people; but the lack of a common political culture meant that individuals interpreted that interest in their own way, leaving the *patria* a prey to ambition, indifference, and malice. It was old-fashioned patriotic sentiment that had sustained the French revolutionary armies, not an abstract political ideology. Yet "far from having this national unity, the Neapolitan nation could be seen as divided into many different ones" (chap. XVI: 92). The kingdom had embraced a bewildering variety of cultures; and the feudal system, which had held the balance between anarchy and barbarism for centuries, had merely reflected the diversity of the established communities. The very first task of the revolutionaries should have been to fashion a coherent political culture out of these unlikely materials. Little could be done to make the doctrine of natural rights a political reality until the people themselves had come to associate their concrete interests with the new political creed. Everything should have been so contrived as to minimize the formal novelty of the new regime; and this could be achieved only by attending to the people's needs, not by trying to secure their rights.

What happened, however, was that the revolutionaries remained faithful to their ideas. If theoretical analysis had shown that established institutions were inadequate, then it behooved them to fashion the social and political world anew. But the commitment to change everything (Cuoco calls it an "obsession") inevitably brought with it the threat of counter-revolution (chap. XVII: 96). As the revolutionaries sought to root out the abuses of the old regime, so the people would be deprived of the petty advantages that could be enjoyed under a corrupt and inefficient administration. It was the very zeal with which the republicans tried to impose a fair and equal legal system that led the people to complain of the new regime's rigour and severity. Law was evident to the multitude only as a constraint, a willful denial of the habitual practices of the old way of life. The advantages of a regular system of law would only manifest themselves in daily affairs after a period of peace and stability. Time, however, was the one thing the republic did not have on its side. The deposed Bourbons were waiting in Sicily, intent upon taking advantage of the first signs of popular unrest on the mainland. At the earliest opportunity they would return; and one could be sure that they would not make the mistake of relying on the people's judgment rather than their interest. Despotism, as Cuoco puts it, always depends upon the support of the "dregs of the people, who, with no care whatsoever for good or evil, sell themselves to whomsoever is best able to satisfy the needs of their bellies" (chap. XVI: 94).

The mistake of the "patriots" had been to treat the creation of a republic as a moral crusade. Close readers of Machiavelli will recognize a familiar dilemma. The problems facing the founders of a "new" republic are similar in kind to those facing a "new" prince. In both cases the pressing task is to create a community of understanding or political culture that would sustain the new regime; and to this end it is essential that what is politically practicable should take precedence over what may be ideally desirable. The "patriots," however, continued to neglect "what is actually done for what should be done"; and they inevitably learnt "the way to self-destruction rather than self-preservation" (Machiavelli 1961: 91).

The Neapolitan republic had shown itself to be lamentably lacking in political realism. But the point Cuoco wants to stress is that the abstract nature of republican ideals effectively precluded the balanced appraisal of different courses of action that might have made a success of the revolution. Time and again the analysis comes back to the contrast between a purely theoretical view of politics and one that is attuned to the traditions of a community. The point is nicely illustrated in discussions of different conceptions of political liberty. The "patriots" would insist that liberty is a good in itself. When we ask ourselves why people actually value liberty, however, we find that a host of other notions have to be introduced. Liberty is seen as a good precisely because it leads to other more tangible goods – such as security, a comfortable way of life, or a flourishing commerce. Indeed, in Cuoco's analysis, it is specifically because people enjoy concrete benefits that they come to love liberty (see chap. XIX: 104; and Cuoco *Fragment* 6, see appendix I). The first concern of a new republican regime should have been to make some of the concrete advantages of liberty available to the people at large. By concentrating on the moral dimension of liberty, the "patriots" had effectively surrendered the political initiative to their Bourbon opponents.

The negative side of Cuoco's argument should by now be clear. Scepticism about the role of ideas in politics, combined with an analysis of the problems of political leadership, had led him to insist that any program of reform should have roots in a traditional culture. What we find on the positive side (though the point is less fully developed in the *Historical Essay* than elsewhere) is a stress on the importance of sound institutions for sustaining a flourishing political life. Where late-eighteenth-century republican thought (largely derived from Rousseau) had set the virtuous individual at the centre of the political stage, Cuoco sounded a warning. In the Neapolitan Revolution, virtue had been entirely on the side of the "patriots"; lacking a viable institutional framework, however, their best endeavours had proved to be self-destructive. Here was another Machiavellian insight (this time drawn from *The Discourses*) that had been obscured by the optimism of the eighteenth century (see Machiavelli 1960: 146–52). In politics we can only take people as we find them and hope that individuals will channel their self-interest in directions that benefit the community as a whole. This might have seemed a disappointing conclusion if one had been brought up on utopian tracts promising heaven on earth; but theorists of the post-revolutionary generation had grown acutely conscious of the hidden pitfalls that could transform the best-intentioned reforms into sinister instruments of social control.

Cuoco focuses specifically on constitutional issues in the "fragments" of letters addressed to Vincenzio Russo published as appendix I to the *Historical Essay*. The tone is sharply focused and more analytical than the treatment of the "patriots" in the body of the text. Consistent with the critique of rationalism that pervades the whole narrative, the *Fragments* make explicit basic assumptions that drive the analysis (see also Battaglia 1925: 50–85).

Some assumptions cluster around individuals. One, they are the basic or constituent units to be considered in the design of political institutions. Two, individuals are taken as they are, self-interested, and are presumed to seek to enhance their relative advantage. Three, human perfectibility is replaced with the assumption of human fallibility with capabilities for learning. Education then plays a chief role in the development of self-regulation and, correlatively, a resultant public spirit. For, individuals "more willingly correct themselves than allow themselves to be corrected by others" (Cuoco, *Fragment* 4: 258, in appendix I). Other assumptions cluster around how to devise institutions in such a way that conditions of reason and justice can be sustained over time. Particularly *Fragments* 3 to 6 turn on what mechanisms create and maintain a logic of mutually productive relationships. Aware that the prerogatives of public authority create unique opportunities for individuals to pursue their advantages at the expense of others, Cuoco is sympathetic to what

Pagano tried to do but thinks that he did not dig deep enough about human motivation, institutional arrangements, and the practice of self-rule. Again, the problem is modelling Neapolitan institutions on those that do not quite fit local conditions.

Cuoco elaborates these points and defends his position through close criticism of Francesco Mario Pagano's proposals for a Neapolitan constitution, very much influenced by successive French republican models (Battaglini 1994; see also Pagden 1994; Pagano's constitutional project in Venturi 1962; and symposium on Pagano in *Pensiero Politico* 1995). Whether Cuoco has faithfully interpreted Pagano is a contentious issue for some (see Ferrone 2012: 153–75). Giole Solari, a distinguished thinker in his own right and a sympathetic student of Pagano's thought, noted earlier that Cuoco was "the most authoritative and fairest of his critics" (Solari [1934] 1963: 289). Certainly, the *Fragments* remain indispensable for a balanced interpretation of Cuoco's political theory and institutional analysis.

A central theme is the need to adapt constitutions to the manners and customs of a people. "Constitutions," argues Cuoco, "have to be made for men as they are, and as they forever will be, full of vices, full of errors; for it as likely that they will want to give up their customs, which I believe to be second nature, to follow our institutions, which I believe to be arbitrary and variable, as it is reasonable for a shoemaker to demand to shorten the foot of someone for whom he had made a shoe that was too small" (*Fragment* 1: 226, in appendix I). A constitution "perfect" in theory would have to be applied to a society that had developed through tortuous adaptation of practices to circumstances over centuries. However sound a constitution might look on paper, it would inevitably be revised radically in practice if it survived for any length of time. A constitutional model for all people, anywhere, at any time, is simply inconceivable. Again adopting a homely analogy, Cuoco insists that "constitutions are like clothes: each individual, each age in which each individual lives, must have its own, which will not fit another if you try to give it to them" (*Fragment* 1: 226). While recognizing that the drafting of constitutions cannot be done by everyone, he recalls that the person who makes the shoe has to take into account the person who wears it (*Fragment* 1: 226), a homely analogy later dear to John Dewey (Dewey 1927, cited in E. Ostrom 1990: 185n10).

From Cuoco's perspective, reform must be piecemeal, respecting established habits without being a slave to them. The rationalist project, by contrast, assumes that defensible change should satisfy the requirements of theory. Theory, however, is a very blunt instrument when confronted with the vagaries of everyday life. Cuoco's worry, echoing the reservations of Burke and de Maistre, is that "to want to reform everything is tantamount to wanting to destroy everything" (*Fragment* 1: 226). It is a recipe for permanent frustration and disappointment.

In terms of constitutional detail, Cuoco's preference, clearly expressed in the second *Fragment*, is that political representation should be "as closely linked to ... the people as possible" (*Fragment* 2: 231, in appendix I). He specifically counters Pagano's suggestion that each representative should represent the "Neapolitan nation as a whole" (*Fragment* 2: 232). In any such scheme, as Robespierre's experience in revolutionary France illustrates so vividly, the authority of the nation overwhelms the constituent interests of the various localities.

Cuoco focuses, instead, on the established institutions that have served communities in some sense over a significant time span. Naples, he argues, idealizing considerably, has the "vestiges of ancient sovereignties," where communities were enabled to defend their interests "against the encroachment of the barons and tax authorities" (*Fragment* 2: 232, in appendix I). It is, no doubt, stretching matters to liken Neapolitan traditions to the robust management of local responsibilities among the "peace-loving inhabitants of the Swiss mountains," but Cuoco is adamant that municipal rather than national representation best secures interests and liberty (*Fragment* 2: 232).

What is most intriguing about Cuoco's position is that, despite his trenchant criticism of (what he sees as) French Jacobin theory, he positively endorses Rousseau's crucial distinction between the "general will" and the "will of all" (Rousseau 1968: 72). Following Rousseau to the letter, he insists that "the law is the general will"; but he is much more accommodating in his account of the "will of all," recognizing that "each individual has their particular will," and insisting that "freedom is no more than these two wills being in agreement" (*Fragment* 2: 236, in appendix I). There is no suggestion that the "general will" trumps the "will of all," or somehow embodies our better selves. And he explains the relationship between the two dimensions in terms of the practical accommodation that is evident in the extended development of communities. The particular wills of individuals always remain plural. If too many identify unconditionally with the singular will of the nation or state, the delicate balance between general and particular wills is undermined, leading to de facto tyranny even in the most enlightened of despotisms.

The priority should always be, in striking anticipation of the modern principle of subsidiarity, to ensure that interests are managed "by those who are most affected by them, and affected by them most closely" (*Fragment* 2: 238). This is a pragmatic criterion. It does not guarantee a qualitative transformation of experience, but it facilitates informed consideration of matters of mutual concern. Above all, it is an institutionalized learning process, reducing the gulf between public and private interests that naturally develops in centralized systems.

With the benefit of hindsight, it is possible to argue that Cuoco may have pressed the argument against centralization too far. His claim that "establishing the Neapolitan republic is no more than a question of restoring matters to their former state" would have astonished generations of enlightened reformers for whom baronial privilege was the principal obstacle to change (*Fragment* 2: 240, in appendix I). What he does grasp, however, is the complex interdependence that stems from regional differences and specialization. Allowing communities to develop in their own way contributes to a wider sum of benefits at national level. And it is simply the case that no central government is sufficiently enlightened to order priorities optimally from a local perspective. Local anomalies may demand central attention, but that is quite different, in Cuoco's view, from central imposition of priorities and rules.

The specific thrust of the *Historical Essay* was a critique of what commentators, at least since Hume, have styled "rationalism in politics" (Oakeshott 1962; Haddock 1996). The central dilemma of Cuoco's political theory is the dilemma that has come to be shared by classical liberalism: given the view of the limited role reason plays in social life, how is it possible to mount a systematic defense of reform without falling victim to the very kind of rationalism criticized (e.g., Kukathas [1989] 1990: vii)? Yet Cuoco was clear that a positive strategy for Italy could be gleaned from the experience of abortive revolution.

Between 1803 and 1806 he immersed himself in political journalism in Milan, coming into direct (almost daily) contact with his politically active contemporaries. He was the founder and first editor of the influential *Giornale Italiano* (1804–6). The political purpose of the journal was clear. Cuoco announced in the first edition that it was not simply "a matter of conserving public spirit but of creating it" (Cuoco cited in Tessitore 2011: 6). The point was to lift the minds of the Italians, to mould the inhabitants of provinces into citizens of a state. To this end he directed the journal to the principal achievements of Italians in the history of philosophy, literature, and politics. There would be articles on different aspects of modern European thought and their significance for Italian culture, together with studies and reviews of current developments in the worlds of politics, economics, the arts, and education – all designed to foster awareness of the central problems facing Italy.

In many of Cuoco's specific articles the themes that had emerged in the *Historical Essay* would be generalized and used as a key to interpret recent events in Italian political history. His range of topics extends from detailed reference to individual writers (notably Machiavelli, Vico, and Pestalozzi), through a general characterization of the Italian political tradition, to analyses of principal developments in Europe, notably the impact of the French Revolution and of Napoleon (Cuoco cited in Tessitore 2011: 35–47, 50–63, 180–2, 247–51). The tone is more didactic than the *Historical Essay*, but the message remains the same. If Italy were ever to revivify her political culture, it would be in terms of the resources of her own tradition.

Nor was Cuoco's exploration of a distinctively Italian tradition restricted to journalism. In the same fertile period in which he was immersed in the *Giornale Italiano*, he produced a philosophical romance, *Platone in Italia* (1804–6), that sought, through a series of mythical dialogues, to unearth a specifically Italian contribution to the Western philosophical tradition at its inception, championing an ancient Italian language that embodied a pristine wisdom later overwhelmed by the impact of Greek philosophy (Nicolini 1924; see also Dainotto 2011; De Francesco 2013). The argument is far-fetched for modern readers, but Cuoco had an exemplary source in Vico's *De antiquissima Italorum sapientia* of 1710 (see Vico 1971: 55–131; Haddock 1986: 58–64). The concept of an ancient, almost primordial, wisdom is, of course, treated with deep suspicion by modern historians, focused as they often are on the discursive construction of cultures in deeply divided contexts. What remains, however, once the stylized structure is factored out, is a sustained rebuttal of a rationalist cast of mind. Cuoco turns the association among his contemporaries of rationalism with enlightenment on its head, highlighting instead a tale of corruption, sophistry, and special pleading. Not only is wisdom lost but also the culture of virtue that sustained it (see also *Fragment* 6, see appendix I).

Cuoco's personal fortune changed abruptly in 1806 with the reassertion of French hegemony in Naples. From 1806 until the Bourbon Restoration of 1815, Cuoco assumed a range of important administrative functions in his homeland, while also continuing with his journalistic work. Nominated as adviser to the Court of Appeal in 1806, he was in

1807 made president of a commission charged with the reorganization of the legal system in the Kingdom of Naples. In 1809 he was asked by Murat to draw up a plan for the modernization of the educational system. The project was to be his most important work of these years, not only as an illustration of his lifelong concern to strike a balance between continuity and change but as a statement which, through Francesco de Sanctis and Giovanni Gentile, was to have a lasting influence on the theory and practice of education in Italy (see Cortes and Nicolini 1924: II, 3–122). Further important administrative responsibilities were to follow, culminating in his appointment as director general of the treasury in 1812. His final eight years, dating from 1815, were beset with mental illness that prevented him from leading any kind of active life. He died in 1823.

Cuoco's life and work spanned an extraordinary period of European political history that set terms of reference for the emerging ideologies that would dominate nineteenth-century political thought and practice. The tensions in his personal position look strained from a later perspective, but what we see in his work is a determined commitment to come to grips with social forces and developments that had yet to assume a settled form. Despite reservations about the wisdom of imitating French thought and practice, Cuoco was thus prepared to exploit the possibilities offered in Napoleonic Italy for reform and development. It was only French dominance that had enabled him to become a public figure in Milan and Naples. Yet he was aware that France had exploited Italian territories and distorted the "natural" evolution of Italian public life.

His *Historical Essay on the Neapolitan Revolution of 1799* remains Cuoco's crowning achievement, not least because it articulated tensions and cross-currents that standard revolutionary and reactionary theory simply could not accommodate. The complexity of the political world resists easy classification. Cuoco, however, offers a perspective that enables theory to build on everyday experience, concentrating on workable rather than ideal solutions. Viewed in this light, much of his journalism, a lifelong commitment, can be read as detailed engagement with a rapidly changing world, very much the message of his early masterpiece. In this book, we offer English-speaking readers the opportunity to study Cuoco's ideas for themselves, in the context of a period in European history that still challenges us politically.

Principal Events in Vincenzo Cuoco's Life[6]

1770	Cuoco is born in Civitacampomarano, then province of Lucera in Capitanata, now province of Campobasso, region of Molise.
1787–1799	Lives, studies, and works in Naples. Initially he assisted Giuseppe Maria Galanti, an Enlightement figure, in his research. Once Cuoco becomes more self-sufficient, he sets out to practise law.
1799	Cuoco becomes involved in the revolution and serves as secretary to Ignazio Falconieri, the organizing commissioner for the department of Volturno. For alerting revolutionary authorities about a Bourbon conspiracy, the Baccher's plot, he is named outstanding citizen by the republican newspaper *Il Monitore repubblicano*, edited by Eleonora de Fonseca Pimentel.
1800	After a nine-month detention, he is condemned to twenty years of exile. In May, he is deported to Marseilles, France. By the end of autumn, after Napoleon Bonaparte's victory in Marengo, Cuoco moves to Milan, in the newly established Cisalpine republic.
1801	In the same year, he publishes the first edition of *Saggio Storico sulla Rivoluzione di Napoli del 1799* (*Historical Essay on the Neapolitan Revolution of 1799*).
1802	He prepares a monograph on statistical observations of the department of Agogna, Draft of the Statistical Observations of the area of Agogna, a river that runs through Piedmont and Lombardy. He completes and submits a statistical study of the Italian republic.

6 This chronology relies in part on the chronology of Cuoco's life prepared by Pasquale Villani ([1966] 2004: 37–9).

1803	He drafts a proposal for the creation of the journal *Giornale italiano,* while writing his book *Plato in Italy.*
1804	Cuoco edits *Giornale Italiano* and publishes by the end of the year the first two chapters of *Plato in Italy.*
1805	In June he oversees the transformation of *Giornale italiano* into a daily, thereby gaining political recognition and prestige.
1806	The Neapoleonic conquest of Naples opens new paths in Cuoco's life. He moves to Naples in July, after overseeing the publication of a third chapter of *Plato in Italy* and of the second edition of the *Saggio Storico.* In August, he is appointed editor in chief of the Neapolitan newspaper *Corriere di Napoli.*
1806–1808	Cuoco is charged by the new king, Joseph Bonaparte, to help reorganize the judicial system of the realm and give a hand to the feudal commission in charge of reforming the feudal system.
1808	He is part of the delegation sent to Bayonne, France, to pay homage to Joseph Bonaparte as the new king of Spain. En route back to Naples, he is received by Napoleon in Paris. In 1808, Joachim Murat succeeds Joseph Bonaparte as king of Naples.
1809	At the request of the new king, Cuoco prepares a draft law for educational reform. In March of the same year, the king names Cuoco rapporteur (*relatore)* at the Council of State, member of the commission for the creation of the Land Register Office, and legal counsel for the Council of State.
1810	In March, he is named major rapporteur of the Council of State, a prestigious political and administrative position which is also taken to reflect positively on the Molise itself.
1811	In January, Cuoco became director general of the Treasury Board, a demanding administrative position taking him away from his more literary interests.
1814	Cuoco takes part in Murat's Italian campaign as director general of the treasury of the army.
1815	King Murat honours him with the title of baron. Following the Bourbon Restoration, Cuoco's illness, which he had been suffering from for several years, worsens with fears of his position under the Restoration.
1823	Cuoco dies following a fall.

Translator's Note: The Words and Structures of Cuoco's Revolution

David Gibbons

Translation is never a straightforward activity; and translation from one language to another at a different stage in its development adds a further layer of complexity, requiring historical as well as linguistic boundaries to be crossed. Translating from early-nineteenth-century Italian to modern-day English offers a particularly acute instance of these difficulties, largely because of the fragmented nature of the Italian language prior to political unification in the second half of the century.

Some of the problems I have encountered in translating Cuoco's *Historical Essay* have been of this kind, that is, instances of language use which look to be non-standard from a twenty-first-century perspective. One such instance involves Cuoco's insistent use of the word *intanto,* which ought to mean something like "meanwhile," but which in his vocabulary often serves a more adversative function, meaning something more like "however"; or, more frequently still, serves as a lexical filler, a pause for thought which in English may comfortably be omitted altogether. I am still not entirely sure whether this is a historical or regional form of language use or is merely idiosyncratic – certainly, I have not encountered it in any other writer of the same period or the same region. In any case, despite the challenges they pose, such instances of language use are in one sense straightforward, for they still result in the customary translational responses, equivalence or omission.

The main problem faced in translating Cuoco, though, is not so much his use of vocabulary that does not have a precise equivalent as that which does, or at least apparently. For there is an entire discourse in Cuoco's *Historical Essay,* the constituents of which, when rendered into their obvious – and in many cases only – modern-day English equivalents, sound anodyne or even innocuous, but which in the original come charged with a series of associations that demand at least acknowledgment and preferably explication. The vocabulary to which I am referring is the political terminology that flooded into the Italian peninsula and, in this case, the Bourbon Kingdom of Naples, in the wake of the French

Revolution and subsequent Napoleonic invasion (for example, see Leso 1991; Dardi 1995; and Stella 1999). This political and social shock had a strong impact linguistically, resulting, for example, in a plethora of foreign-sounding neologisms, such as the "democratizers" Cuoco discusses at some length in chapter XXXI of this *Historical Essay*. But it is more the apparently neutral terms, such as *idea*, *opinione*, and *pregiudizio* that cause the greatest problems in this respect, for the meanings they have in Cuoco's text are more specific than those which their modern English equivalents might suggest. That is to say, these terms do mean "idea," "opinion," and "prejudice" as the English-speaking world today understands them, but for Cuoco they meant a good deal more besides.

Take the case of "opinion," for example. Having or formulating an opinion in Cuoco's Naples was no innocent activity, nor one that was devoid of consequence. Indeed, according to chapter IV of the *Historical Essay*, before the failed revolution took place it was possible to be "guilty of opinion," a crime which involved arrest and imprisonment; while even in the short-lived republic itself, opinion was seen as a commodity to be "taxed." Moreover, opinions in this world were rarely individual, but the opinions of individuals were joined together to become collective or majority opinions and eventually referred to as "public" or "popular" opinion. Much has been written on the subject of popular opinion in recent years, most influentially by Habermas (1989) perhaps. In Italian, Cuoco uses two variant phrases, *l'opinione del popolo* and *opinione pubblica*, the former slightly more often than the latter and generally in close connection with the crucial concept of the "passive" revolution; Cuoco's argument being that the people's opinion has to be won over in cases where the revolution does not arise directly from it. The problem from the translator's perspective is that the only real alternative in English, "opinion," may or may not reflect the weight that the original term carries with it.

A similar problem is first to identify, and then render, the author's often far from impartial stance on the events he narrates, which at times can be implicit in the specific items of vocabulary that he uses. Such a perspective is clear, for example, in the title of his work, for what Cuoco proposes to recount in his work is a "revolution" – nearly always *rivoluzione* in Italian, less often *rivolta*, *insurrezione*, or *sedizione*. Now, a revolution may be a good or a bad thing, depending on whether or not it is "active" or "passive." The Neapolitan Revolution, of course, for Cuoco depended excessively upon foreign imitation, following the principles of the French Revolution too slavishly. Hence it was a "passive" revolution – a bad one, indeed a "revolution of opinion," as he says in chapter XXII – which failed to take due account of the specificities of the Neapolitan context, and which for this reason was to prove unsuccessful. It was still a "revolution" as far as he was concerned, though, and in Cuoco's willingness to use such potentially prejudicial vocabulary he is to be distinguished from, for example, Manzoni, who in rewriting the 1827 version of his novel *I promessi sposi*, studiously avoided such terminology.[7] For the English translator, Cuoco's *rivoluzione* can only be a "revolution," but as the Neapolitan context differs from the Milanese experience in this respect (it is worth bearing in mind that Cuoco's second edition of the *Historical Essay*, translated here, was, like the first, published in Milan), so too the precise stance of the person using such terminology might not be so clear in modern English.

To take another, still more complex example, the main agent of collective action in Cuoco's Naples is *il popolo*, a term which is far from being as straightforward as it looks. Tournier, in his study of 1848 revolutionary texts, argues that use of the term *peuple* in French is never neutral, and draws a distinction between its totalizing significance, which refers to all of the people, and its more limited application, which refers to the "working classes" alone (whoever they may be) (Tournier 1975). This distinction, of course, has its origins in the French Revolution of 1789, and it is implicit in Cuoco's statement in the penultimate paragraph of chapter XXXIV. He writes that, once again, in the context of popular opinion, the "people" as such only ever consist of at most four influential voices and, at times, only one, and it is this voice that must be won over if the revolution is to be embraced collectively. The same use of synecdoche is added as a disclaimer to a footnote in Manzoni's late comparative essay on the French Revolution of 1789 and the Italian Revolution of 1859 (in this case he was prepared to use the term "revolution") (see Ellero 2010, 184; Bardazzi 2003). Quite apart from the problems it

7 The comparison with Manzoni is an apt one, given that Manzoni was friends with Cuoco during the latter's Milanese exile, and that Cuoco is often mentioned as an important influence on Manzoni, his political thought in particular. The bibliography on relations between the two is far from small (and much, indeed, remains to be said), but the following at least should be consulted: Gallarati Scotti (1959); D'Alessio (1960); Biscardi (1962); Possumato (1999); and Cospito (1999). For Manzoni's revision of politically prejudicial terminology from the *ventisettana* to the *quarantana* versions of his novel, see the comments of Angelo Stella in Manzoni (1995: 800), who describes the process as "decolorazione semantica."

causes in the Romance languages, the slippery nature of such terminology is compounded by a second order of difficulties associated with the concept specifically in English, namely, the fact that the term "people" expresses the idea of both a plurality of individual persons (which in Italian would be *gente*) and the collective as a whole (*popolo*). Such confusion is further exacerbated by then having to decide whether the collective noun "people" should be treated as singular or plural. In short, decisions have to be made; hence, in this translation *popolo* in Italian has become "people" and treated as plural, even though an already fine dividing line conceptually and linguistically may become even more fluid as a result.

Another term Cuoco uses on several occasions is *popolaccio*, which, as its etymology might suggest – *popolo* plus the pejorative suffix *-accio* – has unreservedly negative connotations so far as he is concerned. According to Leso's lexicon of Italian revolutionary vocabulary, *popolaccio* is one of a similar group of items, including its variant *popolazzo*, plus *plebaglia*, reflecting a distinction between the category thus identified and the "people" as a whole, which is typical specifically of the Neapolitan context (Leso 1991, 262). Such words thus refer to a sub-group within the collective, a set of individuals with a combined identity as being among the poorer, potentially more criminally minded elements of society, who might also have been more inclined towards violence than others; Victor Hugo, indeed, was to draw a similar distinction in French between *peuple* and *populace* in *Les Misérables* several decades later.[8] In English, however, the term "populace," which clearly derives from *popolaccio*, has lost many of these associations, and even in Victorian times it was little more than a synonym for "people," or possibly even weaker still.[9] Alternative translations might include "mob" or "rabble," terms which certainly convey negative associations of the kind which accompany Cuoco's *popolaccio* (cf. Rudé 1964, 7). Both words are also found in two of the most celebrated English-language fictional representations of crowd violence, the Porteous mob in Scott's *Heart of Midlothian*, and the Gordon riots in Dickens's *Barnaby Rudge*. It is instructive, furthermore, to note that the term *popolazzo* is to be found in at least one of the early-nineteenth-century

8 In *Les Misérables* (1862, vol. 5, bk. 1, chap. 1), for example, describing the barricades of the 1848 uprising, Hugo speaks of the "populace" waging battle against the "people." See Prendergast (2003: 5–6).

9 On the use of this term in the first English-language translations of Manzoni's *I promessi sposi*, for example, see Gibbons (forthcoming).

Italian translations of Scott's novel, at one stage reputed to have been by Tommaso Grossi (cited in Leri 2002, 66).[10] Cuoco's *popolaccio*, however, is not merely an ad hoc phenomenon, assembling on occasion in order to demonstrate discontent. For this reason the term "mob" is inadequate to translate it, and "rabble," while suitably disparaging, lacks the specific connotations that accompany Cuoco's usage. One option would be to leave the term untranslated, as John A. Davis (2006) chose to do when quoting and translating a passage from Cuoco in a recent book on southern Italy in the revolutionary period.[11] But in an attempt to limit the number of Italianisms in the translation so far as is possible, I have chosen to use "populace" instead, albeit not without some misgivings.

Within the sub-group of the *popolo* that is the *popolaccio*, there is also a further sub-group, namely, the *fex urbis*, or *feccia*. Here, too, comparison with Manzoni is instructive, for on one occasion the Milanese novelist deploys unusual violence in referring to "il fondaccio, per dir cosí, del tumulto," a term which all his English translators, from the earliest to the most recent, have rendered along similar lines to the best of them, Alexander Colquhoun, who translated it as "the dregs, as it were, of the commotion."[12] But again, the term *fondaccio* is used less pejoratively than *feccia* is by Cuoco, having more to do in context with considerations of timing – the final elements in a crowd of demonstrators to disperse – than with value judgments; and the force of the terminology is mitigated by the attenuating clause *per dir cosí* ("so to speak"). Cuoco in this *Historical Essay* has no compunction in referring to a collective that included a high proportion of *lazzaroni*, a term by which the Neapolitans themselves referred to the more idle elements of their own society. Unlike with *popolaccio*, I have chosen to leave the term *lazzaroni* in Italian, partly because of its even greater specificity, partly because it was frequently used in the

10 On the translation of *Heart of Midlothian*, published as *La prigione d'Edimburgo o Nuovi racconti del mio ostiere raccolti e pubblicati da Jedediah Cleisbotham, maestro di scuola e sagrestano della parrocchia di Gandercleugh*, 4 vols. (Milan: Ferrario, 1823), see Benedetti (1974: 36–7), who mentions an uncorroborated testimony in the contemporary Milanese newspaper *L'Ape italiana*, arguing that this translation was by the author of the historical novel *Ildegonda* (namely, Grossi).

11 Translating a phrase from Cuoco's preface, "ciò che realmente era impossibile per lo stato in cui il popolaccio si ritrovava," Davis writes "in fact proved to be quite impossible because of the conditions in which the *popolaccio* lived" (Davis 2006: 102).

12 Forgacs and Reynolds (1997: 196) contains a revised versions of the translations of both works, Colquhoun's translation of *I promessi sposi* and Kenelm Foster's of *Storia della colonna infame*.

original by British aristocratic travellers to Naples in their accounts from the early nineteenth century. "Dregs," by contrast, would seem to be an acceptable translation for *feccia*, although it is perhaps worth pointing out that the force of the term reflects the author's intention as opposed to any prejudices the translator may or may not have.

Other cognate terms are also used by Cuoco, one of the most common of which is *popolazione*, or *popolazioni* in the plural. The term covers a somewhat broader spectrum of significances than its English translation does, ranging from "inhabitants" to "community" to "people groups" or "peoples" in this sense (indeed, on one occasion its sense is that of "populousness"). For this reason, it has not been translated with such absolute consistency. In the singular, *popolazione* is at times used in distinction to both *popolo* and *la feccia del popolo*. On one occasion, a particular class, that associated with the law courts, is described as accounting for one-fifth of the *popolazione*; on another, the term is used in opposition to the number of those who were actually in favour of the revolution. In contexts such as these, the term often recurs in connection with markers of entirety, such as *tutta la popolazione*, or *la popolazione intera*. On other occasions the individuality of the population concerned is emphasized through comparison with other populations from the same kingdom; thus there is a population of, say, Caiazzo, just as there is a population of Naples. Indeed, the regularity with which the term recurs in the plural in Cuoco's text is indicative of the Neapolitan kingdom's demographic composition at this time, a conglomeration of different people groups unified to a greater or lesser degree by the years of Bourbon rule. Cuoco himself reflects on this fact in chapter XIII, describing the rhetoric adopted by the defeated royalists in their mass conscription to withstand the advances of the foreign enemy, in which "for the first time we heard our peoples being reminded that they were Samnites, Campanians, Lucanians and Greeks."

Use of the term "nation" to describe Cuoco's *nazione* similarly requires explanation. For if a response to Ernest Renan's famous question "What is a nation?" were to be formulated for Cuoco based on his use of the term in this *Historical Essay*, the answer would be unequivocal but different, perhaps, from what the modern reader of English might expect (Renan 1882; cf. Anderson 2005: 6, 199–201). For when Cuoco speaks of *la nazione*, it invariably refers to the Kingdom of Naples: *la nazione napolitana* (only on one occasion is the modern form of the adjective, *napoletana*, to be found), or, more personally, *la nostra nazione*, but never, unlike in, say, Leopardi or Cattaneo, *la nazione italiana*. This one basic referent for the noun *nazione* is, moreover, mentioned in the same breath as the recognized, established nations of Europe such as France, Spain, and Britain.

As a nation, Naples had distinct borders, geographical as well as administrative and political. However, the fact that the Neapolitan nation was geographically delineated in this way, with distinct physical borders, did not mean it was not also part of the wider reality that was Italy. The relationship between Naples and Italy as Cuoco conceived of it is described in a footnote to chapter XLIII, in which he speaks of the importance of Italian unity, and the crucial role which the freedom of the Neapolitan kingdom, a nation in its own right, had to play in it:

> ... Italy should not be divided, but united: and the unity of Italy depends on the freedom of Naples; a country [*paese*] that France could never keep and which has so many resources, that on its own it could disrupt the peace of all Italy if it is not in the hands of a humane government that is a friend of liberty. The experience of centuries shows us that the conquerors of upper Italy have generally been broken on the banks of the Garigliano; and philosophy explains the reasons why this is so.

All these terms – *nazione*, *paese* ("country," but in some cases "town" or even "village"), and others such as *patria* (literally "fatherland," which I have rendered almost exclusively as "country," to avoid misleading historical and political connotations), and even *terra* (which I have translated as "land," but which, as Filippo Sabetti has pointed out to me, refers to towns and villages and/or their surrounding areas) – are problematic for both the translator and the reader unfamiliar with the Neapolitan usage of such terms prior to the nineteenth century.

A nation in this context, then, can be an individual province or region – this, indeed, is the definition given in the fourth edition of the *Vocabolario degli Accademici della Crusca* (1729–38), and reflected in Baretti's bilingual dictionary of 1760[13] – or a larger kingdom or state, in particular Naples. But it does not, or not yet at any rate, refer to what was to become the nation of Italy. The lexical instability I have been describing, which is inherent in the source text and which the translation itself may or may

13 *Vocabolario degli Accademici della Crusca*, vol. 3 (1729–38), 372: "Generazion d'uomini nati in una medesima provincia, o città"; and Baretti (1760): *ad vocem*: "NAZIO'NE: s. f. [generazion d'uomini nati in una medesima provincia] *nation, people, country*."

not clarify, reflects the fact that with political changes of this magnitude word boundaries had to be renegotiated as much as the territorial boundaries did. What this use of language reminds us of more than anything is the degree to which all borders, territorial and lexical, are conditioned by historical process, and the extensive influence that changes in these boundaries can have on the identities and communities imagined as a result of them.[14]

This translation has been made on the basis of Pasquale Villani's edition of Cuoco's second, revised version published in 1806. It may be worth pointing out, with reference to the translation specifically, that vestiges of Cuoco's revision remain evident in the organization of the second version of his text. At various points the passages between different considerations can seem unusually abrupt, while at others comments may appear to be arranged somewhat haphazardly. In such cases the reason is often to be found in questions of textual history, as a result either of deletions disrupting the original train of thought, or additions which represent afterthoughts in the proper sense of the term. Chapter XLIX of the *Historical Essay* forms a particularly acute instance of this phenomenon, where the additional clauses and sentences serve to confirm and reinforce Cuoco's original argument regarding the mistreatment – or persecution – of those who had professed republican ideals at the hands of the restored Bourbon monarchy; while the deletions work in the opposite direction, helping him climb down from some of his more extreme positions. Such disruptions may explain why the translation might not always read as fluently as might be hoped.

Equally, there are also midway stages between additions and deletions, textual forms that permit or facilitate the process of revision. I am thinking primarily of paratextual phenomena such as footnotes or parentheses that either allow new information to be added or provide a more discreet home for details contained in the original but subsequently deemed to be extraneous. Both phenomena, footnotes and parentheses, have been the subject of serious scholarly attention in recent years,

14 The bibliography on the emerging discipline of border studies is already enormous, but the various essays in the following two works have been of particular use to me in formulating these considerations: Albert, Jacobson, and Lapid (2001), and Wastl-Walter (2011).

while the paratext generally has become an important issue in translation studies, for often such apparently marginal material in the source text is not considered sufficiently important to be transferred to the translation.[15]

This is not the case here, however, where the basic structure of Cuoco's text has been respected. As the preface to the second edition makes clear, the original footnotes have been retained and are marked "V.C." in order to signal their provenance. Likewise, every effort has been made to retain the original format in terms of parenthesis, despite occasional variation for the simple reason that the modern Italian and English conventions in respect of punctuation do not always coincide.[16] Indeed, Cuoco's use of parenthesis can be instructive, for it can provide typographical representation of the different stages in the production and revision of his text. This is the case towards the end of chapter XV, for example, when Cuoco writes, "Hence for five centuries, the kingdom ... was the unhappy scene of an infinite number of civil wars, without even one of them being able to do any good to the country." By the time he came to revise his text for the second edition, he clearly felt that the historical reference required qualification, and hence added a parenthetical comment explaining that the five centuries represented the number between when the Norman dynasty died out and the house of Bourbon was established.

Similar considerations also apply, finally, to certain syntactic structures; for while neither footnotes nor parentheses, theoretically at least, have any affect at the level of syntax – constituting clauses in their own right and for this reason being especially well suited to textual integration – there are specific structures, such as concessive clauses, which are less closely integrated than others into the syntactic fabric of the sentence and, for this reason, perform similar functions to the paratextual phenomena I have been describing (see Gibbons 2011, esp. bibliographical references). Syntax has tended to be the poor relation of lexis in translation studies (and, incidentally, in philological criticism as well). But Cuoco's *Historical Essay* is an interesting example of some of the challenges involved in translating this kind of structure. If we look again at

15 On the footnote, see Grafton (1997); on the parenthesis see, among others, Lennard ([1991] 2003). On paratexts, the discussion of which owes much to the pioneering work of Gérard Genette, see the recent volume by Gil-Bardají, Orero, and Rovira-Esteva (2012).

16 For an introduction to the situation in Italian, see Lepschy and Lepschy (2008).

chapter XLIX, for example, we find two different orders of concession at work: the king's apparent mercy in granting what was effectively a false pardon (as Cuoco says, "the first trait of a coward is to show himself to be better than the just, and to seek to give of his own volition what he is bound to give by law"), and Cuoco's own concession in justifying the republicans' conduct. These two orders are expressed, among other things, through the repeated clauses beginning *ad onta di* or *ad onta che* in Italian, rendered in English as "despite" or "despite the fact that."

On other occasions, these concessions are again textual additions from the first to the second redactions. Such is the case, for example, with the partial admission Cuoco allows in chapter XXII to mitigate his criticism of the decision to allow Palomba to leave without prosecuting his charges against Rotondo. The original version describes merely the attempts made to sweep the episode under the carpet, and Cuoco's criticism that such silence was offensive to both the person accused and to all good men; while the second version contains an entire paragraph conceding that Palomba did have the right to prosecute his charges despite being allowed to escape, plus a strong rebuttal of the significance of this concession (he may have been entitled to prosecute his charges, Cuoco says, but he should have been made to do so, and if he was not prepared to, he ought not to have been allowed to leave).

Such textual features and syntactic structures, then, are an important part of Cuoco's *Historical Essay*, reflecting the spontaneous nature not only of its composition – written *a penna corrente*, Leopardi might have said, or "with the flow of the pen"[17] – but its revision as well, showing the degree to which Cuoco was still emotionally involved in what he had written and was writing, and resulting in a flurry of argument and counter-argument, of first thoughts and second thoughts. A translation, of course, is no critical edition; but it can, at least, offer a snapshot of one particular stage in the process of textual formation, rather than seek to elide it and pretend that the text fell from heaven already made. Indeed, textual formation is as much the result of historical process as the negotiation and renegotiation of boundaries, geographical, and lexical, discussed above.

Hence, if some of the more unusual typographical, syntactical, or lexical aspects of the translation I have described in this note – paratextual

17 As it has been rendered in the first full English-language translation of Leopardi's *Zibaldone*, edited by Michael Caesar and Franco D'Intino (2013).

or pseudo-paratextual disruptions, complicated sentence structures or distracting repetitions – strike the reader as more inelegant than might normally be demanded in English prose writing, my justification is that they are features of the source text, and that I have sought in my translation to provide something similar to the original reading experience insofar as possible. This is not quite the same as to say that mine is a "foreignizing" rather than a "domesticating" translation, according to the influential opposition instituted by Lawrence Venuti (1995), for I hope that it will still be readable. If it does, this will prove the point made most cogently perhaps by Umberto Eco (2003), that every translation is fundamentally an act of compromise between competing claims that often have equal merit. If it does not, all the more reason why a certain amount of prior explanation may prove helpful.

ITALY IN 1797

Map 1. Italy in 1748. From G. Holmes, *The Oxford Illustrated History of Italy.* Oxford, 1997. © Oxford University Press, used with permission.

Map 2. Southern Italy in 1806. From R.M. Johnston, *The Napoleonic Empire in Southern Italy,* vol. 1. London: Macmillan, 1904.

Historical Essay on the Neapolitan Revolution of 1799

Vincenzo Cuoco.
Incisione del 1805.

Author's Preface to the Second Edition (1806)[1]

Cedo cur vestram rempublicam tantam perdidistis tam cito?[2]

When this *Essay* was published for the first time,[3] the judgments pronounced on it were many in number and most varied, as inevitably happens to every book in which the author professes to be impartial, while its readers are anything but. Time, however, and the greater number of positive responses, have done justice not to my intellect or learning (neither of which were displayed abundantly in my book), but to the impartiality and sincerity with which I narrated events, and to which I myself was far from indifferent.

For some time now, the first edition has been out of print, and despite the many requests I have had, I would have postponed the second edition even longer, too, were it not for the fact that some, in seeking to reprint it without my consent, have forced me to speed up the process.

Since the first edition, I have collected the judgments which the public has pronounced, and have sought, insofar as I was able, to use them to improve my book as much as possible.

Some would have preferred a greater number of facts. And, in truth, I do not deny that I omitted some facts in the first edition, for I did not

1 The footnotes by the author are identified as "(V.C.)"; all others are the editors'. The editors' notations are meant to clarify events, personalities, and places cited by Cuoco and to give a deeper context to his narrative for English-language readers. The preparation of these notes has benefited from, but not always followed, the notations in Nicolini's (1913), Cortese's (1926), Villani's ([1966] 2004), and Bravo's (1975) editions of Cuoco's 1806 edition of *Saggio Storico*, checked against the notations by De Francesco (1998) for the 1801 edition.

2 "Tell me, why did you send your republic, which was so great, to ruin?" Pomponius Atticus, in Cicero, *De senectute*.

3 In Milan by Tipografia Milanese in 1801.

know them. For others, I kept my own counsel over, for I felt it more prudent to do so; others I neglected, for I considered them to be of little importance; others still, finally, I barely mentioned. I composed my book with no other guide than my memory: it was impossible to know all the infinite accidents of a revolution and to recall all of them. Many of them I came to know subsequently, and I have added the most important of these to the ones I had already narrated. However, despite all the additions, I well realize that those who desired more facts in the first edition will desire them still in the second. But my design was never to write the history of the Neapolitan Revolution, much less so a legend of it. The events of a revolution are infinite in number; but how could they not be, if an infinite number of men act simultaneously in a revolution? For this same reason, among so many events, there are bound to be some that are unimportant and others that resemble each other. I have neglected the former, and grouped the latter by their respective nature. I have concerned myself more with things and ideas than with persons. This proved displeasing to many, who would perhaps have liked to be mentioned; and pleasing to a great many others, who were very happy not to be. In history, names are of more use to the person who is named than they are to the instruction of the one who is reading. How few are the men who have been able to overcome and dominate things! The majority are slaves to them; they are as the times, ideas, customs, and accidents want them to be. When you have described these aspects properly, what is the point of naming men? I am firmly persuaded that if most histories were written so that the proper names were replaced by the letters of the alphabet, the instruction to be gleaned from them would still be the same. Finally, in considering and narrating events, I concerned myself more with the causes and effects of things than with those minor accidents which are neither causes nor effects of anything, and so please the idle reader for the simple reason that they provide him with a way to use the time he would be incapable of deploying in reflection.

Following these observations, it is plain that the facts left for me to add [in this new edition] were fewer than might have been expected. In reasoning with many of those who wanted more facts, I noted that often what they wanted to find in my book was in fact already there; but they wanted names, details and repetitions, and these had no place in it. Why should I distract the reader's attention with an infinite number of trifles, and divert attention from what I consider to be the true purpose of all histories, which is the observation of the path taken not by men, who shine but for a moment, but by ideas and things, which are eternal? It will be said that my book does not deserve to be called "history"; and

I shall reply that I never proposed to write history. After all, does a book have to be history in order to be useful?

One criticism was made as soon as the first volume came out. As it was born of a misunderstanding, I believed it was my duty to dispel it; and I did so by means of the notice to be found at the start of the second chapter of the first edition, which I now include here:

> Every time that mention is made in this work of "name," "opinion," or "rank," its meaning is always that of the rank, opinion, or name which influences the people, which is the main and only true agent of revolutions and counter-revolutions.
>
> Some, as a result of not having made this reflection, have concluded that when [in the first chapter] I speak of those who were pursued by the state inquisition, and describe them as "young men with no name, no rank, and no fortune," I mean by this to refer to them as persons of no merit, like the dregs of the people, who wanted revolution in order to make their fortunes.
>
> This was contrary to the rest of the work, in which it is repeated a thousand times that in Naples all those who had possessions and fortune were republicans; that no nation could count on so many men who desired reform solely out of love for their country; that the republic in Naples fell almost as a result of the republicans' overabundance of virtue [*soverchia virtù*] ... In the same place it says that the light of philosophy shone more brightly in Naples than elsewhere, and that the wise strove to spread it still further, hoping that one day it would prove not to be useless.
>
> The first republicans were all from the best families of the capital and the provinces: many were nobles, gentlemen, wealthy and very enlightened. Their very enlightenment exceeded the experience of the age and made them believe that what in reality was impossible, due to the state in which the population found itself, was in fact easy. Their desires were good, but they could not bring about a revolution without the people. This was precisely what made the tyrannical persecution unleashed upon them so inexcusable.
>
> Anyone who reads carefully will see clearly that this is exactly what I meant. I did no more than report what Cito, the respectable president of the Council, said at the time in defence of the republicans; and Cito was a long way from not knowing the persons involved or wanting to offend them.
>
> It would be foolish to say that the Carafa, Riari, Serra, Colonna, Pignatelli, etc. families[4] were poor; but, without doing these people any injustice, it may be said that they did not possess the sum of at least

4 They were, in fact, leading aristocratic families of the realm.

30 million ducats required to bring about a revolution, given the conditions in which the Neapolitan people found themselves at the time. Wealth is relative to the object sought after. An income of 300,000 *scudi* would make any man a very wealthy individual, but that would make a king a wretched sovereign.

It is possible to occupy a very eminent position in society and at the same time be unable to bring about a revolution. The president of the Council was one of the leading magistrates in the kingdom, and was unable to do so. It would have been far easier for a regent from Vicaria,[5] much less grand than a president, to move the people, or one elected by the people themselves, far less grand even than a regent.

The same is true of reputation. Who could say that the Serra, Colonna, Pignatelli, etc., families were obscure? That Pagano, Cirillo, and Conforti were men with no name?[6] ... But their reputation was among the wise, who, for the purpose of bringing about a revolution, are useless. They had no reputation among the people, who were needed for this purpose, and to whom they were unknown on account of their being too superior. Paggio, the head of the *lazzaroni*[7] of the Mercato district, is a despicable man in every way; but it was Paggio, not Pagano, who was the man of the people, and the people always curse that which they do not know.

I believe it goes without saying that the judgments of the people are not my own; but it must be pointed out that in a work intended to be truthful and instructive, my own judgments must be reported as well as those of the people. Each will be found in its rightful place: it is necessary to be able to distinguish between them and recognize them; and for this reason it is necessary to have the patience to read the entire work, and not to judge it on individual sections.

---

5 The headquarters of the chief of police of Naples and the realm.

6 Francesco Mario Pagano (1748–1799) was a jurist and author of the constitutional design that prompted Cuoco to write his letters to Vincenzio Russo, presented as fragments in appendix I, *Fragments*; Domenico Cirillo (1739–1799) was a scientist; Gian Francesco Conforti (1743–1799), before becoming interior minister of the republic, had been a widely respected theologian and literary figure who served the Bourbon government in various capacities. See Galasso (1984).

7 The general term *lazzaroni* referred loosely to a group of people in Naples that included labourers, peddlers, beggars, and con men, many without permanent residences who were living on the streets and were unemployed. Socially comparable to the *sans-culottes* of Paris, but unlike their French counterparts, the *lazzaroni* were staunchly monarchist. The term is still used today around Naples, often to describe friends and neighbours in an endearing way.

This *Essay* has been translated into German. I am very grateful to Mr Kellert, who, without knowing the author, believed the work to be worthy of his scholarship. I am all the more grateful to him, for he translated it in such a way as to make it seem worthy of the approval of the German men of letters. Their favourable judgments would be a source of pride to me, if I did not know that their reactions were in very large part due to the qualities that the elegant translator was able to lend to my book. Nonetheless, along with the praise which the book received, some criticism too was forthcoming, written in the style of an errant knight who combines reason with the sword, which may be read in Mr Archenholz's newspaper entitled *La Minerva*.

The article is signed by Mr Dietrikstein, whom I do not know, but who I have reason to suppose is a most valiant writer and warrior, for he shows himself equally willing to argue against me, with both pen and sword, that Baron Mack is an excellent army officer,[8] despite my seeking to argue the opposite in my book. In truth, General Mack's military talents were negligible. When I was writing my *Essay*, I had in mind the Naples campaign and the second Flanders campaign, both of which were led by Mack: I saw the same defeats, and the same causes of defeat, in both one and the other; and I believed it was possible to reasonably assign the blame to the general. Misfortune alone did not repeat itself with such similarity on two separate occasions. When Mr Dietrikstein's article then reached Milan, the final campaign had already begun. The friend who advised me of the article wanted me to make some kind of reply. But two days later, the cannon firing in the square announced the victory at Ulm, and I sent the article back to my friend, having written at the bottom of the page: "The answer has already been given."

This book of mine should not be considered as history, but as a collection of observations on history. Subsequent events have shown that I observed impartially, and not without insight. Many of the things that I foresaw materialized: the experience of subsequent events confirmed the judgments I had made on the former ones. While almost all of Europe held Mack to be a general in great account, I alone avenged the honour of my nation, or was the first to do so, and asserted that the

---

8 General Karl Mack von Leiberich (1752–1823) was the Austrian head of the Bourbon troops that, among others, unsuccessfully fought against the French in the Papal States. Admiral Nelson, who knew him from Naples, had a low opinion of his military skills. General Mack surrendered without resistance to Napoleon at Ulm in 1805, for which he was court-martialed. See also Davis (2006: 75n15).

setbacks which he suffered in his campaigns were not so much the result of misfortune as of ignorance. From as early as 1800, I pointed out the fundamental problem that vitiated every alliance which conspired against France, the reason why every attempt by the allies was bound always to end in failure, regardless of all the victories that might have been achieved. This is so because victories consume forces as much as, or only marginally less, than defeats do, and forces are lost pointlessly if they are without planning [*consiglio*], nor is there planning where either there is no purpose, or where the purpose is such that it cannot be achieved.

My desire is that anyone who reads this book should compare the events spoken of in it with those that have occurred since its publication. He will find that often the judgment pronounced by me regarding them was a prediction, and that subsequent experience has confirmed my earlier observations. The Neapolitan cabinet continued to make the same errors; the same indecisiveness in its conduct, the same alternating between hope and fear, the former always rash, the latter always precipitous; excessive reliance on foreign aid, lack of confidence in, and hence having no regard for, its own forces; never a well-coordinated operation. In the first alliance, the Treaty of Tolentino and the expedition to Toulon were concluded and carried out in such a way as to be beyond all reason and outside of every advantage.[9] In the second alliance, the Papal States were invaded before Austria had thought of moving its armies, and the operations of the small corps which Damas commanded in Arezzo commenced when the Austrian forces no longer existed.[10] Finally, in the third alliance, a treaty was signed with France, when it was perhaps unnecessary, as the Neapolitan royal government was already thinking of breaking it; the Russians and British summoned, when most things had already been decided at Austerlitz. Thus the futile stain of betrayal and the inappropriateness of treachery added to the shame of seeing a king with 7 million men under his command becoming, due to the fault of his ministers, virtually the agent of the British, and ceding command of his own troops in his own kingdom to a Russian

9 This passage refers to the mediation role played by the Court of Naples in the Treaty of Tolentino between the pope and Napoleon in 1797, and to the participation of a Neapolitan contingent to the defence of Toulon against the English in 1793, in which Napoleon distinguished himself as a young officer to gain wider attention.

10 By this point, the war had been decided based on the victory of Napoleon at Marengo in June 1800.

general.[11] Look for the causes of all these events, and you will find that they are always the same: a minister[12] who derived much of his power from Britain, where his own wealth was stored; ignorance of the forces of the Neapolitan nation, lack of interest in improving its destiny, in reawakening in the minds of its inhabitants a love of their own country, arms and glory; the state of violence, which had naturally to arise from the type of struggle inevitable between a people naturally full of energy and a foreign minister seeking to keep it in misery and oppression; the lack of trust which this same minister had inspired in the minds of the sovereigns against the nation. Basically, in saying that the conduct of this cabinet would ultimately lose the kingdom, I predicted what happened, this time irreparably.[13]

I could have added the history of subsequent events up to our own day to that of the revolution. I reserve this task for times in which I will have greater leisure and ease to instruct myself in these matters, once I have returned to my own country. I will write another volume in the same format, paper, and typeface as the present. In the meantime, I have wished to change nothing of the book that I published in 1800.

When I was writing this book, the great Napoleon had just returned from Egypt; when the book was going to press, he had just begun to take matters in hand, and embarked on the magnanimous enterprise of restoring the ideas and orders of both France and Europe. But I may boast of having desired no few of the great things that he later accomplished. In times when all principles were exaggerated, I, for my part, can boast of having advocated moderation, which is the inseparable companion of wisdom and justice, and which may be said to be the greatest director of all the operations that have made human beings great.

---

11 The general went by the name of Lascy.

12 This is a veiled reference to John Acton (1736–1811), a sort of sailor-soldier of fortune. Acton was born in France and descended from an English Jacobite family. He served in the French navy before going to Tuscany to advise the Grand Duke on naval matters, from where he was enticed to do likewise for Naples. In 1779, he was appointed secretary for the Neapolitan navy and in 1780 acquired the posts of Secretary of War and Finances. Within a few years of his arrival, Acton became a most powerful minister at the Neapolitan court and the queen's favourite, to finally become prime minister. In his *The Bourbons of Naples (1734–1825)*, Harold Acton (1956) provides a more sympathetic view of John Acton and his government work in Naples; attention will be drawn to this work from time to time as a contrast to the negative views in Cuoco and in much of the scholarly literature.

13 Or so it seemed in 1806. The Bourbon king was eventually restored.

He has confirmed the Greek adage whereby it is said that the gods gave infinite force to proportional means, that is, to the ideas of moderation, order, and justice. I even kept the letters that I had written to my friend [Vincenzio] Russo on the plans for a constitution drawn up by the illustrious and unfortunate Pagano, albeit now superseded, both as an historical monument and as a demonstration that all those orders which at the time were believed to be constitutional were in fact merely anarchic.[14] France did not begin to have order, and Italy did not begin to have life, until after Napoleon; and among the many benefits which he granted to Italy, that of having gifted Eugène [Beauharnais] to Milan and Joseph [Bonaparte] to my country are certainly not the least important.

14 The fragments of the letters are reproduced as appendix I in this edition.

Letter by the Author to N.Q.[1]

When I began to concern myself with the history of the Neapolitan Revolution, I had no purpose other than to alleviate the leisure and tedium of exile. It is a sweet thing to recall past storms when in harbour. I had achieved my objective. I would not have thought of anything else, if you and the other friends to whom I read the manuscript had not believed it could be useful for some other purpose.

Is it not strange how the world goes? The king of Naples declares war on the French, and is defeated. The French conquer his kingdom, and then abandon it. The king returns, and proclaims it a capital offence to have loved one's country in the time when it no longer belonged to him. All this happened without my having the slightest part in it, without even having predicted it. But all this also meant that I was exiled, that I came to Milan, where certainly, had my life followed its ordinary course, I was not destined to come, and where, as a result of having nothing else to do, I became an author. "All is necessarily linked in the world," says Pangloss: may everything be so for the best!

In other times I would certainly not have allowed this work of mine to see the light of day. Until very recently, rather than having principles, we had but the exaltation of princes.[2] We sought liberty, but had merely factions. Men, who were not so much friends of liberty as enemies of order, invented a word to form a new faction, and proclaimed themselves head of this faction, so that they could feel entitled to destroy anyone who followed a different one. These men, whom Europe will eternally reproach for the deaths of Vergniaud, Condorcet, Lavoisier, and Bailly, were the men who brought the ashes of Marat to the same temple as those of Rousseau and Voltaire but refused to bring those of

1 N.Q. most likely refers to Nicola Quagliarelli, a friend of Cuoco and republican patriot, who later, in 1814, was named Neapolitan ambassador to Tuscany.

2 A play on the word *principi*, which in Italian can mean both principles and princes.

Montesquieu. These were not men, certainly, from whom Europe could hope for its happiness.

A new order of things promises us greater and more lasting benefit. But do you believe that the obscure author of a book can ever produce human happiness? In any order of things, ideas of truth always remain sterile, or generate only some useless desire in the minds of decent men, if they are not listened to and held dear by those entrusted with regulating earthly affairs.

If I could speak to the man responsible for this new order, I would tell him this: the oblivion and scorn in which these ideas were held meant that the new destiny which his arm and mind have given to Italy would almost be destined to become, in his absence, the playing field of desolation, ruin, and death, if he himself does not come back to save it.

One man liberated Italy twice, made the French name known in Egypt, and who in returning, as though carried on the wings of the wind, like lightning dissipated, dispersed, and brought down those who had combined to lose the state which he had created and made illustrious with his victories. I would tell this man that he has done much for its glory, but he still can and must do much good for the benefit of mankind. Having broken Italy's chains, it still remains for him to restore her cherished and secure liberty, so that your gift to her may not be lost by negligence, or taken away by force. For if my country, as a very small part of that great universe with which your thoughts are occupied, is destined also to serve in the great scheme of things, and if it is written in the fates that it cannot have all the good for which it hopes, then may it at least have relief through you for all the ills with which it is currently oppressed! You see, under the fairest sky and on the most fertile soil of Europe, justice becomes the instrument of an evil man's ambition,[3] the law of nations is trampled, and the French name scorned. There is the horrible slaughter of innocent people who, by their death and amid torments, make atonement for sins not their own.[4] And in the very moment at which I am addressing you, 10,000 still groan and call out, if not for liberation, then at least for a powerful intercessor.

A great man of antiquity whom you equal in heart and surpass in terms of mind, one who, like you, first defeated the enemies of his country,

---

3 A veiled reference to John Acton.

4 A reference to those who were executed, imprisoned, or forced to go into exile when the Bourbon king was restored.

then reorganized the country that he had conquered, Hiero of Syracuse, as a price for the victory achieved against the Carthaginians, imposed an obligation onto them to stop killing their own children. He entered into this agreement at the time for the good of all mankind.[5]

If you content yourself solely with the glory of conquest, you will find thousands of others who, like you, have made the earth fall silent in their presence. But if to this glory, you wish to add that of establishing wise governments and bringing order to peoples, then a grateful humanity will award you, in the memory of the living, a place in which you shall have very few or no rivals.

Adulation reminds the powerful of the virtues of their elders, whom they are no longer able to imitate, and philosophy reminds great men of their own virtues, that they should continue ever more constantly in their magnanimous enterprise.

N.B. Every time the currency of Naples is referred to, the number shall always refer to ducats: one ducat is equal to our French livres.

5 This sentence in the original manuscript was italicized.

I

Introduction

I undertake to write the history of a revolution which intended to bring about the happiness of a nation, but in fact caused its ruin.[1] We will see that, in less than a year, a great kingdom was overthrown while it threatened to conquer Italy; an army of 80,000 men was defeated, dispersed, and destroyed by a handful of soldiers; a weak king, counselled by cowardly ministers, abandoned his dominion *(stati)* without any danger; freedom was born and established when it was least hoped for; fate itself fought for the good cause, and human errors destroyed the work of fate, causing a new and fiercer form of despotism to rise up from within liberty.

The great political revolutions occupy the same place in the history of man (*nella storia dell'uomo*)[2] as extraordinary phenomena do in the history of nature. For many centuries, generations follow each other peacefully like the days of the year. They merely have different names, and if you know one, you know them all. An extraordinary event seems to give them a new life; new objects present themselves to our eyes; and amid this general disorder which appears to want to destroy a nation, its character, the customs and rules of that order are discovered, while previously only their effects were visible.

But normally speaking, a physical catastrophe is more precisely observed and more truthfully described than a political catastrophe. In observing the latter, the mind always follows the irresistible

1 This book was written in the year 1800, hence it is easy to understand which ruin is being referred to. (V.C.)

2 It may be useful to recall that "man" in Italian as in Latin and the way it is used here has no gender; that is, it refers to both men and women.

movements of the heart; and for events that are of most interest to humankind (*genero umano*), we tend not to have their history so much as their praise or satire. Too close to the facts we wish to recount, we are oppressed by their very number; we fail to see them as a whole; we are ignorant of their causes and effects; we are unable to distinguish the useful facts from the useless, the frivolous from the important, until time separates them from each other. In causing that which does not deserve to be kept to fall into oblivion, we hand down to posterity only that which is worthy of memory and useful for the instruction of centuries.

Posterity, which must judge us, will write our history. Since we are held responsible for preparing the material of the facts, so too may we be permitted to anticipate their judgment. Without claiming to write the history of the Neapolitan Revolution, allow me to dwell on certain events in it that seem to me more important, and to indicate what I see as praiseworthy in them, and also what may be censured. Posterity, exempt from passions, is not always free from prejudice towards whoever is ultimately the victor; and actions risk being slandered merely because they did not succeed.

I declare that I do not belong to any party, unless reason and humanity have one. I narrate the events of my country; I recount events which I myself have witnessed, and in which I, myself, at one time had some part;[3] I write for my fellow citizens, whom I cannot, must not, and do not want to deceive. Those who, even with the purest of intentions and ardent zeal for the good cause, through a lack of enlightenment or courage, brought about my country's ruin; those who, as victims of the good oppressed party, either died gloriously or still groan – they must forgive me if I do not, even out of friendship, offend that truth which must always be dear to anyone who loves their country. They should rejoice if, having not been able to be of use to those who survived them with their actions, they may at least be useful with the example of their errors and misfortunes.

Whatever party I may belong to, whatever party the reader may belong to, it will always be useful to observe how false counsel, the whims of

3 See especially chapters XXXI and XXXV.

the moment, the ambition of private individuals, the weakness of magistrates, the ignorance of one's own duties and one's own nation are damaging to republics and monarchies alike. Our successors will see from our example that any force without wisdom merely destroys itself, and that there is no true wisdom without that virtue which sacrifices everything to the universal good.

II

Europe after 1793

Before dealing with our own revolution, it is worth going back somewhat further and dwell briefly on the events that preceded it; to see what the state of the nation was, the reasons which caused it to be involved in the war, the ills that it suffered, and the good for which it hoped. In this way, the reader will be better placed to understand the causes and to judge, more soundly, the effects.

From 1789 onward, France had carried out the greatest revolution spoken of in history. There was no example of a revolution which, in seeking to reform everything, had destroyed everything. The other revolutions had fought and replaced one prejudice with another, one opinion with another, one custom with another; the French attacked and overturned simultaneously altar and throne, the rights and property of families, and even those names which nine centuries had made respectable in the eyes of the peoples.

Despite being foreseen by a few wise men, to whom the masses are not usually inclined to pay attention, the French Revolution broke out suddenly and dismayed all of Europe. All the other sovereigns were fearful of an example that might become contagious, partly because of the ties of kinship that linked them to Louis XVI, and partly because of their own interests.

To extinguish the nascent flames was believed to be a simple enough exercise. Much hope was placed in the domestic turmoil agitating France. It never occurred to anyone that all the divided parties would be reunited by national pride at the approach of an external enemy. Much hope was placed in the decline in trade and commerce, in the absolute lack of everything into which France had fallen. In any case, there was hope to defeat the revolution through misery and hunger, without remembering that danger transforms the enthusiastic into warriors, and hunger turns warriors into heroes. A war against external forces which, begun with equal injustice and imprudence, consolidated a revolution that without external threat would have degenerated into civil war.

From the ruin of a nation that at the time was its only rival, Britain contemplated immense conquests and infinite advantages to its commerce. The Court of London, more than any other court in Europe, must have feared contagion from the new opinions, which may almost be said to have been born in the very bosom of England, and found no better means to make them odious to the English people than to reawaken national rivalry, by which another nation could be hated, if not as unreasonable, then at least as French. Pitt[1] saw that the inhabitants of Great Britain, especially the Irish and Scots, were prepared to do something similar; revolution would have broken out in Britain if the British had not almost scorned to imitate the French.[2]

Although Britain was not the first to declare war, it was the first to fan the flames of discord. Austria took up the invitation from its ancient and natural ally. The courts of Europe were not familiar with republics. From France's inevitable loss, they hoped for certain gain. Prussia had already obtained some in the congress at Pilnitz [Pillnitz], with the division of Poland. Britain and Prussia moved to suppress the office of *Statholder*, who wished, by means of a foreign war, to distract the excitable minds of the Batavians, who had recently become his subjects, and had been keen to see destroyed those who might one day be their far-from-weak protectors. Prussia and Austria carried with them the small princes of the empire, who were moved more by the gold of the British, to whom they had been accustomed for some time to sell the blood of their own subjects, than they were by the loss of a few uncertain, useless rights which the French Revolution had taken away from them in Alsace and Lorraine. The king of Sardinia followed the paths of his ancient policy; accustomed to profit from the dissent between France and Austria, to which he alternately sold his favours, he initially supported the alliance party, which seemed to him to be stronger. Finally, Spain too followed the general trend; and war followed.

Hostilities opened with great victories by the allies; but these were soon followed by the most terrible defeats. The French managed to detach Prussia from the alliance; having obtained its portion of Poland, Prussia

1 William Pitt the Younger (1759–1806) was prime minister of England between 1783 and 1801.

2 All of this had been foreseen by Burke. He alone among the British had predicted that the war would necessarily prove to be fatal, that it was in England's interest to halt the revolution by means of mediation, etc. etc. etc. (V.C.)

realized that between two first-ranking powers bent on tearing apart and destroying each other, the best course of action was to remain neutral.[3]

The Court of Spain soon became jealous of Britain, which alone seemed able to profit from the war. The conduct of the British at Toulon[4] caused resentment that had long been simmering to boil over, and Charles IV [of Spain] no longer wished to deploy his forces in support of a nation which he ought to have feared more than the French. While his armies were beaten on land, his fleets remained inactive on the seas; while the French gained in Europe, Charles IV could have received compensation in America, and so put an end to the war by means of a reciprocal restitution, without the losses that he was forced to incur in order to obtain peace. The desire of the French was precisely that many should declare war on them but that none should do so with all of their forces. This way, each new enemy gave the French a new victory, and the alliance that was intended to bring them down served to increase their ascent.

As in ancient Rome, war had now become indispensable to France, partly because it took the place of all the trade and commerce which previously had formed the means of subsistence for the people, partly because an almost always factious government considered it a means by which to distract and preoccupy the too-active minds of the inhabitants, and partly to remove the disruptive elements that are wont to agitate in times of peace. Hence the system of universal democratization developed, which the politicians needed for their own interests, and which the philosophers applauded for its surfeit of good faith; a system which added the force of opinion to that of arms, the former being a force that is accustomed to produce, and indeed sometimes has done, those empires that so much resemble a universal monarchy.

---

3 Treaty of Basel of 5 April 1795.

4 The city of Toulon was a monarchist stronghold, and rose up in 1793 against the republican government. It was occupied by the British troops. Led by Napoleon, then artillery commander of the republican forces at the siege of Toulon, the French forced the British to evacuate the city before capturing it.

III

Italy until the Peace of Campo Formio[1]

In just a short space of time, the French were seen to be victors and lords of Flanders, Holland, Savoy, and the whole immense stretch of land running along the left bank of the Rhine. However, they did not enjoy such swift success in Italy; their armies remained for three years at the foot of the Alps, which they were unable to pass, and which they perhaps might have never been able to, had Bonaparte's genius not called forth victory in these places, too.

When the Italian mission was entrusted to Bonaparte [in 1791], it was virtually a lost cause. He found himself at the head of an army lacking in everything, but which had left France at the height of its enthusiasm and for three years had become accustomed to discomfort and fatigue; he found himself at the head of courageous adventurers, resolved to be victorious or to perish. In addition, he had every talent, especially that of getting his soldiers to love him, without which every other talent is worthless.

If Bonaparte's campaigns in Italy are to be compared with those that the Romans made in foreign countries, they may be said to resemble only those by which Macedonia was conquered. For instance, Scipio had to fight against an outstanding commander who had no nation; many others did not have to face either generals or warring nations. Only in Macedonia did the Romans encounter a well-ordered power, a fierce nation eager for fresh triumphs, and generals who, while not blessed with genius, at least knew how to practise their art. Bonaparte changed tactics, changed the practice of the art [of war]; and the Germans' powerful manoeuvres became as useless as the Macedonians' phalanxes were against the Romans. He crossed the Alps and descended on

1 The Treaty of Campo Formio between the French republic and the Austrian empire was signed on 17–18 October 1797. It brought the Italian campaign to a final close, dissolved the Venetian republic and redrew the map of Europe, as Cuoco here notes.

Piedmont. He forced the king of Sardinia, perhaps tired after five years of war, deprived of a good portion of his dominions, and abandoned by the Austrians who had been reduced to defending their country, to sign an armistice, possibly necessary but certainly not honourable. He also forced the king of Sardinia to cede, by way of a down payment until peace was achieved, those cities that they were still able to defend, and should have defended to the death. After this the campaign was a series of continual victories.

Italy was divided into many small states, which, however, when united, were still able to put up some resistance. Bonaparte was skillful enough to divide up their interests. This is the fate, says Machiavelli, of those nations that have already earned the reputation of arms: everyone desires their friendship, everyone takes steps to avert a war that they fear.[2] So, too, the Romans always fought their enemies one by one, and defeated them all. The pope sought to bring together an Italian alliance. The Courts of Naples and Sardinia contributed willingly to this alliance, the former of which took it upon itself to invite the Venetian republic as well. But the sages[3] of this republic replied to the Neapolitan representative's propositions that no mention had been made of an alliance in the Venetian senate for almost a century, and that there would be no point in proposing it; but that, if the alliance with the other princes was entered into, the republic might well have joined it. When the Viennese cabinet came to hear of these negotiations, it opposed them bitterly and showed by words and deeds that it feared Italian unity more than it did the French Revolution!

Hence it became evident how unhappy the political situation of Italians was. They were divided into so many small states (for even being divided would not have been the worst of all ills), and for 200 years they had been either conquered or, worse still, protected by foreigners in the shadow of the general system of Europe. Without wars between themselves or fearing wars from abroad, and poised between servility and protection, they had lost all love of their country and every military virtue. In recent times, not only have we been unable to renew the examples of

2 See *The Prince*, chaps. 8, 12, and 17 (Machiavelli 1961). Machiavelli's influence on Cuoco has been noted and documented by several intellectual historians (e.g., Di Maso 2005: chaps. 2–4).

3 It may be worth noting that the sixteen sages were elected annually and constituted, with the Doge, the six district councillors and the three chiefs of the Quarantia, the Signoria, or the executive, of Venice.

our most ancient forebears, who came together and conquered much of the globe. We have also been unable even to imitate our less illustrious forebears of more recent time, when, though divided among ourselves, we were at least independent from all the rest of Europe – when we were Italians, free and armed.

The Austrians, isolated, were unable to withstand the enemy's momentum. All Lombardy was invaded, Mantua fell, and the Austrians were driven back as far as the Tyrol. Bonaparte was already not far from Vienna. Europe was anticipating more dramatic action at any moment, when France stopped hostilities and signed a peace treaty granting it possession of the left bank of the Rhine and the important city of Mainz, while Austria acknowledged the independence of the Cisalpine republic, in return for which it was given the dominions of the Venetian republic. By resolving to go to war too late, Venice had merely given the stronger powers a plausible motive for accelerating its ruin.[4]

By what force of destiny could a government continue to exist, when for two centuries it had destroyed all military virtue and valour, reduced the entire state to the capital, and concentrated the capital into the hands of only a few families which, feeling weak faced with such a great empire, had no principle other than jealousy, no confidence other than the weakness of its subjects, and more than any external enemy feared the virtue of its own citizens? I do not know what will become of Italy. But the fulfilment of the Florentine secretary's prophecy, the destruction of that old, imbecilic Venetian oligarchy, will always be a good thing as far as Italy is concerned.[5] And I, who of all the benefits that peoples can receive, assign first place to those of the mind, that is, to judging rightly, from which virtuous and noble actions ensue; I believe it to be great profit already, to see the old error whereby the Venetian noblemen enjoyed the reputation of wise governors of state removed from the minds of the people.

The Treaty of Campo Formio was advantageous to both parties. Austria in particular gained a great deal; and if some other object remained to be

---

4 Here Cuoco accepts the questionable justification used by Napoleon to disband the republic of Venice, to turn much of the Venetian republic's territory over to Austria and to move many of its treasures to France. Most historical accounts of events prior to the Treaty of Campo Formio do not accept Napoleon's view that Venice had a leading part in bringing about its own ruin.

5 For Machiavelli, the two most dangerous forces in Italy were the papacy and Venice. (V.C.)

determined, it was not hard to see that it could have gained even more, at the expense of the minor princes in Germany. But equally, it was not hard to see why Britain was a long way from entertaining thoughts of peace. It was the only ally to have gained from the war and the only one to have to make restitution.

Whatever many people believed, the government in power in France at the time had renounced, at least for a while, its plans for universal democratization, which as the French conceived them, could be enforced only in a moment of enthusiasm. The Romans showed that they were giving peoples the institutions (*ordini*) they desired, but they were not obsessed with the idea of exporting Roman institutions (*ordini*) everywhere. Hence the Romans managed to preserve, better and for a long time, the appearance of being liberators of peoples. But the French government retained its initial language, in order to sell its promises and threats more dearly. There was always a contradiction between the generals' proclamations and the ministers' negotiations, between the words given to the peoples and those given to the sovereigns.[6] Amid these continuous contradictions there was a continuous exchange of hopes and fears, now with the peoples, now with the sovereigns.

Even from this, everyone could see that the Treaty of Campo Formio suspended the democratization of all Italy only briefly. The king of Sardinia now was merely the French republic's minister in Turin, while the duke of Tuscany and the pope were nothing. [General Louis-Alexandre] Berthier[7] eventually occupied Rome; and the only cost of destroying that old, theocratic government was to want it. Such is the state of Italy that whoever wants to save it or occupy it has first to unite it, and it cannot be united without changing the government of Rome.[8] The indifference with which Italy regarded this occurrence shows clearly how much progress the new opinions had made in the minds of Italians.

6 Like the secret annex of the Treaty of Campo Formio stipulated between Napoleon and the Austrian emperor.

7 The French occupation of Rome led by general (and future Marshal) Louis-Alexandre Berthier (1753–1815) in February 1798 was the pretext for the French-Neapolitan war, which was catastrophic for Naples.

8 That is, without suppressing the temporal power of the papacy then considered essential to the freedom of the Church.

IV

Naples – The Queen

There remained the Kingdom of Naples; and at that time at least, the French possibly had neither the interest nor the desire to attack it. But familial relations with the sovereigns of France, the preponderant influence of the British cabinet, the queen's character – everything conspired in the Court of Naples to fuel that hatred which, right from the outset and more passionately than in any other court in Europe, had been displayed against the French Revolution.[1] On her journey through Germany and Italy upon the occasion of her daughter's marriage, the queen had been the prime mover in the alliance that would later attack France. The Naples court was forced to subscribe to neutrality when [French admiral] La Touche came right up to the capital with a squadron [in 1792].[2] Perhaps the court was more afraid than it needed to be; if negotiations had lasted for two more days, the season and winds would have avenged a fleet that had imprudently sailed too far into a perilous gulf in a highly dangerous season.

The taking of Toulon caused the neutrality to be broken once more. Like the other courts, the Court of Naples sent troops to support an unhappy enterprise that was more mercantile than belligerent and which, in the way that it was conceived and executed, could have been

---

1 Maria Carolina, queen of Naples (1752–1814), was the daughter of Maria Theresa, the empress of Austria, and the sister of Marie Antoinette of France. Maria Carolina's view of France rapidly changed for the worse when the French monarchy was abolished in September 1792, and when her own sister was beheaded in October 1793. It should come as no surprise – so Harold Acton (1956: 237) reminds us – why King Ferdinand and the queen loathed the French Revolution and why this loathing affected their disposition, behaviour, and course of action.

2 He threatened to bombard the city if the king did not agree to his ultimatum – that the king recall the Neapolitan ambassador from Constantinople and send an ambassador to Paris on a French frigate. To add to the imposition, Admiral La Touche also prevailed on the king to grant an audience to a French ambassador dressed for the occasion as a grenadier of the French national guard.

useful only to the British. The following spring, Naples sent two cavalry detachments to the Cisalpine republic to help the emperor, which conducted themselves excellently. But Bonaparte's victories in Italy plunged the court back into fear, and it hurriedly sought to conclude a peace precisely at a time when the emperor needed help most; at a time when Mantua had still to be taken, when the [Austrian] imperial forces in Italy had not yet all been destroyed, when troop deployment could have brought about a powerful and possibly dangerous distraction. To a court that did not know how to wage war, the French government was able to sell a peace which it should have bought or been perhaps prepared to buy.

Why were they so afraid of La Touche's fleet? Because they thought that there were 50,000 men in Naples ready to take up arms in his favour. There was no one, no one.[3] In the negotiations for this peace, what was the great object with which the Court of Naples concerned itself? It was the release of around 200 schoolboys,[4] who were being held under arrest in its fortresses. What was not done, what money was not paid, to ensure that the Directory did not insist, as was the fashion at the time, on the release of those "guilty of opinion"? The queen did not approve of this peace, and perhaps she was right; but she believed she had obtained much in having obtained the right to show needless cruelty against a handful of young people whom it was more advisable to despise. These facts should never be forgotten. The Neapolitan court did not know what to fear or what to hope for: how could it have been expected to act wisely?

The Court of Naples was the court of indecision, of cowardice, and, consequently, also of treachery. The queen and the king were agreed only in their hatred of the French; but the king's hatred was indolent and the queen's very active: the former was happy to keep them at bay, the latter wanted to see them destroyed. In moments of danger, the king listened to his fears, or more than his fears, his indolence. At the first favour of fortune, at the first glimpse of new and felicitous hopes, because of his indolence he again abandoned affairs to the queen.

---

3 Generally, the growth of Jacobin clubs in Naples has been dated to the time when Admiral La Touche was there. There is now a huge literature on this topic. For an initial overview, see Galasso (1984), Giarrizzo (1994), and Pedio (1978).

4 Cuoco uses the term schoolboys (*scolaretti*) to minimize the fact that the young people had been arrested for their presumed sympathies for the French Revolution and to exaggerate the counter-revolutionary fears and policies of the Neapolitan government.

[John] Acton encouraged this indolence in the king, for it increased his influence and that of the queen. Because of her desire to rule, the queen did not realize that Acton was disrupting all things and driving the king, the kingdom, and herself to inevitable ruin. The queen was ambitious; but ambition can be both a vice and a virtue depending on the paths chosen, and according to the good or evil it produces. She came from Germany originally with designs on the throne, and did not desist until, by means of intrigues, and with the advantage her cultured upbringing gave her in the mind of her husband, she was able to change domestic and international relations of the realm.

Marquis Tanucci[5] foresaw the dire consequences of the young queen's reforming spirit, and sought to oppose it from the time when she demanded to have access to the Council of State and to vote in it. This was unheard of in the Kingdom of Naples, and much more so in the Bourbon dynasty. However, the queen was victorious, and swore vengeance on Tanucci. Neither his age, nor his merit, nor his years of long, loyal service could save this old friend of Charles III and practically his son's tutor, from humiliation and disgrace.

Under a king who was a weak enemy and unfaithful friend, everyone saw that there was both nothing to fear and nothing to hope for, except the queen; hence everyone sold themselves to her. She created new support for the empire, even from outside.

All political interests joined the Kingdom of Naples to those of France and Spain, and these ties could have formed the nation's prosperity through the benefits of commerce and peace. But while the nation's interests might well have coincided with the king's, they could never have been the same as the queen's. She wanted new political relations to support her against the king, if the need arose, and even against the nation if that were possible. The country became loyal servants of Austria, a distant power, from which our nation had nothing to hope and everything to fear: a power which, as it was involved in continuous wars, at every moment dragged us into participating in others' interests, without ever

5 Bernardo Tanucci (1693–1783) was the king's chief minister. Originally from Tuscany, he brought enlightened government to the Kingdom of the Two Sicilies first under Charles III and then under his very young son Ferdinand IV. Tanucci's power began to decline around 1774, and he was dismissed in 1777. For an appreciation of Tanucci as a statesman, literary figure, and jurist, see the two volumes of papers presented at a 1983 conference celebrating the second centenary of his death, edited by Ajello and D'Addio (1986).

being able to hope that our own might be defended. The predominance that Austria was acquiring over our affairs offended Spain; but far from fearing its scorn, the queen instigated it, and pushed it to the extreme, in order to close all roads for the king to reconsider this course of action.

The king's ministers should have been the queen's favourites; but she always sacrificed her favourites for her designs. The last of these [i.e., Acton] was the most fortunate of all, not because he had greater merit, but because he was more daring than the others, who did not fight with him on equal terms, because they did not dare to do all that he did. They still retained some vestige of justice, of friendship, of the public good. How could they stand against someone who had sacrificed everything to the destruction of his enemies and to the favour of his queen?[6]

John Acton came from Tuscany, that is, from a state which had no navy, to create one in Naples. He had two titles by which to merit the queen's favour, as well as a third one assigned to him by reputation. He was the only one of the king's ministers who was a foreigner, and he understood before the others did that in Naples the queen counted for everything and the king counted for nothing. He arrived at a time when disgust with the Spanish court was at its highest. Sambuca,[7] who was prime minister at the time, took the Spanish side: he was unwitting and cowardly; he lost the queen's favour, and shortly afterwards, as was inevitable, also that of the king. Caracciolo[8] was his successor for a brief period: but broken by his age, and inclined by nature to indolence, in a court where good was not wanted and truth was not suffered, he was but a shadow of his great name, and served, involuntarily or at least not deliberately, to allow Acton to shine, whom the queen wished to exalt but who as yet was unable to defeat his elders' reputation. Caracciolo's death finally paved the way for her designs. Acton was placed at the head of affairs, old [Carlo, Marquis] De Marco was confined to the minute details of the royal house, and all the other ministers were merely Acton's creatures. The only part of genius that Acton truly possessed was that of knowing men. No one was better than him at identifying the moral character of

6 The long favour enjoyed by him might make some think that he had some talent, at least courtly talent … he has none … merely evil. He would have fallen a thousand times, if he had had another evil man as his opponent. (V.C.)

7 Giuseppe Baccadelli-Bologna Marquis of Sambuca (1726–1813) replaced Tanucci as prime minister.

8 Before becoming prime minister, Marquis Domenico Caracciolo of Villamaina (1752–1789) distinguished himself as Neapolitan ambassador in Paris and as viceroy of Sicily.

his favourites. He considered Castelcicala[9] to be cowardly, and cruel in his cowardice; Vanni[10] to be enthusiastic, ambitious, and cruel in his fury, as much as Castelcicala was in his reflection; Simonetti[11] and Corradini[12] he considered to be both good men, but the former indolent, the latter pedantic, and both of them incapable of opposing him. He used Castelcicala from the time when he had been minister in London.

---

9 Fabrizio Ruffo, prince of Castelcicala (1763–1832), was a minister who over time also served as Neapolitan ambassador in important capitals, such as London, Paris, and Vienna.

10 Carlo Marquis Vanni was a judicial officer who gained a reputation of being a fanatical royalist.

11 Saverio Simonetti was a high-level functionary who served the government in various capacities.

12 Ferdinando Corradini (1731–1801) was a practising lawyer who became a high-ranking civil servant.

V

State of the Kingdom – Humiliation of the Nation

It was almost as though Acton and the queen conspired to lose the kingdom. The queen displayed the highest disdain for everything that was national. Was a genius needed? He had to come from the Arno.[1] Was a good man needed? Then he had to come from the Danube.[2] We were inundated by a horde of foreigners, who occupied every post, took up all the incomes without having any talent or manner (*costume*), and insulted those whose means of subsistence they were robbing. National merit was forgotten, depressed, and could think itself fortunate when it was not persecuted.[3]

What was extinguished entirely among us was that noble sentiment of pride, which alone inspires great actions, causing us to believe we are capable of them; that sentiment which alone inspires public spirit and love of one's country; that sentiment, which in other times caused us to be great and which today makes so many other nations of Europe, of which we were both masters and lords, great. We became alternately French, German, and British; we ourselves were no longer anything. For twenty years, it had been repeated to us so many times and so loudly that we were worth nothing that we had almost begun to believe it.

The Neapolitan nation developed a frivolous mania for foreign fashions. This harmed our commerce and manufacturing. In Naples, a tailor was no longer able to sew a garment unless the design had come from London or Paris. From imitating clothes, we soon passed to imitating customs and manners, and from here, to imitating languages: French

1 Allusion to Acton who had been at the service of the grand duke of Tuscany.

2 Allusion to General Mack.

3 One example: the king once appointed Michele Arditi as secretary to the magistrate of commerce; he appointed him on his own initiative and without the prior prompting of Acton. (V.C)

and English were learnt, while it was more shameful not to know Italian.[4] The imitation of languages eventually brought with it imitation of opinions. The mania of imitating foreign nations first of all humiliates, then impoverishes, and finally ruins a nation, extinguishing love for its own things. The queen was the first to open the door to these novelties, which she then pursued with much ardour. A nation, which admires foreign things excessively, comes to add to its own causes of revolution that emerge in the course of its own life those of other peoples' revolutions. How many of us were democrats simply because the French were? Out of a hundred people in every nation, you must count fifty women, and forty-eight men more frivolous than the women, who reason only this way: "In ... they do their hair better, dress better, cook better, speak better: this is proved by the fact that we do our hair, eat, dress the same way they do. How could that nation possibly not think and act better than us?"[5]

4 "Omnia graece, cum sit nobis turpe magis nescire latine" [Everything is Greek, when it is more shameful to be ignorant of Latin; Juvenal, *Satire* VI.] This has been a distinguishing feature of every corrupt nation, from the time of Juvenal to the present day. (V.C.)

5 In France itself, the revolution was preceded by fifty years of Anglomania. Those who are well versed in French literature may easily note this. For fifty years until this time, the French themselves despised their own things excessively. (V.C.)

VI

State Inquisition

Once our emotions take a certain direction, they cannot be halted. Hatred follows scorn, and after hatred come suspicion and fear. The queen, who did not love the nation, feared being hated by it; and like any other, this emotion, albeit pitiful, needs encouragement. Anyone who spoke ill of the nation was well received by her.

The novelty of political opinions increased her suspicions, and provided new means for the courtiers to win her affections. Acton used them in order to have Medici[1] and some of his other illustrious rivals defeated. In doing so, he opened the floodgates, and desolation was brought into the heart of all families.

Let me give an example. In those years, it was the fashion among our young men to hold horse races through Chiaia and Bagnoli. Acton was believed when he said, or rather Acton wanted to have the court believe, that they were seeking to replicate the Olympic races. What relationship could there be between our young Neapolitans' races and those of the Greeks? And even if there was an imitation, where was the evil or the danger in that? In the meantime, Acton charged the police with monitoring these races, as though they were the march of twenty enemy squadrons descending on the capital.

Some young enthusiasts, their heads full of new theories, read about the events of the French Revolution in the periodical broadsheets, and spoke of it among themselves, or worse still, spoke of it with their beloveds and their hairdressers. They committed no other crime than this; nor

---

1 Luigi de' Medici (1757–1830), a member of the nobility, occupied several positions in government, and died in office as president of the council of ministers. During the first wave of anti-Jacobin repression in 1792–4, he was the chief of police (*reggente della Vicaria*) and then became a member of the State *Giunta* (High Court). Accused of Jacobin sympathies, he was able to prove that he did not support that cause, though it is not clear what new ideas he professed. He was imprisoned during the republic. He was an important political personage between 1794 and 1830.

could any young person without rank, fortune, or opinion attempt anything else. A court of blood was erected to judge them under the name of the High Court (State *Giunta*), as though they had murdered the king and overturned the constitution.[2]

A few of the magistrates who made up the *Giunta*, true lovers of the king and country, saw that the first, true, and only crime of the state was that it sowed mistrust between sovereign and nation, and dared to defend the innocent. They suggested to the king that the laws punishing state criminals did not fit the few, inexperienced young men, guilty of no other crime than having spoken of things about which they would have done better to keep quiet, and having approved of things which they would have been better to examine. Such crimes of young men would have naturally been corrected with age and experience, which would have belied the brilliant but misleading theories that captivated their minds in their youth. Ills of opinion are cured by scorn and oblivion; the people will never understand, and never follow philosophers. But if you persecute opinions, these turn into emotions. Emotions produce enthusiasm; and enthusiasm is communicated. Those who are persecuted become hostile, so too those who fear persecution, and the neutral man who condemns it. Ultimately, the persecuted opinion becomes widespread and triumphant.

But where crimes of state are concerned, the most obvious reasons remain ineffective. For rarely does such a crime exist, and rarely does a man make an unequivocal attack on the constitution or the sovereign of a nation. On most occasions it is a question of words or thoughts; words are worth less than threats, or thoughts, which are worth even lesser than words. Such things are worth as much as the fear of the person governing allows them to be.[3] Woe to him who listened once to the voices of fear! The more he feared, the more he must fear. The queen of Naples feared much, and Acton wanted her to fear even more. The frequent impressions of suspicion and fears which she suffered changed her almost physically, and entirely disturbed the sequence and association of her ideas. Persons worthy of credence tell me that it was not without the risk of displeasing her that some attested to the faithfulness of her subjects.

---

2 In reality, while new judges were named, new directives were given. There was already a tribunal in place to deal with the offence of lese-majesty.

3 Julianus had a purple garment sent as a gift to the wretched madman who almost publicly aspired to seize the empire. Tiberius would have had him hanged. (V.C.)

Blood was desired, and it was obtained. Three unfortunate men were condemned to die, including the virtuous Emanuele de Deo, who was offered the chance of living if he revealed the names of his conspirators. Instead, he opted for death over infamy.[4]

Here is an example of what fear can and does produce in people's minds, once disturbed. On the day when the sentence was executed, precautions that at other times had been neglected, and which then too were superfluous, were taken. It was feared that the people wanted to save the three wretches, whom they barely knew; there was fear of sedition by around 50,000 revolutionaries that were said to have been in Naples. Meanwhile, the troops were virtually besieging the city and the government was issuing threatening orders. Everything alarmed the imagination of the people; the slightest tension, to which at other times they would have been indifferent, could not help but disturb them; they feared the rioters, they feared the government's orders, they feared everything; and the slightest fear could produce an uprising in a great mass of people, as indeed it did. Thus the government's suspicions make the people suspicious. From that time on, the Neapolitan people, who prior to this largely contained themselves without policing, were harder to manage. Public festivities were carried out with greater precautions, but were no more peaceful because of fear.

The High Court (*Giunta*) was dissolved. It was hoped that some breathing space might finally be achieved after so many horrors; but just a few months later, a new conspiracy, and another High Court, more terrible than the first one, came into operation. Attempts were made to remove all those magistrates who still retained some semblance of justice and humanity. It became clear that villains were wanted, and, as a result, villains came forward in great numbers. Castelcicala, Vanni, and Guidobaldi[5] were at their head. The nation was besieged by an infinite number of spies and informers, who counted steps, recorded words, noted the colour of faces, and even observed sighs. There was no longer

4 For a contrary view: "The three young men went to the gallows with Christian resignation. While their fate was lamentable, we must bear in mind the verdicts of the French Revolutionary Tribunal of which they and their accomplices approved. Between 6 April and 28 July 1793, it sent 2,625 persons to the scaffold: during that period 80 per cent of those accused before it, were sentenced to death. The *Giunta di Stato*, which Cuoco called the 'Tribunal of Blood,' only sentenced three persons" (Acton 1956: 270). See also Croce ([1896] 1961) and Pedio (1978).

5 Baron Giuseppe Guidobaldi was head of the secret police.

any security. Private feuds found a sure way to obtain vengeance, and those who did not have enemies were oppressed by their own friends, who had sold out to Acton and Vanni because of their thirst for gold and ambition. Indeed, what good can be preserved in a nation where the person who reigns bestows riches, titles, and honours only onto informers? Where, if an honest man comes forward to ask for the reward of his labours or virtues, he is told that he should "first acquire merit"? Acquiring merit here meant to become an informer, that is, to bring about the ruin of at least ten honest persons. Many had this kind of merit, and the just vengeance of posterity must not allow their names to be forgotten. The queen took umbrage against the sentiment of virtue retained by the majority of the nation, and publicly declared that she would "one day succeed in destroying that old prejudice whereby the profession of informer was held to be infamous." All these and many other similar things were recounted: perhaps, as is often the case, a small part of them true, but the majority of them false, and made up out of hatred. But these things, whether true or false, are always harmful when spoken and believed by many, for they make the wicked bolder and the good more timid. If they are false, the ministers whose conduct gives rise to their being articulated, and grounds for their being believed, are doubly deserving of public execration. For because of these rumours, one part of the nation took up arms against the other; there were now only spies and honest men, and a man who was honest was consequently also a "Jacobin." Vanni had told the queen a thousand times that the kingdom was full of Jacobins; Vanni wished to appear truthful, and, by his conduct, created them.

All the castles, all the prisons were full of these wretches. They were thrown into horrible prisons, deprived of light and everything else that was necessary for life. They languished there for years, unable to obtain either absolution or condemnation, without even being allowed to know the cause of their misfortune. Almost all of them emerged free as innocent men four years later; and all of them would have been released, had they not been deprived of the legitimate means of defence. Vanni, who at the time was the supreme director of such affairs, no longer preoccupied himself with those who were in prison; his only thought was to imprison others: he even said that "they should have arrested at least 20,000 of them." If the brother, son, father, or wife of some poor unfortunate soul applied to him to speed up the decision on their dear one's fate, this act of humanity was charged against them as a crime. If the king was petitioned, and the king did sometimes call Vanni to account, this too was useless, since the queen answered for Vanni, as she believed Vanni's work to be good. Vanni always said that there were other ranks of the conspiracy to be discovered, other criminals to be arrested; and the queen approved everything, for she was always fearful of other criminals and conspiracies.

Vanni, who knew better than anyone else what arts were required in order to put together an inquisition, tended more to incite the queen's fears rather than placate them, and trembled each time he heard mention of examination and sentence. He wanted to find the criminal, but was more afraid of the truth being sought.[6]

All that I recount here of Vanni will seem implausible to some. And indeed, this man was singular in terms of his moral character. He combined extreme ambition with extreme cruelty, and to compound mankind's misfortunes, was an enthusiast. Every affair with which he was entrusted was enormous; but he always wanted to appear larger than them. Such men are always lethal, for they do not know how, or are unable, to satisfy their ambition with truly great actions, and so strive to ensure all the acts which they do know and are able to perform appear great, and in so doing corrupt them. Vanni began to gain a reputation as a magistrate of integrity and strictness in his conduct with the prince of Tarsia, who for some years had been the director of the silk factory which the king had set up at San Leucio.[7] The first mistake was perhaps committed by the king in entrusting this enterprise to the prince of Tarsia rather than to a manufacturer; the second was by Tarsia himself, who, not being a manufacturer, ought not to have accepted the appointment. What was bound to happen did happen. Tarsia was an honest gentleman (*cavaliere*), that is, an honest, carefree man who was incapable of misappropriating even a penny, but at the same time was also incapable of preventing others from doing so. A shortfall of around 50,000 *scudi* was found in the accounts. Vanni was appointed to settle them. Nothing could have been simpler, for Tarsia was a man who was both able and willing to pay. And yet Vanni protracted the affair for an

6 Instead of the many satirical commonplaces which were published against the king's government during the early days of the republic, not even one person thought to publish a faithful excerpt from the State *Giunta* trials! It is so much easier to make declamations than to recount facts! But declamations pass, and facts reach posterity. (V.C.)

7 For a most recent assessment of the business operation of this royal factory and the Capodimonte porcelain works, see Musella Guida (2012).

unconscionably long period of time; the king fell, and the Tarsia issue was still not resolved; meanwhile, Tarsia's family was subjected to every kind of harassment and insult, because, it is said, this was Acton's intention. Among the men of good sense, some of them said: "What a fool!" While others said: "What an imposter!" But in the court they made sure it was said: "A judge of such integrity! How zealously, how firmly he confronts the prince of Tarsia, who is a grandee of Spain, a great royal palace official!" As though an injustice perpetrated against the great cannot derive from the same causes, and be equally cowardly, as one which is perpetrated against the small.

A state inquisitor was required, and Vanni was chosen for the very reason that he ought not to have been. The first time Vanni entered the assembly of magistrates who were called to judge, he was visibly anxious, his eyes half wild, and in commending the judges to justice, he added: "I have not slept for two months, because of the dangers which my king has faced." "My king": this was the way in which he referred to him, once he had been entrusted with the state inquisition. "Your king!" shouted the president of the council, Cito, to him one day. Cito, a man to be respected because of both his office and his century of blameless life, said: "Your king! What on earth do you mean by this phrase, which with its appearance of zeal conceals such pride? Why do you not say 'our king'? He is king over us all, and we all love him equally." These few words are sufficient to allow the two men to be judged; but in a weak government, it is the man who shouts "my king" loudest who usually has the upper hand over the one who contents himself with saying "our king."

Vanni's attention was always focused on himself: his face was pale and ashen in colour, like the usual colour of atrocious men; his gait was irregular, with what were like jumps, the gait of a tiger in other words: all of his actions were intended to dismay and frighten others; all of his emotions dismayed and frightened himself. He was not able to live in the same house for more than a year, and in each house where he lived, he did so in the same way that the lords of Pherae and Agrigento[8] are said to have lived in theirs. This was the man who was supposed to save the kingdom!

But the machinery of four years had to be wound up eventually. The interested parties shuddered. Men of good sense laughed about a new kind of state crime that had not yet been discovered in four years of

---

8 Both are ancient Greek towns; the former is in Greece itself, the latter is in Sicily.

inquisition. Among the populace itself, the heated passion shown initially against the criminals was cooling, and in seeing so many unfortunate persons not being sentenced, they began to believe they were innocent and almost started to feel pity for them. Acton, who from the outset had been the main author of the inquisition, having used it sufficiently for his own designs, and seeing it go on more than was fitting and not wanting or being able to halt it, handed it over to Castelcicala. This man, the most cowardly of all men to gain the queen's favour, needed that means which Acton had used only to bring down his rivals, and therefore had to push the abuse further, and did so. He did everything to ensure that the cabal was not discovered: he even came to denounce the religiosity of those who made their vow in favour of the truth as though it were a crime. He even threatened to punish the lawyers, whom he had appointed to defend the criminals zealously. But the nation was oppressed, not corrupt. If it gave great examples of patience, it also gave very many and equally splendid examples of virtue. Nothing could unsettle the judges' constancy or the lawyers' zeal. When the truth was seen to triumph, and those whom he had wanted dead walked free, to justify himself in the eyes of the public and of the king, who had finally occupied himself with this affair, Castelcicala sacrificed Vanni, and all the blame fell on him.

Before the king, Vanni had accused all the judges, the president of the [royal] Council Mazzocchi, Ferreri, Chinigò, possibly the most respectable men[9] that Naples had both in terms of doctrine, integrity, and loyalty to their sovereign; and for a time there was a question mark as to whether they would be punished or Vanni. If Vanni had been victorious, he would have completed the task of losing the kingdom and ruining the throne. Fortunately he had come to the brink, and ruined himself by wanting too much. But before this came to pass, how many other useful men did he deprive the state of, and how many faithful servants were removed from the king? Even if the throne of Naples had not been overthrown as a result of the war, Vanni on his own would have been sufficient to do so, and would have done so.

Vanni was deposed and banished from the capital: secret attempts were made to sweeten his exile, but to no avail. Vanni's ambitious mind fell into a melancholic fit that ultimately drove him to seek his own death,

---

9 In fact, Filippo Mazzocchi had such a good reputation that during the republic he served on the Supreme National Council (*Supremo Consiglio Nazionale*); the marquis Gioacchino Ferreri came from Sicily with a similar reputation, as did *cavaliere* Chinigò.

which, if justice were to be done, for the good of mankind, he deserved to receive from the hand of another and far sooner. His death only just preceded the arrival of the French in Naples. He feared them, had applied to the court for asylum in Sicily, and had been denied. Before killing himself, he wrote a note in which he said: "The ingratitude of a treacherous court, the advance of a terrible enemy, and the lack of asylum have led me to take my life, which is now a burden to me. Let no one take the blame for my death; and may my example serve to make the other state inquisitors wise."[10] But the other state inquisitors laughed at his death. Castelcicala laughed at it; and the inquisition continued with the same fury until the French reached Capua.

10 The authenticity of the letter Vanni wrote on 21 December 1798, expressing these thoughts, remains in doubt.

VII

Causes and Effects of Persecution

I shall stop; my mind recoils at the memory of so many horrors. But where did so much hostility towards the French Revolution in the minds of the sovereigns of Europe come from? Many other nations had changed form of government. There is barely a century that cannot count such a change: but those changes had never affected anyone other than the courts directly attacked, nor had they produced any suspicion or persecution in the other nations. A few years previously, the American sages had carried out a revolution that was not so different from the French one, and the Court of Naples had publicly applauded it. No one at the time had been afraid that the Neapolitans might want to imitate the revolutionaries of Virginia. Did the danger faced by sovereigns perhaps grow in proportion to their fears?

The French deluded themselves over the nature of their revolution, and believed that the effect of the political circumstances in which their nation found itself was caused by philosophy itself.

France, which was presented to us as a model of monarchic government, was a monarchy that contained several abuses and contradictions. The revolution was merely an accident waiting to happen. The main accidents which caused the revolution were: the king's weakness; the arrogance, at times overweening and at other times equally a sign of weakness of the queen and Artois;[1] the ambition of the wicked and inept Orléans;[2] the public debt; Necker; the assembly of notables, and much more so, the Estates General. But before these causes existed, ancient and infinite material for revolutions had accumulated over the course of many centuries: France was resting on deceptive ashes that concealed a devastating fire.

---

1 Count d'Artois (1757–1836), brother of King Louis XVI, later reigned as king of France between 1824 and 1830.

2 Louis-Philippe Joseph d'Orléans (1747–1793); his sympathy for the French Revolution did not spare him from being guillotined.

Among the many who have written the history of the French Revolution, can there really be no one who has expounded on the causes of this event, seeking them not only in the deeds of men, which can change only the appearance, but in the eternal course of things themselves, which alone determines their nature? The legend of popular uprisings, of massacres, of ruins, of the various opinions, and of the various parties forms the history of all revolutions, not just the French one, and tells us nothing of what made the French Revolution different from all the others. No one has described to us the absolute monarchy created by Richelieu, and reinforced in a moment by Louis XIV; a monarchy which arose, like all the others in Europe, out of feudal anarchy but without destroying it, because, while all the other sovereigns had been elevated to their position by protecting the peoples against the barons, the sovereigns of France had both feudatories and enemies, more powerful than elsewhere, and the people were still oppressed; the many different constitutions which each province had; the silent but continual warfare between the different social classes of the kingdom: a singular nobility, which, without being any less oppressive than in other nations, was more numerous, and to which anyone who wanted to could belong because any man became noble as soon as he became rich, and to which the people lost their wealth as well; a clergy which believed itself to be independent from the pope, and which thought it did not depend on the king, hence it was engaged in a continual struggle with both king and pope; the military ranks which were the property of the nobles, the civilian ranks which were venal and hereditary, made it so that the man who was neither noble nor rich had nothing to hope for; the disputes which all of these conflicts caused to arise; the urge to write, which was born from this and which in France had become a means of subsistence for those who had no other, of whom there were a great many; the discussion of opinions to which the disputes gave rise and the danger which was born of these same opinions, because they were founded on real class interests. All of this led to the strongest persecution and the utmost intolerance, by both clergy and court, at the very same time that the philosophers were preaching the utmost tolerance; to the greatest contrast between the government and the laws, between the laws and ideas, between the ideas and customs, between one part of the nation and another; contrast that was bound to produce shocks in all parts alternately, a state of violence throughout the entire nation, and, consequently, either the torpor of destruction or the outbreak of revolution. This would have been the stuff worthy of Polybius's history.[3]

At the same time France had an infinite number of abuses to reform. The greater the number of abuses, the more abstract the principles of reform to which it was necessary to resort, as those which must take in the largest number of special ideas. The French were forced to deduce their principles from the most abstract metaphysics, and fell into the error to which men who follow abstract ideas excessively are prone – that is, to confuse their own ideas with the laws of nature. They believed that everything they had done or wanted to do was the duty and right of all men.

Anyone who compares the *Declaration of the Rights of Man* made in America with the one made in France will find that while the former speaks to the senses, the latter speaks to reason. The French declaration is the algebraic formula of the American one. Perhaps the other *Declaration,* which Lafayette had designed, was better.

Ideas as abstract as this lead to two different kinds of problem: it is easier for the evil to avoid them, and for the powerful to adapt them to their whims. The turbulent and factious always find something in them to support the oddest claims, and decent men receive no protection from them. Anyone who looks at the events of the French Revolution will be persuaded of this.

The sovereigns believed, as the French did, that their revolution was a matter of opinion, a work of reason, and so they persecuted it. They were ignorant of the true causes of the French Revolution, and feared its effects for the very reason that they ought not to have. When and where

---

3 Many, including Rousseau, predicted the French Revolution from these observations. More detailed is the prediction of Mercier in his *L'An 2440*, a work that at one time was attributed to Rousseau; an attribution at which Rousseau blushed, almost as though the work was unworthy of him. It seems that [Louis-Sébastien] Mercier was not party to the revolutionary secret, like also the author of the *Remonstrance to be Read in the Private Council of H.M.*, who sought to warn the king of the imminent revolution, as Mercier had warned Europe. Among those who before others predicted that the French Revolution would arise within the French state for domestic reasons was our own Antonio Genovesi. He saw the direction in which both the writers' opinions and the course of events were heading: his prediction was worthy of Vico ... I would not know if the king of Prussia also foresaw the revolution. He certainly did, however, foresee the haste and the urge to reform everything philosophically. He treats very harshly the metaphysical reformers, whom he refers to as "encyclopédistes." See his *Dialogue between Prince Eugene, the Duke of Marlborough and Prince Liechtenstein.* (V.C.)

has reason ever had its own following? The more abstract the ideas of reform are, the further removed they are from the imagination and senses, and the less likely they are to move a people. Have we not seen this in Italy, and in France itself? Given the way in which the French had expounded the sacred principles of humanity, it was as likely that other peoples would rebel as it was that our pictures of carriage wheels would be perfected by the principles of perspective, as demonstrated through differential and integral calculus.

If the king of Naples had known the state of his nation, he would have realized that it would never have been able or have wanted to imitate the examples of France. The French Revolution was understood by only a few, was approved of by even fewer, and wanted by almost nobody; and if there were some who wanted it, their desire was in vain, for no revolution is possible without the people, and the people are not moved by ratiocination but by need. The needs of the Neapolitan nation were different from those of the French nation; the revolutionaries had become so abstruse and mad that they could no longer understand them. This was true of the people. As for the class above the people, I believe, and believe firmly, that the majority of them would never have approved of the French revolutionaries' theories. The Italian school of moral and political sciences followed other principles.[4] Anyone who had filled their minds with the ideas of Machiavelli, Gravina, and Vico could not lend credence to the promises, or applaud the operations, of the French revolutionaries once they abandoned the ideas of constitutional monarchy. In the same way, the old school of France, that of Montesquieu for example, would never have applauded the revolution. It resembled the Italian school, for both of them greatly resembled the Greek and Latin ones.

The working of a revolution must be distinguished from its principles. Operations are the product of circumstances, which are never the same from one people to another; while principles differ even more, for the number of ideas is always much greater than the number of operations, and consequently, it is easier to find diversity and harder to find similarity. There is no people that has not had many revolutions in its history. When the workings of revolutions are compared, they are found to be similar; when ideas and principles are compared, they are always found to be quite different.

4 There is a rich literature tending to support this view. See, among others, Battaglia (1925); Haddock (2005: 34–41); Giarrizzo (1981: chap. 5); and Sabetti (2011a).

Anyone who witnesses a revolution in a neighbouring state must fear either its operations or its ideas. The means for opposing the operations are entirely military: whatever ideas the two peoples follow, the one which is better able to wage war will be victorious; and the people which is better ordered, more patriotic, braver and more disciplined, is the one who will wage war more effectively. The means for opposing the contagion of ideas (shall I say it?) is but one alone: to allow them to be known and discussed as much as possible. Discussion will give rise to opposing ideas. It is a matter of pride: two men are always more in agreement at the start of a discussion than they are at the end. Once such opposing principles have been conceived, they will become national in character; they will increase the love of one's own country, because nations which are more different from others will have more of these principles; they will increase hatred for foreign nations, reliance on one's own forces, and national dynamism; not only will the contagion of opinions be avoided, but shelter will be provided from the force of operations as well. I am told that when the marquis of Gallo[5] read the list of those who found themselves under arrest as conspirators, he laughed about it like all good men did, and suggested to the king that they be sent on their travels. "If they are Jacobins," he said, "send them to France: they will come back royalists." Such advice is full of reason and common sense, and does honour to the marquis of Gallo's heart and mind. A revolution is defeated by the one who fears it least. By persecution, sovereigns turn ideas into emotions, and emotions are then transformed into factions. Their fear betrays them, and they sometimes fall victim to their own excessive precautions. All periodical broadsheets were prohibited in Naples; the people were not allowed even to have news of the French. Thus an object which, if observed from close up, would have aroused pity or laughter, was seen like Aesop's pieces of driftwood,[6] which looked like an enormous ship while far out to sea. An indomitable curiosity drives us to want to know what is concealed, and man assumes that what is hidden behind a veil is always better and more beautiful than it is.[7]

5 The marquis and later duke del Gallo (1753–1833) was Marzio Mastrilli, a Sicilian-born aristocrat. A much experienced Neapolitan diplomat, he was at one point a favourite of Queen Maria Carolina.

6 Aesop, *Fables*, no. 258.

7 The paragraph continued in the first edition with the observation that the sovereigns of Europe believed they were kings by the grace of God alone, and not by the grace of their subjects. Cuoco noted that such a belief was as ancient as it was weak, and was an unreliable justification for rulership. It is not clear why he omitted this passage from the second edition.

But sometimes I imagine Philip of Macedonia rather than our kings in the current crises of Europe. Greece in his time was split between the Spartans and Athenians, who waged war because of differences of opinions over governance, and in conjunction with the philosophers who, at the time, were discussing the Greek constitutions like our own philosophers do today, and wearying the Greeks with bloody wars and petty controversies. This is what always tends to happen: in the various revolutions, ancient ideas are forgotten and the people's ways of life (*costumi*) are lost. Once things have been reduced to this state, schemers, the foremost among whom are the powerful, always profit, for ultimately the peoples lower themselves to follow those who offer them the most material goods at the time. Hence the utmost love of liberty generates an exaltation of principles but also accelerates their destruction and leads back to an even harsher form of servitude. It is by these means that Philip won the Greek empire.

It is a misfortune for humankind (*genere umano*) when a war leads to a change in either the form of government or religion. In such cases it loses its true objective, which is the defence of a nation, and the ills of a foreign war are compounded by the even worse ones from within. Hence the partisan spirit makes persecution necessary, and persecution itself incites a new partisan spirit; hence such times are cruel even when there is peace. Northern Italy repeated the examples of Sparta and Athens for us when, rather than closing ranks to defend their respective constitutions, its republics sought first under the name of the Guelphs then of the Ghibellines to reform one another's. The same errors had the same effects in Italy. Scala, Visconti, Baglioni, etc. repeated the example of Philip.

Such political eras are less adverse to sovereigns who know how to reign than is presently thought. But in such periods, the most humane and if, I dare say, the most just, always wins. Today the republicans are more generous and forgive the royalists; with foolish cruelty, the kings never grant any truce to the republicans. This means that they will soon have indifferent friends and fierce enemies. When the pretender's fleet descended on England, he had all the Hanoverian prisoners hanged; while George released all of them. This alone, as Voltaire well says, is sufficient to allow the justice of the two sides to be determined, and their future destiny to be surmised.[8]

8 When I consider all that the kings' cabinets in this time could have done and have not been able to, I wish for a book that was entitled: *History of the Errors of Those Who Were Great without Being Great Men.* It was with this idea in mind that one of the most sensible books of the last decade of the century was written: *Everyone Is Wrong*; but much still remains to be added to the series of its observations. (V.C.)

VIII

Public Administration

While the nation was humiliated and oppressed through various means (*arti*), increasing misery was wrought by the disorder found in every branch of public administration. From the arrival of Charles III,[1] the Neapolitan nation had begun to find relief from the incredible ills it had suffered through two centuries of vice-regal government. The authority of the barons, who previously had not allowed the inhabitants to have either real or personal property, was diminished. Ordinary taxes were made certain by means of a new land register, which, if not the best that there could be, was at least the best there had been until that time. Moreover, the use of extraordinary taxation was abolished, which, under the name of *donativi*, had removed huge sums of money from the nation and transferred them to Spain for no profit.[2] Once the nation was free of the barons' oppression, the burdens of the tax authorities, and the perennial withdrawal of money, its activities began to develop. Agriculture became resurgent, and commerce picked up once again; existence became more comfortable, minds became more cultured, and intellects more refined; a Neapolitan kingdom separate from Spain was created, Spain was taken away from the Austrian dynasty and given to the house of Bourbon, the [royal] family separation agreement restored the very peace to our nation needed to recover from the ills suffered, and allowed us to maintain neutrality in the last war between Spain, France, and Britain for the American colonies. All these factors produced a considerable increase in our nation's wealth. In fifty years we

1 He arrived in1734, at the same time as the proclamation that Naples was an independent kingdom with its own king.

2 Montesquieu says that Spain kept Italy and made it wealthier. The authors whom Montesquieu consulted on our history could not have been very accurate. (V.C.) Cuoco is probably referring to Montesquieu's *The Spirit of the Laws,* bk. 8, chap. 18. For a more general discussion of Montesquieu's views on Italy in his work, see Felice (1995) and Sabetti (2011b).

made very swift progress, and there was every reason to hope we would be able to make more.[3]

Our nation went, so to speak, from infancy to youth. But this state of political adolescence is precisely the most dangerous, and the one from which it is easiest to fall back into torpor and desolation. Nations escape barbarism by increasing their strength and hence making their existence more secure. They do not become more cultured [or civilized] without increasing their needs. But needs grow more rapidly than forces do, partly because these needs depend on our ideas alone, partly because other nations willingly share their ideas, customs, orders, and vices with us, without sharing their forces, and these new ways become a source of new needs for us. This way, if we do not also take care to increase our forces while our needs are growing, we will never have that balance between needs and forces that alone brings about the health of individuals and the prosperity of nations. The steps we take in being open to other cultures may merely make us more enslaved to foreigners, and a precocious and sterile new culture will prove more harmful to us than barbarism. A state which does not do all that it can do is diseased. Such was the state of all Italy; and this state was most dangerous for Naples, because it had more natural resources, and its sphere of activity was wider.

But the Neapolitan government caused many of its resources to be lost, and, by humiliating the public spirit, suppressed the development of individual abilities. Everything was left for the government to do, but the government did not know how to do anything, nor could it do everything.

Nations which are still barbarian love to be relieved of taxes, for they have no superfluous desires. Cultured nations are content to pay much, provided that this increase in tax increases national strength and the standard of living. The secret of a good administration is to increase production in proportion to taxation. It is not so much the sum of the taxes, as the use of them in relation to the nation, which determines the state of its finances.[4]

---

3 For a more recent discussion in English of the positive developments connected with Naples ceasing to be a province of Spain and with the growth of the Enlightenment in Naples between 1680 and 1760, see, among others, Astarita (2013); Calaresu (2013); Robertson (2005); Sabetti (2012).

4 Necker was unable to recognize this truth, when he made the comparison between the finances of France and Britain. The British paid more than the French, but the nation increased its wealth, while France could not grow any further as a result of its political circumstances. Taxes were useful in Britain, but harmful in France. France had run its political course, it had become decrepit; hence if no new order of things arises, it will remain but a step from death. Necker indeed could find no remedy for this ill. Experience showed the fallacy of his theories. "If Britain can cope," he would say, "France will be able to cope much more easily." While France failed, Britain is still coping. (V.C.)

A wise and active government would have corrected the old administrative abuses, developed national energy, exempted us from the duties we paid to foreign countries for their products. A wise and active government would have protected our own trades, improved our produce, and extended our commerce. The government would have become richer and more powerful, and the nation, in turn, would have become happier. This was exactly what the nation desired.[5] The period when Acton arrived was the time of useful plans.[6] He passed himself off as a "planner," and as such he was received. But his plans, which were either impossible to follow, not followed at all, or poorly executed, became the causes of new disasters, because they were the cause of new and useless expenditures.

Acton wanted to give us a navy. Nature had formed the nation for the navy, but had not formed Acton for the nation. The navy first of all had to protect the trade we had at the time, which, as it involved foodstuffs (over almost all of which the kingdom had a monopoly), could arouse only minor envy in the other nations, or none whatsoever, for they largely had trade that involved manufactured products. Our enemies were the Barbary pirates, against whom a large navy was of less use than the small corsair navy that Acton destroyed.[7] The armed navy should have grown in proportion to the mercantile and commercial navy, without which the former is useless and cannot be sustained. Instead of extending our trade, Acton restricted it with his diplomatic errors, his despotic tendencies, his ill faith, and the cowardice with which he espoused foreigners'

---

5 Who can guess the degree of prosperity and power to which the Neapolitan nation could have been directed by wise government? I am no visionary, but I believe that even more than what [Carlo Antonio] Broggia, [Antonio] Genovesi, and [Giuseppe] Palmieri hoped for was possible. But this nation has the misfortune of being despised because it is not well known: the Spanish knew it and feared it; only Emperor Frederick the Second knew it and loved it. But the great days of Frederick were but a brief flash of lightning as far as we were concerned, to be followed by a stormier night. (V.C.)

6 It may be worth recalling that it was Queen Maria Carolina of Naples who persuaded her brother Grand Duke of Tuscany to release John Acton from his duty there and come to Naples in 1779 to reorganize the Neapolitan navy. As Davis (2009: xii) notes, the monarchy was then embarked in efforts to modernize and professionalize its army and navy.

7 Perhaps the most effective method against the Barbary pirates was the one adopted by the British under Charles II, that is, to build all merchant ships so that they were armed with ten cannons, and so make the ship owners themselves responsible for defending their property. Our merchant ship owners applied for permission to do this on thousands of occasions; and on thousands of occasions they were denied it. They had courage and good will, but Acton did not want them to have it. (V.C.)

interests in preference to our own. Acton knew neither the nation nor things. He wanted a navy, but we had no ports, which are necessary for it. He was not even able to refurbish the ones at Baia and Brindisi, which nature itself had formed, and which at one time had been so famous, and could have become so once again at minimal expense if, rather than following the plans of Acton's creatures, we had followed the Romans' plan, which was the same as that of nature.

The navy, as Acton had conceived it, was a giant with feet of clay. It was too small to do us any good, and too big to harm us. It excited rivalry on the part of the great powers, but without giving us the force required, if not to defeat then at least to withstand them. Without a navy, we would have remained profoundly at peace. With a large navy, we might have been victorious; but with a small navy we were bound, sooner or later (as indeed proved to be the case), to be dragged into the maelstrom of the great powers, suffering all the ills of war without ever being able to hope for the advantages of victory.

Acton followed the same plan in reforming the infantry. Charles III[8] had set the number of ground troops at around 30,000 men. But, as always occurs in small states that enjoy prolonged periods of peace, the war orders had been dismissed, and the actual number of troops totaled no more than 15,000 men. We were totally lacking in artillery, and this was organized so that there was nothing left for us to envy the foreigners. The number of the other troops increased only apparently, to conceal high misappropriation and extravagance that knew neither laws nor limits. Acton devoted himself to this more than the other ministers; and this was not the least of the reasons why he merited such powerful and long-lasting protection.

Habits and tactics began to be reformed, from the death of Jaci on.[9] A new general would arrive each year, from Spain, France, Germany, or Switzerland, who would order that the caps should be raised by two inches, that the uniforms should be shortened by two inches, and so forth ... A soldier would shudder at seeing himself subjected to such

8 As noted earlier, Charles III (1716–1788) was king of Naples and Sicily from 1735 to 1759 before he was king of Spain from 1759 to 1788. He acquired a reputation as an enlightened despot.

9 Jaci was Charles III's commander-in-chief, and remained so until his death, including under the reign of Ferdinand. He had great authority, and knew how to use it; he opposed Acton for as long as he was alive. (V.C.) Jaci's full name was Stefano Reggio e Gravina, Prince of Jaci and of Campofiorito.

novelties, when he knew that but a year later, these would be declared useless.[10]

These generals always brought foreigners with them, who would occupy the first ranks among the troops. The other ranks were accorded to the pupils of the military college,[11] whose graduates were indeed well trained but did not possess that ability to endure fatigue, which is acquired only with age and long service. Intelligence and knowledge should be what forms generals; but courage and love of fatigue are what forms officers. The great principle, which says that in peacetime, seniority should be the norm in determining promotions, did not fit with Acton's mentality. When Acton did not have despotism in his heart, he had it in his head. Old captains, abandoned to their misery, were seen having to obey inexperienced and weak young men, who knew no more than theory, and many others (for once the sensible norm of justice is removed, the way is opened to favour and intrigue) who did not even know the theory, but who had been raised to that rank through money, espionage, and in some cases even more infamous qualifications. The ranks which could not be occupied by such people remained unfilled, and entire regiments were seen to be missing half of their officers, while those who should have been promoted requested in vain the reward of their labours. Acton replied to them, that they should "wait for their plan to be published"; an admirable plan, which cost Acton twenty years' meditation, and which, without ever being published, disorganized the troops, appalled the nation, and wasted the state's tax revenues!

Everything in the Kingdom of Naples was misappropriation, or illusory projects that were more harmful than misappropriation, while all that was necessary was left undone. We needed roads: the marquis of Sambuca saw the need, a tax of approximately 300,000 ducats per annum was imposed [in 1778]: the work was started, some stretches were completed, but shortly afterwards the work was halted and the money paid in tax was used for some other purpose. Entire provinces applied for permission to build roads at their own expense, promising to continue

10 Initially, a soldier had the hope of being rewarded, for low-ranking officials were entitled to regular promotion. Instead of obliging everyone to be low-ranking officials, Acton took away all hope of promotion from them. A sergeant had to die a sergeant, and was obliged to serve twenty years. This was equivalent to wanting neither decorated sergeants nor brave soldiers. (V.C.)

11 Cuoco here is referring to the Nunziatella Military Academy established in 1786. It still exists.

paying the road tax in any case, even though this had already been earmarked for some other purpose; promising to pay it indefinitely, even though when the tax had originally been levied, it had been promised that the imposition would end when the roads had been built. Is it possible to believe that this proposal was rejected? Is it possible to conceive of a more reasonable or better nation than this, or a more foolishly evil ministry? In the Kingdom of Naples, there were errors in the principles and flaws in the organization, which hindered the progress of public happiness. These had originated in different times and different circumstances; the circumstances and times had changed, but the errors and flaws continued to exist.

Like all governments with an empire larger than their own strength, the government of Spain took steps, in the times of the Austrian dynasty, to destroy what could not be preserved. All military valour was extinguished. In order to contain a generous and powerful nobility, the first of the Spanish viceroys, Pedro de Toledo,[12] thought it a good idea to entangle them in the snares of nitpicking jurisprudence. This offered easy and abundant wealth to those who had none, but it deprived those who had riches in abundance of their wealth, and unduly multiplied a class of persons who are dangerous in every state, because they were able to become rich without being industrious, or without their industry producing anything (which amounts to the same thing). All the kingdom's affairs were debated in the courts; and what was debated above all in the courts was affairs. Many ills derived from this. Everything that was not the matter of forensic disputes was neglected: agriculture, the arts, commerce, useful sciences, all this was considered the object of sterile or greedy curiosity rather than as areas of study useful for public and private prosperity. For centuries a Latin distich was written above the entrance to our schools, in which the clumsiness of the style is matched by the stupidity of the thought which says: "Galen provides riches, Justinian the honours; all the others provide nothing but straw." And if anyone, despite their lack of education, conceived some idea of public utility, they could not execute it without first subjecting themselves to an examination, which always became a dispute given that it had to be taken before judges with all the legal formalities. Did someone want to build

12 Pedro de Toledo (1484–1553), generally known as Pietro de Toledo, was viceroy of Naples from 1532 to 1552. He was responsible for many changes in public life and administration. Perhaps he is most remembered for his unsuccessful attempt to institute the Spanish Inquisition in Naples in 1547.

a bridge? Litigation was necessary. Did someone want to build a road? Litigation was necessary. Every member of the Neapolitan people had the right to oppose the good that some wanted to pursue.

Charles III did wonderful good for the kingdom. He overhauled the administration of justice, removed the abuses of ecclesiastical jurisdiction, restrained those of feudal jurisdiction, and protected the arts and industry. He would have done more, too, had his reign lasted longer, and had many of the ministers serving him not still followed most of the principles of old Spanish policy. For example, his friend Tanucci,[13] the one out of all his ministers to whom the kingdom is most indebted, was wrong to believe that the Kingdom of Naples should never be a military kingdom. The answer he used to give to anyone who spoke to him about war is well known: "Big princes need big armies and big cannons; little princes need little palaces and little villas." His maxim was wrong, both because the king of Naples could not be described as a "little prince" (*principino*), and because even little princes are not exempt from providing for their own defence. Tanucci, who was more of a diplomat than a military man, trusted in treaties more than his own strength. He ignored the fact that it is might (*forza*) alone that causes advantageous treaties to be obtained. He did not know the power (*forza*) of the kingdom he administered, and rather than giving it a secure existence of its own, he made its existence dependent on the uncertain judgment of others.

Tanucci continued to confuse administrative with judicial authority, and the court system continued to be the centre of all affairs. By its intrinsic nature, judicial authority aims to preserve things in the state in which they are found; administrative authority tends, instead, to change them, for it aims to improve them. The former always pronounces irrevocable sentences; the latter merely makes attempts, which can, and, at times, must change every day. If one combines these two sets of authority, their very nature, being so different, ends up corrupting them both.

Everything in Naples had to be done by the judges and by judicial proceedings. This meant that all administrative operations were slow and produced bad outcomes. The government was so far removed from true principles of administration that various objectives of administration were either entrusted to no one, or committed to the judges themselves.

---

13 As may be recalled, Charles III appointed BernardoTanucci (1698–1783) to bring enlightened government to the kingdom: Tanucci served first as councillor of state, then as superintendent of posts, then minister of justice, foreign minister, and finally as prime minister. See also chap. IV, note 5.

Hence there was either no one to promote useful administration, or it was promoted exceptionally slowly by those who had many other things to do.

The other failing in the organization of the Neapolitan government was the lack of a common centre on which all branches of the administration would converge, like the many spokes of a wheel. This should have been the Council of State. But in Naples there was a Council of State in name only. Each minister was independent. The general regulations ought to have been the result of common deliberation by all ministers, but each minister made them himself. As a result, each minister made them as he wished; and the regulations made by one minister were the opposite of those by another, for each minister's main concern was always to usurp as much of his colleague's authority as possible, and to destroy the work of his predecessor. Hence there was no unity or coherence in government performance: the war minister destroyed what the minister of finance did, and the minister of finance destroyed what the minister of war did. Among so many ministers, there was always (and this was inevitable) one above all others in the sovereign's favour, and this minister was the one who, as they say, set the "tone" and the "character" for all affairs. This tone and character changed from one moment to the next, because the favour changed too. Nor was it sufficient for a regulation or law to be reasonable for it to endure. Was there ever a law more just than the one that obliged judges to give reasons for their rulings, so that there were truly rulings rather than mere whims? Tanucci had imposed this obligation on the judges: Simonetti exempted them from it. Can it be believed that Simonetti held, in good faith, that the judges were not obliged to offer reasons and obey the law? Thus, Simonetti betrayed his own conscience, and betrayed the king, for the law which he abolished was not his own work but that of Tanucci.[14]

There are an infinite number of similar examples, but I have restricted myself to this one alone because, as it is so obviously at odds with common sense, it suffices to demonstrate that the organizational flaws of which we are speaking had gone so far that not even common sense was respected any longer. It should be added that all the ministers were

14 As noted earlier, Saverio Simonetti was the Secretary of Justice. Colletta ([1838] 1858: I: 146) and Imbruglia (2000: 18) effectively convey the dilemmas that public officials faced as subordinates to John Acton and as servants of the king.

ministers of justice, because administration of justice was not organized according to the nature of things or actions, but based on the individual nature of persons, as had been the case among the northern barbarians, our forefathers. This way, justice was different for the soldier, the priest, the man who possessed a flock, the man who did not, etc., etc. Specialized courts proliferated in Naples more than gods proliferated in Rome at the time of Cicero, whence this great man had bemoaned the fact that he could not take but one step without fear of bumping into some divinity. And in the continual clashes between so many courts, it was often very hard to know which one had the authority to judge. I have examples of "court disputes" that lasted eighteen years.

New, and greater, disorders. In a monarchy, what in the Roman jurisprudence was called the *rescriptio princeps*[15] has the force of law. But wise princes make very few rescripts and only ever under very special circumstances. This is why virtually all monarchies, by an almost fundamental law of state, established that rescripts should never be transferred from one case to another. In the Kingdom of Naples the number of rescripts had been multiplied to an infinite degree. Every minister issued them, and every minister issued rescripts rather than laws. As was always the case, the rescripts were the work of clerks, and among these there was one who for many years had been the true and only legislator in the whole kingdom.

I have dwelt at considerable length on what may seem to be minor things, because the more important things depend on them. Change the former, and imagine that Tanucci had understood the kingdom's potential, and had established military order and education there; that administrative power had been separated from judicial power, and that the former had become more active, and the latter more regulated; that all parts of the administration had a common centre, a permanent council with the king at the head of it; and that the ministers were no longer independent of each other and rivals, but forced to work to a single, coherent plan. Imagine, in other words, that rather than allowing first one, then another, minister to dominate, the king had wanted to truly be the king: everything would have changed. For I am persuaded that in the present state of ideas and customs in Europe, it is very rare, and virtually impossible, to find a king who does not want the good of

15 This means that a ruler had supreme authority to issue an order on his own authority to resolve any contentious case.

his kingdom;[16] but this good is not allowed to be produced, for it has to be done by individual ministers, who love their position more than the kingdom and themselves more than their position. They must therefore be compelled to do so by using the forces of public order, the true purpose of which, for those who understand it, is none other than to protect the king against the negligence and malevolence of the ministers. With very minor reforms one can achieve a huge amount of good. Said reforms implemented in a state point to a single goal, namely that the king should truly be king. But for this reason the ministers always oppose such reforms; thus the ills become bigger, and it is impossible to avoid those huge crises whereby ten generations often have to sacrifice themselves for the good, perhaps, of the eleventh. A gloomy truth, this, for both princes and peoples! The ruins of both one and the other are usually the work of ministers and those who boast that they are the king's friends.[17]

16 It may be worth recalling here that when work on the royal palace at Caserta began in 1752, the then king Charles III had the Latin motto *Deliciae regis felicitas populi* (The king's pleasures are the people's happiness) stamped on a coin placed under the first stone of the palace.

17 See C. Bonnet, *Art de rendre les révolutions utiles*, a book full of common sense. (V.C.)

IX

Finances

Anyone who compares the sum of the taxes which we paid with that paid by the other nations in Europe will believe that we were not the most oppressed. Anyone who compares the sum of the taxes we paid at the times of Charles III with those which we paid subsequently in the times of Ferdinand will perhaps see that the difference was not that great. But in the meantime, the needs of the nation had grown, and those of the court had grown too. The nation came to pay more because in reality it had less to spare, while the court was effectively demanding less. But the little which was demanded was misappropriated. No thought was given to the possibility of restoring to the nation what was taken from it. It was easy to predict that the revenue would soon be inadequate, and that the need for new taxes in the court would be as great as the people's inability to pay them.

They started by speculatively changing some of the indirect taxes which seemed to be higher (e.g., those on tobacco and manna ash) and which were converted into direct taxes yielding almost twice as much. A duty was levied on hunting, which until that time had been free; but no thought was given to regulating it, because the duty concerned the court and regulation concerned the nation. A duty was imposed on the export of domestic foodstuffs when there should have been a duty on the import of foreign foodstuffs. Use was even made of the "crusade tax,"[1] and I do not believe there can be a more cowardly resource than this, whether or not the government believes it to be in the honour of Catholics' godliness that on certain days of the year they should eat only bad food that the heretics sell us.

Lands which two, three, four, ten centuries previously had been possessed by the tax authorities were sought throughout the kingdom, and a

1 A tax originally reserved to cover costs associated with the fight against infidels, and awarded by the papacy to various sovereigns from time to time. This tax was granted to the Neapolitan government by Pius VI in 1777.

persecution which was less cruel than the persecution carried out against persons had begun against things. Insofar as the persecution was against fief owners and clergy only, it was tolerable. But once the tax agents had been assured of authority over the king's dominion, as they called it, they pitilessly cancelled all contracts and, mocking all good faith, came to disturb the poor tenant, who was forced to buy back, by means of an altercation or with money, the land which had been watered by the sweat of his elders' brows and which was to form his sons' only means of subsistence.

Perhaps one day it will not be believed that the frenzy over these claims had reached the stage where the knights of the Constantinian order,[2] imagining goodness knows what kind of kinship between Ferdinand IV, the great master of the order, and St Anthony the Abbot, managed to persuade the king that all estates in the kingdom over which this saint's name was invoked belonged to him; and that he, in return for the advice and care which these knights provided in seeking out such estates, wherever they were, believed it useful to the state, and therefore right, to remove them from those who were cultivating them profitably, and to give them to others who, being Constantinian knights, were entitled to live idly.

Our municipalities had many public lands (*fondi pubblici*)[3] which the populations themselves administered, the return on which served to pay the public debts. There were also many others, which under the name of "pious places" (*luoghi pii*), were devoted to public beneficence and dated from the times when religion alone, under the name of "charity," had been able to induce men to perform works useful to their peers, and merely the name of some saint was sufficient to restrain the still barbarian Europeans from usurping them. There were thousands of abuses, both in the object and administration of these lands; but they formed part of the national heritage, and to deprive the nation of them,

---

2 This is the Constantinian Order of Saint George, which dates back to the eleventh century; in the 1720s, it became associated with the Neapolitan Bourbons. It continues to exist now under the aegis of the Spanish Bourbon monarch, though it split into two branches in 1900.

3 These *fondi pubblici* include the "commons" and often took such different forms as *terre civiche, demani civici, usi civici, terre comuni* and the like. For an introduction to the variety and often contentious governance of the commons in the Italian South, see Bulgarelli Lukacs (2011); Corona (2004, 2010); Genuardi (1911); Salvioli (1909); and Trifone (1974). For a more general discussion, see Grossi (1981) and E. Ostrom (1990), as well as the many publications of the *Centro Studi sui Demani Civici e le Proprietà Collettive* of the University of Trento, directed by Pietro Nervi.

without there also being any increase in trade and commerce with which to replace them, was effectively to impoverish it. Time, which reforms all ills better than man, would have corrected this one too.

Part of these public lands came to be occupied by the court, and this was not the least of the ills; the other part, on the pretext that it was poorly administered by the populations, came to be administered by the chamber of accounts (*Camera de' conti*),[4] and by a court defined as "mixed" which, however, in the composition of its employees, consisted of people who were anything but honest. Administration passed from the hands of the municipalities to those of the clerks of these courts, who went on stealing with impunity. The only advantage that derived from the new reforms was that now it was the few who were robbed, whereas previously it had been the many; now it was the idle who were robbed, whereas previously it had been the industrious. The money was frittered away between the vices and luxury of the capital, whereas previously it had been used in the provinces. The nation became poorer, but the state became no richer.

The same thing occurred with the allodial and Jesuits' lands.[5] Everything in the Kingdom of Naples tended towards all branches of administration being concentrated in the hands of one person. But as one person could not do everything alone, disloyal agents had to be used, and the nation fell into that deplorable state, in which its employees are not expected so much to bear the honour of serving their country as the right to despoil it. Thus the nation was invaded by the very judging "wasps" that make us laugh so much in the comedies of Aristophanes.

Our capital began to be crowded with these insects, who neglect every form of work in the hope of obtaining some miserable, subordinate position. Meanwhile, vices and whims increase with idleness, and because their wretched salary does not increase proportionately, they are forced, in the exercise of their employment, to adopt such conduct as to ensure

---

4 Since about 1444 and until the Napoleonic reforms of 1807, this chamber of accounts was known as the *Regia Camera della Sommaria,* the top fiscal and financial council in the kingdom's government. For a history of the finances of the Kingdom of Naples, see Bulgarelli Lukacs (2011); Bianchini ([1839] 1983); and Calabria (1991).

5 Here is an example of the waste that took place in the administration of these estates. When the Jesuits were driven out of Sicily, they possessed lands which in the first year of royal administration yielded 150,000 ducats of income, in the second year 70,000, and in the third year 40,000: and they were valued on this basis when they were sold. *Ab uno disce omnes* [from one you know them all]. (V.C.)

that their fortune increases at the expense of the state's, and of the mores of the nation. I judge the corruption of the government by the number of persons applying for posts in order to make a living. Honest citizens should not think of serving the country without first having obtained the means of subsistence. Rome, in the ancient sanctity of its customs, did not concede this honour to anyone who had not. Disorder in government administration is thus the main cause of public corruption.

To begin with, the disorder in public finances affected the richest; but since theirs was also the class of the industrious, and the rest of the population lived off of them, disorder affected the heart of the state, and soon all its members felt it equally.

Nothing was sufficient in the Court of Naples. The money received from despoiling Calabria was not sufficient. The *donativi*[6] were reinstituted. Not a year went by without there being one. Eventually not even the *donativi* were sufficient, and the operations involving the banks commenced.

The Neapolitan banks were private individuals' cash deposits, to which the government provided no more than its protection. There were seven foundations, which together possessed approximately 13 million ducats, and to which the nation had entrusted 24 million. Their paper enjoyed the highest credit, partly because it was secured against huge lands, partly because a foundation believes itself to be immune from those accidents to which a private individual might be subject, and partly because the banks always held the money of which they were the depositaries themselves, and were not allowed to put it to other uses. Until 1793 they were held to be sacred.

The queen had the idea of turning them from private banks into court [or royal] banks. The first use she made of them was to burden them with the odd pension for some favourite; the second was to force them to lend money to some other favourite who was less cowardly or more cunning; the third was to have large sums contributed for Acton's projects, which were called "state needs," almost as though the banks' money was not in fact the money of the same private individuals who had already been taxed. Thus, the secret operations commenced. Immense amounts of money were withdrawn: when there was no more money, paper was

6 Literally, a voluntary donation, a gift, *donativo* came to stand for parliamentary aids and special taxes, which were no longer freely given. For a list and discussion of *donative*, Bianchini ([1839] 1983: I, bk. 6, chap. 3) remains a good source.

printed in order to be sold as cash. Paper in issue reached the level of approximately 35 million ducats, not even a penny of which existed.

At this point a charge hitherto unknown was introduced to the nation, which soon grew until it absorbed two-thirds of the value of the paper. Far from seeking to remedy the ill when it first appeared, the court increased it by continuing to issue the worthless paper all day long, and having it converted into cash through its agents at whatever margin was requested. The sovereign himself thus became a speculator: he would have done exactly the same if he had wanted to make an enemy nation go bankrupt.

The charge was all the more onerous, because it was not share certificates or sovereign notes that were involved, the fate of which was of interest to but a few investors. It meant attacking the entire money supply in one go, and overthrowing all the estates, commerce, and trade of an agricultural nation, which by nature always had more sluggish circulation than others. The court awoke from its slumbers when the damage was irreparable. It gave its allodial lands as security for the worthless paper; but these lands could not so easily find buyers, nor, once sold, were sufficient to repair the ill will. The people should have been persuaded that no more worthless paper would be issued, that is, either that the court no longer needed it, or, if it was still needed, that the expedient of issuing new paper would no longer be used. The state of affairs would have created concerns over the need, but the court's conduct caused doubts to arise over its good faith. How was it possible to trust a court which, having already started the sale of ecclesiastical properties, rather than tearing up the two and a half million notes received from the disposal, put them back into circulation again? Hence this portion of the public debt was effectively doubled, for the paper remained payable by the nation while the equivalent amount in land was sold.

There were also some who believed that the sale of the ecclesiastical properties was not the result of the concern to meet the banks' deficits, but of fear that they might be used as a pretext and stimulus for revolution. The less there is to gain, it was said, the fewer the number who will want a revolution. Did the man said to be the author of this advice know anything about revolution, men, or his country?

X

Trade

Fifteen years previously, the banks' disorder would perhaps either not have taken place or would have been more tolerable, for the nation's tax revenue at that time was sufficient to fill the hole made by the banks, or at least to keep as much money in them as was required for circulation. It is a truth universally acknowledged that part of the cash may be missing from the public deposits without the paper losing its credit; but circulation must be fully operative, and while part of the nation is returning its paper, another has to be depositing new bills. Now the introduction of new funds in Naples had ceased several years previously, for all national industry had been extinguished, and the only trade relations with other nations that remained all showed a deficit. The earthquakes of 1783, and more than the earthquakes, the destructive economy pursued by the court,[1] had ravaged Roman and Greek Calabria: two of the most fertile provinces had become deserted. The reclaiming of the Pontine Marshes and the crops which Pius VI introduced there had removed, or at least diminished, a very useful market for exporting our wheat. In other times we had enjoyed lucrative trade with France, and what we gained from France offset what we lost from the British, the Dutch, and the Germans. In destroying the manufactures of Marseilles and Lyons, the French Revolution caused

1 Cuoco is referring here to the work of the *Giunta di Cassa Sacra di Catanzaro* and its central corresponding agency in Naples, created in 1784 to help the population in Calabria after the earthquake. The main task of the *Cassa Sacra* in Catanzaro and its corresponding agency in Naples was to devolve funds expropriated from church property and religious organizations to the reconstruction of Calabria, which was easier said than done. In order to appreciate the radical nature of the government policy one must keep in mind that church expropriation and confiscation tooke place before the French Revolution by an otherwise very Catholic monarch. See Bianchini ([1839] 1983: 186); and, for a more recent account, Placanica (1970).

our trade in oil and silk to decline. More business should have been given to our silk manufacturers, and soap factories should have been set up. We would have virtually had a monopoly over them, and we could at least have taken this advantage from the French Revolution.[2] But this objective was of no importance to Acton. Strict neutrality should have been maintained, which in the first years of the French Revolution would have ensured that our wheat had a huge market. But Acton and the queen thought they could starve the French to death. Meanwhile, the French roused the Dalmatians and Levantines, from whom they received wheat, and did not starve to death. We thus lost all the profit for which we might reasonably have hoped, and today find ourselves having acquired competitors in this branch of commerce, who are all the more dangerous because they inhabit a soil which is equally fertile and are poorer than we are. Only trade with the English was allowed, for trade with the Netherlands was also in British hands; that is, only trade which should have been forbidden was permitted. Indeed, just as the opinion of the court was sold to the British, so too was that of the nation; and the brilliant trifles of the Thames had never been so fashionable on the banks of the Sebeto.[3] We have never been so indebted to the British as we were at precisely the time when we could least afford it. This trade imbalance removed almost 10 million [ducats] of the Neapolitan nation's actual money in the space of eight or nine years, in addition to the same amount, and possibly more, which it could have and should have earned if the nation's true interest had been preferred over the whim of the persons governing it.

To all these ills was added that of an imaginary war, carried out so that it destroyed the kingdom without ever giving us hope of victory or peace. An army of 60,000 men was kept idle on the borders for four years, and retaining it cost as much as it would have done to retain any army active in campaign. To preserve the kingdom's peace, as they called it, which could be based only on the king's good faith, fresh help was sought from the people; and was duly obtained. Not only was the church's silver

2 The king had established an excellent silk production factory in Caserta; but silk was produced only in Caserta, and could not be produced anywhere else. Who could ever have competed with a king? The sovereign should be the manufacturers' protector, not their rival. (V.C.)

3 Sebeto is the name of the river in the eastern part of the city of Naples.

asked for, but also that of private individuals, who would receive worthless paper in return; and this too was obtained.[4] A tithe [in 1796] was imposed on all the kingdom's lands, which produced almost one-quarter of all the other taxes already being paid. But all these resources, which were not inconsiderable, were wasted, lost, passing through negligent or unfaithful hands.

The countryside was robbed of horses, mules, oxen, some of which died from the lack of food, while others were sold by those who requisitioned them.

In the first conscription, the best labour was removed from agriculture, the state was deprived of its most useful youth; having been torn from their families, they were led off to die at San Germano, Sessa, and Teano. The plague-ridden air of those places, and the lack of all things necessary for life, destroyed more than 30,000 of them in the space of one summer. A defeat would not have caused as many to be lost.

In this way it became clear how reasonable the Neapolitan nation was, how much the Neapolitans loved their country, but at the same time how hostile they were to oppression and injustice. Two years had passed since a conscription of 16,000 men had been ordered, but this conscription, which had been entrusted to corrupt agents, was not completed. The nation had put so many obstacles in the way that very few communities (*popolazioni*) sent barely even their own contingent of recruits. The inhabitants of the Neapolitan kingdom's provinces did not want to act as mercenary soldiers, or be slaves to the whims of a German general[5] who knew no other law than his truncheon. The court saw the problem; the new conscription was entrusted to the municipalities, or to the populations themselves, and the new conscripts were declared "volunteers,"

4 The nation merely allowed itself a small laugh when it read in the edict [dated 28 March 1798] which removed silver from private individuals, that "the king was minded to reinstate the old sumptuary laws, which had been so profitable to the State." Who on earth was the minister who persuaded the king to lend his holy name to so blatant a lie? And in what other case has a king been permitted to expose his own needs to his peoples, save when these needs are the needs of the State? Why did they not say: "The country is in danger; the country's needs are my needs and your needs: let us save the country"? What idea of honour and what generosity could there have been in the mind of a minister, to counsel such treachery? Now, are not the sense of honour, and the nobility and generosity of ideas, of its ministers the most accurate measure of a State's true strength? (V.C.)

5 A reference to the Austrian head of the Neapolitan army, General Karl Mack von Leiberich (1752–1823), who was born in Bavaria.

who had to defend the country until peace was achieved. Everyone rallied under the banner of the "country," under the name of "volunteers," and in a few days almost double the number stipulated in the conscription order had signed up. But one year later most of these same men deserted, appalled at the poor treatment they received from the court, and even more so by its bad faith. They were volunteers required to serve until peace was achieved; when peace was concluded, they duly applied for leave. A wise government would willingly have granted it, certain in the knowledge that they would return when a new need arose. But the Neapolitan government knew the power of neither good faith nor justice. It felt safer being feared by its people than being loved, and so was detested by them. To avoid the rigours of persecution, many deserters fled to the countryside. The kingdom was full of thieves, and the borders remained unpatrolled.

The courtiers held the soldiers to be wrong, because they wanted to fawn over the court.[6] The foreigners held the soldiers to be wrong, because they wanted to humiliate the nation; and many of our own people, even those known to be thinkers, held the soldiers to be wrong, as they did not know the nation and fawned over the foreigners. These small traits are what characterize nations, the men who govern them, and those who judge them.

6 Here again it may be noted, once and for all, that in this history, "government," "court," and also "king" and "queen" are all synonyms for "Acton." Only in a few cases do they need to be distinguished. (V.C.)

XI
War

Such was the state of the kingdom at the end of the summer of 1798, when Nelson's victory on the seas of Alexandria,[1] the lack of French troops in Italy, the mercenary promises of some Frenchman, the new alliance with Russia, and above all the British cabinet's intrigues, led the king of Naples to believe that the time had come to reshape Italian affairs.

On the one hand, the Roman republic, the scene of the first [Neapolitan] military operations, resembled a desert more than it did a state, and rather than opposing invaders, the few men who inhabited it were forced to receive anyone who was able to offer them bread. On the other, the German emperor[2] was turning his thoughts again to war. Neither he nor the Directory wanted peace any longer; and while the two powers' plenipotentiaries sat idly in Rastadt [Rastatt], the French were occupying Switzerland and the Russians were marching towards the Rhine.

To complete his army, the king of Naples ordered a conscript of 40,000 men, and this was accomplished throughout the kingdom in the space of just one day. Hence around 70,000 men found themselves assembled on the borders at the end of October.

These troops, however, lacked a general, and in the belief that none could be found in Naples, one from Germany was asked for. Mack arrived as the genius who would protect the kingdom.

The plan was for the king of Naples to advance his troops at the same time as the emperor was opening the campaign on his side. The duke of

---

1 The jubilation at this victory went beyond the limits of decency; not even a semblance of neutrality was maintained. The British fleet had been summoned by the court of Naples, and had been provisioned by the same court, albeit under a private name. (V.C.)

2 Cuoco is referring here to Francis II, emperor of the Holy Roman Empire and future emperor of Austria, as Francis I. In 1806, Napoleon forced Francis to renounce the crown of the Holy Roman Empire.

Tuscany and the king of Sardinia were also to take part in the operation; to this end, they made secret conscriptions in their own states. Seven thousand men were sent from the court of Naples under the command of General Naselli, who occupied Livorno; at the right moment he was to march on Bologna together with the Tuscan troops and join up with the great army there. Under the guise of defence, it was deemed necessary to occupy Tuscany, because out of all the Italian governments, it was the one whose thoughts were furthest from war, and this rendered the Tuscan minister so odious to the Neapolitan government that it was not far short of sending detachments of troops from Naples to Livorno, solely in order to oblige the grand duke to depose Manfredini.[3] Thus the French, surrounded and attacked at all points, would have no choice but to decamp from Italy.

But the emperor was not moving, possibly because the time was not yet right, possibly because he was waiting for the Russians, who had still not arrived. The Council of Vienna had resolved not to open the campaign before the month of April. It is not known how, but letters more authoritative than the Council's resolutions were received, which allowed the Neapolitan army to move earlier. These letters had been applied for and obtained with such secrecy that the minister of Vienna himself knew nothing of them until the same day on which he heard of both the troops' march and their defeat. Those who sat in Vienna on behalf of the Neapolitan court at the time were reproached bitterly because of it. Minister [Johann] Thugut said that the court had betrayed the cause of all Europe, and that it deserved to be abandoned to its own fate. The protection of Emperor Paul I,[4] mediated with the help of Grand Duchess Elena Paolowna, at the time the Palatine's archduchess, saved the court from the effects of this threat. The Neapolitan ambassador justified himself by showing orders, faced with which the council members had to fall silent. But it remained uncertain and disputed, and will always do so, why, against their own interests, secret orders were applied for by Naples, and granted by Vienna, that were contrary to the plan which had been publicly resolved, agreed to by all, and universally acknowledged as the most advantageous. Was the intention with this to deceive the enemy or themselves?

3 Marquis Federico Manfredini (1743–1829), risen to prominence as a military commander in Austrian service, was now the wealthy and influential counsellor of the grand duke of Tuscany.

4 Paul I (1754–1801) was the emperor of Russia.

The Court of Naples probably burnt with excessive impatience to expel the French from Italy. Such impatience, again probably, was born not only of hatred but also of the desire to derive from a victory, held to be certain, a gain which Austria might perhaps not willingly have conceded, but which, in finding it already taken, it might have tolerated. As in alliances more is never given than one party takes, so too each allied party hurries to take for itself as much as it can, as quickly as possible. Mutual jealousy creates mistrust *(malafede)* on both sides, and while each party thinks only of itself, the interests of all are forgotten. But assuming this was the case, why did Austria consent to the demands of Naples? It is likely that Mack, who was always full of plans, felt it would be easy to expel the French, and having become confident as a result of his early successes (and who would not have believed him, when Mack was still unknown?), was keener to invite the emperor to enjoy the fruits than to share the glory.

Above all other speculation, however, it is probable that the Court of Naples often acted without the German emperor's intelligence, because while he lent his name to the alliance that had been formed in the north, the principal centre of which was in Vienna, he also retained an ambassador in Paris, who, when the peace had already been broken, still could obtain orders from the Directory to prevent the general at the head of the army of Italy from invading the Kingdom of Naples, and limit his military operations to merely resisting aggression. By means of an accident, the nature of which is unknown, the courier bringing these orders was assassinated in Piedmont. Now orders of this nature, even if the negotiations that precede them are unknown, could certainly not have been obtained without supposing that either the Directory was entirely unaware of the Neapolitan cabinet's designs and movements (which is inconceivable) or that it had resolved to abandon Italy. This way, the Court of Naples set its hopes of advantages more on the French government's abandonment than on help from its allies, and hence it sought to procure such advantages itself, so as not to be forced to share them with others. What is certain is that the war with Naples was made against the Directory's orders; that Championnet[5] had no one else to authorize him to wage war than the commander-in-chief, Joubert, and had to apologize

5 General Jean-Antoine-Etienne Championnet (1762–1801) was in charge of the French troops on the Neapolitan front. He was sympathetic to the Neapolitan aspirations to have their own independent republic.

to the Directory, citing that need which often pushes a general to go beyond the limits of his superiors' instructions as the reason; and he was absolved, because all daring which achieves prosperous success is easily justified.

But all these things stirred in the secrecy of the cabinet, nor were they entrusted to all the king's ministers. Wretched condition of the times, when the fate of peoples depends more on intrigue than on true bravery, and when a government which reasonably has everything to hope for from its own forces and from favourable circumstances humiliates itself in seeking victory from the whims and promises of men, which are less stable even than fortune! If the Court of Naples, in consulting its own forces and reason, had actually waged war rather than frequenting taverns, it would have obtained more successful, or less disastrous, results. Indeed, the majority of the king's councillors stood firm in their opinion of peace, either because they were unaware of the secret reasons on which all hopes of success were founded, or because they did not set much store by them. But Acton took care to have these men removed. When it was decided to go to war, not many of the old councillors intervened. Marquis De Marco, General Pignatelli and Marquis del Gallo were in favour of peace; as were Marshal Parisi and General Colli, who were summoned to the Council despite not being councillors. But the queen, Mack, Acton, and Castelcicala formed the majority, and turned the king's mind to their view.

"What do you think of this war, which has been decided?" the queen asked Ariola many days later, Ariola being the minister of war, who as of yet knew nothing about it. Ariola, who would have preferred to remain silent but was encouraged to speak, replied that there was more to fear than to hope for from such a war.

"The king could sustain a defensive war to some advantage," said Ariola, "but lacks everything he would need for the offensive. He does not fight on equal terms. The French are few in number, but they are soldiers used to war and hard work. Our army is half composed of recruits snatched barely a month ago from the arms of their families, and the fact that there are more of them will merely serve to embarrass the good veterans among them, and to make our shortage of good officers the more keenly felt, for we have not been able to double the number of these in the space of a moment the way we have doubled the number of troops. Why not wait until these troops have been trained? Why not wait for the emperor to move first? Are we in such a hurry to win that we do not even take care to make victory certain? Is Mack so sure of victory that he sets off without even contemplating the possibility of defeat? If a war is commenced on the borders, one of the two states must immediately be invaded; while he has taken no care to defend the interior of the kingdom, which is entirely exposed; with the first reversal we suffer, the enemy will be in the heart of our state. It will not be easy for us, alone and without the emperor's help, to expel the enemy from Italy, and until this has been achieved, nothing may be said to have been accomplished. We need many victories: one alone will be sufficient for the enemy. The further the enemy advances, the easier he will find the path to victory; but the further we advance, the larger and more numerous the obstacles we encounter will be; the fate of the enemy is decided in a moment; ours, even if favourable, will require a great deal of time. Meanwhile, as though he were able to end the war in but a few days, Mack heads off towards a desolate country, where there is a shortage of everything, without first having thought about provisioning, in a season when transport is difficult and food is in short supply. He is heading off to conquer others' territory, and could end up losing his own."

What effect did this speech have? Mack and Acton took offence, Acton threatened Ariola, Ariola complained to the king, the king sided with him [Acton], and Acton, in the king's presence, removed his portfolio from him [Ariola]. A few days later, experience confirmed the veracity of his predictions. The king, having fled from Rome, reached Caserta: he recalled Ariola, and appealed to him as the only one who could free him. Ariola left for the battlefield in order to agree with Mack on the means for defending the kingdom from an invasion. He found the general staff in Terracina, but Mack was not there, nor could anyone give any indication as to where he might be. Meanwhile, he saw the dispersed army returning. He thought it necessary to return to Caserta so as not to waste time. A few hours after his departure, Mack arrived. He wrote to the king that the minister of war was a coward who had abandoned his post. And Ariola was arrested. Nor is it unlikely that Acton had a hand in Ariola's misfortune, if what some say is true, that having been accused of having directed certain military preparations poorly, he wanted to make Ariola take the blame for it, and grabbed the opportunity to have his papers seized, so that the true author should never come to light. Did he think that by means of a courtier's crime, he would be able to retain the reputation of a general?

XII

War (cont.)

War was resolved upon. A proclamation was published, in which the king of Naples declared in equivocal terms that he wished to preserve the friendship which he had with the French republic, but that he felt slighted by the occupation of Malta, an island which belonged to the Kingdom of Sicily; and that he could not allow the pope's lands to be invaded, for he loved him as his old ally and respected him as the head of the Church. He would have his army march in order to restore Roman territory to its lawful sovereign (though it was not specified whether this sovereign was the pope or not); and invited any armed force to withdraw from Roman territory, for otherwise war would be declared on it. No similar proclamation has been seen in any century of diplomacy, unless the Romans made one when they ordered the other Greek peoples not to disturb the Acarnanians, who had been the only ones not to send troops to the siege of Troy.

This proclamation was published on 21 November. The whole army left on 22 November, divided up into seven columns, entering Roman territory at seven different points. The columns which moved from San Germano and Gaeta advanced rapidly. Neither the very wet weather nor the rivers which they encountered en route, with the difficulty of transporting artillery and provisions along roads that were impracticable due to the deep mud, were sufficient to stop Mack's troops. He just kept going. He left the artillery behind, supplies started to dwindle, the soldiers were deprived of all comfort and needed to rest; but on Mack drove. Micheroux's and Sanfilippo's columns had already been defeated in Abruzzo.[1] Public opinion blamed the generals for this setback; but it cannot be disputed that Micheroux's conduct was subsequently examined by a council of war, and was found to be blameless. We know nothing of Sanfilippo. But in such cases public opinion is never entirely deserving of

1 Respectively, on 28 November and 25 November 1798.

credence, for the people usually judge according to the outcome, and often apportion greater praise and blame than is merited. Mack, who had never thought to establish firm communications between the various detachments of his army or to coordinate their operations, heard late of an event which should have changed his plans entirely, but continued to push on regardless. He reached Rome on 27 November. They took five days over a route that should have taken fifteen. The troops were allowed only five hours' rest under arms, and were then forced to push on to Civita Castellana.[2] En route the provisions were completely exhausted. In vain the army's provisioners asked Mack where they should send the supplies. The general's orders were so rapid that while the first was being carried out, the second, third, fourth, and fifth had already been given. The supplies lay wastefully by the roadside, while the soldiers and horses were starving to death. When they reached Civita Castellana our men had not seen bread for three days. They were absolutely unable to stand against a fresh enemy familiar with the territory, and the enemy destroyed our army, duping them here and there in places where numerical advantage was of no use. Mack was unable to inspire courage in the new troops even to put them into action in minor skirmishes against the small enemy detachments they encountered between Terracina and Rome. Instead, these were released as a result of senseless advice, which had two major negative consequences. The first was that our troops did not become accustomed to victory, when victory was easy and assured. The second was that the enemy's numbers were swollen at the point where they were about to launch major attacks. Mack was unable to have two columns fighting at the same time: they were all thoroughly routed. Mack was unfamiliar with the places in which he found himself, and as he teetered on the edge of a precipice, persuaded himself, and managed to persuade the king as well, that everything was going fine. Because of the resistance which the French had put up against the king of the Two Sicilies' army, the latter declared war on them on 7 December, that is, when the war was already over because of the defeats that had been suffered, and when it was necessary to be thinking of peace. After two more days the entire army had been routed, and Mack could find no response other than to rush back, just as previously he had rushed forward. In the space of less than a month Ferdinand left, drove on, reached his destination, conquered someone else's kingdom, lost one of his own, and being

2 A town about sixty-five kilometres north of Rome.

unsure of the other, was almost on the point of fleeing to the third of his kingdoms, in Jerusalem,[3] in order to seek asylum.

I am no man of war: others will read the history of these events in Bonamy's *Memoirs*, and in those of our own Pignatelli, who saw the facts and was able to judge them. Mack also published his own *Memoir*. In it he slanders both the nation and the army. But was not the army, which was defeated with him at its head, the same one with which he said he intended to conquer Italy in 15 days, while some were advising him to proceed more slowly?[4]

This man, who previously was challenging all the earth's powers, lost all his genius at the first setback. Though defeated, he still retained infinitely superior forces; and while unable to win, he could at least have put up some resistance. With his army's advances, he might have stopped at Velletri or at the Garigliano, where he could have disputed the pass for some time; he could have saved Gaeta and saved the kingdom. But if, while his luck (*fortuna*) was in, Mack had done nothing but press forward; when it left him he could do no more than flee. He stopped only when he got to Capua, where he thought he could defend himself but where, in fact, he did not stay.

Capua could easily have been defended, and on that side the fate of arms might have been tested once more, with greater hope of success this time. When a proclamation for mass conscription was published, the whole kingdom was in arms. The Abruzzesi opposed Rusca's division,[5] and while they did not succeed in stopping him from passing, they did at least make sure that it cost him dearly. In the impassible mountains in the province of L'Aquila, the insurrection was never effectively extinguished, and the provincial capital itself was under French control for only a few days; they were reduced to defending it from within the castle. The other division which came via Terracina and Gaeta advanced as far as Capua, but was unable to impede the insurrection that had broken out at Itri and Castelforte. The insurgents, who ceded the plains for a

3 A play on the title of King of Jerusalem with which the Neapolitan monarch styled himself, as did other monarchs.

4 Mack slandered the nation to save his own reputation. Bonamy seems more inclined to do justice to Mack than to the nation, because he does not know the nation, and it was in his interest, after the victory, to talk up the general whom he had just defeated. It seems that Pignatelli, who knows both the nation and general equally, does equal justice to both, as they deserve. (V.C.)

5 Jean-Baptiste Rusca was a French general in charge of French forces there.

while, took refuge in their mountains, before returning shortly afterwards to overrun the rump of the French army, which thus had all its communication with upper Italy broken. A detachment of troops bravely and successfully defended the pass at Caiazzo. Capua had almost 12,000 men garrisoned. All the inhabitants of the districts of Nola and Caserta had risen up en masse, and there was still a detachment of troops there intact under the command of [Luigi de] Gams.

What I say now will doubtless appear implausible to posterity, but virtually all the Capuans have sworn to me that it was so. If Capua was not taken by surprise, this was not the merit of Mack but of a humble drummer or gunner (whichever it was),[6] who, of his own accord, fired one of the advanced posts' cannons in the direction of San Giuseppe, and made sure that the French halted. Mack had certainly not given any orders to defend.

I repeat: I am no man of war, nor do I undertake to examine the operations and accidents of the campaign one by one. But I do believe that these accidents must be reckoned, and that the final sum of the result depends less on the accidents than the general plan. Mack naturally erred in extending the line of his operations too far, so that even the smallest enemy attack was sufficient to break it. He paid more attention to the enemy in front of him than the one at his flanks, when the latter was possibly more to be feared than the former. This is why he always advanced so rapidly, and this same speed (which some call victory) was the main reason for his unanticipated and irreparable defeats. Defeated at one point, Mack was defeated along the whole line, because the whole line was broken. When Mack was drawing up a huge plan to defeat a weak enemy, many called him a great general, for there are many who measure the greatness of a mind by the forces it moves. I called him unwise, for wisdom involves achieving the maximum effect with the minimum of forces. Mack is the kind of general who shines in a cabinet, for the cabinet is the place where, before the action begins, the minds of the majority tend to confuse the greatness of the machine with the greatness of its builder. Mack is not lacking in that theoretical knowledge of military science by which the majority are so easily impressed. A general who always speaks to them of mathematics, geography, and history, who

---

6 Anna Bravo (1975: 135) suggests that this may have been Pietro Colletta, the future general and author of *The History of the Kingdom of Naples 1734–1825,* who at the time was a young artillery officer.

reminds them of the ancient names of all the Scythians, lists all the great battles they have illustrated to him, and who, to confirm every development he is asked to imagine, brings forward the examples of Prince Eugene [of Savoy], Montecuccoli, Caesar, Hannibal, and Scipio, is sure to receive the majority of votes in his favour. Common sense, meanwhile, should really lead us to mistrust campaigns that are too erudite; they are also necessarily too well known to the enemy, and are consequently useless. The whole true secret of war, says Machiavelli,[7] consists of two things: doing everything that the enemy cannot suspect you will do, and allowing him to do everything you have predicted he will do. With the first of these precepts, his entire defence is rendered useless; with the second, his entire offence. These overly systematic commanders also have another shortcoming, which is that their ideas are too rigidly interconnected or linked to each other. They commit their plan to memory, and if the fortunes of war happen to impinge upon it, they become like little boys who have lost the thread of their lesson, and are forced to halt. What are the unmistakable signs of one of these commanders?

He will be extremely intolerant of contradiction and advice from others. For him, the criterion of truth is not that his ideas correspond to reality, but that the ideas correspond to each other. Before starting engagement, they are extremely bold; afterwards, they are extremely timid. They are bold, because they do not think that events could be different from their ideas; they are timid because, having not foreseen that there could be such a difference, they are unprepared. They affect extreme precision in their speeches; but this precision is itself imprecise, for it takes no account of the differences existing in nature. They count men but do not value them; more than in men, they trust in the army; more than in virtues of the soul they trust in those of the body; and more than in bravery they trust in tactics. Such leaders, who are more powerful in words than in deeds, always prevail, to the detriment of the nation. The same can be said when a state's military orders are such that the entire execution of a war depends on an assembly or council, or when those who govern the sum of things are not free from partisan spirit; and this is certainly not the least of the ills which partisan spirit and ill-conceived orders are accustomed to produce.

7 In "The Art of War" (Machiavelli 1965).

XIII
The King's Flight

Governments are like men, in that all passions are useful to the wise and disastrous to the foolish. Rather than inspiring prudence and caution, the Neapolitan court's fear of the French was the cause of disastrous cowardice. By fearing them, they made them more terrifying than they were.

A few days before war was declared, someone at the court told me it was wise counsel not to let the soldiers know they were going to fight the French. It was with this in mind that the ambiguous terms in which the proclamation was couched were conceived, namely, to conceal the true object of the expedition until the moment of the attack. "But they told us we weren't going to war with the French!" the soldiers said when they found out. This was not the least of the reasons why the mass conscripts in Naples showed more courage than the regular troops, and why such courage increased with the defeats rather than diminished. It would have increased even more, too, had Mack not been the general. There is a difference between accustoming a people to despise the enemy and causing them to believe that there is none. The former produces courage, the latter carelessness, which in situations of danger gives way to dismay. Caesar did not comfort his soldiers (who at times were frightened by the enemy forces' reputation) by diminishing it but by exaggerating it. Once Juba [of Numidia]'s arrival was feared to be imminent, Caesar summoned the soldiers and harangued them as follows: "Know that in a few days' time, the king will be here with 10 legions, 30,000 horses, 100,000 light infantry, and 300 elephants. So stop daydreaming and start realizing what forces he has." Caesar exaggerated the real danger, which however great it might have been, was still limited, in order to remove the imaginary danger, which was limitless.[1] This is how all peoples want to be governed.

---

1 Juba had supported Pompey against Caesar, 60–46 BC. When Caesar was victorious against overwhelming odds, Juba killed himself.

The same fear which the court experienced with the first setbacks inspired it to counsel a mass conscription. An edict was published, in which the peoples were invited to take arms and defend their property, families, and the religion of their fathers against the enemy. For the first time we heard our peoples being reminded that they were Samnites, Campanians, Lucanians, and Greeks. The priests were entrusted with the duty of awakening such sentiments in the name of God. Operations of this kind never fail to produce great results. The greatest disturbance was in Naples, where a huge populace, with no true profession or education, lived only at the expense of the government's disorders and the prejudices of religion.

But this same disturbance, which should and could have preserved the kingdom, through the fault of Acton and the court's fears, became the principal cause of its downfall. The people rushed to the royal palace in numbers to offer themselves for the defence of the kingdom. A king with mind and heart needed only to get on horseback and take advantage of the moment's enthusiasm; he would have gone to certain victory. But Acton held him back. The people wanted to see him. He did not want to show himself, and had General Pignatelli and Count Acerra go out instead. Among the many words spoken on that occasion, as everyone can imagine, one member of the people said that all the kingdom's problems were caused by the foreigners who had come to serve as ministers; that whereas previously profound peace and general abundance had been enjoyed, in the last fifteen years everything had changed; and that the foreigners were all traitors. Then, either out of a patriotic sentiment not unknown to the Neapolitan people, or a spirit of adulation for two popular knights, he added: "Why doesn't the king make General Pignatelli prime minister and Count Acerra minister of war?" These words, which were recorded by Acton's cronies and repeated back to him, moved his suspicious mind to speed up the departure. On what things does the well-being of a kingdom depend!

It was easy enough to persuade the queen in favour of this course of action. But in order to persuade the king as well, the popular insurrection was stepped up. The following morning, Acton's agents encouraged him to arrest Alessandro Ferreri, a courier for the cabinet who was taking papers to Nelson. Many have reason to believe that he had been chosen as a designated victim a long time beforehand, because he was aware of the secret of the letters from Vienna altered upon the occasion of the war. I would not dare to pronounce on this issue. Whether by chance, or as the result of the minister's policy or vengeance on the part of one or another of his own personal enemies, he was arrested on the pier at the point when he was about to board Nelson's ship, murdered, and his bloody corpse was dragged as far as the royal palace and shown to the king amid shouts of "Death to the traitors!" "Long live the holy faith!" "Long live the king!" The king was standing at the window; he saw the imposing force of the people, and doubting that he could govern it, began to fear it. At this point departure was resolved.

The most precious items of furniture from the palaces of Caserta and Naples were loaded onto the British and Portuguese ships, along with the most valuable rarities from the museums at Portici and Capodimonte, the crown jewels, and 20 million and possibly more in coin and precious metals still to be minted, the spoils of a nation which remained in misery. The Neapolitan court had many useless treasures, but at the same time had ruined the nation with the general disorder in its administration, the hole in its finances, and the banks. The court had also ruined the nation, when it could have increased its power, making it more prosperous. The Neapolitan court had always thought more of fleeing than remaining! They boarded at night, as though fleeing an enemy already at the gates. The following morning (21 December) a notice was read in Naples, which made known to the Neapolitan public that the king was going to Sicily for a short while, in order to return with powerful reinforcements, while General Pignatelli[2] would remain as his vicar general until his return.

The people displayed that silent consternation which springs less from fear than surprise at an unexpected event. In the first days when the king remained in the harbour due to adverse weather, everyone rushed to see him and begged him to stay; but the British, who already considered him their prisoner, sent them all away as cowards and traitors. The king either did not want to show himself or was not allowed to. This hard, unmerited scorn; the memory of past events; the loss of so many national riches; present, past, and future ills gave cause for thought and diminished compassion. The people witnessed him depart on 23 December[3] without displeasure or joy.

---

2 General Francesco Pignatelli di Strongoli had earlier served as vicar general in Calabria in 1783. Acton (1956: 323) writes that "the choice of General Francesco Pignatelli as the King's Vicar or Regent proved as disastrous as the choice of Mack. He was prematurely old at sixty-five, and all his actions were defeatist." In fact, he was also deeply unpopular before he assumed the office of vicar general of the king.

3 Drawing on a chronicler of the time, Villani ([1966] 2004: 135n5) suggests that this date is incorrect, for the event described by Cuoco took place the day earlier, 22 December 1799.

XIV

Anarchy in Naples and the Arrival of the French

In the history of Italy, the events at the end of the eighteenth century resembled those seen at the end of the fifteenth. In both periods, the same events were produced by the same causes, followed by the same effects. In both periods, the kingdom was lost by the work of a small number of enemy forces. In the fifteenth century, the parties which divided the kingdom were the ones which attracted the war; in the eighteenth, war and defeat were what caused the parties to arise. In the former, the king tried every means to avoid war; in the latter, he deployed every one of them to bring it about. The Aragonese and Bourbon kings were both equally discouraged after their defeat; but before the war, the latter showed more courage than the former. In both periods, though, the kingdom was lost when events subsequently showed it was easy to keep, for it is impossible to believe that the kingdom could not easily have been kept when it was so easily won back even after having been lost. In both periods, the loss of the kingdom was preceded by mutual, fatal diffidence between the king and the peoples, not unreasonable during the period of the Aragonese but without any foundation in our time. Ferdinand of Aragon had treated the barons cruelly, and they plotted a conspiracy and waged civil war; Vanni[1] punished a conspiracy that had yet to be plotted, and the idea of a rebellion that could not have been executed. In both periods, the defence of the kingdom was lacking in energy, in terms of the counsel given to the king, rather than the actions of the peoples. Lastly, in both periods, the kingdom was abandoned by the victors, who were forced to withdraw their forces into upper Italy.

---

1 In his *History of the Kingdom of Naples 1734–1825*, vol. 1, Colletta ([1838] 1858) noted that it was the king who in 1793 instituted a tribunal for the trial of persons accused of treason and composed of seven judges, including Marquis Vanni. The judges, Colletta noted, "afterwards attained celebrity for the iniquitous deeds they sanctioned or committed" (198).

Every time a similar event occurs, the following lesson or prophecy (I am not sure which) by Machiavelli should be read again. He says:

> Before they had felt the blows of the Transalpine wars, our Italian princes believed that a prince need only know how to dream up witty replies in his study; write a beautiful letter; display intelligence and readiness in his conversation and his speech; weave a fraud; adorn himself with gems and gold; sleep and eat in a more splendid style than others; surround himself with a large number of courtesans; conduct himself in a miserly and arrogant manner with his subjects; rot in laziness; give military positions as favours; despise anyone who had shown them any praiseworthy path; and expect that their pronouncements be taken as oracles. Nor did these wretched men realize that they were preparing themselves to become the prey of anyone who assaulted them. This resulted in the great terrors, the sudden flights, and the miraculous losses of 1494; the three powerful states of Italy [Florence, Milan, and Naples] were sacked and despoiled many times.[2]

It is no wonder that the same errors in 1798 had the same effects, and that a powerful kingdom was ruined precisely when, with wiser orders, it should have expanded (such was the political state of Europe). "What is worse," Machiavelli continues, "is that those who still remain persist in the same errors and live in the same disorder."[3]

The "City"[4] had taken over the municipal government of Naples. A national militia[5] had been formed to keep order. In the early days, the

---

2 Machiavelli, "The Art of War" (1979: 515). This essay was first published in 1521.

3 Ibid.

4 "The City (*la città*)" in Naples was the name given to a group of seven people, six of whom were nobles, with one from the people. The nobles were elected from the five "seats" (*sedili*) into which the entire nobility of the kingdom was divided (the seat of Montagna elected two, but these had only one vote), and these seats succeeded the "fraternities" in a city that had been Greek until the eleventh century. The popular member was supposed to be elected by the people, who had just the one *sedile* despite their being a thousand times more numerous than the nobles; but in fact he was appointed by the king. The City represented both the municipality of Naples and the whole kingdom. When the national parliaments were abolished in the viceroy's government [in 1642], the City continued to be the repository of the nation's privileges. But under Ferdinand IV the City was nothing but an empty name. (V.C.) For a background discussion of issues of citizenship, representation, and culture in the kingdom, see Balbi and Vitolo (2007); Marino (2011); Naddeo (2011); and Ventura (2007).

5 Established on 3 January 1799.

people had recognized the City's authority; everything was apparently quiet; but below deceptive ashes a fire was burning. Pignatelli [as vicar general with full powers] must have realized that the dangerous honour reserved for him was perhaps his rival, Acton's, last throw of the dice in order to ruin him. He could have taken revenge on his rival, performed one of those remarkable and extraordinary services to his king by which a man can virtually acquire the name and rights of the founder of a dynasty, and at the same time provide an equally great service to his country. He could have won the war or ended it, sparing the nation anarchy, and all the ills which this entails: the circumstances in which he found himself were extraordinary, but the thoughts he was able to conceive were only ordinary.

It is said that the queen, in leaving, had left him secret instructions to stir up the people, consign arms to them, generate anarchy, have Naples burned, and not allow a living soul to remain "from the notary upward." Whether these rumours were true or imagined, as though inevitable consequences of the insurrection which the queen had organized in leaving, they were nonetheless certainly repeated by all, and believed by all; and in observing the events of a revolution, true and false rumours deserve equal attention, because unlike in peaceful times, popular opinion is a major cause of all events, hence both what is true and what is believed to be such take on equal importance.

A few days later the first grim effects of the queen's orders were seen in the burning of vessels and gunboats which it had not been possible to transport to Sicily because of the excessive haste of the flight. A few hours were sufficient to consume what many years and treasures had cost our nation. Count Thurn[6] directed operations from a Portuguese ship, watching the fire calmly; and it seemed that the Neapolitan people saw in the feral splendour of those flames both the government's errors and the miseries of their future destiny.

The people no longer loved the king, they no longer even wanted to hear his name; but their minds were still full of so many years' impressions, so they still loved their religion, their country, and hated the French. Some advantage could have been gained from these dispositions. Rivalries arose between the City and the vicar general [Pignatelli]. The latter wanted to usurp rights which he did not have, as if it would not have been

---

6 Antonius Count of Thurn and Valsassina (1723–1806) was the then commander of the navy of Naples and Sicily.

more useful and also more glorious for him to have ceded those which he did have. The City recalled that its privileges included not ever having to be governed by a viceroy. The City displayed considerable energy at the time. So why did a republic not arise? The people would undoubtedly have followed the City party. But among those who governed it, some inclined towards an oligarchy, which could not have supported itself against the provinces, where hatred for the barons was common to all populations; hence in the state in which minds and affairs found themselves, in wishing to establish an oligarchy it would have been necessary to renounce feudalism. Others did not have the courage; and there were even those who proposed that the kingdom would have to be offered to a Spaniard, as though such a project at the time were even feasible if not laudable. In moments of great trepidation, when ideas are divergent and there are many factions, it is always difficult to find the middle way, and it was more difficult in Naples than anywhere, as the majority believed that in order to found a republic the French were indispensable.

In the meantime Capua was holding out, and the people were applauding its defence. They even deluded themselves with the prospect of greater advantages, for it is always easy for the people to hope, and there is never any shortage of people to encourage it. However, on 12 January [1799] a notice was affixed throughout Naples announcing that an armistice had been concluded between the French general[7] and Vicar General Pignatelli, whereby the French came to acquire all that stretch of the kingdom which lies to the north of a line drawn from Gaeta through Capua as far as the mouth of the Ofanto [river]. Furthermore, to obtain two months' armistice, the vicar general had undertaken to pay the sum of two and a half million francs.

No vicar general ever concluded such an armistice. Glory counselled him to oppose the French advancing on the walls of Capua, and to die there; prudence counselled him to cede everything and save his country from new, useless misfortunes. What could be hoped for from a brief armistice of two months? There were not even any grounds to hope for a treaty. The fatal counsel by which the king had put himself into the hands of the British placed him in the harsh necessity of losing either the Kingdom of Naples or the Kingdom of Sicily. The king had committed the same error by which the last king of the Aragonese dynasty was defeated, that is, to put himself in the arms of one of the two contenders

7 General Jean-Antoine-Etienne Championnet.

for his kingdom; the error which the wise Guicciardini[8] repeats was what ultimately ruined that dynasty, because through it they were prevented from taking advantage of those opportunities which fortune would subsequently offer them to win back their throne. Why, then, did the viceroy wish to put time between surrender and possession, and grant free rein to the populace's hatred for the French, when they were near enough to arouse it, but not near enough to restrain it? Did he want civil war, anarchy? Were these the queen's orders?[9]

The people believed they had been betrayed by the vicar, the City, the generals, the soldiers, by everyone. The arrival of the French commissioners, sent to demand the sums promised, increased their suspicions and fury. The next day, the people hurried to the castles to take up arms; the castles were opened, and the troops put up no opposition, for they had not yet received orders to do so. The vicar general fled, just as the king had done; the populace hurried to Caivano[10] to depose Mack, who despite being at the head of the troops, was unable to do anything but flee.[11] Every social bond was broken. Senseless mobs of the populace raced menacingly through the city streets shouting out, "Long live the holy faith!" "Long live the Neapolitan people!" Moliterni and Roccaromana[12] were chosen as their commanders, young cavalrymen who at the time were the people's idols for the bravery they had shown against the French at Capua and Caiazzo. They

8 In his *The History of Italy,* bk. 5, among others.

9 Not so, according to Cortese (1926: 103).

10 A village about twelve kilometres from Naples. (V.C.)

11 It is well known that at this point he laid down his uniform as the king of Naples's general to take up that of an Austrian general. He presented himself to Championnet, and claimed that, as an Austrian general, he should not be made a prisoner of war. Championnet did not listen to this wretched example of sophistry. But this episode clearly showed the nature of the man, who ten months later challenged [Girolamo Pignatelli prince of] Moliterni to a duel and then himself pulled out of it. Challenging a man to a duel is not, in my view, an act of bravery. It might perhaps be an act of imprudence; but to challenge a man to a duel and then refuse to fight is an act which combines imprudence with cowardice. It showed the true nature of a man who, having been made prisoner and released on his word of honour, would then flee. (V.C.)

12 Both were noblemen with Jacobin sympathies. The former was Girolamo Pignatelli, prince of Moliterni, who had lost an eye while fighting the French in Lombardy (Acton 1956: 327), and the latter was Lucio Caracciolo, the young duke of Roccaromana who cut a dashing figure.

managed to restrain the popular disturbance for a short while, but the calm lasted only two days. The French were already almost at the gates of Naples.

A deputation was sent to the French general quarters, consisting of the leading demagogues, to persuade them to give up on their idea of entering Naples, offering them what had been promised under the terms of the armistice agreements plus a sum or two more. The French response was negative, as might have been expected, but not as it should have been; while many agreed that the demand was reasonable, the odd Neapolitan *émigré* added threats and insults to the negative response; which ended up making the people even angrier.

There was no shortage of court agents urging the people on to new frenzies. There was no lack of that rapacious spirit common to all peoples of the earth. There was no shortage of fanatical priests and monks, who, in blessing the weapons of superstitious people in the name of the Lord of armies, increased their audacity with hope, and their frenzy with audacity. The City, which had met until that day, met no more. The people believed they had been abandoned by everyone, and did everything on their own. The entire city offered nothing but a vast spectacle of looting, burning, mourning, horrors, and repeated images of death. Among the victims of popular fury who do not deserve to be forgotten were Duke della Torre and his brother Clemente Filomarino, whose talents and virtues should have earned them respect but who were wretched victims of treachery by a wicked servant.[13]

Some republicans, and in Naples at the time everyone who had property and morals was a republican, prevented worse ills by mixing with the people and feigning the same sentiments in order to lead them. Others, with the help of Moliterni and Roccaromana, made their way into the Sant'Elmo fortress under various pretexts and false names, and managed to drive out the *lazzaroni* who were commanding it. Championnet had wanted to make this castle, which dominated the whole city,

---

13 This is how Acton (1956: 327–8) reports the chain of events: "The mob broke into the palace of the scholarly Duke della Torre, whose barber had spread a rumor that he was in touch with the enemy. The house, which contained a valuable library and a collection of pictures and scientific instruments, was looted from top to bottom; the harmless Duke and his brother Don Clemente Filomarino were tied to chairs and shot, after which their bodies were burned. This was one of the several outrages which inclined law abiding citizens to wish for the French to restore order since nobody else could do so."

secure before moving off towards Naples. Many others rushed to join the French and came back fighting with their columns.

All good men wanted the French to arrive. They were already at the gates. But the people, defending stubbornly despite being poorly armed and without any leader, showed such courage that they proved themselves worthy of a better cause. In an open city, they held back the arrival of the victorious enemy for two days, contesting the ground inch by inch. When eventually they realized Sant'Elmo had been lost, that the republicans were opening fire at their backs from all points of Naples, defeated but not discouraged they retreated, less humiliated by the victors than they were indignant towards those they considered to be traitors.

XV

Why Did Naples Not Become a Republic after the King's Flight?

The king had departed, the people did not want him any longer. He had taken the love of national independence (which some considered to be a form of attachment to the old slavery) to the point of madness. When the Neapolitan people sent their deputation to Championnet, they meant to say only this: "The French republic was at war with the king of Naples; and the king has now departed. The French nation had no war with the Neapolitan nation, so why do the French soldiers want to conquer those who voluntarily offer them their friendship?" Such language was wise, and the Neapolitans were less far from the republic at this stage (without knowing its name) than is believed.

But as strength and ideas are required in every human operation, so too, in order to produce a revolution, numbers are necessary, along with leaders to present the ideas to the people, who sometimes glimpse them instinctively and on many occasions follow them enthusiastically, but are rarely able to formulate them on their own. Revolutions are easier to carry out in a people that have recently lost their own government, for in such cases the ideas of the people are easily taken from the government that was abolished, the memory of which is still fresh in the mind. Hence according to Machiavelli, "every revolution paves the way for another."[1] The longer the oppression from which a nation rises up, the greater the difference between the form of government destroyed and the one which it is desired to establish, the more uncertain and unstable the ideas of the people are, and the more difficult it is to bring them to unity, to have consensus, and to ensure effectiveness in its operations. This is why revolutions are swifter and more successful among peoples where either the memory of a better government is still fresh, or where

1 Cuoco paraphrases Machiavelli, who in chap. 2 of *The Prince* had actually warned that "every change in government creates grievances that those who wish to bring about further change can exploit" (see Machiavelli 1995: 7, translated by Wootton).

the revolutionaries attach themselves to certain rights (like the Magna Carta, which has been the guiding principle for all English revolutions) or certain magistratures or customs (as the Dutch did), which they managed to preserve virtually in the face of the encroaching despotism.

The ideas of the Neapolitan revolution could have obtained popular consensus if they had been taken from the nation's own foundations. But instead they were taken from a foreign constitution, and hence were far removed from our own. Founded on principles that were too abstract, these ideas were too remote from sensory [practical] experience, and moreover were compounded by all the customs, whims, and at times flaws of another people imposed as though laws, which were thoroughly alien from our own flaws, whims, and customs. Disputes and disagreements multiplied in accordance with the number of superfluous matters, which ought not to have come into the plan of operation, but which did so.

The greater this variety, the greater the difficulty in uniting the people, and the greater the force required to overcome the variety. If the ideas are the same, everyone could act without any need for consensus, for they would all be acting in accordance with their own ideas; but when the ideas are different, one person alone has to act. A revolution can rarely be completed, save by one person alone: liberty itself can be brought about only by despotism. For a long time the people waver in factions: you might almost say that the nation is set to destroy itself, you can see the bloodshed already; until one person rises up, acquires leadership over the people, establishes the ideas and assembles the forces. With time, this person either brings about the country's welfare, or, if he seeks to oppress it, sometimes ends up being oppressed by it himself. But he has shown the way, after which the people can act on their own.

Such a man is found only after repeated unsuccessful experiments, after a long period of contrasting events, when his own deeds have revealed him; civil wars put everyone in their rightful places. If someone wishes to make himself known and be followed by the people in the first stirrings of a revolution (unless the revolution is religious), it is not sufficient for him to have a great mind and heart: he must also have a great name; and this name is often acquired in every way other than by merit.

The most certain and effective method by which to gain public opinion is through regular jurisdiction, which some preserve in passing from the old to the new order. The City was in a position to ensure it was followed by the whole people, and after the City, Moliterni could have done so: but Moliterni had no mind to do anything, and the City too, in wavering between so many ideas (virtually all of which were illusory), was unable to decide on those which the times required.

It seems that no one in Naples was prepared for this situation; and when they found themselves in the midst of this maelstrom, everyone simply abandoned themselves to the waves. It is not very honouring to humankind to say this, but it is still true: virtually all nations, in their political crises, achieved their objectives more easily when a profoundly ambitious man was found among them, who, having foreseen events from afar, prepared himself for them, united all forces to his own advantage, and then brought about an advantage for the nation. Either he was wise and virtuous, and established his own greatness on the basis of the country's welfare; or he was foolish or wicked, and fell victim to his own designs. But by this stage, I repeat, he had shown the way.

In Naples, Viceroy Pignatelli did not even think of doing anything; the City was unable to make up its mind; Moliterni did not dare; no one else came forward; the many republicans who made a great deal of noise were more French[2] than republican, and the genuine republicans at the time had become mixed with an endless crowd of revolutionary mercenaries, who sought change for their own calculating purposes. The first moment had passed; the people had gone too far; even the wise men despaired of being able to hold them back, while even the good men sought an external force to restrain them.

Perhaps the French themselves were already too near. An operation which could have succeeded on 25 December, when the City was acting as king, ordering the departed sovereign's hunting reserves to be opened,[3] could hardly be carried out once the French were in Capua. However impartial the City was in its operations and however remote in its ideas of oligarchy, in wanting nonetheless to establish the nation's

2 This expression is merely intended to refer to two categories of people: the first, those who wanted change for the sake of change, rather than change which was beneficial; the second, those who felt they should imitate France in everything, even in those things which they were unable to or should not have imitated because of the differences between the two nations. The first category was made up of calculating men, the second of dreamers. Naturally I do not mean to refer to that reasonable form of attachment which even upstanding men had to experience for the victorious nation, on which the welfare of the country at the time depended. But the noble attachment of such men did honour to both nations, whereas the cowardly or foolish partisanship of the former categories was unworthy of both liberated and liberating nations. (V.C.)

3 Cortese (1926: 110n1) and Bravo (1975: 154n1) suggest that the order from the City came on 17 January 1799.

welfare, it could not and should not have departed from national ideas; and these ideas would have been too far from those of many others. Now even the slightest disagreements are hard to reconcile when an external force is ready to support one party. Parties surrender only because of disparity in terms of force or through being mutually tired of fighting: many offences can be tolerated, and in tolerating them, many ills avoided, simply because we cannot avenge them there and then; and harmony between men is less the result of wisdom than necessity. Foreign powers, ready to take sides at all times, first in the rivalries between opposing factions in the same city, then in the disputes between one state and another, have destroyed first the freedom and then the independence of Italy. No nation has experienced the unhappy effects of this more than the Neapolitan nation. Among the many foreign powers boasting claims over this kingdom, there was always one taking part in every rivalry between citizens: sometimes it was the foreigners themselves who instigated the rivalries. The citizens, in order to be stronger, joined their designs with those of the foreigners (like the horse [in Aesop's fable], which gave itself to the hunter to avenge itself of the stag). Hence for five centuries, the kingdom (five being the number of centuries between when the Norman dynasty died out and the house of Bourbon was established) was the unhappy scene of an infinite number of civil wars, without even one of them being able to do any good to the country.

Perhaps I am merely deluding myself with sweet illusions. But if we ourselves had founded the republic; if the constitution, guided by eternal ideas of justice, had been founded on the needs and customs of the people; if an authority which the people believed to be legitimate and national, rather than speaking an abstract language to them which they did not understand, had procured real benefit for them and released them from the ills from which they suffered; then perhaps the people would not have been so alarmed at the appearance of novelty, of which it had heard so many bad things said, and in seeing its ideas and customs defended without suffering the discomfort of war and the dilapidation that war brings with it. Perhaps ... who knows? We would not now be bemoaning the miserable remains of a desolate country deserving of a better fate.

XVI

State of the Neapolitan Nation

The French army entered Naples on 22 January [1799].[1] Championnet's first concern was to "install" an interim government which, while serving the nation's temporary needs, at the same time was expected to prepare the state's permanent constitution. Such an important responsibility was entrusted to twenty-five[2] persons divided up into six "committees," which concerned themselves with the details of the administration, and exercised what was called "executive power." When gathered together, they constituted the legislative assembly.

The six committees were: 1. central; 2. domestic; 3. war; 4. finance; 5. justice and police; and 6. legislation. The persons elected to the government were: Abamonti, Albanese, Baffi, Bassal (who was French), Bisceglia, Bruno, Cestari, Ciaia, De Gennaro, De Filippis, De Renzis, Doria, Falcigni, Fasulo, Forges, Lauberg, Logoteta, Manthoné, Pagano, Paribelli, Pignatelli-Vaglio, Porta, Riari, and Rotondo.

But to devise plans for a republican constitution is not the same thing as to establish a republic. In a government where the public will, or rather the law, does not and cannot have any support, guarantor, or executor, apart from that flowing from individual consent, the only way to promote freedom is by forming free men. Before the edifice of liberty could be constructed on Neapolitan territory, there were a thousand obstacles that needed to be removed from the ancient constitutions, from the out-of-date customs and prejudices, and from the inhabitants' current interests, which needed to be understood. Ferdinand looked sullenly at our nascent liberty; from Palermo, he engaged in all kinds of machinations to win back the kingdom he had lost. He had powerful allies, who were terrifying enemies as far as we were concerned, especially the British, rulers of the sea, and hence also the trade

1 Actually, it was on 23 January 1799.
2 It was in fact twenty-four.

of Sicily and Apulia, without which a huge capital city like Naples would struggle to exist.

Since Roman times, the fate of southern Italy largely depended on that of Sicily. The Romans made Italy into a garden, which very soon was transformed into a wasteland. After the first Roman conquests, the saying began to be heard, for the first time, that Sicily was the grain store of Italy: a saying as glorious for the former as it was injurious for the latter. Such a statement would not have been made before the fifth century of Rome, when Italy alone was sufficient to feed 30 million industrious, belligerent men, with simple, magnanimous customs. In the Middle Ages, whoever was lord of Sicily could disturb Italy at will. From Sicily, Belisarius destroyed the kingdom of the Goths; from Sicily, the Arabs plagued Italy for three centuries, until the Normans reunited it with the kingdom of Naples, to which it remained joined until the time of Charles I of Anjou. And who could deny that this separation did not have an effect in delaying the progress of that civilization in the Kingdom of Naples, which the great Frederick of Swabia and his unfortunate progeny had inspired there earlier than in any other region in Italy? The two kingdoms were reunited under the long domination of the Austrian house of Spain. During this time, Naples began to expand and became a huge capital, which, in order to exist, required wheat and even more oil from those distant provinces bathed by the Adriatic, which cannot easily be traded, nor can the capital easily survive, without free passage through the Strait of Messina. It should also be added that the true ruler of this strait is the one who holds Sicily: this is so because in Messina he has a large, convenient port, whereas the Calabrian side has only small and unsafe harbours.

The king still had more than a few supporters left in the kingdom who loved the old government more than the new one. In what revolution are such men not to be found? Many populations were openly in counter-revolution, for they had not yet laid down the arms they had taken up when invited and urged to do so by the king's proclamations. At the same time, others were ready to take up arms once they had both recovered from the stupor inspired in them by so rapid a conquest and realized how weak the French forces were, and once they had found both a schemer for their leader and some apparent injustice by the new government as a pretext for an uprising.

The number of those who had decided in favour of revolution was very small compared to the entire mass of the population; and as soon as the matter was entrusted to the decision of arms, it was inevitable that they would succumb. Here is an example in the province of Lecce, where an uprising was produced by an accident that is worth recounting because of its singularity.

Seven Corsican *émigrés* found themselves in Taranto, having come there in order to secure a passage to Sicily. The continual *scirocco* winds, which prevent ships from leaving the port there, prevented the Corsicans from departing. Hence despite themselves, they were still there in Taranto when the republic was proclaimed. Afraid that they might be arrested and fall into French hands, they left on the night of 8 February 1799 and headed for Brindisi, hoping to find a passage to Corfu or Trieste. After walking for several miles, they stopped at a village named Monteasi [Monteiasi]. Here they lodged with an old lady, and to ensure that she served them well, they told her that one of them was the crown prince. This was sufficient for the woman to leave and run to a relative of hers named Bonafede Girunda, the chief farmer in the village. Girunda immediately rushed to the Corsicans, knelt down before the youngest of them and professed every act of reverence and vassalage to him. The Corsicans were taken aback, and fearing worse disasters, they escaped as soon as Girunda had left, without waiting for daybreak. Once Girunda had been informed by the same old woman that the alleged crown prince had departed, he mounted his horse quickly to catch up with them, but went by a different route. Not meeting them, he asked all and sundry if they had seen the crown prince and his entourage, hence a rumour started and soon spread, and was sufficient for all the villages he passed through to take up arms and to cause the populations to rush to meet him. The alleged prince was reached at Mesagne, and was forced by the circumstances of the moment to maintain the comic part he had begun with; but believing himself not to be safe in Mesagne he withdrew swiftly to Brindisi. Here he shut himself up in the fortress and began to issue orders. One of the despatches provided that, as he had to depart for Sicily in order to meet up with his distinguished parent, he was leaving his two commanders-in-chief as viceroys in the kingdom, whom the people subsequently believed to be two other blood princes. These two impostors, one of whom had the surname Boccheciampe and the other that of De Cesare, soon put themselves in charge of the insurrectionists. The former remained in the province of Lecce, while the latter headed for the province of Bari, taking Girunda with him, proclaiming him general of the division.

With this troop, composed entirely of policemen, the barons' men of arms, convicts and prisoners who had escaped from the prisons and courts, and all the rioters of the two provinces, it was easy for them to take charge of all towns that had proclaimed the republic and to take Martina and Acquaviva by siege – these cities having sworn to die rather than recognize the impostors. Emboldened by the successes they enjoyed, they took on the French who already ruled a good portion of the Bari province. When, however, they encountered a small French detachment in the woods at Casamassima, they were thoroughly defeated, and fled – Boccheciampe to Brindisi and De Cesare to Francavilla. The former fell into the hands of the French; while the latter, who was the more astute, after hearing the news of his companion's imprisonment, managed to escape to Torre di Mare, the ancient Metaponto, and went to join up with Cardinal Ruffo near Matera.

Our revolution was a passive revolution, and the only way for it to be successful would have been to win over popular opinion. But the patriots[3] and the people did not hold the same views: they had different ideas, different customs, and even different languages. The admiration for foreigners, which had slowed down our culture at the time of the king, now formed the greatest obstacle to the establishment of liberty at the birth of our republic. The Neapolitan nation was split into two peoples, separated by two centuries in terms of history and two degrees in terms of climate. As the cultured part of the nation had been formed on the basis of foreign models, its culture was different from the one that the nation as a whole needed, one that could come about only through the development of our own faculties. Some had become French, others British; and those that stayed Neapolitan – most of the people – were as yet uncultured. Thus the culture of the few had not benefited the nation as a whole; which, in turn, virtually despised a culture that was not beneficial to it and which it did not understand.[4]

---

3 "Patriot." What on earth is a "patriot"? The name ought to describe someone who loves his country. In the past decade it has been synonymous with the term "republican"; although obviously, not all republicans were patriots. (V.C.) See also Rao (2012a).

4 The basis of the manners and customs of a people is always originally barbarian, but the multiplication of men, time, and the efforts of the wise equally can soften every custom, and civilize every manner. The Apulian dialect, for example, was the first to be written down in Italy, and was as suited as Tuscan to become cultured and noble; that it did not do so was the fault of our own people, for we abandoned it in order to pursue Tuscan. We admire foreigners' manners, without reflecting that it was precisely this admiration that prejudiced our own manners, which would have been equal and perhaps even superior to the foreign manners had we cultivated them. A nation that

The misfortunes of peoples are often the clearest demonstrations of the most useful truths. One cannot ever be of use to one's country without loving it, and one cannot love one's own country without esteeming the nation. A people can never be free if the part of it which nature has destined – because of its superior reason – to govern the others by its authority and example has sold its opinion to a foreign nation. In such a case the whole nation loses half its independence. Also, the majority remains with no precepts to follow, the ambitious take advantage, the revolution degenerates into civil war, and the ambitious, who in surrendering still always manage to gain, the wise, who always choose the lesser of two evils, and the indifferent, who only ever calculate based on the need of the moment, are united in receiving their law from a foreign power, which never fails to profit from similar turmoil either for its own benefit or to re-establish the exiled king.

That love of country which is born from public education and which generates national pride is alone what caused France to survive despite all the ills it suffered because of its revolution, and despite all of Europe being allied against it. A thousand Frenchmen would have elected another king, but not one of them would have wanted to receive him from the hands of the Germans or British. No one should have been more convinced by the domestic examples than Pitt, even if avenging Bourbon rights had been the cause rather than the pretext for the alliance, that such a war, with the pretext of restoring the king, was useless.

Far from having this national unity, the Neapolitan nation could be seen as divided into many different ones. Nature seems to have wanted to bring together all its varieties in a very small expanse of land: the sky; the soil that is different in every one of its provinces; the taxes imposed

---

develops on its own acquires a civilization that is equal in every one of its parts, and culture becomes a general asset for the nation as a whole. Hence in Athens, a little lady spoke with the same elegance as Theophrastes, and the cobbler could stand in judgment of Demosthenes. In admiring and imitating foreign nations, not all men who make up a people become cultivated, nor do those who do so become well cultivated: not all, because not all men are in a position to see and imitate foreigners; not well, because by an eternal law of nature, the imitator always remains inferior to the model. A foreign culture brings divisions rather than uniformity to a nation, and is therefore acquired only at the expense of force. Which are the dominant nations in Europe today? Those which not only do not imitate others but despise them. And we wanted to make an independent republic by starting with despising our own nation!

N.B. For the avoidance of all doubt, this note applies to all Italy, to a greater or lesser degree. (V.C.)

by the revenue authorities, which have always followed such varieties to find reasons for imposing new duties wherever they found new benefits of nature; and the feudal system which in previous centuries, between anarchy and barbarism, was always different in the various places and circumstances. All this meant that properties and consequently also human mores, which always follow property and means of subsistence, were also different everywhere.

Amid such contrast, some common interest should have been found to rally and unite all men to revolution. Once the nation was united, all the powers on the earth would have allied themselves in vain against us. If the state of our nation presented great obstacles, at the same time it offered great resources with which to carry out our revolution.

We had a population that, while it would never have started a revolution on its own, was nonetheless docile enough to receive it from the hands of another. Neither of the two determined parties was adequate: the majority of the nation was indifferent. What could this mean? That they were not moved by any party, and were not animated by any passion? Impartial and hence fair judges of the two pretenders, they would have followed the party that offered it the greatest advantage. Such people are hard to deceive but easy to govern.

They did not yet understand their rights, but did have a sense of their own worth. They believed it was sacrilege to attack their own sovereign, but believed that another sovereign could do it, using the same right by which the Austrians had succeeded the Bourbons; and when this new sovereign restored their rights to them, they would gladly accept the gift.

The insurrections burned in only a few places, which, because they had been the scene of the war, were still animated by the king's proclamations, by the war itself (which, in forcing us to feign hatred, eventually led us genuinely to hate) and by the conduct of some French officials, who, armed and victorious, did not always remember what was right. The great majority of the nation understood the revolution peaceably and remained in its place; the insurrections broke out only much later.

There were also many people who pushed their enthusiasm for liberty so far that they prevented the French from reaching the capital, and resisted with merely their own forces against every weapon mobilized by the king, even after the capital had surrendered. All these forces joined together could have formed a single imposing force, had it been known how to gain advantage from them.

The capital's huge population was more dumbstruck than active. It still looked with wonder on a change that it had scarce thought possible.

In general terms it may be said that the capital's population was further from the revolution than those of the provinces, because it was less oppressed by taxes, and more flattered by a court which feared it. Despotism is founded mostly on the dregs of the people, who, with no care whatsoever for good or evil, sell themselves to whoever is best able to satisfy the needs of their bellies. Rarely does a government fall without being bemoaned by the worst elements of society; but the new government must also take care to ensure that the same fate is not desired for them by the good elements as well. But the excessive fear that was conceived of this population meant that possibly too much heed was paid to it, while the provinces were neglected which alone were to be feared, and were in fact the source of the counter-revolution.

XVII

Ideas of Patriots

What should have been done, then, to propel the revolution in the Neapolitan kingdom?

The first step was to ensure that all the patriots were in agreement on their ideas, or at least that they agreed on the government.

Of our patriots (if I may be permitted an expression appropriate to all revolutions, and not offensive to those who were good patriots), many had the republic on their lips, many had it in their heads, but very few had it in their hearts. For many the revolution was a question of fashion, and they were republicans only because the French were. Others were republicans out of a longing of their spirit while others were because they were irreligious, as though a certificate from the government was necessary to be free of superstition. Some confused liberty with licence, and believed that the revolution would allow them to insult public customs with impunity. And for many, still, revolution was a matter of calculation. Each of them was moved by the disorder that had affected them most during the old regime. By this I do not mean to offend my nation; it is typical of all revolutions. Indeed, which nation other than our own could boast an equal or greater number of persons who loved only order and their country?

As usually happens, however, that which was merely ancillary was taken to be the principal object of reform, and the principal object was sacrificed for the ancillary. In following the ideas of the patriots, no one knew where to start or where to stop.

So what is a revolution in a people? You will see a thousand heads, each with different thoughts, interests, and designs from the others. If a commander (*capo*) arrives seeking to unite them, unity will never ensue. But if it happens that people share a common interest, revolution will follow and will be carried on only for that purpose which is common to all. Does this mean that the other objectives will perhaps be neglected? No; but each will adapt their own private interest to the public. The particular will follow the general, ancillary issues will be reformed imperceptibly over time, and all will proceed in an orderly fashion.

No government is free of those disorders which cause great discontent. Equally there is no government that does not also do much good to many people, and does not also have many supporters. When the leader of a revolution seeks to reform, that is, to destroy everything, then it happens that the same people who desire revolution for one reason then detest it for another. Once the initial wave of enthusiasm has passed and the main objective has been achieved, that is, the one which is always necessarily desired more vehemently and achieved earlier than all the others, because it is common to all, then the pain of all the other sacrifices required by the revolution starts to be felt. Everyone says, first to themselves then to others: "Perhaps that might be enough now … The other things we are seeking to achieve are useless, harmful." Private interest begins to make itself felt. Everyone would like to obtain what they desire for the lowest possible cost; and since sensations of pain are stronger than those of pleasure, everyone considers what they have lost to be worth more than what they have gained. Individual wills change, and they start to disagree with each other, in a government where the general will must not or cannot have any guarantor or executor other than the individual will. Laws become unenforceable, and are in conflict with the public customs. Authorities (*poteri*) start to languish; and such languor leads to anarchy, or, if anarchy is to be avoided, law enforcement has to be assigned to an external force, which is no longer that of the free people; and you no longer have a republic.

The secret of revolutions is this: to know what all the people want, and to do that; then the people will follow you; to distinguish between what the people want and what you would like, and to stop as soon as the people no longer want something; for at this point they will abandon you. When Brutus drove the Tarquinians out of Rome, he thought to provide the people with a *rex sacrificulus*: he knew that although the Romans were tired of having a king on the throne, they would still think it necessary to have one on the altar.

The obsession with reforming everything leads inevitably to counter-revolution. In such cases the people are not rebelling against the laws, for it is not the general will they are attacking, but the individual will. Do you know why a usurper is followed? Because he relaxes the severity of the laws; because he concerns himself with only a few matters that he subjects to his own will, and it is his will that takes the name and place of the "general will." All other matters are left up to the individual will of the people. "*Idque apud imperitos 'humanitas' vocabatur, cum pars servitutis esset.*"[1] What a strange characteristic this is, common to all peoples of the earth! The desire to give them excessive liberty reawakens the desire in them to be liberated from their own deliverers.

1 "All this in their ignorance they called 'civilization,' when it was but a part of their servitude." From Tacitus, *The Life of Gnaeus Julius Agricola,* chap. 21.

XVIII

The French Revolution

I thought I was reflecting on the Neapolitan revolution, but in fact I was writing the history of the revolution of all peoples of the earth, especially the French Revolution. The misconceptions that our own people had of this revolution contributed in no small measure to our ills.

They wanted to imitate everything in it. There was much as good as was bad, which the French themselves would one day realize; but our people were not prepared to wait for the judgments of posterity, nor were they able to predict them. They believed that the French Revolution was the work of philosophy, whereas philosophy did little more than ruin it. They judged its current state, without remembering what it had been at one point and without foreseeing what it might one day become.

The French Revolution had an almost lawful origin[1] that was lacking in ours. Its first purpose was to remedy the ills of the nation, on which point both people and king were in agreement. The people recognized the legitimate authority of the Estates General and later of the assemblies, in exactly the same way they respected the authority of the king, by whose command, or at least with whose consent, both the Estates General and the assemblies had been convened.

This same political state in France, which for some time had caused the wise men to predict that a revolution was inevitable, resulted in the breakup of the Estates General. The National Assembly was formed, and the king was on the Assembly's side. Whether he was so in appearance only, and constrained by fear, matters little; at this point there was still no revolution.

The revolution began when the king distanced himself from the Assembly: at this point civil war commenced, and the Assembly party was able to win the people over by appealing to the idea of justice.

---

1 Cortese (1926: 123n1) recalls that in the 1801 edition, Cuoco noted that he had used this expression following De Lolme ([1771] 2007).

Up to this point the French people had at all times, we might say, acted in accordance with their ideas. The Estates General appeared just to them, because the memory of other Estates General was still fresh in France, and because they had been convened by the king's authority, which the people considered to be legitimate. The king himself authorized the National Assembly; the king negotiated with it when he became constitutional monarch; and when he was sentenced, it was on the grounds of not having kept the promise to which the entire people had been witness. And what was this promise? It was the one whereby he himself had acknowledged the nation's sovereignty and sworn an oath to its welfare. In following the Assembly party, the people believed they were following the party of justice as well as their own interests. When I compare the English Revolution of 1649 with the French Revolution of 1789, I find that they are more similar than is often believed. Reformation is started in the king's name; the king is arrested, judged, and condemned almost by the king himself; the people move gradually from the old ideas to new ones, and the new ideas are in turn supported by the old ones.[2]

There is method in the operations of peoples, in precisely the same way that there is in the ideas of men. If reversed, that is, if the order and sequence of them is upset, and if you seek to expound the ideas of 1792 in 1789, the people will not understand them; and instead of seeing a throne overturned, you will see a half-wise man or corrupt orator exiled. And to the same degree as a man in his ideas, so too a people in their operations are slaves to the external forms with which they are clothed. An externally precise syllogism allows an error to be swallowed without being noticed; the external solemnity of the formalities sustains a manifestly unjust operation. Inadvertently or maliciously, you start from a very slight error: the further you go, the more you depart from that straight line where the truth lies; and you proceed so far that even if you come to realize the error, you will not know the way back. Thus a few ambitious men will declare that what is merely a whim and ambition of theirs is in fact justice and public necessity; and the crime will be perpetrated not because the people approve of it, but because they do not know how legitimately to prevent it. When the error stems from a wrong method, to go back is more difficult, for it is necessary to revert to the point, by this stage often distant, where the line of fallacy begins to diverge from the line of truth; but once minds have been changed, they will destroy the

2 For Cuoco, both revolutions fit his concept of active revolution.

entire system because of a single error. Contrary to all the laws which it had itself proclaimed, the National Convention condemned Louis XVI. On that occasion the troublemakers among them reasoned as Virginius had done at the time when Appius made his appeal to the people; and no "worse example can be set in a republic," says Machiavelli, "than to make a law and not to observe it; and when it is not observed by the man who made it so much the worse."[3] All the good that the French Revolution might have done was destroyed with the very ruling that condemned the unfortunate Louis XVI.

In the same period that France thought it was acquiring full liberty, those reforms that we call superfluous were also beginning. What effect did these reforms produce? There was a continual struggle between the parties; eventually the parties no longer understood each other, and the people understood no one. They chased after a word, which represented a person rather than a thing, and sometimes did not represent either; and those controversies that could not be decided with reason were decided by force. Robespierre emerged; he had the greatest force, and restrained all other forces through fear.

Robespierre retained the words to defeat his rivals, but attached material things to them, albeit different ones, to win over the people. The people did not understand either Robespierre or Brissot,[4] but realized that Robespierre was granting them more licence than the others, and so slaughtered everyone whom Robespierre wanted slaughtered. Robespierre could not last long, because his deeds bore no relationship to his ideas, and the things could be preserved without preserving the ideas. What else, indeed, could the term *ultra-révolutionnaire* mean, which his rivals invented in order to describe and defeat him?

Robespierre saved France, by causing all parties to rebel against him and uniting them as a consequence;[5] but Robespierre did not and could not save his own person, ideas, or constitution.

---

3 Machiavelli, *The Discourses* (2003: bk. I, chap. 45). Here Machiavelli also recalls the story of Virginius and Appius.

4 Jacques Pierre Brissot (1754–1793) was a leader during the French Revolution. With moderate views, he became associated with the Girondins and died by the guillotine.

5 The effect that Robespierre had on France was comparable to that which a stimulus has on human excitability in Brown's system. (V.C.)

Cuoco refers here to the Scottish doctor John Brown, who in 1780 published the medical manual *Elementa Medicinae* that became well known in Naples; it also became a popular text for the so-called Brunonian system of medicine, according to which physical life consists in a peculiar excitability of all the agents which affect the constitution of the healthy conditions of the body, whereas all diseases arise either from deficiency or from excess of excitement.

Ideas had reached an extreme, and had to turn back. More had been reformed than the people wanted; and since these superfluous reforms did not have public custom in their favour, observance of them had to be coerced through the use of fear and force: laws are always crueller, the more capricious they are. The moderates' system brought things back to their natural state, and attached no importance to them other than that attributed by the people themselves; hence the severity or lenience of the laws were the severity or lenience of the people themselves.

The nature of man is such that all his ideas, all his affections, change, weaken, and are extinguished when they reach their extreme. By wanting too much to be free, man tires of even the sentiment of liberty. "*Nec totam libertatem, nec totam servitutem pati possumus*"[6] said Tacitus of the Roman people; it seems to me that the same may be said of all the peoples on the earth. Now what else had Robespierre done, in pushing the sense of liberty to such an extreme, but accelerate its demise?

The life and fortunes of peoples can be measured and calculated by their ideas. Between extreme slavery and extreme freedom there is a course that all civilizations have to run, and the lives of all peoples may be said to consist of precisely this course. The Roman plebs were merely the serfs of a handful of patricians; they had no property of either goods or persons. They began by demanding certain laws; the security of goods and persons was instituted, but they were still without marriage, patrons, and magistrates. They sought – and obtained – participation in all these things, but they sought them with temperance, and were granted them in moderation. This not only prolonged the life of the republic, but as a result of the parts which composed it seeking to emulate each other, made it more energetic and glorious. Having achieved what might be called "*de jure* equality," the courts also demanded *de facto* equality. Agrarian laws[7] began to be mentioned, and the republic perished. An extreme point had been reached, beyond which it was impossible to progress. In the first year of the French Revolution, the only thought was to establish *de jure* equality, towards which the public orders of all of Europe were irresistibly progressing. By the third year, however, *de facto* equality was demanded: in three years you go from the age of Menenius Agrippa to that of the Gracchi. What am I saying? In the age of the Gracchi, while equal property was being demanded, the legitimacy of civil ownership

6 "We cannot bear either absolute slavery or absolute freedom," Tacitus, *Historiae*, I, 16.

7 The agrarian laws were those promoted by Tiberius and Caius Gracco (133–123 BC).

was acknowledged. Thus the respect that the people continued to have for the law on dowries held them back from actually dividing up the properties. In France ideas had gone much further; the legitimacy of dowries had been questioned, as had that of wills and even the basic law of ownership, without which there is no property. The ideas of the French Revolution were a century further forward than those of the Gracchi; which is why, starting from this period, the French republic survived for a century less than the Roman republic did.

When the demands for equality go beyond the confines of the law, the cause of liberty becomes the cause of the wicked. The law, Cicero said, no longer distinguishes between patricians and plebeians: why, then, should there still be disputes between plebeians and patricians? This is because there are still, and always will be, the few and the many: a few rich, and the many poor; a few industrious, and many idle; very few wise, and a great many foolish.

Robespierre's ideas could not stand with the other ideas of the French nation or with those of the other European nations. In removing trades, commerce, and navy from his nation, if this were possible, he would have turned the French into so many Gauls: he would have made them better warriors, but less able to sustain war; he could have invaded the whole earth in a moment, but in time all the earth would have taken its revenge, and the French nation would have been destroyed. It was said of one of the ancients that he must either have been Caesar or mad; of Robespierre, it might have been said that he was either the dictator of the world, or mad.

I have looked for a man in history with whom to compare Robespierre. Some of his friends, and also his enemies, compared him to Sulla;[8] but we may say that the former did not know Robespierre and the latter did not know Sulla. Robespierre has many similarities with Appius. They differed in the principles which they preached; I do not know if they differed in the purpose they set themselves, because for me it is far from clear that in preaching liberty, Robespierre did not in fact tend towards despotism. But both were equally ambitious, and in their ambition, equally cruel and equally foolish. Both wanted, by means of the laws, to establish that form of despotism which is precisely the force that destroys the law. Both had that authority that Machiavelli[9] described as "highly

---

8 Lucius Cornelius Sulla (ca. 138–78 BC) was a Roman military and political leader who came into prominence during the Social War (91–89 BC). He had the distinction of holding the office of consul and that of dictator twice.

9 In *The Prince,* chaps. 8–9.

dangerous," free in its power but limited in time, which creates in man the desire to perpetuate it, and nor does he lack the means by which to do this; but as these means were not given by the laws for the purpose to which he is directing them, they necessarily become tyrannical. Neither understood the principle of either not offending anyone, or causing offence at one point and then providing reassurance, giving men reasons to calm and quieten their minds; but every day, with new cruelties they added new fears in the citizens, and rendered fearsome the people they wished to dominate. Both wished to establish their empire by terror; neither of them was a military man, nor did they suffer the army, which they feared. They replaced it with the inquisition and a travesty of judgments, which is crueller than any standing army, for it is forced to punish the crimes that the other prevents, and increases the suspicions that the other reduces. This kind of tyranny, which may be described as "decemviral," is the most terrible of all, but fortunately is also the most short lived.

For thinking men, "moderatism" was only an intermediate stage that ought to produce another. The nation paused for breath after the struggle it had gone through with Robespierre, but had not yet settled on the point at which it was to rest. An excess of energy had to produce a surfeit of relaxation. The war against Robespierre had been desired by the nation; but it had been waged by one party, which then, as is often the case, had entrusted government to treacherous and wretched hands. Under Robespierre, the nation was forced to save its liberty; under the Directory, its independence.[10]

This is the ordinary course of all revolutions. The people are restless for a long time without knowing where to stop: they always go to extremes, knowing only that happiness lies somewhere in the middle. And woe if, as happened to the Florentine people in other times, it never manages to find this point!

---

10 This point has been proved today. (V.C.)

XIX

How Many Ideas Did the Nation Have?

The damage that excessively abstract ideas of liberty do is that they displace liberty as they seek to establish it. Liberty is a good thing, because it produces many other benefits such as security, comfortable existence, populousness, moderation in taxes, increase in industry, and many other tangible benefits; and because the people love such benefits, they also come to love liberty. A man who comes and orders a people to love liberty without procuring such advantages for them would be like Marmontel's Alcibiade, who wanted to be loved "for himself."[1]

The Neapolitan nation wished to see several things: order re-established in its finances, which were troubling (*incommode)* more because of the poor distribution than the burden of taxation; an end to the disputes arising from feudalism, which held the nation in a state of civil war; and the immense lands that had accumulated in the hands of the clergy and the revenue authorities divided up more fairly.[2] This was the desire of everyone: and this was the use which those populations that became democratic on their own made of their liberty, and that which the government agents and the French were unable to achieve, or achieved only too late.

Many communities divided up the lands that previously had belonged to the "royal hunting grounds."[3] Many claimed the disputed feudal lands. But I do not know all the events, nor is it of any importance

1 Jean-François Marmontel (1723–1799) was the author of several literary works. A contributor to the *Encyclopédie* and a friend of Voltaire, he was at one point editor of the journal *Mercure de France.*

2 Villani ([1966] 2004: 168–9n3) recalls that in the first edition Cuoco had used much stronger language in this sentence: "The Neapolitan nation wanted to have taxation reduced, to be free of the yoke of barons, to share in the land now resting in the hands of barons, ecclesiastics and the fisc."

3 A huge hunting reserve that the king kept in the province of Salerno, surrounded by the populations referred to in the text. (V.C.)

The hunting reserve was known as the Persano forest.

to repeat them, for they are all the same. In Picerno,[4] as soon as the people realized that the French had arrived, they rushed to church, following their parish priest, to give thanks to the "God of Israel, who has visited and redeemed his people." From church they went to assemble in parliament, and their first act of freedom was to ask for an account of the use made of public money in the previous six years. No riots, no massacres, no violence accompanied this claiming of their rights: those who were present at the assembly listened with pleasure and admiration to hear the majority respond as follows to someone who proposed the use of violent means: "Is it not right that we who complain of others' injustice should set an example?" The second use to which they put this liberty was to reclaim what had been usurped by the landowners. And what was the third? To do miracles in the name of liberty itself, to fight as long as they had ammunition, and when the ammunition had run out, in order to obtain lead, they resolved in parliament to melt down all the church organs ... "Our saints do not need them," they said. They melted all their domestic utensils, even the most vital medical instruments; the women, dressed as men in order to frighten the enemy, fought so hard that the latter was deceived more by their bravery than by their clothes.

Are these not the extremes to which the love of freedom leads? Many other populations would have taken matters to the same degree; and they would all have done so, for they all had the same ideas, the same needs, and the same desires.

But while all had such desires, a great many also desired useful reforms that would reawaken the nation's activity, remove the monks' idleness and the uncertainty over property, assure and protect agriculture and commerce; and these people formed the class which in all nations lies between the people and the nobility. While this class is not as powerful as the nobility or as numerous as the people, it is everywhere the most sensible. Freedom of opinions, abolition of worship, and exemption from prejudices were demanded by very few, because they were of interest to only very few. This last reform should have followed on from liberty once this was established; but to establish it, force was required, and this could be obtained only by following the ideas of the majority. But the order was reversed, and they tried to gain the minds of many by presenting them with ideas that were those of the few.

4 A small rural town in the province of Potenza, in the region of Basilicata.

What could be hoped for from the language used in all the proclamations addressed to our people? "*Finally you are free*"[5] ... The people did not yet know what liberty was; it is a sentiment, not an idea; it is experienced with facts, not demonstrated with words. "*Your Claudius has fled, Messalina is trembling.*" Did the people have to know Roman history in order to know happiness? "*Humanity wins back all its rights.*" Which ones? "*You will have a free and just government, founded on principles of equality; positions will no longer be the exclusive privilege of the noble and wealthy, but the reward for talent and virtue.*" A powerful motive for the people, this, who pride themselves on neither virtues nor talent, who want to be governed well and do not aspire to hold positions! "*Let a holy enthusiasm be manifested in all places, let tricolor flags be hoisted, let trees be planted,*[6] *municipalities, civic guards be organized.*" What a collection of ideas, which the people neither understood nor cared about! "*The destinies of Italy must be fulfilled. Scilicet id populo cordi est: ea cura quietos sollicitat animos.*"[7] *Prejudices, religion, customs* ... Gently, my dear orator! Up to this point you have been only useless; now you risk also doing some harm.[8]

---

5 Italicized in the original text to draw attention to the language used in the proclamations: *Istruzioni generali del governo provvisorio della Repubblica Napoletana ai patrioti,* 25 January 1799.

6 This tradition can be traced back to the first and famous Liberty Tree that stood on the Boston Common before the American Revolution and came to stand for a place for people to gather on their own terms and for their own purposes against the rule of Britain over the American colonies. Inspired by the American example, the Liberty Trees became a symbol of the French Revolution and, soon afterwards, of other revolutions taking place, such as the creation of the Batavian republic in 1795 and of the Roman republic in 1789. The Neapolitans followed that tradition which may have originally also been inspired by Thomas Jefferson's well-known quotation, "The tree of liberty must be refreshed from time to time with the blood of patriots and tyrants." The planting of "Liberty Trees" in the major squares and public sites of Naples and provincial towns became a key symbol and ritual of the revolution and the new regime. The clergy and the civil authorities were expected to, and did, participate in these rituals, often singing the obligatory *Te Deum* to consecrate the new regime and to celebrate the public event. See Bronzini (2002), and Davis (2006: 100); as well as www.quotedb.com/quotes/2074

7 "This is certainly dear to the heart of the people: this is a concern to trouble the calm of their minds," adapted from Virgil, *Aeneid* IV, 380. Translator's note.

8 This kind of language may be fitting to the mouth of a conqueror wishing to talk up his conquests, to an orator addressing an assembly of idlers, to a philosopher speaking to other philosophers; it may also be the language of the historian handing down the results of events to posterity: but it ought never to be the language of a man

The course of ideas is what must guide the course of operations and determine the degree of force in the effects. The first ideas that must be caused to prevail are the ideas of all; then those of the majority; and lastly, the ideas of the few. As those who lead a revolution are always fewer in number and have more ideas than the others, because they see more problems and perceive more benefits, the republicans therefore often have to forget themselves in order to establish the republic. Brutus suffered many hardships for a long time, and foresaw a great many, but as long as he alone suffered and saw, he kept silent; the patricians suffered many hardships before the people complained; and finally the rape of Lucretia caused each one to remember that they too were husbands: Brutus addressed the people first and moved them, after which he spoke to the senate, and when the revolution had been accomplished, finally he listened to himself.

Everything can be done: the only difficulty is how. With time we can arrive at those ideas which it would be madness to want to arrive at today: once the mechanism has been set in motion, you go from one event to another, and man becomes merely a passive being. The whole secret lies in knowing where to start.

A revolution can never be produced, unless it is a religious revolution, by following ideas that are too general, or by following a single plan. At every step you will encounter a thousand obstacles that had not been envisaged; a thousand conflicts of interests, which have to be reconciled because they cannot be abolished. The people are like a child, and often make difficulties for which you are not prepared. Many of our populations did not like the tree as a symbol because they did not understand its purpose, and some, who went to pains not to understand it, criticized it

---

speaking to the people and seeking to move them. We have lost every idea of popular eloquence: ours is only the eloquence of the schools; this is why the barely credible effects witnessed among the ancients are no longer repeated among us. Now that the mechanics of speech have been analyzed by pedants, then the scholars, then the philosophers, its force has been calculated, and the principles established whereby it can be directed in order to produce the maximum effect, it seems to me that there is still a book to be written in which the force of eloquence on nations rather than individuals is counted, where the relation which the state of the nation can have on eloquence and the nature of the latter on the state of the former are shown. In this way the difference could be appreciated between that secret but irresistible force and the pompous proclamations that have invaded Europe since 1789. Pericles thundered, roared, upset the whole of Greece, and the sons of Isaac and Ishmael divided the empires of the earth and the centuries among themselves. (V.C.)

as magic; many would rather have had a different symbol from the tree. It makes no difference whether a revolution has one symbol or another, but it does have to have one that the people understand and want.

In many populations there was a problem to be solved, a benefit to be procured in order to entice the people: in other populations there were not the same resources; and the law or the government could not occupy itself with such objectives until after the revolution had already been completed. Active revolutions are always more effective, because the people on their own direct themselves immediately towards what affects them most closely. In a passive revolution, the government's agent has to try to guess the mind of the people and present them with what they want but would not be able to procure on their own.

Sometimes the general interest (*bene*) clashes with the interests of the powerful. Abolition of fiefs, for example, damages the landowner significantly; but those who live on the fief are to be feared more than the landowner himself. The people usually derive their sustenance from the landowners; they realize that after a year they would be better off without them, but they cannot live without them for a year: the need of the moment causes them to neglect future benefits, however much greater they may be. The reformer's talent is therefore to break the bonds of dependence, to know people as well as things, to cause the respect, friendship, or dominance which, for good or ill, someone at times may enjoy over a population to be heard.

Often I have noted that one population likes a reform more than another does. Many populations wanted the monasteries to be abolished, whereas many others did not want this yet. More than superstition, it was the greater or lesser need that they had of lands that influenced their spirit. Do not clash with public opinion: the need for it will grow with the new order, and you will be asked to destroy what was wanted to be preserved just a moment previously.

It is sufficient to set things in motion: the necessity or usefulness of many will not be understood today, and will be understood only tomorrow. In this way you will have the advantage that the people will do what you yourself would want to.

You do not concern yourself with ancillary matters when you have obtained the main one. I, who wished to examine the revolution from the point of view of the peoples' ideas more than those of the revolutionaries, have noticed that most times discontent was born from seeking to perform certain operations without certain appearances and formalities which the people felt necessary. The same thing occurs in revolutions as in philosophy, where all the disputes arise less from ideas than from words. The reformers call the audacity with which they attack the ancient rituals "force of spirit." I call it the "foolishness" of a spirit that cannot reconcile them with new things.

The great talent of the reformer is to lead the people in such a way that they do on their own what you yourself would want to do. I have seen many populations do by themselves things that they would have condemned, had they been done by the government. "To keep the people ... from favouring a man in his errors, the great remedy is to manage that the people judge him."[9] But this great objective is achieved only by whoever has already defeated both the childish vanity of preferring appearances to reality, and the vanity of those men who are doubly childish in that they do not know true glory, and believe it to consist of doing everything themselves.

Since the great danger in passive revolutions is that of going beyond the point where the people want to stop and after which they would abandon you, the best course of action in the majority of cases is to stay this side of it. The government had ordered many monasteries to be abolished immediately; and this, which was entrusted to persons who were not always loyal, had failed to produce the advantages that had been hoped for. The convents could have been allowed to remain, but with the law that they could not admit new monks; under another law, their estates could have been assigned to those who were renting them, with the freedom to acquire ownership of them. In this way the lands would have been divided up and the monasteries abolished in the space of just a few years, and in any case the monks could have been made to pay dearly for this extension of their survival. Wanting to do all you can in the space of a moment is not always without danger, because a situation where the people no longer have anything to fear or hope from you is not without danger.

The people are often wiser and more just than is believed. Sometimes misfortunes themselves can correct them of their errors. I have seen populations become republicans and take up arms, because in their indifference they were plundered by the insurgents. In Caiazzo[10] some of the vilest dregs of the people rose up and attacked the authorities that had been established. All others were indolent spectators, and the insurgents

9 Cuoco is quoting Machiavelli from "The Art of War" (1965: 691).

10 A town near Caserta, the seat of the royal palace.

alone were the strongest; they wanted to plunder, and this broke the lethargy of the others. Then the insurgents were no longer alone; the entire population defended the authorities established; and, educated by danger, Caiazzo became the population most devoted to the republic.

Profit can be taken from everything; everything can be useful to an active government, which knows the nation and does not have systems. All peoples resemble each other; but the effects of their revolutions are different, because those who lead them are different, too. I could tell of many events to demonstrate what I have just stated; but could it all be recounted without mortal tedium? For the foreigners, the results are sufficient; the compatriots (*nazionali*), if they want to, can apply the events and names that they already know to each of them.

XX

Project of an Interim Government

In the state in which the Neapolitan nation found itself, the choice of those who would form the provisional government was more important than might be thought. In this connection, we shall report what some proposed to Championnet and his advisers.

The first step in a passive revolution is to win over popular opinion; the second is to involve the highest number of people in the revolution. These two operations, while apparently different, are in practice one and the same, because the same step that involves the highest number of persons in a revolution also allows popular opinion to be gained. As the people are seldom able to judge a revolution or government based on principles and theories, and in the early days cannot judge it by its effects either, they must judge it on the basis of persons, and approve of the government that they see is committed to the persons they themselves are accustomed to respect.

Among those employed by the king of Naples, there are many who have never waged war on the revolution, who are friends of the country because they love what is good, and who are attached to the king's government only because it provided them with an honest means of making a living. Many of them deserve to be employed because of their talents, and can win the opinion of many popular classes over to the revolution.

The legal profession (*foro*) employs a great number of people; and once the legal class has been won over, it will bring with it one-fifth of the population. The ecclesiastical class also employs a great number of people, and here too something similar might be hoped for; the rest would come from the nobility (I shall use this term for the last time to indicate a class that ought no longer to exist, but which did exist until this time) and the merchant class. The nobles will be less upset when they see they have not been forgotten completely; and the merchants, who until now have been despised by the nobles, will be proud of an honour that puts them on a par with their rivals, and the nation may hope for great help from them in its needs. In Naples it is this class that is on friendly terms with the people, because all those in Naples who are fishermen, sailors, porters, and other such, and who form that numerous and ever-mobile part of the people known as the *lazzaroni*, depend on and live off this class. The many rich landowners in the provinces would also be useful, for they could do there what the merchants can do in Naples, and enlighten the government where it is unenlightened, and has no other way of being enlightened, regarding the provinces.

As an effect of our ill-directed public education, knowledge of our affairs has become linked to power and wealth: those who concern themselves with knowledge for the most part know everything save that which they are supposed to know. Raised in reading English and French books, they will know all about the manufacturing industries of Birmingham and Manchester but not those of Arpino; they will speak to you of the agriculture of Provence and know nothing of that of Apulia. There is not one of them who does not know how a Polish king or a Roman emperor is elected, but very few will know how the administrators are elected in one of our municipalities; everyone can tell you the degrees of longitude and latitude of Tahiti; if you ask them those of Naples, no one will be able to tell you. Once upon a time our people would concern themselves with such matters, and we had writers on these subjects before the other nations of Europe had even thought about them. Today no one deigns to deal with them, eager as they are for foreign glory, almost as though it were possible to obtain greater esteem from other peoples by repeating badly to them what they themselves know well, than in telling them what they do not already know. But in any case such knowledge is necessary and, in order to have it, one has to either resort to muddled, inelegant books written two centuries ago or rely on those who know both men and their state as a result of having handled the kingdom's affairs and seen several of our regions. Through the fault of our education system, the knowledge we have is useless, and we are forced to beg useful information from others.

But in order that knowledge of our patriotic matters does not remain separate from the light of universal European philosophy; or that those whose opinion we require do not become our masters out of necessity; or that the old interests do not oppress the new ones (for these people too had an interest in the old government), they will be joined by double the number of wise and virtuous patriots. In this way we will have the advantage of patriotism in decision making, and patriotism will have the advantage of local knowledge at the review stage and of public opinion in execution.

Instead of making an assembly that might be called "constituent," consisting of twenty-five persons, it could be made of eighty, and in this way all these advantages could be combined. A provisional assembly of eighty is not too large for a nation that should have a constitutional assembly more than twice the size: one of twenty-five could prove to be too small for requirements, especially if the constitution has not yet been published. The people might believe they are being mocked, and that the intention is to exclude them from everything. A foreign general who came on his own to dictate law to us would be tolerated as a conquering king, and the oppression in which everyone would see all the others would make their own tolerable; but as soon as the nation is a part of the sovereign body more care must be taken; you should give to everyone or no one; compromise solutions do not remove oppression and add envy.

It was possible to name the true patriots in each of the classes, who, without being members of any club, loved the country and could have brought it prosperity. But it would be culpably imprudent to reveal the names of them now.

XXI

Principles That Were Followed

I beg all those who read this chapter not to think that my intention is to write a satire of the patriots. If a patriot is a man who loves his country, then am I myself not a patriot? How could I condemn a name that honours so many of my friends for whose distance or loss I now beweep? We may be proud that our class of patriots in Naples was the best. There, and perhaps there alone, the revolution was not carried on by those who wanted it merely because they had nothing to lose. But amid such great political turmoil, it is impossible for the wicked not to become mixed up with the good; as when a vessel is shaken, it is impossible for the dregs not to become mixed up with the liquid. The great objective of the laws and government is to ensure that, despite the common names with which they may clothe themselves, the good can always be distinguished from the evil, and that only the man who is worthy of the name "patriot" is recognized as such. Then the wicked will no longer corrupt the work of the good. Then the government made up of patriots will be the best of all governments, because it will be a government of those who love their country. Such is the harsh necessity of human affairs, however, that often the greatest precautions taken to ensure that the good prevail merely alienate them, and confirm the old adage that in revolutions it is always the worst who triumph.

In other revolutions, revolutionaries who were not good men caused bad principles to emerge. In the Neapolitan revolution, principles that were neither our own nor good caused the good men to be lost. Nothing was better than the individuals we had, for their principles were upright. If the political operations failed to match up to their ideas, this was because the public principles were not their own, and were wrong. These political principles could not help but corrupt everything.

Some false patriots or malicious speculators, who had hardly any followers among the class of good men and members of the government, said that all the aristocrats, bishops, priests, and the wealthy had to be destroyed. They were not content with them being brought down to the same level as the others. The Florentine republic once operated on the same principles; and the Florentine republic was in a state of perpetual civil warfare as a result, which was what eventually brought about its downfall. This inevitably occurs each time that a republic is not founded on justice. And it never is, each time that individuals continue to be persecuted once their class has been destroyed, not because they continue to enjoy the distinctions of the destroyed class, but simply because they belonged to it at one time. The Romans contented themselves with ensuring that the plebeians could attain all positions. This was right and constituted liberty. If they had wanted to exclude the patricians only because they were patrician, it would have been the same as to seek to restore the patriciate after having destroyed it and seeking to cause civil war to commence.

They claimed they did not have to employ any of those who had served the king well. It was right for them not to employ those – if there were any – who had served him in his whims, in his dissoluteness and tyrannies; who owed the honour of serving to the infamy with which they had covered themselves. But many, in serving the king, had served the country; and many others, by contrast, had not been able to serve the king, for they had not been worthy of serving the country. Excluding the former, admitting the latter, only because one set had served the king and the other had not: was this not the same as betraying the country and causing it to be served by those who were incapable of doing so?

Who, then, should they have employed? Only those who were patriots. The Neapolitan republic was seen as a quarry in which only a few were entitled to share; and this was the signal – could it have been otherwise? – for civil war between the more numerous part of the nation and the weaker part.

This meant that the republic was deprived of all good representatives: for if a man of genius and honesty is a rarity among human beings, how could such a man be found easily in a class that is not numerous? It is true that the crowd's clamour did not express the opinion of good men, nor was it the norm among the government. But in precipitous and uncertain circumstances, when public curiosity is extremely high and the principles of a new government are still unknown, and there is neither the time nor the means to compare rumours with facts, such clamours, even if false, can do real damage, for the people consider them to be government principles and take offence at them. The most difficult thing, in such times, is to allow an opinion that might be described as public to develop; to ensure that many people can speak, because voices joined together produce a greater effect, and at the same time that their words are in harmony, so the effect is not destroyed by them being in conflict with each other. This, incidentally, was more difficult to achieve in Naples than elsewhere: because the revolution was not active but passive, hence there was no dominant opinion. Rather the opinions of France were imitated. These were many and varied, hence some were "terrorists," others "moderates," etc.; opinions were not free, and the one which was not the most widely held often prevailed by force; and time was so limited that it did not allow directionless public opinion to form.

It has generally been observed that the people are never deceived in the details; but a faction may be deceived, and all the more so a faction which reduces all virtues and talents to a single name, using "Cataline" and "Cato" interchangeably. True "patriotism" is love of one's country, and he who seeks its good and has the talents to procure it may be said to love his country. If patriotism were separated from these concrete ideas, it turns into an illusory word which paves the way for slander, and prevents the good man who is not part of a faction from becoming part of the government. Genuine merit is replaced by merit of opinion, which everyone is capable of feigning, and genuine merit ranks behind that of the charlatans.

By these means we saw the virtuous Vincenzio Russo[1] and others, including one who under the circumstances could have been useful to the country, alienated from the legislative body.

If our revolution had been active, our patriots would have come to know each other during the preceding action. This would have left no room for deception, as they each would have been known for their worth. It has rightly been said that civil wars cause the talents of a nation to develop, not in the sense that they cause them to be born but in that they make them known, for in action, everyone is given the place their talent assigns to them, and the choice is mostly successful because men are judged by their deeds.

In Naples, a man was considered to be a patriot as long as he formed part of a club. But even if this British invention of a club could have

1 Vincenzio Russo (1770–1799) was a prominent Jacobin extremist, both for his writings and for his political activities in France, Rome, and Naples. Benedetto Croce described him as a "socialist moralist" (Croce [1896] 1961: 96). More recently, another Neapolitan historian, Giuseppe Galasso (1989: chaps. 18–20), has offered an in-depth and sympathetic assessment of Russo's ideas and actions. See the letters that Cuoco addressed to Russo in appendix I.

brought about a revolution eventually, nonetheless, when it failed to do so, it meant that men could be judged only by words. Our clubs had not yet come through the first test of conspiracies, that of maintaining secrecy among their ranks; initially consisting of a few individuals, they dissolved when the persecution began. When the revolution came, many were found who had done nothing but put their names forward only recently, men who did not even know each other, and it was easy for anyone with audacity to mingle with them and declare themselves to be patriots.

In this way, the country was in danger of falling victim to private ambition, for it was not a question of satisfying the country with services rendered to it, but with those which someone might want to render. Those with skill or ability were not sought. In this kind of contest, the most audacious liar, the most bare-faced braggart, was bound to overcome merit and virtue, which is always modest.

XXII

Accusation against Rotondo: The Censure Commission

From the first days of the republic,[1] a war began to be waged against all public employees: accusation upon accusation, deputation upon deputation. All that anyone who aspired to hold a position had to do was to put himself at the head of a number of patriots and make some noise. Since everything revolved around vague words that no one understood, there was no place for reason. Number and noise, the first force that men turn to in civil conflict until they move on to others which are crueller and more effective, had to prevail. All a reasonable and decent man could do was to wrap himself up in his cloak and keep quiet.

Prosdocimo Rotondo, an elected representative, managed to arouse the envy of some of his enemies. Nicola Palomba made an accusation against him.[2] Palomba, who did not know Rotondo but was enthusiastic and therefore unwise, believed Rotondo to be unworthy of his post only because some of his friends thought him such. An accusation of this kind should never have been entertained, for if a person is unworthy, this might result in the sovereign not appointing him; but once appointed, a crime would have to have been committed for that person to be dismissed before the term set by law. Once the accusation had been entertained, however, it had to be taken seriously. In a republic, accusation should be free but slander must be punished. I do not know whether Rotondo was guilty, but I do know that he insisted on being judged; I do know that once dismissed, he published an account of his administration, at which point everyone fell silent. The then chairman of the central committee saw from this apparently private affair how important it was that the law

1 The republic began on 23 January 1799.

2 Prosdocimo Rotondo (1740–1799), a lawyer from Gambatesa, Campobasso, was a friend of Cuoco and a member of the interim government; Nicola Palomba (1746–1799), a priest from Avigliano, Potenza, was a designated official in the Basilicata area. Both died in the repression that followed the collapse of the revolution.

should continue to be respected, without which there is no government; and realized that a crowd of patriots could become a faction, as soon as they stopped being the nation. But soon afterwards, some who despaired of being loved and of increasing their standing with the nation sought to fawn over the faction instead, and so did not allow the Rotondo affair to be spoken of any further. Palomba departed for the department of which he had been appointed commissioner. Admittedly, he did have the right to continue with the accusation, including by means of his attorneys. It should not, however, have been a question of him having the right; he should have been made to follow through. Palomba should not have been allowed to leave without first having fulfilled the duty which his accusation imposed on him. Under a just government, the accuser is himself at the same time accused; and while Rotondo's fitness to sit as one of the legislators was being questioned, Palomba had no right to be appointed commissioner. A silence in which the government was sacrificed to a faction and the faction was sacrificed to an individual was offensive both to Rotondo and to all good men.

Once the secret was revealed, there was no end to the intrigue. Naples became filled with patriotic assemblies, which started to criticize the government's operations and representatives. But they did not content themselves with thus restraining the conduct of those who might have abused their power, one excellent effect produced in a republic by having free parties; they were not content merely to observe each other; they wanted to fight with each other, they wanted to defeat each other; they wanted their criticisms to have the force of accusations, and hence such scrutiny of the parties was bound to degenerate into civil war.

Now it seems all were accused, but as the accusations were not directed by love of country, they were not founded on reason: personal motives were what caused them to arise, and the same ones also caused them to be abandoned. Furthermore, on the majority of occasions the disputes were decided on the authority of foreigners. Although their decisions were sometimes just, they could never have the force of law, because even when the law was enforced it was only a man who was speaking. Thus men never got used to believing that there was no other way for their desires to be satisfied than by legal means; and that, without this intimate and profound conviction, there is no republic. Public morals become corrupt; factions no longer serve the country but the man whom they believe to be above the law, and in secret this man incites a division which consolidates his own empire. The parties corrupt the man, and the man corrupts the nation. The conspirators take their measures, the good men find themselves defenceless, the factious triumph (regardless of which party they belong to; anyone who is not in the country's party is factious); and given that the only means to keep them quiet is to give them a position, many are promoted who are either not wanted by the nation or who then cause the nation's ruin.

A deadly ill, this; not the least cause of our ruin, and one that good men would do well always to remember, to be more cautious in giving their confidence to the wicked, who are always pushed high by the force of a revolution! They should be feared in all different types of revolution. They are much more to be feared, too, in a revolution of opinion, where a sentiment that cannot be seen and a name that can be feigned often take the place of true virtue and real merit; in a revolution brought about by foreign arms, in which the reckless profusion of positions is inevitable; by the conqueror, who often does not know what is being given or who it is being given to, only that what he gives is not his own; and by the first to be employed by him, who are quicker to recall the needs of a friend than the needs of a state which they hated, and who, full of impatience to obey, are rarely able to control themselves in their use of command.

To quieten the rumours a little, the government instituted a commission of five persons[3] to examine those who were to be employed. Only those approved by the commission were employed; anyone who was censured was ruled out permanently.

This commission was the result of circumstances. The accusations and complaints were infinite; time was short; the need to know people well was urgent. The institution of which we are speaking was conceived for good purposes; very few instructions were given to it, mostly in private. Contrary to the government's intention, it became a magistrature which had and exercised regular jurisdiction, kept an office, received petitions, issued decrees. The institution was transformed from its original nature, which always happens in all similar institutions. If Palomba had been forced to continue with his accusation or if Palomba or Rotondo had been sentenced instead of a commission being instituted, much of the clamour would have ceased and the government would have come to know both its people and affairs better. When a disturbance takes place, especially in the early days of a new government, the people rarely know

3 This was the commission of the *informi* (the inquiring commission); it lasted no more than one month.

the real reason for it. They attribute everything to the government: an inevitable and serious ill, which ought to persuade us of several things: that not everything the people complained of was always the government's fault; that the intentions were always pure but the institutions were not always good; and these were not always good because the principles on which they depended were wrong; and finally, that in a new government, as far as possible, it is necessary to do without institutions that can become arbitrary. Everything must be firmly grasped by the hand of whoever is governing.

XXIII

Laws – *Fideicommissa*

I am following the course of my ideas rather than that of the times. So many events accumulated and meshed together into so short a space of time that, rather than follow each other, they overlap to the point that it is impossible to judge them properly unless we observe how they relate to each other.

The moment when a people rise up in revolution is like the moment when an assembly is in uproar. Disagreements and the heat of the dispute arouse so much and such varied clamour that the voice of reason cannot be heard. If a man, who on account of his prudence and morals is reasonable, then presents himself, minds become calmed, and everyone listens to him. His name wins him the attention of all, and he can cause the voice of reason to be heard. At first, opinion is needed to pave the way for reason; but later reason has to support and confirm opinion.

The events recounted thus far served to win the confidence of the people before the government acted; but eventually the government had to act, and had to earn by its deeds the confidence it had already won ... It started to tackle the abolition of the *fideicommissa*[1] and feudalism, which were the greatest obstacles to equality and republican government among us.

The institution of *fideicommissa* involves the spirit of keeping property within families, which is incompatible with the equality of well-governed republics. In Rome, as in Sparta, the love of equality itself may have caused the spirit of keeping property to emerge. But our *fideicommissa* had nothing Roman about them, save for the name and the external form, which is called "substitution." These ancient substitutions, along with the idea of hereditary nobility and feudal succession, produced a monster among us, for which we wrongly blamed the Romans. In the

---

1 A legal mechanism whereby the aristocracy was able to prevent alienation of property or the break-up of inherited family demesne. Rao (2012b) offers a good introduction to this issue.

Kingdom of Naples, where all wealth is territorial, *fideicommissa* multiplied to an extreme degree, as did the number of single people, idlers, paupers, litigants, etc.

Reform was simple and reasonable. It did not retroactively annul the will of testators who had ordered *fideicommissa,* partly because a new law must never annul the previous facts, and partly because reform of property must not destroy its foundation, which is simply possession authorized by public custom.[2] With the estates covered by the *fideicommissa* remaining in the hands of their holders, and a law preventing new ones from being ordered, a single generation would have sufficed to bring about the redistribution that was desired, something that would have been ill accepted if imposed by the public authority.

For second-born children and legatees, it was ordered that the part of the *fideicommissum* from which they were entitled to draw an income would be given to them as capital. In this way they too would have property for their children to inherit. It was further ordered that the capital should be calculated based on the income from the property, at a rate of 3 per cent. Thus in a nation where estates traded at no less than 5 or 6 per cent, the legatees' portions came indirectly to be doubled, and the inequality that the spirit of primogeniture reserved to the portions inherited by the same father's children was corrected without violence.

This law was wise and acceptable to all. The holders of the *fideicommissa* did not lose as much with the concessions made to the legatees as they gained by acquiring ownership of their properties in a nation where the market in land sale was beginning to develop. The ties of the *fideicommissa* were already ill tolerated, both by prodigals wishing to squander their property, and by the wise who sought to use it well.

Perhaps it would have been fair to add to the law the condition appended by Emperor Leopold when he implemented his reform of the *fideicommissa* in Tuscany. This fine sovereign judged that it was an injustice to deprive a man of the right to succession to which he was entitled and had come to expect. He therefore reserved the right not just for the

2 As Machiavelli says, a law which looks a long way back is always tyrannical. (V.C.) Here Cuoco paraphrases Machiavelli who said, "No law more damaging for a republic can be made than one that looks back a long time," in *The History of Florence* (1965: 3: 1143, Gilbert translation). See also Machiavelli, *The Discourses* (2003: bk. 1, chap. 37).

holders to succeed to the *fideicommissa*, but also for those already born or still to be born from marriages contracted before the law, many of which had been made in the hope of this kind of succession.

There were still other matters to be decided. Measures remained to be taken on the many wealthy marriage dowries in Naples which in reality are merely the *fideicommissa* of families and other people … But such matters depended on testamentary law, the state of the nation, and so many other considerations that it was better to wait for a more appropriate time. Rarely in the French Revolution, and those which broke out subsequently, was the sin of undue sloth in making laws committed. Much more often it was that of undue haste.

XXIV
Feudal Law

Feudal law required lengthier revision and involved interests harder to reconcile. The law on *fideicommissa* took little away from those who possessed them, and what little it did take from them was given to their children and brothers. The law on fiefs took a great deal from the landowners and gave it to outsiders who at times were also their enemies. However, to abolish the fiefs was the general wish of the whole nation. The inhabitants of the provinces burned with such impatience that they had virtually forced the king to strike blows against feudalism, blows which seemed to favour democracy more than monarchy. I say this as a figure of speech, but I am not sure whether feudalism is more appropriate to one or other forms of government. The form of government to which feudalism is most appropriate is aristocracy: all the governments of Europe at the time when feudalism prevailed were aristocratic. The European monarchies were built on the ruins of feudalism. Where this remained intact, the government remained aristocratic, as it did in Poland; where it had been altered but not destroyed, a kind of hybrid government had arisen, as it did in England and Sweden; where it had been destroyed entirely, a monarchic government had arisen, as it did in most of Europe; and in those parts which earlier made up the immense monarchy of Spain in particular, feudalism remained in a unique situation: having lost all the rights it had vis-à-vis the king, it retained all those which it once had vis-à-vis the people. If a feudal vassal of the Swabian emperors were taken as the term of comparison, a British lord resembled such a person more than a Neapolitan did when he was in parliament, but the Neapolitan resembled him much more than the British lord when in his own lands.

But while the former rights are glorious for the landowner, and can be of great use to both sovereign and state, the latter rights are shameful to the landowner, because that which is oppressive and harmful to the state never brings glory to the sovereign or the barons themselves, and because these rights tend to destroy the industry on which the true prosperity of a nation alone depends. They are the rights of barbarian peoples. Wherever industry develops they are forgotten, and it is in the landowners' own interests that this should happen. In Russia, even the great landowners have begun to grant freedom and property to those who live on their lands. With this measure alone, they have virtually tripled the value of their lands.

The landowners had foreseen that the revolution would oblige them to make fresh sacrifices, and wanted these to be as few as possible. Some excessively ardent republicans were keen to take everything away from them. Between these two extremes, the middle ground was hard to find. There was not even a precedent to follow. France, where the great landowners had been destroyed by the civil war, had no need of laws once force had done its work.[1] Joseph II[2] in Lombardy had long before sought to equalize possession of land by dividing large estates.

Many of the populations began with action, taking possession of the barons' estates. If everyone had done the same, the law would have been less difficult to devise. Force authorizes many things which reason would never order, and the people themselves love to see many things approved by events which they would shudder to order.

The discussion of the draft law was interesting. The two opposing parties followed different opinions according to their interests; the principles were conflicting, as usually occurs if one goes to extremes, and were not always true or appropriate to the question.

The landowners believed that conquest could be a right; the republicans believed it was always a matter of abuse (*forza*), and that even if it could become a right at the time of conquest, now it was the nation that had conquered the barons. A new conquest would despoil the usurpers in the same way and with the same right with which they themselves had previously despoiled other, older usurpers.

The landowners believed that all titles dependent on the *ancien régime* were legitimate, for that regime, they believed, was legitimate. The patriots, instead, believed everything that had not been done by a republic was illegitimate. If we listened to the landowners, everything had to be

1 In France, there was a feudal law in the early days of the revolution, but it only reformed the most horrendous disorders which no longer existed here. Feudalism was more burdensome in France than it was in Naples. We had to start from precisely the point where the French laws had stopped. This second reform in France was accomplished by the civil war. (V.C.)

2 Joseph II (1741–1790), ruler of Lombardy as part of the Habsburg domains, had a reputation for being an "enlightened despot."

preserved; if we listened to the patriots, everything had to be destroyed, because once a government was declared illegitimate, there was no reason why some of its deeds should be abolished and others kept.

This way was the same as taking the side of usurpers and governments, rather than humanity and the nation, which were betrayed through an excess of zeal by their defenders. Today, the saying is: "A king should not have done this"; tomorrow a king will say: "This should not have been done by a republic." When will we take the welfare of the people as our principle, and examine not what a government could do, but only what it should do?

To look for a title of property in nature is tantamount to seeking to do away with property. Nature recognizes nothing but possession, which becomes property only with the consent of men. Such consent is always the result of the circumstances and needs in which the people find themselves. Everything which public welfare does not imperiously require cannot be reformed without tyranny, for men, after their needs, have, or should have, nothing more sacred than the customs of their fathers. If what does not need reform is reformed, the revolution will have many enemies and very few friends.

Feudalism in Naples consisted of an immense bundle of possessions, properties, exactions, privileges, and rights, acquired, received, usurped by different hands at different times. The landowners originally were merely the owners of estates with an obligation to fealty; and following the law of devolution, they differed from other owners only in the sense that they had received their lands from the hand of destiny while others had received theirs from the hands of men.

But at the same time, the large landowners were major officials of the Crown, and in times of anarchy or weakness, these representatives of the sovereign were powerful and unmovable, causing the sovereign they represented to be forgotten. The rights they exercised as officials of the Crown became the rights first of the landowner, then of his family, and finally of the fief. In times of continual civil warfare, the few free men who had remained in our regions, with neither security nor property, turned to the powerful for protection, at the expense of their liberty.

These abuses were undoubtedly great. But such was the unhappiness of the times, such was the condition of these men, and such the desolation of our districts, that they must have seemed like tolerable effects. Sometimes, when these conditions reached an extreme, they even resulted in properties being returned. As men multiplied in number, they also extended their industry, and reclaimed their civil liberty: this is the first step which nations take towards culture. A generous-spirited king, who wanted to rise up, gained strength through the favour of the people, by defending them against other minor tyrants. Thus the monarchies of Europe arose from the ruins of feudal aristocracy. In our history we see the steps taken by the people, the baronial opposition, and the sovereign's perpetual wavering according to which he feared most, the barons or the people, and the rapacity of the tax authorities, eternal traitors to barons, peoples, and kings. History itself shows the route to follow, in line with the ideas of the peoples. The feudal laws themselves suggest how to reform feudalism: that reform which the people desire, and which the barons cannot oppose.

It was not sufficient to have a law which declared feudalism to be abolished. Such a law was pompous rather than useful. Little in Naples still had the appearance of feudalism; the difficult part was to recognize feudalism where there apparently was none. The landowners had acquired rights as officials of the Crown and protectors of the peoples. Such rights could no longer exist in a form of government where sovereignty was restored to the people and the citizens had no protector apart from the law. The barons possessed lands. It was not sufficient that these should be made equal in condition to the others. If the reform remained on these terms, the barons, released from the burden of the *adoa* [the tax which the barons paid to the king each year in return for the military service provided by them] and devolution of [the tax on all fiefs payable from the time when the heir to the sixth degree died], having become the owners of free lands, would have gained much more than the exaction of uncertain, fluctuating, and odious duties gave them, while the people would have gained nothing. In a nation where industry is active, it is to the landowner's advantage to have his lands farmed by freemen as opposed to slaves. An idle and poor nation asks to be released from its taxes. A wealthy, industrious nation is content to pay them, provided it has the means to increase its industry. In the huge swathes of lands which the barons possessed, there were only a few which belonged to the fief. In the others, what you saw was an accumulation of sundry rights stacked on top of one another, belonging to different people. It was easy to recognize that the most powerful of these must have been the usurper. Much of that mass of feudal lands which was called "the fiefs' estates" [*demaniali de' feudi*] and which formed the majority of them, was therefore returned to the local populations, with the woodlands left to be publicly monitored. The landowners were also left with sufficient land to be wealthy, provided industry displaced idleness. With the agrarian laws, the nation stood to have, if not perfect equality, at least that division of property which in a great nation is more useful, less dangerous, and closer to true equality.

Never was it more clearly seen how a formal and constant examination is more dangerous to usurpers than hot-headed, momentary enthusiasm. The barons would have preferred a thousand times to return to the principles of "conquest" and "legitimacy," which, while apparently more destructive, were easier to combat, easier to be avoided in the execution. But how could they oppose evident principles, which they themselves had acknowledged even under the abolished government?

Despite all this, the bill was not passed without considerable dissent; even on its deathbed, feudalism had many defenders. Some legislators believed that nothing could be decided about feudalism, for France had decided nothing: an irresistible argument for the representative of a free and independent nation! Pagano believed that the time had not yet come to decide the controversy. He acknowledged that the abolition of feudal rights was necessary and proper, but did not want the lands to be touched, as though a people should not be oppressed but might legitimately be wretched. Some wanted the matter committed to a tribunal, which would be appointed to deal with it; but while the laws are made for the people, sentences are made for the powerful, who, with their possessions, their quibbling, and, at times, abuse of power, could, with the judges' decision, win back all that the people had gained by law.

This is why it is so important that the legislator's ideas should be consistent with those of the nation, and that the draft laws should contain those moderate ideas felt and agreed on by all men! If we had remained with extremes, there would have been no law, or the law would have resulted in civil war and would have carried with it the appearance of injustice. Founded on undeniable principles, it would have been tolerated by even the barons most opposed to revolution, if not with indifference (for who could require that some should remain indifferent to the loss of so much wealth?), then at least with decorum.

But precisely when the government was discussing this draft law, Championnet was recalled, and Macdonald,[3] who succeeded him, was far from

3 Jacques-Etienne Macdonald (1765–1840) was a French general who distinguished himself in several campaigns in Belgium, Holland, and Italy, and served as governor of Rome in 1789. Upon being sent to Naples, he sought to apply the directives from the French Directory, thereby alienating many Neapolitan patriots. When named Marshal of France by Napoleon, he switched loyalties with the Restoration to serve the Bourbon dynasty in France.

keen to rubber-stamp the government's operations. It was necessary to wait for Abrial, who was reasonable and just.[4] But meanwhile time passed, and the fear of upsetting 10,000 powerful men caused the French and the republic to miss the opportunity to gain the minds of 5 million.

It is worth noting the difference between the debate on feudalism in France and Naples. In speaking of the former, Anquetil[5] says that the discussion in the Assembly began from a proposal made to ensure that the tax due on the incomes of those who owned the rights could be collected more reliably, and, in progressing from idea to idea, ended up abolishing all rights. In France, they started out from moderate principles and ended up with extremist ones; in Naples, we returned from the latter to the former. And this was in the order of nature, for we took those ideas from the point at which the French left them. Hence in Naples, the opinions of private individuals were more extreme than those of the government. The government followed the principle that the laws on property have their own justice, which consists of ensuring that everyone loses as little as possible, and in the case of feudal reform, it is possible to ensure that both parties gain. I personally am convinced that the landowners would have gained more from a new law than the old ones. Feudal rights were sustained solely by judicial rulings. From the time when the judges in Naples were obliged to draw their judgment on the text of the law, feudal rights have gradually been abolished, and in time they will all die out. But a new law must be conceived as a negotiation rather than a decree; and through it, long-term possession may come to acquire the force of ownership. The new feudal law did not claim to have as its aim a mythical equality of property or the upholding of old claims of ownership. Its chief aim was to release the people from everything which disrupted the exercise of public authority, restricted and destroyed industry, and prevented the free trade of property.

---

4 André-Joseph Abrial (1750–1828) was sent by the French Directory to organize the Neapolitan republic on the model of the French republic. He worked closely with General Macdonald. According to Colletta ([1838] 1858: 1, 336), "Abrial was reputed an honest man, a friend of liberty, and a thoroughly versed in the subject of the people's rights and modern theories of government, and his residence in Naples only served to increase his already high reputation."

5 Louis-Pierre Anquetil (1723–1806) was a priest, theologian, and historian. He wrote, in collaboration with others, a history of France at Napoleon's request.

XXV

Religion

Today, the ideas of the European peoples have reached such a state that a political revolution is virtually impossible without also leading to a religious revolution, whereas in the past it was mostly a religious revolution which ushered in a political one. Can we perhaps infer from this that modern revolutions are more short-lived than ancient ones?[1]

In France, the religious part of the revolution had to be violent, because the state of the nation in this sense was violent. All extremes were united in France. France had exalted papal authority in Europe. It had also been the first to shake off its yoke, but in doing so, it did not break it completely, as England had done. Rather, the old ideas remained as a matter for eternal dispute, on subjects usually left to faith. While the clergy was continually at odds with Rome, the parliaments were continually at odds with the clergy; and the Court wavered between the clergy, the parliaments, and Rome. But once the first steps had been taken, the nation could not stop there. Reflection was followed by incredulity. As the latter was born among factions, it helped to arouse the jealousy of the powerful. Thus there came to prevail in France the utmost tolerance among the philosophers, and the utmost intolerance in the government and the nation. When it comes to barbarian intolerance, few nations in Europe can compete with the cultured, humane French.

The Neapolitan nation was in a less violent state. Religion was an individual matter; and since it affected neither the government nor the nation, any insults made against the gods were left to the gods themselves. The Neapolitan people loved their religion, but the people's religion was no more than a series of feasts. Provided these were not

1 Rousseau, when asked by the author of the *Études de la nature* [Bernardin de Saint-Pierre] why, with such love for humanity and such distaste for men, he had not imitated Penn and retreated with a few sages to found a colony in America, replied: "What a difference, though! In Penn's century people believed, in mine they no longer do!" (V.C.)

taken away from them, the common people cared about nothing else. In Naples, there was no need to fear any of the ills to which the excesses of religion encouraged so many other peoples.

The foundation of religion is one, but it takes different forms in different regions according to the character of the peoples. It is very much like the language spoken. In France, for example, religion is like the language, more didactic than in Italy; in Italy, religion is more poetic, that is, more liturgical, than in France. In France, religion involves the spirit more than the heart and the senses; in Naples, more the senses and the heart than the spirit.

What other nation in Europe can boast of never having produced a heretical denomination while ready to rebel each time it heard the name of the Holy Office and the Inquisition?[2] The nation which, going against the king's wish, set up a tribunal against this barbarous institution, which all other nations of Europe recognized and tolerated (at least for some time), must be the most humane of them all.

In Naples it was easy to make reforms of both the diocesan and the monastic clergy's wealth. Respect for religion and its ministers did not stop much of the nation from seeking to deprive the clergy of their revenues.[3] Why, then, were these reforms so unpopular when they were attempted by the republic? Because our republicans, again following ideas that were too extreme, sought to take two steps simultaneously when they should have taken one; the other step should or would have followed naturally. While they sought to despoil the priests, they also sought to destroy the gods. By coupling the interests of the former to those of the latter, they strengthened the cause of the former. Hence we always come back to the same principle: there was an attempt to do more than the people wanted, when it would have been more prudent to retreat; it was possible to reach the destination, but how to get there was not known.

Conforti[4] believed that a religion can be reformed only from within. When the Christian religion has been gradually brought back to the

---

2 A reference to the successful Neapolitan opposition to the introduction of the Spanish Inquisition in Naples proposed by Viceroy Toledo in 1547. For Croce ([1925] 1970: 113), "the protest of 1547 was the last evidence of Neapolitan independence and political vitality."

3 The South never had heretical sects of great importance; and even the abbot Joachim of Flora was only a philosopher who generated interest in other parts of Italy but seldom in Naples, his own country. (V.C.)

4 Gian Francesco Conforti (1743–1799) was a priest and civil lawyer, sometimes referred to as the Paolo Sarpi of Naples for his defence of Crown supremacy over the Church. He lent his support to the Neapolitan republic and served briefly as interior minister. Imprisoned and hanged after the Restoration, he became a martyr of the revolution.

simplicity of the Gospel; when the excessive wealth of the few among the clergy has been reformed, along with the indecent misery of the many; when the number of bishoprics and idle benefits has been reduced; when all these factors have been removed, which at present unduly separate the clergy from the government and make them virtually independent, always indifferent, and often even hostile, our religion is better suited than any other religion to a moderate and liberal form of government.[5] No other known religion encourages the spirit of liberty to the same extent. The pagan religion had brute force as its fundamental dogma: it produced unteachable slaves and tyrannical masters. The Christian religion has universal justice as its foundation: it imposes duties on the peoples as it does on kings, makes the former more teachable, and the latter less oppressive. The Christian religion was the first to say to men that God did not approve of slavery. It is thanks to the Christian religion that we have a different kind of liberty in modern Europe from the ancient one. In all likelihood, the earliest Christians were people who, living in the most corrupt times, wished to bring the most superstitious idolatry back to the simplicity of pure, eternal reason, and the most horrible despotism that ever oppressed humankind (which is what Roman despotism was) to the norms of justice.

But men always go to extremes (Conforti said). Having preached tolerance, philosophy itself became intolerant,[6] without recalling that, if forcing religion on people is unworthy of religion, it is equally unworthy of philosophy. It has yet to be demonstrated that a people can survive without religion. If you do not give it to them, they will form one by themselves. But when you give it to them, it becomes a religion analogous to the government, and both will work for the good of the nation. If the people acquire it on their own, their religion will be indifferent and at times hostile to the government. Thus all the abuses of the Christian religion were born from those same measures which today they want to use in order to repair them.

Conforti believed that France itself would one day go back on its principles. When it believed it had destroyed the priests, it had, in fact, increased the desire for them. France would have to restore them, with

5 These ideas were already popular in Naples. The dispute over the *chinea* [tribute paid by the king of Naples to the Papal States; from the English *hackney*] had taught everyone about the legitimacy of a national council. An important prelate had preached against abuse of the indulgences and celibacy, without causing any scandal. (V.C.)

6 Christianity, which originally was but philosophy, also took the same path. It began by preaching tolerance: it had not come only for the sons of Abraham, but for all peoples; but later, when it came to dominate, not even the sons of Abraham were spared by it. (V.C.)

the government restricting itself to those reforms at which originally it should have stopped.

But the others were far from sharing Conforti's ideas; nor were they ever able to make a general policy on this subject.[7] Caught between the state of the nation and the examples of the French Revolution, they abandoned this important matter to the conduct of subaltern agents: the worst party to which they could have attached themselves. An act of force would have made the government hated and feared: but such indolence caused the government to be both hated and despised at the same time.

The people were weary of so many contrary opinions among the government agents, and hated the republicans more as they came to see their actions as the mere result of their individual will. Hatred of the individuals who govern, which has little effect in an old government, is highly dangerous in a new government, because, as a new government, it is formed by the individuals who compose it. The people expect no help against individuals from a government they know, and hatred for the one becomes hatred for the other.

It is an indelible characteristic of man to argue his own opinions with greater conviction than those of others, the opinions which he believes to be new and specific more than those which are old and common. I believe, I firmly believe, that if the acts in which some agents indulged against the priests had been ordered by the government, they would have been less zealous. The law determined nothing: its silence protected the clergy's person and property; so those few government agents who wanted to give free rein to their own ideas had to confine themselves to insults. Now insults are made most directly against the gods, and operations against men. The conduct of many republicans was all the more dangerous, because it was restricted to mere words. Though the priests were threatened, they were not dealt with; and they repeated to the people that the government agents were more concerned with religion than the religious, because, while they left properties alone, they attacked opinions. If precisely the opposite had been done, everything would have been in order.

Too late the government realized its error. It tried to make amends, but did worse. The people understood that the government was acting more out of fear than conviction, and when this was understood, all was lost.

---

7 Let us be fair to the best of our men [i.e., Pagano]. They understood the importance of religion among our people. (V.C.)

XXVI

The Troops

A new government has more need of force (*forza*) than an old government does, because however just the law may be, its implementation can never be safely entrusted to public custom.[1] Under a new government, the wicked, who are never in short supply, have greater scope for slandering and shirking, while the weak are all the more easily seduced or led astray in the doubtful wavering between old and new opinions.

The French, however, obstructed every attempt at organizing a force in the Neapolitan republic. Their first mistake was to fear the capital too much; the second, not to fear the provinces sufficiently. They did not have any troops to send there, for which they cannot be condemned; but they did not allow our own troops to be organized to go in their place, and for that there is no excuse.

From the remnant of the king of Naples's army, a corps of 30,000 men might have been formed on the spot, consisting of persons who asked no more than to earn a living. They were the cream of the king's army, for they had been the last to lay down their arms. Of these, the *camisciotti*[2] distinguished themselves by their courage, contending the terrain up to Castello del Carmine inch by inch. This should have caused them to be respected, but instead they were hated for it. They were imprisoned when they should all have been enrolled as soldiers for the republic, or dismissed. They were eventually released into

1 By "custom" here we take Cuoco to mean the mutual expectations built into the practice of life. In this sense, he implied that, in an established regime, institutions are self-enforcing. On this see, among others, Knight and Johnson (2011).

2 Originally the term referred to Albanian soldiers in the service of the Neapolitan king because of the type of long shirt they were wearing, but soon the name was extended to other Bourbon soldiers. In the 1848 revolts, the term, now *camiciotti*, came to refer to a volunteer group of revolutionaries who waged stiff resistance against the Bourbon troops in Messina; after 1860, the Messina city government later named a street after them to remember their valour. There is still a street named *Camiciotti* in Messina today.

Naples, and paid by those secretly plotting a counter-revolution. Thus the counter-revolutionaries were kept within the capital itself.

The king's soldiers began to gather in Capua, and from there once again in Portici. The Neapolitan republic was in a position to maintain them: they could have saved the country, saved Italy; but as soon as the operation began, it was outlawed. The few soldiers who were retained were grudgingly permitted to have arms, which were in the castles occupied by the French.

At the same time they wanted to disarm the population.[3] How could this be done without forces? The French feared both the populations and the patriots; and this excessive fear meant that in time the populations managed to arm themselves and attack them while the patriots were without arms to defend themselves. General disarmament was ordered, for the French custodians of the weapons, not knowing the country, its practices, and its people, sold them. The buyers were equally the republican government, to whom the weapons should rightfully have been returned free of charge, and the traitors, to whom the arms should have never been sold in the first place. The mercenaries, who could have become our friends, had nothing to live off and so went over to double the force of our enemies.

A gendarmerie as well as front-line troops could have been organized promptly, at the time when all the barons were ordered to dismiss their armed guards. These would willingly have entered the republic's service. They knew no other profession. Abandoned by the republic, they joined the insurgents, when they could have formed a corps of 5,000 to 6,000 brave men.

The barons' guards were ordered dismissed, and no thought was given to their livelihood. The provincial courts were discontinued, and no thought was given to the livelihood of the many individuals who made up the judicial forces, greater in number than even the baronial guards. "They are all criminals," someone said, who idealized the gendarmes as heroes. But these criminals continued to exist, for it was impossible and inhuman to destroy them, to the detriment of the republic. The great principle whereby "all the world has to earn a living" was forgotten.

It was entirely forgotten by De Renzis,[4] when he published the edict informing the king's officials that "for anyone who had served the tyrant,

3 The republican government wanted to disarm the population, fearing that it would turn against the revolutionaries.

4 Leopoldo De Renzis, baron of Montanaro from 1751 to 1799, and one-time colonel in the Bourbon army, directed the republic's military committee. In spite of the edict he published, De Renzis fought valiantly at the battle of the Maddalena Bridge, and was executed by the restored Bourbon government.

there was nothing to be hoped for from a republican government." Such language, in the mouth of a war minister, signalled to the 1,500 influential families and their many followers in the capital that "If you want to earn a living, see to it that your king returns." This edict marked the period of the royal officials' conspiracy. The edict was corrected by the government in practice, because many of the king's officials were in fact employed by the republic. It was quite clear to those with common sense that the edict had been rather strong in both words and concepts, an effect of that type of rhetoric that prevailed at the time, whereby the more forceful word was always preferred to the more precise one. But, I repeat, in passive revolutions, when opinions are varied and still uncertain, words that are not measured can do serious damage. The exceptions, held always to be the product of favour, did not destroy the impression produced by the general law. Many continued to waver; many others still found themselves having already taken steps that could not be retracted against a government they believed to be unjust. Our republic lasted no more than five months: in the first months, the officers were unable to obtain ranks; in the last months, they no longer wanted to accept them.

Shall I go on? Many friends could have been made from among the insurgents themselves. They were following a leader who for the most part was merely a man with ambition. If this leader could not be removed, he could have been bought, and his forces could have been called upon to defend the republic which he had shown he wanted to destroy.

XXVII

The National Guard

Our government reduced itself to placing all the country's hopes on the national guard. But the national guard is the strength of the people, not that of the government.

All was lost in France when the government believed it did not need any other force. The Vendée rebellion was never tamed; murderers filled the streets; there was no longer public safety, and instead of calm there were uprisings. The first shortcoming of every national guard is that it is more inclined to enthusiasm than to hard work. The second is that when it does not defend the entire nation, or at any rate when one part of the nation is armed against the other, it is impossible to prevent each party having its own followers among the guard who can impede, or at least delay, operations.

The true strength of the national guard comes from having a uniformity of opinions. Where such uniformity has not been achieved, a good deal of discretion has to be used in forming its rank. Only those who apply out of voluntary attachment to the cause should be admitted, or who have had honest principles in their upbringing, and who in their civil status have the caution gained with responsibility. Those whom Aristotle would say form the class of optimates in each city might not be enthusiasts, but they will at least rarely be traitors.[1]

I am still speaking about the principles of a passive revolution. In the early days of the republic, an infinite number of people put their names forward for the national militia: respectable magistrates, thoroughly honest citizens, the leading nobles – in short, the cream of the city, who despaired of the abolished government and sought to gain merit with

1 The point that Aristotle made in *Politics* was that stability is most likely to be found in a city dominated by the aristocracy, that is, by a group of people between the rich and the poor.

the new one. They should have been admitted. This would have achieved the dual intention of involving many people while winning over popular opinion. In every unhappy event, the book which contained their names might perhaps have formed the salvation of many. But instead, partiality was shown even in the formation of the national guard. Thus most of them withdrew, and no one had the foresight to keep the book containing their names.

Four companies of patriots were formed. These were all enthusiastic, all good men. But four companies were too few. It was necessary to return to the point from which we had started and admit those who had been excluded. But by this stage they were no longer willing to return. Orders were given that no one could be admitted to civil and military posts until they had served in the national guard. This was right, and should have been sufficient. But they wanted to order everyone to enrol, and at the same time imposed a tax on those who wanted to be exempt. I say "wanted" because the reasons for exemption were such that anyone could feign them, anyone could admit them without fear of being contradicted if they were feigning, or rebuked if they admitted them. So what happened? Those who might have been moved by the desire to hold positions were doubtless the best in the country, but most of them were rich, and they bought their exemptions. By contrast, those who had neither patriotism, nor honesty, nor property were forced to enrol, and in this way the law caused weapons to pass into the hands of our enemies.

They wanted to compel the nation, when it should have been merely invited. The imposition was very heavy in the provinces. The government had gone from one extreme to another: first they wanted no one, later they wanted everyone. It should be noted, though, that this measure was taken when it had already become apparent that the whole state of affairs was turning to inevitable ruin. In such a situation, those responsible for weighing the pros and cons before acting had little room to manoeuvre, and for those judging to avoid being taken over by the system. So the government bet all for nothing, as they say. It is a sad condition of the times, when a man is forced to want what he cannot do because he is unable to do what he wanted! Different principles, a different direction in the first operations, would have avoided the need to place all the country's hopes on the national guard; and perhaps the country might have been saved.

If the national guard in France had proved useless, it was inevitable that in Naples it would be harmful, because, as the revolution was passive, the majority of the nation should have been presumed to be at best indifferent and inert. Having observed the national guards in many parts of the provinces, I always found them to be most diligent and energetic either where there had been suffering or where insurrections were feared. Love of self reawakened love of their country. And yet, despite all this, the national guard never produced any disturbance among us, even when in the capital it was more numerous and active than could have been hoped. In short, there was no lack of good intentions on the part of the government, nor of good will on the part of the people. The mistake was entirely in the principles and the direction first given to affairs. As we approach the end of this *Essay,* we see ills multiplying: they are like so many rivers, all different, but which all derive from the same source; and the greatest profit that may be derived from the observation of these events, I believe, is precisely that of seeing how many kinds of ill can derive from a single mistake. Men will become wiser when they come to realize all the consequences that one small event can produce.

XXVIII

Taxes

On entering Naples with his victorious army, Championnet imposed a tax of two and a half million ducats, to be paid within two months. Such an imposition was utterly exorbitant for a city already decimated by the immense depredations perpetrated by the previous government. Championnet could have asked for double the amount gradually, over a longer period of time. When Championnet realized this, he repented and showed repentance about it, but he did not withdraw the tax. Instead, he taxed the province for 15 million in turn.

But who could explain what I might describe as the almost capricious way in which the already excessive burden was shared? Nothing was simpler than to follow the plan of the tithe exacted by the king, and in this way to make the new tax proportionate to the number of properties already taxed through the office of the tithe. Instead, we saw families with millions taxed just a few ducats, while those which possessed nothing were taxed the most exorbitant sums. I saw the same tax imposed on people with annual incomes of 60,000, 10,000, and 1,000 ducats. They wanted to exempt the families of the patriots from paying the tax, whereas perhaps it might have been more appropriate for them to be the first to set an example, in contributing generously to the country's needs. All the ideas were changed: a tax was considered to be a punishment, and it was not so much properties that were counted as the ranks of aristocracy which a person carried in their heart. "We tax opinion," said the tax collectors to a woman who complained of the tax imposed on her husband, who had nothing but an officer's wages, and so lost everything when the king fled. The principles adopted by those to whom the government had entrusted the matter would scarcely have been tolerated had they been used by a victorious enemy army general. A tax imposed on thought made the whole affair a matter of judgment. This is the damage that ill-conceived, poorly directed taxes produce; even if injustice is avoided, the suspicion of injustice that the effects themselves produce on the people cannot be avoided.

In fact, there was not enough money in Naples to pay the tax. It could be paid in precious metals and jewellery. The persons appointed to collect them were at once treasurer, collector, and beneficiary, and the people believed that everything was transacted not with the scales of equality but in the exactor's own interest. It is not my intention to affirm what the people believed. But to put an end to so many complaints, the government appointed a commission made up of persons beyond suspicion.

While a tax such as this was being exacted in Naples, the provinces were vexed by an order from the new government obliging the populations to pay also the arrears owed to the old government. This ill-fated order must have been signed in a moment of distraction and out of habit. The old style was followed, the style of all governments. Indeed, the decree was signed by one government member alone. I know for a fact that he did not consider it to be sufficiently important to merit discussion with the rest of his colleagues. He did not realize that such a style did not befit a revolution. Slightly beforehand, the government had abolished one-third of the tithe, and raised hopes that all of it might be abolished. The tithe involved the capital city more than the provinces, and by eternal destiny our government has always been more concerned with the former than the latter. But should the provinces ever have expected such language from a new government which needed to earn their affection?

In Ostuni, Giuseppe Ayroldi, one of the leading figures of the city and a man who knew men, opposed the publication and execution of the order. He foresaw the disastrous consequences. The government did not back down; and what was the result? Ostuni rebelled, and Ayroldi was the first victim of the popular fury.

At the same time the provinces were tormented by the arbitrary requisitions of certain commissioners and generals. Ills are unavoidable in any war, but always worse when the victorious nation does not have that energy of government to attract everything to itself and to ensure that the passions of private individuals do not disrupt the unity of public operations. If the army of a republic is not made up of the most virtuous of men, it will always do more damage than that of a king. Such ills always cause the people to become disgusted with the victor, and oblige the latter to make infinite redress to humanity: this alone can vouchsafe the conquest and render the use of force almost legitimate.

XXIX

Commissioner Faipoult[1]

Eventually Faipoult arrived. He issued an edict, repeating a decree made by the executive Directory, which stated everything that the conquest had given the French nation. Conquest was mentioned, after freedom had been promised so many times; and to reconcile the edict with the promise, everything that belonged to the fugitive king was referred to as the "fruits of the conquest."

But which of the king's properties did not belong to the nation? The royal palace, which his father had certainly not brought with him from Spain, was called "the king's land." The lands of the Order of Malta and the Order of Constantine were certainly private and were called "the king's properties";[2] the monasteries too, which belonged to the monks, and which, even if there were no longer any monks, did not for this reason become the king's properties; and all the allodial lands, of which the king was no more than the administrator, were called "the king's properties." The matter went so far that the banks (where the private individuals' money was deposited), the porcelain factory, and the remains of Pompeii still buried in the bowels of the earth, were all declared to be the king's property. The king himself, even in those moments when he was most intoxicated with his own power, had never used such language, and perhaps it would have been less damaging to the nation and less odd

1 I use [Guillaume-Charles] Faipoult [1752–1817] as the name of the executor, possibly involuntary, of the French Directory's orders. Faipoult was a fine man, who loved and esteemed our nation; but as the commissioner of his government, he did no more than execute orders that were not his. The government which France has today [1806] would certainly have given him different orders. (V.C.)

2 When the French assigned the Order of Malta's properties to the nation, they demonstrated that they belonged not to the Order but to the French nation. If the Order of Malta's properties belonged to the nation in France, those of the same Order in Naples must have belonged to the Neapolitan nation. (V.C.)

coming from the mouth of a king: less damaging, because however much he took, it still all belonged to the nation, while he himself remained there; less odd, because he was in fact the head of the government, and his statements did not contain the same contradiction as Faipoult's edict.

This edict could have caused the nation to rebel. Championnet foresaw this, and withdrew the edict; Faipoult objected, and Championnet exiled Faipoult.

Oh Championnet, you are no longer alive; but may your memory receive the praise it deserves for your firmness and justice. What does it matter that the Directory chose to dismiss you? They could not humiliate you. You became the idol of our nation.

Championnet's recall to France was a bad thing for the Neapolitan republic. I did not wish to pronounce judgment on his military merit. But he was loved by the people of Naples, and this was a great credit to him.

XXX

Provinces – Formation of the Departments

What, meanwhile, was the state of the provinces? Eventually they attracted the attention of the government, which until that time had been perhaps excessively preoccupied by the capital alone. The best course of action would have been to make as few changes as possible; but as is always the case, they began by making as many as possible, and the least necessary ones at that. Most revolutions have unhappy results because of undue pressure to change the names of things.

They started with reform of the departments. The Frenchman Bassal,[1] who had arrived with Championnet, wanted to take charge of this task. What madness so many have, they want to do everything themselves! This man, who had no knowledge of our territory whatsoever, made a ridiculous, unrealizable [territorial] division. A traveller sitting on top of a mountain, who draws the valleys below him at night time without ever having seen them, could not have done a more inept job.[2]

Nature itself has divided the territory of the Neapolitan kingdom: an uninterrupted chain of mountains divides it from west to east, from Abruzzo to the furthest tip of Calabria; the rivers which flow from these mountains to the two seas that bathe our territory to the north and south, form the minor subdivisions. Nature itself therefore indicated the departments: the population, the physical and economic relations

---

1 Jean Bassal (1752–1802), a committed Jacobin, was the only Frenchman to serve as member of the Neapolitan provisional government and minister of finance in 1799. Earlier he had briefly worked in Rome for the Roman republic.

2 The work of dividing up the *départements* in France was well executed, but the Frenchmen who sought to direct the same operation in other nations clearly showed they had neither the knowledge nor the common sense of those who had performed the task in France. What sense did it make to divide the territory of Liguria up into twenty departments? The same errors were made in the Cisalpine republic [a republic formed by Napoleon in June 1797 in conquered territories centred in the Po valley of northern Italy]; the same errors were made in Roman territory as well. (V.C.)

of each city or land should have indicated the capital cities and cantons. But instead, departments were instituted which alternately overlapped with and cut into each other; one area, a few kilometres away from the capital of one department, was made to belong to another 160 kilometres away. The populations of Apulia were forced to become part of Abruzzo; the capitals of the departments were not in the centre but on the edges; some cantons had no inhabitants, while a great deal had too many, because the map showed the names of the towns, but not their features. Shall I go on? Many capitals of cantons were uninhabited lands, either mountains or valleys or rural churches, etc., which had names on the maps; many areas [*terre*] which had two names were made to belong to two different cantons.

After a month, the government, which had been unable to prevent citizen Bassal's work, formally dismantled it and used the method it should have begun with, that is, to appoint Neapolitan geographers to carry out the land survey. Meanwhile orders were given that the old provincial division should be maintained, which, while not perfect, was at least tolerable. In the meantime, is it a minor problem for the government to lose the confidence of its population (since the people neither knew Bassal nor were obliged to him) with poorly conceived, unenforceable, and strange orders?

XXXI

The Organization of the Provinces

Perhaps the best method for organizing the provinces was to use the constituted authorities already in place. All the provinces had recognized the new government. The old authorities should have been destroyed or maintained. I do not know which of these alternatives was preferable. But I do know that neither was followed, and the compromise solutions neither removed enemies nor added friends.

The new government issued an edict ordering the old authorities in the provinces to remain in operation until new arrangements had been made. Meanwhile "democratizers," who clashed with the old authorities' jurisdiction on every occasion, were sent everywhere; and given that the latter were still active, they devoted all their energies to obstructing the new democratizers' operations. In this way, they were allowed to retain power, to use it against the republic when they became fed up with it; and the democratizers were sent out so that they might have an opportunity to become fed up.

What a strange idea this was, that of the democratizers![1]

I never understood what the word means. Perhaps it was meant to refer to those who went around organizing a government in a province? But there was certainly no need for one in every town (*terra*). Perhaps it was meant to refer to the persons who went round organizing the people, so to speak, and making their minds republican? But they could not hope to achieve this in so short a time, nor did it require a government commissioner to do so. Good laws, the considerable advantages which a new fair, humane government procures for the peoples, and the words of a few wise citizens living modestly with their families, managing to earn the love and trust of their peers by their virtue, would have done

---

1 During the republic, Cuoco himself served as secretary to the democratizer for the Volturno territory, so he was speaking with some direct experience.

what a government on its own should never have attempted or hoped to achieve.[2]

When you want to effect a revolution you need partisans; but when you want to support or continue a revolution already carried out, it is the hostile and indifferent who have to be won over. To start a revolution you need war, which can be produced only by factions. To sustain it, you need peace, which is obtained only when the passion of partisanship has subsided. Partisans are less able to persuade the people than the indifferent are, for the people are more suspicious of the former than they are of the latter. Hence, in a passive revolution greater account must be taken of those who are not yet on your side than of those who already are. Also, mistakes were made both in establishing the censure commission[3] and in the practice initially adopted in order to form the national guard, because matters tended to be restricted only to those who had openly espoused the good cause. Likewise, it was mistaken, and a mistake commonly made among us, to employ the person who volunteered freely rather than the one who would have liked to have been asked, and to use the efforts of young men rather than those of mature men. Those who hold sway over the minds of people are not those who are gained easily, but those who are hard to win over. There is never any shortage of young people in a revolution; Russo[4] believed they were best suited for it. If he meant that they were the most able to bring it about, he was right;. if he believed that they were most able to sustain it, he was wrong. Young people can achieve much when there is need for an uprising, but not when there is need for forming public opinion.

Young, inexpert men, with no experience of the world, flooded the provinces with a "charter for democratization," which Bisceglia,[5] who was then a central committee member, granted to anyone who asked for it. They could not count on influential names for introduction, and could count themselves lucky when the reputation that preceded them

2 Cortese (1926: 195n1) notes that the intentions of the republican government were good but impractical or unrealistic.

3 See chapter XXII, and *Fragment* 6 in appendix I.

4 Vincenzio Russo (1770–1799), as noted earlier, was a most prominent figure of the Jacobin Left.

5 Domenico Bisceglia (1756–1799) was a lawyer and member of the provisional government from Calabria; he died on the scaffold in November 1799.

was not an impolite one! They had no instruction from the government: everyone operated according to their own ideas; everyone believed that reform should be what he himself wanted: one waged war on prejudices, another on the provincials' simple and strict customs, which he termed "uncouthness." They began by scorning the very people they wanted to raise up to provide energy for the republic. They spoke highly of a foreign nation [France] unknown to ordinary people except that it had won militarily. Everything the people held most sacred was attacked, their gods, their ways of life, their name. And then there was the occasional instance of embezzlement, and abuse by the new authority. This reawakened the partisan spirit, which was not extinguished between the main families of small towns. Minds were embittered. The second government[6] saw the damage that was done from the mistake of the first. Abamonti[7] in particular called back as many of these democratizers as he could. But the damage had been done. The social ties that had bonded departments were broken, as the uniformity of the law and the union of forces was removed. We were only one step away from civil war, which indeed soon broke out.

And how could this not have happened? One population shook off the young men's yoke; others followed it: the populations which were republican, that is, which had the fortune not to have democratizers or to have wise ones, armed themselves against the insurgent populations.[8] But the latter had ideas widely held, since the ideas of the old government were common to all the populations. They understood each other; their operations were coordinated. The republican populations had none of these advantages. The old constituted authorities, which still retained considerable power, were on the side of the insurgent populations, at least in

6 The second government refers to that constituted by the French political commissioner Abrial, see chapter XXXIX.

7 Giuseppe Abamonti (1759–1818) was a member of the provisional government in Naples. A journalist by profession, he had been involved in the 1794 conspiracy and managed to escape to Milan where, with other Neapolitan expatriates – Salfi, Galdi, and Lauberg – he engaged in political activities and worked for the Cisalpine republic. Jailed after the collapse of the Neapolitan republic, he was subsequently released and went back to Milan where he stayed. He returned to Naples with the later French rule, entering the judiciary and serving on the Council of State.

8 That is, the royal insurrectionists who were led by Cardinal Ruffo of Calabria. For some earlier accounts, see Croce ([1943] 1989) and Gutteridge (1903); for a more recent and balanced account, see Davis (1991).

secret. What wonder was it, then, when these, albeit originally inferior to the republican populations in terms of number and forces, began to overtake the republicans?

The opposite route from the route of nature had been taken. Nature forms its operations spontaneously, and the design of the whole always precedes the execution of the parts. In Naples, they [the republicans] tried to fashion the parts before the design had been made.

XXXII

The Expedition against the Insurgents in Apulia

The Neapolitan nation was no longer one: its territory could be divided into democratic and insurgent. The insurrection was gaining grounds in Abruzzo, and becoming linked to those in Sora and Castelforte. These insurrections were in large part due to the lack of foresight and numbers on the part of the French. Determinedly pushing their conquest forward, they did not leave sufficient troops behind to achieve staying power; nor did it occur to them to organize a government. So what did they leave behind? Anarchy. It is not possible for anarchy to last long, more than five days. What had to happen happened. After a few days, an order of things emerged, which resembled more the old government people knew than a new one which they did not know; and the idea of the new conquerors could not help but become associated in their minds with the memory of all the ills produced by the anarchy.

Cardinal Ruffo in the first days of February occupied Calabria near the Sicilian side.[1] He led another insurrection towards the north, and joined with the others in Matera. Too late the government sent two commissioners to Calabria, of exactly the kind that the inhabitants did not want, in that they were without forces and hence were obliged to flee; and anyone who managed to save his life could consider himself fortunate. Monteleone, a rich and populous city, full of republican spirit, put up stubborn resistance against Ruffo; but isolated and without communication, it was forced to surrender. And all the other communities of Calabria surrendered in the same way.

The republican supporters of the other provinces – isolated, surrounded, pressed on all sides by the insurgents – saw themselves threatened

---

1 Cardinal Fabrizio Ruffo di Calabria (1744–1827) led the pro-Bourbon uprising, labelled *Sanfedismo* after its full name in Italian, *Armate della Santa Fede*; its members were called *sanfedisti*. For some earlier accounts, see Croce ([1943] 1989) and Gutteridge (1903); for a more recent and balanced account, see Davis (1991).

with the same fate. Moreover, the insurgents were looting, getting their hands on everything; while the republicans were virtuous. But when, as a result of factions, the wicked can no longer be restrained, they give themselves to the faction whose principles most resemble their own, and force, so to speak, the gods not to be for the cause of which Cato approved.

It was decided to destroy the insurrections in Apulia and Calabria, as these were the most dangerous, the most distant, and the hardest to defeat, for they were closest to Sicily. Two small columns left from Naples: one French, which took the route to Apulia, the other made up of Neapolitans, led by Schipani,[2] who took the route to Calabria via Salerno. The Apulian column was also to pass along the Adriatic and Ionian coasts to reach Calabria and join up with Schipani's column.

The commander of the French column, aided by the patriots and soldiers led by Ettore Carafa[3] and by the patriots of Foggia, destroyed the formidable insurrection in San Severo. From there, he pressed further and took Andria and then Trani, and it was he who destroyed the Corsican army near Casamassima. But he abused his strength. He took 7,000 ducats which the public courier was transporting, and which should have been sacred; and when asked to account for them he was unable to show that they belonged to the insurgents. Perhaps he was deceived by his own excessive zeal to punish them! He was unable to distinguish friend from foe, and where taxes were concerned, the former were no better off than the latter. Bari, a province in full insurrection, had done wonders to defend itself. When he arrived, he had to liberate it from the close siege that had lasted forty-five days. When he came in, he started to treat it as if it were an enemy city, and imposed a payment of 40,000 ducats on it. He did the same in Conversano, where, despite the city having been besieged by insurgents, he imposed a payment of 8,000 ducats. There were no more than a couple of silver buckles left in the province of Bari. Everything was given to pay the contributions that had been imposed.

The first weapons in a virtuous revolution ought to have been prudence and justice; and our compatriots who had lost their way deserved

2 Giuseppe Schipani (1758–1799), originally from Calabria, had been an officer of the Bourbon army; jailed for his Jacobin sympathies, he was released in 1798 and took part in the 1799 revolution for which he paid with his life on 19 July of that year.

3 Ettore Carafa, count of Ruvo (1763–1799), was imprisoned in 1795 for his anti-Bourbon and republican sympathies. Following the collapse of the revolution, he was beheaded in September 1799.

correction more than destruction. By doing otherwise, they appeared to have been defeated, when in fact they had only been dispersed. Trani was looted; this handsome, populous, wealthy city was destroyed; but the insurgents of Trani were still there. When the French approached, they set sail, ready to return more ferocious as soon as the French abandoned their houses.

Shall I say it? The many victories achieved against the anti-republican insurgents destroyed more good men than wicked ones. The latter, conscious of their crime, always think ahead to save themselves. Good men are caught unawares and defenceless: their houses are looted to the same degree and possibly even before those of the insurgents, because the good men are almost always wealthier, and when the insurgents return, they find them appalled by those responsible for the looting.

A good government should be strong but not cruel, strict but not such as to induce terror. The [anti-republican] insurrections in Naples could be reduced to a calculation. They had few focal points, and whoever knew those places saw that they were the same ones that under the old government had been full of the idlest and most corrupt men, and for this reason were also the most wretched and unruly. The places that during the king's time used to have most thieves, traffickers, and other similar types were now the places with the greatest number of monarchical insurgents. Atina, Isernia, Longano, the Albanian colonies of the Sannio, San Severo, and others were places of insurrection. Where the people were industrious, and consequently well off and orderly, one could bet a hundred to one that peace prevailed.

The prime movers in the [anti-republican] insurrection were those who had lost everything with the downfall of the old government, and who had nothing to hope for from the new one. If there were many of these, much of the blame lay with the government itself, which proved unable to give them anything to hope for, and gave rise to the fear that the republican government was a faction. And yet the republic had so much to give that it was dangerous folly to believe it should always be partial to republicans!

The major instruments in the counter-revolution included the provincial tribunals' militias, the barons' private guards, the veteran soldiers whom the new order of things had left penniless (*senza pane*), the assassins who enthusiastically pursued an insurrection that gave them an opportunity to continue with their thieving while almost ennobling them. The scenes of the greatest [anti-republican] insurrections were therefore almost all provincial capitals, such as Lecce, Matera, Aquila, and Trani, where the presence of the provincial authorities, their forces, and all the criminals of the provinces who were in prison there, and who, in the anarchy that accompanied the change in government, were all released, brought together various discontented and disruptive elements. They led astray all the other peaceful and merely passive individuals, who were equally intimidated by the brigands' audacity and the new government's weakness.

Against such insurrections, a military expedition sent to destroy is worth less than a sedentary force which is able to contain. The insurgents fled at the sight of an army; once the army had passed, a small but permanent force would have prevented the insurgents from regrouping and acting. But the soldier does not suffer being stationed. He desires war, and loves the enemy to become so strong that it requires an expedition, in order to have the opportunity of measuring himself against them, the glory of defeating them, and the pleasure of despoiling them.

The French commander in charge of Trani was ordered by Palomba,[4] commissioner of the department of Lucania, to march on Matera and prevent an insurrection arising there that could become dangerous for that department. But as Matera had not yet risen up, he did not go there because he could not have it looted. And when, at the repeated petitions of Palomba, he did finally set off with all the forces at his disposal, he was called back to Naples. The insurrection in Matera, which was quite ready, and restrained only by the fear of the proximity of superior forces, when these were far off did in fact break out, and joined up with the one in Calabria.

But why did Palomba himself not march with his forces on Matera? Because Palomba, as commissioner, had been unable to find a way to unite and sustain them; because his general Mastrangiolo [Mastrangelo][5] was anything but a general. Both of them burned with the purest republican zeal, with the purest of intentions, but did not carry that public opinion which alone is capable of joining other forces to ours, and that counsel without which neither our forces nor those of others are worth anything. Neither was able to do anything but cry "Long live

4 He is the Nicola Palomba (1746–1799) whom we met in chapter XXII.

5 Cuoco incorrectly identifies him as Mastrangiolo, but his name was Felice Mastrangelo (1773–1799). A medical doctor, he came from a strong republican family. Named commandant of the national guard in Basilicata, he unsuccessfully opposed the advance of royalist forces under Cardinal Ruffo.

the republic!" and wait for the French to establish it, as though it were possible to found a republic with another nation's forces! In the most democratic department on earth, with the imposing forces of Altamura, Avigliano, Potenza, Muro, Tito, Picerno, San Felè, etc., etc., Mastrangiolo wasted his time in indolence. The good officers around him warned him in vain of the danger that was facing him: the insurrection grew, and forced him to flee.

XXXIII

Schipani's Expedition

Schipani[1] was like Cleon[2] of Athens and Santerre[3] of Paris. Full of the most passionate zeal for the revolution, highly qualified to take the stage and play the leading character in a tragedy on Brutus, he was appointed commander of an expedition to pass through Roman and Greek Calabria, that is, through the two hardest provinces to bring under control and to govern, due to the harshness of the terrain and the character of the inhabitants. He only had 800 men with him, but they were all brave, and only slightly fewer in number than the enemy forces.

Schipani marched. He took Rocca di Aspide, and then Sicignano. At Castelluccia he found men gathered and fortified in highly inaccessible land on top of a mountain. But there were a thousand ways to bring it under control. Castelluccia was a small land, which could have been left behind without any danger. He should have marched straight to Calabria, where 10,000 patriots were awaiting him; where Ruffo was not yet very strong and was barely attempting a counter-revolution of which he himself possibly despaired; if Ruffo had been forced to flee, all the insurrections in the southern part of our region would have surrendered. But Schipani did not even know the enemy he had to fight, nor was he able, like Scipio, to disregard Hannibal in order to gain Carthage.

All the places around Castelluccia were full of friends of the revolution. Campagna, Albanella, Controne, Postiglione, Capaccio, etc. could have provided more than 3,000 well-trained men: the commissioner of

---

1 Giuseppe Schipani (1758–1799), a Calabrian officer of the royal army, took part in Jacobin plots and was jailed until June 1798. In 1799, he was named commandant of the national guard for Calabria Ultra and later general of the Bruzia Legion and president of the war council of the republic. See also chapter XXXII, footnote 2.

2 Cleon of Athens was the demagogue who dominated Athens between 429 and 422.

3 Antoine Santerre (1752–1809) took part in the storming of the Bastille and escorted King Louis XVI to the guillotine. One account has it that he ordered a drum roll to be played during the speech the king made before he died in order to drown out his voice.

the Cilento had another 400 men ready, and could have assembled more had he wanted. If Schipani had had more than a fair desire to fight and be victorious, and if before destroying his enemies he had first thought to make himself secure with the help of his friends, he could easily have formed a force infinitely superior to the one he had to fight.

He could have brought Castelluccia under control by starvation, for they had only a few days' provisions left. He could have taken it by surrounding and defeating it from the top of a hill overlooking it; and this advice was given to him by the citizens of Albanella and La Rocca, who even volunteered for the enterprise. What a shame that such counsel did not arise on its own in Schipani's mind! He had a romantic idea of glory, and considered it cowardly to follow advice other than his own.

This character of his led him to reject the offer from the inhabitants of Castelluccia, who were prepared to surrender provided that the troop did not enter the town; and the other, made to him by Sciarpa, head of the whole insurrection, to unite his troops with those of the republic, provided he received compensation.[4] Schipani replied as did Godfrey of Bouillon: "I fight [in Asia], and sell not war for gold or good."[5]

This same character caused him to dream up a plan to assault Castelluccia from precisely the side from which it could not be taken. Our men performed valiantly, but the enemy, from the strength of its position, destroyed our troop with stones. Schipani was forced to retreat; plunging abruptly from daring to desperation, his retreat was almost a flight.

The expedition led by Schipani should have been commanded by the valiant Pignatelli di Strongoli.[6] It was a shame for our republic that Pignatelli, because of the illness that befell him, was at that time unable to devote himself to the government's orders and the wishes of good men.

---

4 Sciarpa, one of the greatest and fiercest of the counter-revolutionaries, became so through calculation. He had been a subaltern officer in the court of Salerno's militias: with the new order of things, he could have moved across to the police force. He was not admitted. Sciarpa was neither courted nor dealt with [republican revolutionaries]. (V.C.) The real name of Sciarpa was Gerardo Curcio; for his support of the monarchical cause, he was named baron by King Ferdinand in 1800.

5 Tasso, *Jerusalem Delivered / Gerusalemme Liberata* ([1580]1624), XX, 142, 8.

6 Cuoco here is referring to Francesco junior, prince of Stromboli (1775–1853), who initiated his military career in Austria. Converted to revolutionary ideas, he enlisted in the French army in 1795. He returned to Naples with Championnet and gained fame for his valour in the defence of the republic. Condemned to death with the Restoration, he managed to escape that sentence and lived through the revolutions of 1820 and 1848.

After this operation, Schipani was sent against the insurgents in Sarno. He reached Palma, set fire to two portraits of the king and queen which happened to be there, harangued the people and went back again. The French went there instead, looted and set fire to Lauro, from where all the inhabitants had fled, and did not kill a single insurgent. Hence the insurgents of Lauro and Sarno, not defeated but merely irritated, joined forces with those of Castelluccia and the districts of Salerno, already victorious.

XXXIV

The Organization of the Provinces (cont.)

This was the state of things when the departmental authorities, who had already been sent into the departments, started work on organizing the municipalities.

For a revolution, no subject is of greater importance than the selection of town councillors. On them depends the government's ability to ensure its authority is applied appropriately in all places; on them depends the government's ability to ensure it is loved or hated. The people know only their municipal council, and judge those whom they do not know on the basis of that.

To elect the local councillors in a nation which had had a municipal government even under the old constitution, it was decided to follow the method of another nation which before the revolution did not have the experience of municipal government; and so while new rights were promised to the people, the old ones were removed from them. It was almost as though it were our destiny to follow the ideas of our liberators, even if the ideas were not particularly good!

The town councillors were elected by an electoral college, the members of which were chosen by the government. "What then is this liberty and sovereignty you promised us?" the population said. "Before it was we who elected the councillors; we have suffered so much and fought so hard to preserve this right against the barons and the revenue authorities! Now we have it no longer. Before, the councillors were accountable to us for their actions; now they are accountable to the government. Have we then lost rather than gained with the revolution?"[1] Attempts were made to explain the electoral system to them; attempts were made to ensure they understood how those who were elected by their electors could still be said to be elected by them. But the populations did not believe a constitution that had not yet been published, nor were they

1 Italics in the original.

under any obligation to do so. They were told that one day the electors would be elected by the people, but meanwhile the people could see that they were elected by the government: the facts belied the promise. Even if the constitution had already been published, the peoples still believed it unnecessary to form an electoral body in order to elect those who had previously elected themselves in more popular manner, and still considered it a loss to go from the law of immediate election to that of merely mediated election.

I noted on that occasion that the choices of councillors made by the people were less inferior than those made by the electoral colleges, not because the colleges intentionally did wrong but because it was impossible for them to do good. For they did not know the individuals they were electing and often they elected individuals whom the people did not know. I continue to repeat the same thing: in our revolution the men were good, but the orders were bad. I appreciate that a departmental electoral college to elect or propose magistrates to govern the entire republic could be useful; but a departmental college that comes down to the level of electing municipal magistrates seems to me an illogical institution. Rather than proceeding upwards from ideas of the species to the idea of the genus, the intention is to proceed downwards to those of the individuals, which should in fact precede the idea of the species. It is true that at some times many qualities are asked of men who hold public office, which the people themselves either do not know or do not appreciate; but you, who hold the government of the nation, know very little if you are unable to ensure that persons who are worthy of your confidence are elected without having to alter the appearance of liberty.

So what happened? The electoral colleges destroyed the elections which were made by the people, and appalled the people and the popular men whom the people had elected. If the electoral college wanted upright men, these were better known to the people who lived with them than to six individuals sent from Naples, who neither knew nor were known by the people. If it wanted men who were useful to the revolution, who could have been more useful than the men whom the people loved and respected?

This word "people," in all places and at all times, denotes no more than four, three, two, and at times even one single person, who, by their virtues, talents and manners, sway the minds of an entire population: if these individuals are not won, there is no point in trying to win over the people, and to deceive oneself that they have been is not without danger.

After some time the electoral colleges were abolished; but the old right was not restored to the populations. It was believed that the bad came from men when in fact it came from things. Organizing commissioners were sent, who were given all the powers of the electoral body; the right which was previously exercised by at least six people was entrusted to just one individual; and with this, such exercise, even if it was more just, appeared to be more tyrannical and capricious. The people would have judged differently if these commissioners had been sent earlier. Their institution was more in conformity with nature, with the peoples' old ideas, and the needs of the revolution.

XXXV

Lack of Communication

While the government was concerning itself with the appearance of organization, it was neglecting, or rather was forced to neglect, the most essential part of true organization, which consists in keeping the lines of communication open between the different parts of a nation. The government would have been without excuse had such neglect been deliberate; but it was, rather, an inevitable consequence of the feebleness of power and of being poorly directed. If a small force, apportioned well, and acting continuously on all points (or at least the main ones), would have been sufficient to prevent, obstruct, and remove ills, a great force, acting in mass and at times on one point alone, was able only to produce a weak and transitory effect.

The provinces were unaware of what was being ordered in the capital; the capital was unaware of what was happening in the provinces. Can you believe it? Not even the laws were published. Two months after the feudal law was released in Naples, it had still not been published in the whole of the department of Volturno,[1] that is, the nearest department; and in our revolution the feudal law was everything.

This law, which should have been known to the peoples to whom it was useful, was known only to the barons whom it attacked, because they alone were in the capital. This circumstance alone would have greatly accelerated the counter-revolution, if a small part of the leading nobility had not been attached to the republic out of a sentiment of virtue, and despite the not inconsiderable sacrifices it cost them.

In the meantime, papers defaming the new order of things circulated freely throughout the departments, passing through the hands of the royalists, who, with insidious interpretations, increased the suspicions every people has for facing novelties.

---

1 Cuoco was briefly stationed in Volturno to work on behalf of the government.

Lack of communication facilitated the attempt by the Corsican impostors Boccheciampe and De Cesare in the province of Lecce; and Cardinal Ruffo and all the other insurrectionist leaders too profited from it. It was easy to get people to believe that the king had returned and the republican government had been dissolved in Naples. They were believed, because in the provinces the government was silent, and its voice was no longer heard. Ruffo persuaded the provinces that the republic had been wiped out, while the *Monitore repubblicano*[2] onvinced the capital that Ruffo was dead. But Ruffo's mistake spurred men to action, while the republicans' caused them to slumber in their indolence; and Ruffo was helped equally by the errors of both royalists and republicans.[3]

2 The official newspaper of the revolution directed by Eleonora de Fonseca Pimentel. What Croce ([1896] 1961: part I, chaps. 1–4) wrote on both the newspaper and its editor remains valuable. See also chapter XXXVIII, note 4.

3 As noted in the Introduction, John Davis (2006: 119) has drawn attention to the challenges and difficulties Cardinal Ruffo faced in coping with different and conflicting pressures coming from several sources. That Ruffo succeeded is a tribute to his skills.

XXXVI
Police

The royalists had freer and more extensive communication throughout our territory than the republican government. All of Calabria was open to them; the whole Mediterranean coast from Castelvolturno to Mondragone was open, with the result that the insurgents in those places were strengthened by, and received arms and munitions from, the rulers of the waves, that is, the British. Proni, too, who commanded the uprising in Abruzzo, opened up the sea.[1] All these insurrections were converging on Naples, and they had secret correspondents within Naples itself giving them reliable news of the internal weaknesses.

Nothing was neglected as much as the police force in the capital. To begin with, no thought was given to winning over the only persons who were able to maintain it. The police force, like any other civil service, requires the right officers, because not everyone knows the country and the often tortuous and obscure roads trodden by schemers and villains. Happy is the nation where the ideas and customs so correspond to the public order that there is no need for a police force. But wherever there is one, such a force does not, and cannot, consist of anything more than the practice of making a handful of villains useful by deploying them to observe and contain the many. But in Naples the villains and schemers were hated, persecuted, abandoned. All the new officers of the republican police force were educated and upright, because they were the only ones who loved the republic. The conspiracies were plotted between the populace and those who were neither upright nor educated. These were

---

1 Proni, I am told, was an arms bearer for the marquis of Vasto: his crimes had seen him sentenced to prison, from which he escaped. In the anarchy he had put himself at the head of other murderers, and later became a general. Others say he was a priest. (V.C.)

His name is usually given as Giuseppe Pronio (1760–1804). There is uncertainty about his life before 1799, but he was a leading participant in the royalist insurgency, and for this, he was later named colonel, not general, of the royal Neapolitan army.

the only ones the gold of Sicily and Britain had been able to buy. Hence the conspiracies were plotted in what was virtually a different country, with the inhabitants and language unfamiliar to the police officers. The morality of the republicans, which was far superior to that of the people, was one of the causes of our ruin.

The second cause was that the majority of the republicans were too separate from the people, while the people always had reliable information about whom to be aware of. Thus the part of the police force responsible for keeping the peace was very busy, for in order to have peace it was sufficient to be feared; the other part dealing with security was ill used, for to have security confidence was required. The people were peaceful because they were afraid; but because they were distrustful, they were not talkative. What they were doing was known, but what they were plotting was not.

The French perhaps feared more than they should have a lively and even garrulous people. They believed it was dangerous for the people who following the necessities of the climate and their ways of life tended to extend its entertainments until the early hours of the morning.[2] The people felt that they were being obstructed in their pleasures, which they believed to be, and which were, innocent. They became depressed (always a dangerous state in any people, and a prelude to despair); and those places where plots are usually discovered, amid frivolity and wine, no longer existed. The character and intentions of peoples can be known only when they are at leisure: in an oppressed people conspiracies are plotted more frequently, and they are more difficult to uncover.

There is no doubt that a great conspiracy had been plotted in Naples. One of the main agents involved was a certain Baccher,[3] who was arrested relatively early on; the ranks of conspirators were not discovered, but the conspiracy remained without effect.

---

2 In March 1799, they ordered the closure of drinking places like *cantine* by two o'clock in the morning, and prohibited card playing and games of hazard.

3 Vincenzo Baccher was a rich Neapolitan merchant and a friend of Acton. His family and especially his sons were active in organizing counter-revolutionary activities in Naples planned for 2 April 1799. Cuoco had a direct part in the discovery of their plans for which the Baccher brothers and other monarchist sympathizers were arrested and condemned to death. Croce (1912: 115–92) remains a good introduction to the Baccher conspiracy.

XXXVII

Procida – Expedition to Cuma – Navy

The [anti-republican] conspirators' first plan was for the British to occupy Ischia and Procida, as they did, to make it easier for them to maintain contacts in Naples and to lend a hand in other operations at the appropriate time. This inconvenience was anticipated, but the government did not have sufficient forces to retain Procida; and the French did not understand the danger of losing it.

Once the British became rulers of Procida, they attempted a landing on the coast opposite at Cuma and Miseno. A detachment consisting of a few of our men occupied the coastline and thwarted it. The Court of Sicily was given cause to shudder on more than one occasion as a result of the defeats suffered by its proud ally.

We might even have succeeded in banishing them from the island. But our navy had been destroyed by the king's last orders; and in the early days of our republic, the exorbitant expenses which a new order of things always brings with it had removed all means of building even a single gunboat. The few, wretched scraps of the old navy that remained were squandered through indolent military administration; and the wood, ropes, and even the nails of the arsenal were seen being sold publicly.

Caracciolo, back from Sicily[1] and restored to the nation, gave us back our hope. Caracciolo was worth a whole fleet on his own. With a few, ill-equipped, and poorly served barges, Caracciolo dared to take on the

---

1 Caracciolo was officially released by the king: the king himself allowed him to return to Naples. (V.C.)

The Caracciolo Cuoco refers to is Admiral Francesco Caracciolo (1752–1799) who served the royal government well and accompanied the king to Sicily. He returned to Naples with the king's permission and soon became head of the republican navy which he reorganized to oppose the British, not without success. With the collapse of the republic and Restoration, he suffered the fate of other patriots: condemned to death, he was hanged on a ship.

British: the navy officials, the whole navy showed themselves worthy of following Caracciolo. They attacked, and endured an unequal battle for many hours. We won even though we were weaker. But at the decisive moment, the wind came to snatch it from our grasp. Caracciolo was forced to withdraw, leaving the British the worse for wear, and we might even say defeated, had the only objective of victory not been to gain Procida. A minute longer and Procida would perhaps have been occupied.[2] How many great battles fought on the immense fields of the ocean can compare with this small action for its intelligence and the courage of those who fought it!

The wind which prevented Procida from being won back was a true ill wind as far as we were concerned, because through it the dangers facing our country increased. Misfortunes poured in; after two or three days there were other ills more urgent than Procida to be rectified; and our indivisible navy was forced to defend the crater that the capital city had become.

2 The event Cuoco describes here took place on 17 May 1799.

XXXVIII

Ideas of Terrorism

The history of a revolution is not so much the history of its facts as that of its ideas. As a revolution is no more than the effect of a people's common ideas, those who through repeated observation come to know the course of such ideas may be said to have gained every profit from its history. For individuals, the history of facts is the same as the history of ideas, for individuals cannot help but be consistent with themselves. But when nations operate en masse (which is what happens in a revolution), there are inconsistencies and uniformities, similarities and dissimilarities, on which depend the delay or celerity, the failure or success of the course of events (*operazioni*).

The Baccher conspiracy, the occupation of Procida, and the rapid progress of the insurrection shook the patriots. In the deep slumber in which they had hitherto rested, comforted by the French generals' and their government's words, they finally realized the danger surrounding them. The first sentiment of a man who has been, or who fears he has been, offended is vengeance, and this, if it becomes government policy, results in terrorism.

Although made up of individuals who had suffered much as a result of the unjust persecution under the monarchy, the Neapolitan government felt it was cowardly to seek vengeance, even though power was in their hands and so the only cost of the vengeance was to want it. Pagano[1] was always talking about the noble letter which Dion wrote to his enemies when he restored liberty to Syracuse,[2] and the divine gesture of

1 As noted earlier, well before 1799, Francesco Mario Pagano (1748–1799) had become the leading proponent of reforms. A student of Antonio Genovesi, during the republic he played a leading role in the design of laws intended to abolish feudal arrangements, to reform the judicial system, and to remodel the constitutional order. On the latter, see Cuoco's *Fragments* in appendix I in this edition.

2 Overthrowing his uncle Dionysus II around 357 BC.

Vespasian, who, once he had risen to the position of emperor, sent notice to one of his enemies that he no longer had anything to fear from him.[3] Whenever we look for examples of individual morality, our governors are always to be found.

But many patriots accused the government of being unduly relaxed in the "moderatism" to which the republic's ills were attributed. Since "terrorism" in France had been followed by a fatal, lethargic relaxation of all principles, it had remained almost anathema to the most ardently patriotic souls. Perhaps this was partly because the human heart considers it almost noble to support an oppressed party, and in this way to take vengeance on the triumphant party which it envies. As a result, some people may have been saved in Naples, even though public opinion and public welfare would have preferred to see them destroyed or at least removed.

But between the two extremes there is a happy medium. Terrorism is the system used by men who wish to dispense with the need to be diligent and rigorous; who not knowing how to prevent crimes prefer to punish them; who unable to make men better, remove the embarrassment caused by the evil ones by destroying indiscriminately both the wicked and the good. Terrorism flatters pride, because it is closer to domination; it flatters the natural laziness of men, because it is so easy. But it always has to be accompanied by force: where there is none, you will merely accelerate your own downfall. Such was the state which Naples was in.

In Naples the first martial laws issued by the generals in charge were terrorist laws, for the laws of war are always such and perhaps must always be so. However, they did not produce any effect, and could not have, for how can you enforce the law, how can you apply it, when the entire nation has conspired to conceal the facts from you and to save the guilty parties? Robespierre had the whole nation enforcing his terrorism. When the punishments are not in line with the peoples' ideas, the excess of the punishment itself renders its enforcement more difficult, and to make the punishments more effective, they have to be made more clement.

Towards the end, a "revolutionary tribunal" was instituted in Naples, which used the same principles and the same type of process as Robespierre's terrible committee. By the time it was set up it may have already

3 Emperor Vespasian sought to maintain something of the Roman virtue of his time, ruling the empire wisely between AD 70 and 79.

been too late, and perhaps did no more than dip itself pointlessly in the blood of the evil Baccher family, in the twilight of our civil existence, when prudence counseled forgiveness which could no longer be harmful. But if such a tribunal had been instituted beforehand, the very law which ordered its institution would have served as a warning to the nation to beware of such a tribunal.

Terrorism always proved useless against the insurgents. "What is this?" wrote the wise, unfortunate Pimentel:[4] "When one cure does not work, can another not be tried?"

Indeed, an amnesty for the [anti-republican] insurgents was agreed on. Not for all of them, which would have been pointless, but for those whom the government thought worthy, whereupon each of them made haste to earn their pardon. This desire caused suspicion and division to arise among all of them. But such pardon should have been applied by means of wise and energetic people who had access to every part of our territory and could carry out government orders. I will say it again: the lack of communication between the various parts of the state, the lack of forces distributed in many areas to maintain such communications, and the lack of diligence and rigour, to all intents and purposes, were the origin of all our problems, and caused some to believe that terrorism was necessary, while terrorism itself did no more than increase them.

---

4 Eleonora de Fonseca Pimentel (1751–1799), born in Rome of Portuguese nobility, moved to Naples as a child. By the 1770s, she had become a leading literary figure in Naples, and by the 1790s was involved in the Jacobin movement seeking to overthrow the monarchy. As noted in chapter XXXV, she edited the official newspaper of the republic, thereby to be one of the first women journalists in Europe. Following the Restoration, a royal tribunal condemned her to death and she was executed by hanging. Writing in 1837, Pietro Colletta noted that in her case "vengeance outweighed prudential motives" (Colletta [1838]1858: I, 378). In his account of the revolution, Croce ([1896] 1961: 3–83) portrays her sympathetically. Her extraordinary life as a woman, journalist, poet, writer, revolutionary, and martyr of the Neapolitan revolution has more recently been captured in the form of a novel by Spriano ([1986] 2013).

XXXIX

The New Constitutional Government

The patriots also demanded reform of the government, and perhaps there was something to that. Leaving aside the private motives which led some to shout louder than was necessary, a reform was certainly needed. Abrial eventually arrived as the commissioner charged with organizing our state, and set about doing so.[1]

But in the old government there were many who enjoyed the public's confidence, either because they deserved it, or because they had usurped it; and as is always the case, the latter (who in fact were very few in number) were more accepted, more illustrious than the former, for the praises they gave themselves did not go unrewarded. "These are the first ones I would get rid of," citizen Mazziotti[2] remarked sharply in a patriotic society meeting, but in vain. A government formed by an assembly is no more than five or six heads that control the others; if these remain, you change the whole assembly but it will be to no avail.

Abrial's intentions were upright: Abrial was the one who wanted our welfare most sincerely and with whom the nation was happiest. His choices were much better than the first ones, and if they were not all excellent this was certainly not his fault, because it was impossible for him to come to know the country in the space of a moment, nor did he stay here long enough to know it.

Abrial divided up the powers [i.e., the legislative from the executive] which Championnet had grouped together. The government formed by him was as follows:

- In the executive commission, Abamonti; Agnese, a Neapolitan who had lived for thirty years in France, where he had property and

1 The need to form a new constitutional government to replace the interim government established by Championnet was widely discussed.

2 Gherardo Mazziotti (1775–1854) was a patriot from Celso, Salerno area, and served as justice of the peace in the republican tribunals. He was exiled for his participation in the revolution.

family; Albanese; Ciaia; and Delfico, who was never able to come to Naples because of the uprisings in Abruzzo.

- The ministers were: 1. home office, De Filippis; 2. justice and police, Pigliacelli; 3. war, navy, and foreign affairs, Manthoné; 4. finance, Macedonio.
- The members of the legislative commission again included Pagano, Cirillo, Galanti, Signorelli, Scotti, De Tommasi, Colangelo, Coletti, Magliani, Gambale, Marchetti, etc. The others changed frequently, and we shall not give their names; all the more so, because in the state in which our nation found itself at the time, legislative power could do little, and all the good and the bad depended on the executive.

In this way Abrial sought to give us the appearance of the constitution before giving us a constitution. In so doing, he rendered the powers [of constituted authority] inactive and conflicting. This involuntary mistake was the cause of no few problems, for the division of powers made our operations weak at the very time when we needed the unity and energy of a dictator; which, incidentally, he was unable to give us, because, having been appointed to carry out the French Directory's instructions, he could indeed modify the directives established in France but only in part, not in full. Hence all the facts bring us back once again to the idea, which may be said to be fundamental to this *Essay*, that the first principles were wrong, and even the best architects were unable to construct an edifice that could last.

XL

Patriotic Salons

Some felt that the revolution could be made more "active" by adopting the tactic of patriotic salons; hence these were instituted. But how on earth could they hope to achieve that? I can see no other way of making a revolution active than by persuading the people to take part in it. If the revolution is active, the people join forces with the revolutionaries; if it is passive, the revolutionaries must join forces with the people, and in order for them to do so, they must distinguish themselves as little as possible from them. In either case, the real patriotic salons must be the public squares (*piazze*).

What good did they[1] ever produce in France? As Machiavelli would say,[2] they caused the partisan spirit, which is always found in republics, to degenerate into factions, and as is always the case, they drove principles to extremes, causing the constitution to be changed three times, effectively delaying the revolution and possibly even destroying it. Without patriotic societies, the other European nations had used wiser principles to lead their revolutions to a more successful conclusion.

But the mistake made in using the salons to render the revolution more active depended on a still more distant principle. The object of democracy is equality. Given the fact that in every society there is considerable inequality between the various classes, orderly government is achieved either by bringing the optimates down to the level of the people, or by elevating the people to that of the optimates. But as the optimates still have principles and customs to go with their rights and riches, when affairs are taken to an extreme, not only are they forced to cede their rights and share out their riches (which would be correct), they are also forced to abandon their customs.

---

1 The salons.

2 Machiavelli, *The Discourses* (2003, bk. III., chap. 1).

It was deemed important to fraternize with the people, but "fraternizing" meant taking on the vices of the populace, adopting their manners and customs; methods which may sometimes work in an active revolution, in which the people will forgive a lack of decency on account of the partisan spirit, but never in a passive revolution, in which the people are free from violent passions and therefore better able to judge what is right and good. Should the people have been despised, then? No, but all that was needed in order to be popular was to love the people, to abolish the privileges in order for the people not to be despised, and to retain some manners so as to be esteemed by them and do them some good at the same time.[3]

The Roman republic was admirable and successful because the patricians, in ceding their rights, caused the people to love and respect them for their talents and virtues. The people became free and better because of it. In the Florentine republic all the revolutions were guided by the same principle of "fraternization," which was understood in Florence as it would later be in France; hence the Florentine republic oscillated between continual revolutions, perpetually restless and never content. Sooner or later the people became bored with their leaders, who had obtained their favour only because they had humbled themselves. Once bored of their leaders, the people became bored of the government, which is rarely known by anything other than the idea that is entertained of those who govern.[4]

---

3 The objective of fraternizing with the people was to become united with them; and in order to be united with them, it was necessary to be as indistinct from them as possible, that is, to do as little that was new as possible. Those who try to climb too high seek to distinguish themselves as much as those who attempt to come down too low, and the people are equally wary of both. The duke of Orléans never showed his desire to ascend the throne more clearly as when he lowered himself to be called *Citoyen Égalité.* (V.C.)

4 This comparison between the Roman and the Florentine republics was made by two great men of Italy. Machiavelli agrees with us, and says that the desire which the plebeians in Rome had to imitate the patricians was what perfected the Roman institutions. [Tommaso] Campanella, by contrast, argues that liberty was lost in Rome and preserved in Florence for the simple reason that in the latter the people forced the nobility to abandon their morals. Here, in a nutshell, are the two perspectives from which democracy has alternately been viewed. But Rome had customs, constitution, military, and power, and did so for a long time; while Florence had nothing but disorder, revolutions, licentiousness, and weakness. Machiavelli has on his side both the facts (which are against Campanella) and the judgment of wise men, among whom not one would not have preferred to live in the Roman republic rather than the Florentine one. (V.C.)

In this edition Cuoco removed the concluding sentence found in the first edition: "Campanella is a genius but Machiavelli is wiser." The passage, including that which

Some *lazzaroni* from the Mercato district[5] were taken to the salons; but most of them had been bought, and as can readily be imagined, served only to further discredit the revolution. The man of the people is not always, indeed almost never, a popular man.

The patriotic salons made the revolution active by attracting a crowd of idlers, who rushed to spend time there which they did not know how to use otherwise. Young people in particular always rush to wherever there is action, and simply repeat everything they hear being said to them. However, a few clever, ambitious men called themselves leaders or moderators of the salons in order to acquire merit; and it is merit such as this, which is useless to the nation, which a wise government should either not allow or should disregard (which is the same thing). If they do not, the factious will take advantage in order to obscure, humiliate, and oppress genuine merit. Some good men, who saw how the salons were open to abuse, thought it was advisable to set one salon against another, and if possible unite them all with those where the spirit was purest and the principles most upright; the desire for medicine was so strong that it was believed health could come from the illness itself. But I repeat: when the institution is evil, good men become useless, for they are either corrupted by the institution or forced by it to serve the designs of the evil under the appearance of the good.

"Your elders," the consul Postumius said to the people of Rome, "apart from when the banner was raised over the Tarpeian Rock to invite you to conscript an army, or the tribunals called the plebeians to a council, or another of the magistrates summoned the whole people to be harangued, did not want you to assemble randomly and spontaneously. They believed that wherever there is a multitude, there must be someone to govern it legitimately." In France the popular societies, rendered constitutional by Robespierre, who almost wanted to make anarchy constitutional, either did not produce many ills to start with, or the ills which

---

was removed for the 1806 edition also evinces Cuoco's knowledge of early modern political theorists and various articulations of Italian and Neapolitan liberties. In fact, Campanella (1568–1639) was not the obscure figure he would later become. Born in Calabria, he was known in his time as a brilliant if controversial philosopher, theologian, astrologer, and poet. He died in France. John M. Headley's *Tommaso Campanella and the Transformation of the World* (1997) is the best modern treatment of this thinker.

5 A popular district of Naples, near the port and built around the Church of Our Lady of Carmen. It was in the piazza there that, following restoration, many revolutionaries were publicly hanged.

they did produce went unnoticed. This is so, for when a nation suffers many ills, often one serves to rectify another. In Naples, where the salons were less necessary because of the nature of the revolution, they were corrupted more quickly.[6]

Anyone who is truly patriotic does not waste his time chattering in salons, but rushes to confront the enemy face to face, fulfills the duties of a magistrate, seeks to make himself useful to the country by cultivating his spirit and heart: where the country's need is you will find him, not where the crowd calls him; and when there are no citizen's duties to be fulfilled, he has those of a man, father, husband, son. The government does not see him; but woe to them if they are unable to recognize and find him! The only good government is that in whose eyes no other man can be confused with him, and the esteem which is due to him can be usurped only by doing the same things he does. Hence the first part in a good (*ottimo*) government is to ensure that there are no classes, no divisions other than those of virtue, and to this end to avoid every other

---

6 When I reached this point, I received a memoir of the popular societies by citizen Baudin. I beg leave here to quote an excerpt from it, which describes the effects that the societies produced in France, and confirms what I have always said, that the errors were in the principles.

> The desire to join up with these new societies was fuelled by many causes, which made them almost universal. They opened up a career for ambition and provided a means for emulation. They gave the weak cause to hope for support that they were better off seeking only in the protection of the laws. They gave the patriots a meeting point which, with their similar interests and principles, they ought to have wanted and which should have helped the revolution to succeed. But they also promoted that prejudice with which we are too familiar and which is to some degree national, which causes many to believe that the theory of government is an innate science, that can be discussed without having studied it and without any experience ...
>
> We all, in the cradles of our youth, imitated religious ceremonies and changing of the military guards; but the bishop and his chapter were never seen kneeling before a young pope, dressed in cloak and mitre made out of golden paper, swearing loyalty to him and entrusting him with the care of his diocese and the collection of benefits. Yet the most eminent authorities humbled themselves to this point with the popular societies!
>
> Soon the societies gave up debating the theory of political issues, on which their members were able to say very little that was tolerable, and the salons became a centre for informers, a powerful tool which certain skillful, ambitious men used for their own promotion, all the while enticing the minds of the blind multitude with the two illusions by which even the wise often allow themselves to be deceived, namely, hope and adulation. Each club was flattered by its orators with the idea that it was sovereign; and the club often conducted itself in accordance with this doctrine, issuing orders, distributing favours, demanding respect and submission ... (V.C.)

institution whereby the virtuous might become mixed with those who are not, even avoiding all names that might risk confusing them.[7]

I am not confusing the patriotic salons with those "circles of instruction,"[8] where the youth go to learn, to prepare themselves to handle affairs, to hear the words of their elders and become inspired to follow their example, to make themselves useful to their peers and acquire that esteem from their contemporaries which one day they will earn from their country and government. One of these circles was opened successfully in Naples; its aim was to propose charitable works to be carried out on behalf of the people. The needy were helped, and medical and obstetric assistance was provided to the lowest class of the people free of charge. This was the institution that should have been perfected and multiplied.[9]

---

7 The patriotic salons, modelled on the Parisian clubs, were opened on 7 February 1799. They never worked as intended.

8 The Hall of Public Education in Naples was opened on 10 February 1799, aiming to establish links with the youth and emancipate them. The opening speech was made by Carlo Lauberg, followed by Vincenzio Russo and Eleonora de Fonseca Pimentel. For more elaboration, see Rao (1999), which was part of the special issue of the *Journal of Modern Italian Studies* commemorating the Second Centennial of the Neapolitan republic. For a biographical sketch of how Lauberg became a revolutionary, Croce ([1943] 1989: 365–437) can still be read with great profit.

9 In my view every republic should have halls of education based on the "young republic" model found in the old Bern republic. This seems to me to have been an admirable institution for forming men of state. I do not know if it was preserved with the Swiss Revolution. (V.C.)

XLI

Constitution – Other Laws

Such were the ideas of the people. Since the powers had been divided, the cares of the republic were divided too. Released from the cares of governing, the legislative commission had concerned itself solely with the constitution, the plans for which, drawn up by our Pagano, had already been completed. But judgment on this matter will be given elsewhere,[1] for the constitution, having neither been published nor executed, had no part in the events of our republic.

Other more urgent needs now demanded the legislative commission's attention.

It concerned itself with repairing the mess that had been made of the banks.[2] From the first days of the revolution, the government's priority had been to reassure the nation, unsure and agitated over the fate of the banks' debt, on which the fate of one-third of the nation depended. Such debt was declared a national debt. This move was praised by some, criticized by others, depending on whether the benefit or difficulty of the enterprise was considered. All, however, agreed that a mere promise could calm the nation for at most a moment, but would then become twice as dangerous if the means with which to fulfil it were not forthcoming. Then all the shame and the hatefulness of the bankruptcy would fall on the new government, and the single opportune moment would be lost, that of the revolution, when the blame for the ill and the hatred of it could have been deflected onto the fugitive king. Men would have patiently endured it, as one of those events that are inseparable from the downfall of an empire, more an effect of the irresistible course of affairs than wickedness on the part of those who govern. Hence the

1 In the letters to Vincenzio Russo that Cuoco penned and probably never sent. The letters are reproduced in appendix I at the end of this book.

2 See also chapter IX.

government at the time did no more than make a promise, when the law still remained to be made.

But when the government did come to concern itself with the law, the time was perhaps not right. The nation was oppressed by a thousand ills, opinions were wavering, and everything was restlessness and agitation. In such a state of affairs, the best counsel is to make laws that are strong and useful; in this way the burden of ills oppressing the people is relieved, and the reason for the discontent fades. To make useless, ineffective laws is dangerous, because the uselessness of the remedy adds desperation to the discontent already experienced as a result of the ill. If you are unable to do good, do not do anything; then the people will complain about the illness, rather than the doctor.

The legislative commission did no more (and in truth, what more could it have done?) than renew, for the properties that had become national, the mortgage that the king had granted over them when they were royal estate. Previous examples would have shown that this on its own was useless. These properties could never be sold, because they were concentrated in huge masses in just a few points of the Neapolitan territory; whereas the holders of paper money were many, spread over all points, and unwilling to make huge, distant purchases. When the ecclesiastical properties, which did not have this disadvantage, were put up for sale during the king's reign, buyers were easier to find. Added to this was the uncertainty as to how long the republic would last, which further put off potential buyers; and the uncertainty over the fate of the properties being mortgaged, as though the Neapolitan and the French nations were contending for them. For sales to be completed amid such risks, huge advantages would have had to be offered to buyers, hence all the nation's properties would not have sufficed to meet a small portion of the public debt.[3]

The national debt in Naples was not so great that it could not have been met. It was more of a nuisance than a burden. More ordered

3 What has France gained from the sale of its immense national properties? What horrendous squandering I myself have witnessed [Cuoco was in France between May and December 1800]! Into whose hands has the public welfare been entrusted! This unfortunate tactic, to which a government sometimes resorts, always proves useless. A government should sell the national properties (because it ought not to have any), but it should sell them in times when it does not need to; then, if no buyers are found, they should even be given away. (V.C.)

administration was necessary, and this there was.[4] Indeed, in five months of the republic, with the income of just two provinces, the government managed to remove a million and a half's worth of paper from circulation. With such morality in the government, it might even have been possible to do without the law, which was intended to remedy an illness from which it might have been possible to recover by events alone, and from which we doubtless would have recovered, if the nation's domestic and external circumstances had been less infelicitous. At the same time the whole nation should have met the national debt. The debt should have affected the nation at every point; and, whereas previously only the money supply was affected, part of the burden should have been borne by agriculture and property as well. In this way the debt, shared among many, would have become easy for all to bear.

The Neapolitan nation is an agricultural nation. In such nations the circulation of money is always more sluggish than in manufacturing or merchant nations; and the cash sooner or later starts to fall into the hands of the landowners and to stay there. Indeed, in Naples, and especially the provinces, there was no shortage of money, but this accumulated in the hands of just a few, while only the paper circulated. The entire nation should have been involved, and the landowners should have been offered opportunities to spend the cash which they had accumulated to no profit. I say, "should have been," for I am not writing a financial treatise. I am writing only what can make my nation known.

4 This was our governors' triumph. I challenge any other nation to propose morality and economy equal to ours! What could the king, with thirteen provinces, in peaceful times and with all powers in his hands, not have failed to achieve? And what did he achieve? This is the triumph of our cause. (V.C.)

XLII

Abolition of Head Tax and of Duties on Flour and Fish

For a legislator to be judged fairly, it has to be independent; for its laws to be effective, it has to be free. When other men or other matters work to restrain its thoughts and deeds, when sovereignty is divided, demanding to see a legislator that holds the heart of the nations in its hands is pointless. [In such a condition] timid counsel is given, half-way measures are adopted; between imperious necessity and precipitous occasion often the best counsel cannot be followed, or can only be followed when the opportunity has passed; and in its transactions (*operazioni*), only purity of heart and nobility of intentions can be noted.

In this way, as with the law on the banks, virtually all the other laws devised to relieve the peoples of the burdens they suffered under the old government proved useless. The only exception I would make is the law that abolished the duty on fish, which produced an immediate effect, and won the minds of virtually all sailors and fishermen in the capital over to the republic.

When the duty on flour was abolished, it did not achieve the intention of reducing the price of grain in Naples, which could not receive fresh supplies from outside because the insurrections had closed all the provincial roads, while the existing stocks of grain on which duties had already been paid were now dwindling. Hence the Neapolitan people said that "the duty was removed when there was no longer any flour."

Since 1764 the price of grain had risen considerably in Naples;[1] and though this was in part the result of the nation's increased wealth, there is no doubt that the price of other goods did not rise in proportion with the price of grain.[2] The latter was no different from the price of grain

---

1 This is in reference to the disastrous harvest of 1763 and the 1764 famine and epidemic that ensued. See Gentilcore (2013).

2 This phenomenon, which was most marked in Naples, deserved greater attention from our economists. I believe that it derived from a variety of causes: 1. From grain being one of the few foodstuffs which we exported abroad: oil was in the same situation for

in the other European nations; but it was very different compared to the price of other goods in the nation of Naples. The whole problem arose from the fact that industry, and hence wealth, was not developed or diffused among all goods and persons. The problem was tolerable in the provinces but insufferable in the capital, not because there was a shortage of grain or because the price of it was much dearer than in the provinces; but because Naples contained a huge number of rentiers, idlers, or persons who without being idle still produced nothing and did not participate in the increase in industry and the national wealth. To keep the Neapolitan people happy on the issue of bread, either the people had to be improved and made more active and wealthier, or the provinces made more wretched. The former course of action would have made the Neapolitan people happy with the new prices; the latter would have restored the old prices.[3] To merely abolish the duty (*gabella*) was, as far as the capital was concerned, a gesture more pompous than useful.

Look at the provinces. To abolish the duty in places where it was not paid, which were the majority, was useless; to do so in places where it was paid was damaging. Collection of the duty served to pay the public obligations. To ban the former and demand the latter was a contradiction in

---

the same reason, and had suffered the same fluctuations in price. A foodstuff for which there is demand from a high number of people cannot help but increase in price; and if it forms all or a very large part of a nation's foreign trade, it becomes a form of currency and appreciates in value, not just because of the demand from buyers, but also due to speculation from the sellers. Grain today is a currency in Sicily, and oil in Naples, because oil in Naples ranks first among the foodstuffs exported, and grain second. This phenomenon has been noted by no one, but deserves to be. 2. The Neapolitan nation's consumption of pasta. 3.The monopoly that exists in the lands, which are owned by a few and sought after by many, given that there is no other means of investing one's own money either in rents, which are few, or in items of manufacture and commerce. Had such items been promoted, I am convinced that the price of lands would have reduced which in turn could have influenced the price of grain. 4. The lack of understanding of agriculture, whose cultivation requires great expanses of land. (V.C.)

3 It is astonishing how writers on public economy fail to distinguish between the two types of famine, one real, the other apparent but which nonetheless produces real hardship. Real famine may be divided into the shortage of the commodity itself and changes in its price. All flaws in regulations on food are born of seeking to remedy an apparent famine as though it were a real one, and this first mistake gives rise to a second one, which has more to do with the change in price than a shortage of the commodity. Anyone acquainted with the history of the food institutions in Naples knows the truth of what I am saying. But such institutions are similar to those in all other parts of Europe; they were born of the times and the ideas of those times. Our mistake is in seeking to follow them even when the times and ideas have changed. (V.C.)

terms; to forgo the latter was impossible, amid so many urgent needs by which the government was pressed at the time; to oblige the population to replace the old method with a new one, and to oblige them to replace it on their authority (since provision had not yet been made for it by law) was dangerous, at a time when the partisan spirit meant that what is right was neither known nor loved. Only a god could have persuaded the population at this time that an innovation was not a patriotic injustice. Indeed many, as a result of their proximity to the capital city and accustomed to bring their complaints to the government, asked for the duty on flour to be reinstated.[4]

In the ancient constitution of the Kingdom of Naples, where the taxes were direct, the sovereign did virtually no more than impose the taxation. Distribution was determined by an almost fundamental law of state, and the method by which it was exacted was left to the discretion of each population. Hence it was not exacted in the same way in all places: one population had one duty, another had another; one did not have duties but paid a tithe of the grain harvested, another paid based on property, one in one way, another in another according to their circumstances, products, needs, customs, and at times prejudices. This method of administration had its inconveniences; but these could have been corrected, and a method preserved which, while it did not remove the problem, at least made it less pronounced.

This state of the nation meant that the law abolishing the head tax (*testatico*) also proved useless. "No head tax, no personal tax will be imposed in the Neapolitan nation." The same thing, in the same words, had been said almost three centuries previously. That law was still in force in the kingdom, but the personal tax continued to be paid despite the law. In a few places it was exacted under the name of "head tax"; in many others, it was paid under the name of "industry"; in still more it was paid by means of an indirect duty on commodities of primary necessity, consumed equally by those who had possessions and those who did not. In one place in one way, in another in another, the head tax was paid everywhere but not named anywhere. The law existed; but abuse defrauded the law by changing the words.

It would have been better to become acquainted with our old financial system before reforming it. Reforms should have been simultaneous and exhaustive. All parts of a financial system are closely linked to

4 Palma and other lands. (V.C.)

each other and to the state of the nation as a whole. Most of the states of Europe were born not from spontaneous unions, but from conquest: the lord of one small state oppressed the others by different means at different times. For the most part, settlements were reached with the populations, which thus retained their habits, duties, and customs. A great nation was merely the aggregate of so many small ones, which considered themselves to be separate from each other; and the sovereign considered himself to be separate from all. People requested "privileges" rather than laws. The financial system was merely a combination of different bits made by different hands at different times. The needs of the moment, which are never those of the nation, meant that instead of old abuses being corrected, new ones were added. All this produced that awful financial chaos in which, as Vauban[5] said, anyone able to devise new names with which to impose a new tax without altering the old ones was considered to be a great man.

The happy period of reform had arrived; but such reform ought not to have been carried out with special laws that sooner or later would be repealed, or carried out in the space of just a short time. It was a work that required a long time. To begin with, to satisfy the people, who amid such novelty are always impatient to see tangible signs of usefulness, all that was needed was to ask them to pay just two-thirds of the old taxes. This reduction of all taxes by one-third would have won more people over to the revolution; while abolishing the head tax and flour duty was of use only to the poor. Later on, when the favour of the wealthy was no longer as necessary and their hatred not so dangerous, the poor could have been relieved of their burden entirely. An established government must be fair; a new government must make itself popular. The former must give to each its own; the latter must give to all. A commission set up for this purpose later on would have made the old finances and the new needs of the state known, and a general, enduring system would have been formed, on which the prosperity of the nation could have been founded.

5 This is Sébastien Le Prestre de Vauban (1633–1707), a prolific writer on many subjects, including political economy. In 1707 he published a study, *Projet d'une dixme royale,* on the unequal incidence of taxation, advocating the repeal of all taxes and the imposition of a single, 10 per cent tax on all agricultural output and on income from trade and manufactures. Hence Cuoco's recalling his work. Vauban was a Marshal of France and a famous designer of fortifications and breaking through them.

XLIII

The French Are Recalled

But now we have reached the unhappy days of our republic. The ills so long neglected, now enormous, overwhelmed us and threatened to oppress us. Calabria was lost entirely, and the insurgents there were already communicating with those of Salerno and Cetara, reaching as far as Castellamare occupied by the English. The flag of the proud Britons was seen flying victorious opposite the capital city.

The French took back Castellamare and Salerno; Cetara was destroyed. But a few days later the French were called back to upper Italy and were forced to abandon Neapolitan territory. They sought to portray their retreat in a more favourable light by making pompous declarations, but the insurgents well understood the reason for it and derived increased confidence from it. Salerno was taken back: a strong garrison was sent from Naples to Castellamare, but was reduced to defending just the city, virtually besieged by the insurrections surrounding it.

Macdonald, in departing, left a garrison of 700 men in Sant'Elmo;[1] some 2,000 remained to defend Capua, and another almost 700 in Gaeta. He had promised to leave a strong flying column; but in effect this was no more than a weak column of 400 men detached from the Capua garrison who came to Sant'Elmo, from where another 400 men in turn departed for Capua.

This force would have been superfluous had we been allowed to organize our own national force from the outset. As we had been deprived of this possibility, the force that remained was insufficient.

The defeats in Italy were already an indication of the sluggish state into which the Directory's lax government had plunged France. France declined in strength as it grew in size; the new republics organized in Italy, which should have been its allies, were its provinces; instead of

1 Sant'Elmo was a fortress in Naples sitting on a hill by the same name. The fortress was also used as a prison for several Neapolitan patriots before and after 1799.

being loved, the French were hated by them, for instead of loving the new republics, the French feared them.

The Romans, whom the French wanted to imitate, derived strength from their allies. The Spanish took a different line, humiliating those nations which ought to have been their friends. But what proved successful for the Spanish for some time, given the state in which Europe found itself then, could not be successful for the Directory, which had regular, powerful governments everywhere on its borders.

It is always more difficult to organize a republic following a conquest than when a king does the conquering. A king must accustom the peoples to obey, for all he has to do is make slaves; a conqueror who wishes to make citizens must accustom them to lead as well as to obey. But one cannot accustom peoples to lead without giving them independence; this requires the conquering party to sacrifice its own authority, which is usually painful. This is why liberty received as a gift from other peoples almost always proves to be vain, for one knows neither how to lead nor how to obey. Instead of wise orders being issued by the government, these are merely the momentary desires of those leading the occupying force; desires which are as disastrous as the leadership is weak, which the merit of good conduct barely serves to prolong. Liberty is jealous, and the law removes even fine men from their positions of employment.

These changes produced others, equally rapid, in the government of the new republics. The governors in the Roman republic changed virtually every month. What hope could there be for that stability of principles, that consistency of operation that alone can make republics firm and energetic?

Sometimes the constitution as well as the governors was violated; and the Directory itself, which had already violated the French constitution, overturned the Cisalpine one as well. Heroic individuals were found who managed to resist both intrigues and force, and chose the freedom of their own oath in preference to the conqueror's favour. In Naples, when it was feared that the nation's independence and prosperity might not be the Directory's priorities, all the governors took an oath to resign their post. Not one of them hesitated for even a moment. But is it possible to count on a people of heroes? The majority are always weak; how can a whole people love a constitution which they have not chosen themselves and which can only be preserved or destroyed by the will of another?

In addition, while the fundamental principle of a republic, namely respect and love for its citizens, ensures that a republican government pays great attention to every injustice committed among its own people, it makes it negligent over the fate of foreigners. In Rome a proconsul was judged by his peers, who were more concerned about him than they were about the desolate provinces. The Italian republics became increasingly sluggish with age. Rather than becoming more established as the years passed, the longer they lived, the closer they came to dying. After four years of freedom, the other republics of Italy were as weak as ours had been at the start of its political revolution.[2]

If the French had allowed the Cisalpine republic[3] to organize a regular force, if they had allowed the Roman republic to do so, they could have resisted far longer the Austro-Russian forces in Italy: if they had not prevented the Neapolitan forces from organizing themselves, these same forces would have ensured victory for the republican party. But to seek to defend the Cisalpine, Roman, and Neapolitan republics with only their own forces; to be as fearful of friends as they were of the enemy, was the policy of a government seeking to increase the number of its subjects without increasing their force.[4]

People often speak of Schérer's treachery.[5] Schérer did indeed betray the government, but the conduct of that government had already betrayed a great nation.

The Neapolitan Revolution alone could have secured the independence of Italy, and only the independence of Italy could have vouchsafed the French. The much-vaunted equilibrium of Europe rests only on Italian independence; that independence which all powers, if they were following their own genuine interests rather than merely their whims, should have helped to procure in full. Anyone capable of reflection will agree that in the great political struggle rocking Europe today, the party which most sincerely favours Italian independence will be victorious.[6]

---

2 In practice, they were French protectorates.

3 In northern Italy.

4 The clearest proof that the First Consul [i.e., Napoleon] gave of his sincere desire for the freedom of Italy was to assign the Polish legion to the Cisalpine republic. The reader who reads this chapter and the whole book carefully will see how the events themselves justify the new order of things, desired so much by justice and humanity. (V.C.)

5 Barthélemy Louis Joseph Schérer (1747–1804) was the commander of the Army of Italy in March 1799 who proved unable to stop the Austro-Russian advance. The Austro-Russian coalition force, led by Russia's Count Suvorov, took Milan on 27 April 1799. By failing to respond effectively to changing conditions of war, Schérer was accused of treachery and forced to appear before a committee of inquiry which eventually acquitted him.

6 If I were to address the French government on behalf of Italy, I would tell them freely that they should either liberate the country fully or not touch it at all. If it were to form a single government, France would acquire a very powerful ally; by rendering

Destiny had finally caused the moment to arrive; but the government that France had at the time was unable to execute destiny's orders, and the pro-Directory governments of Italy were unable to grasp its intentions.

Harsh necessity caused us to neglect those external relations that might have ensured our political survival. We were ignorant of what was happening in the rest of Europe, and what Europe knew of our revolution was from the mouths of our enemies. All we heard of even the Cisalpine republic or the French army was from gazettes or reports more frivolous and mendacious than even a gazette. In them the French generals wrote only of their victories, for this was imposed on them by reasons of war: but it was in our interests to know also of the defeats; and the ignorance in which the government remained and the false promises of imminent help accelerated the loss, if not of the republic, then at least of the republicans. Naples could have saved Italy, but Italy fell and engulfed Naples in its ruin.

---

just a part of it democratic, since this small part could neither hope for peace from the other powers nor defend itself on its own, it would either perish abandoned by France or cost France an endless, useless war. This is why despite his ambition, when Genoa offered itself to Louis XI, he replied that they should "go to hell." This is why it is said that holding possessions in Italy was of no use to France. Possession of Milan cost it two hundred years of destructive war. At the time the French sovereigns had failed to understand two truths, the first of which is that Italy is of more use to France as a friend than as a slave, hence it is better to make it free than a province. This truth has been apparent for some years now, although the Directory was behaving as though they had not understood it or did not want to, and the new, more just order of things is now the only hope for it to yield useful effects. The second is that Italy should not be divided, but united: and the unity of Italy depends on the freedom of Naples; a country that France could never keep and which has so many resources, that on its own it could disrupt the peace of all Italy if it is not in the hands of a humane government that is a friend of liberty. The experience of centuries shows us that the conquerors of upper Italy have generally been broken on the banks of the Garigliano; and philosophy explains the reasons why this is so. (V.C.)

The Garigliano River marked the border between the Papal States and the Kingdom of Naples.

XLIV

Ettore Carafa[1] Recalled from Apulia

The French had to use arms to open a way for themselves to retreat, and they lost quite a few men on the island of Sora and in the valleys of Castelforte. As soon as they left, new insurrections broke out in many places.

Roccaromana[2] instigated an insurrection in his territories, near the walls of Capua. He became the main instrument of the nobility, to which he belonged, and the people, with whom he had standing. The government had disgusted him, having downgraded him because of suspicions possibly entertained too early:[3] but they were unable to keep him under observation, find him guilty, or defeat him. They offended him, but were unable to put him in a position from which no damage could be done. At the same time, Luigi de Gams[4] organized an insurrection in Caserta. These uprisings, along with those in Castelforte and Teano, interrupted all communications between Capua and Gaeta and between the Neapolitan government and the rest of Italy.

The French retreat from the province of Bari caused the province of Lecce to rise up again. Ettore Carafa was still in Apulia with his legion, and even apart from the legion, had a reputation and many followers there. But whether out of imprudence, or jealousy on the part of the government as some would have it, Carafa was recalled from a province where he could have been useful. He was sent to garrison the fortress

---

1 Ettore Carafa, count of Ruvo (1763–1799), jailed in 1795 for his Jacobin sympathies, headed one of the three republican legions during the revolution, especially in Apulia where his family had a fief in Trani. For his republican activities, he was later sentenced to death and beheaded.

2 Cuoco is referring here to Lucio Caracciolo, duke of Roccaromana (1771–1836), cavalry colonel; see also chapter XIV.

3 He in fact switched sides and went to fight for the return of the monarchy, alongside Cardinal Ruffo. This did not, however, earn him any favour from King Ferdinand.

4 Not much is known about him.

of Pescara. Carafa's withdrawal was a real disaster for those provinces and the republic as a whole. The disaster could have been repaired in part, had Federici[5] been able to force his way into Apulia, and Belpulsi[6] into the county of Molise; but their expeditions were unduly delayed. They were only undertaken once the French troops had departed, that is, when they could no longer be carried out.

Hence there remained barely pockets of democracy across the whole of the Neapolitan territory. But in these pockets there were heroes. [The town of] Venafro, in the heart of Campania, put up a lengthy resistance on its own against Mammone, the leader of the Sora uprising; with only slightly greater reinforcements it could have gone on the attack.[7] The villages of Lucania performed valiantly, preventing Ruffo from joining up with Sciarpa.[8] If fate had not caused the good, virtuous Vaccaro brothers[9] to perish, if the government had sent them even just 100 line troops, the odd officer plus the war munitions they were lacking, the cause of liberty might not have been lost. Similar examples of bravery were provided by the republican populations of the Cilento, which for a long

---

5 Francesco Federici, marquis of Pietrastornina (1739–1799), a Prussian-trained military officer, filled important positions in the republican army, including that of enticing royal officers to defect. He was beheaded following the Restoration.

6 Antonio Belpulsi (1760–??), Bourbon military officer, was involved in Jacobin conspiracies as early as 1793. He was in charge of the republican legion named after the Apennine area of Sannio. It is not clear what happened to him after the Restoration and when he died.

7 Gaetano Mammone, a miller by trade, became the head of the Sora uprising. He is an evil monster, whose equal it would be hard to find. In two months of his command in a small area of land he had 350 unfortunate men shot; possibly more than double this number were shot by his henchmen. This is not even to mention the looting, violence and arson; nor the horrendous prisons into which he threw the unfortunate souls who fell into his hands, or the new kinds of death which his cruelty invented. He reinvented the ideas of Procustes, Mezentius ... His thirst for human blood was such that he drank all the blood shed by the unfortunate individuals he had slaughtered. I myself witnessed him drinking his own blood after it had been let, and greedily thirsting after that of others who had their blood let with him. When he dined, heads still pouring blood sat at his table; he used to drink from a skull ... The man responsible for these monstrosities was the one Ferdinand addressed from Sicily as "my general and my friend." (V.C.)

8 Gerardo Curcio, nicknamed Sciarpa, see also chapters XXXIII and XLV.

9 The two Vaccaro brothers, Girolamo (1773–1799) and Michelangelo (1774–1799), came from a wealthy family from a town now in the province of Potenza in Basilicata. They both first espoused Jacobin and republican ideas as university students.

time prevented the insurrections of Calabria from joining up with that of Salerno. Foggia, finally, was a city full of democrats: it had a national guard of 2,000 men; it was a city which, because of the political and economic state of the province, could bring the whole province with it; and an almost unbroken line ran from Foggia northwards towards Abruzzo, where Serracapriola, Casacalenda, Agnone, Lanciano, and so forth could be relied on. On the other side, through Cerignola and Melfi, Foggia communicated with the many democratic populations in the province of Bari and in Lucania [Basilicata]. We would like to be able to name all the populations and individuals; but we do not know everything in such detail, nor can everything be said so openly without being imprudent. Perhaps one day these things will be known, and justice may be done to these people.[10]

But what could be done? There was no mind to direct these forces, no meeting between all these points, no common plan to their operations. It may not seem credible, but it is true nonetheless: one of the chief reasons for the downfall of our republic was the lack of people in the provinces to coordinate and lead operations. The insurgents had all these advantages.

10 There is now in fact a rich literature on this subject, mostly in Italian. See, for example, Rao (1986, 2002). For an English-language overview of this literature, see Davis (2006).

XLV
Cardinal Ruffo

Meanwhile Ruffo was triumphing in Calabria. From Sicily, where he had followed the court in its flight, he returned to Calabria virtually alone; but the lands where he stopped were those of his family, where his reputation gave him some followers. They were joined by those in the Sicilian islands who, sentenced to prison, were now promised pardon. The criminals who had been banished or exiled from Calabria were promised immunity. Ruffo was joined by the provincial governor Winspeare[1] and the auditor Fiore.[2] Immunity, plunder, looting, easy promises, and superstitious fanaticism; all helped to increase the number of his followers.[3] He began with small operations, with a view more to testing out minds and matters than invading. But once the republican forces had been overcome as a result of being divided and poorly directed, once he had got past Monteleone, he attacked and took Catanzaro, capital of Greek Calabria, and then, moving on to Roman Calabria, attacked and took Cosenza, a long-standing seat of ardent republicanism. Cosenza fell victim to the errors of the government, which alienated the lower popular classes by ordering that even the arrears on the taxes due to the king

1 Antonio Winspeare (1740–?), a royal official from a Catholic English family that settled in Naples, had joined the king in Sicily with the French advance, now returned and served, among others, as the royal official responsible for the province of Calabria. An engineer, he served the king as a capable administrator and was the founding director of the realm's National School of Bridges and Roads. His son Davide (1775–1847) became the author of a well-known history of feudal abuses, *Storia degli abusi feudali* published in 1811.

2 Angelo di Fiore, royal prosecutor attached to Catanzaro, followed Ruffo as a military judge. Not much is known about him except that he was a royal magistrate who strictly and severely applied the law. It was often said then that his behaviour betrayed his sweet name, "flower."

3 This man caused the credulous inhabitants of Calabria to believe that he was the pope. Cardinal Zurlo, archbishop of Naples, had the courage to excommunicate him. (V.C.)

had to be paid, and by making Lieutenant De Chiara[4] commander of the national guard there, a thoroughly evil man with leanings towards the old government. When Ruffo was nearing Cosenza, De Chiara was at the head of 7,000 to 8,000 patriots, determined to be victorious or perish. Ruffo had barely 10,000 men. When these troops were in sight, De Chiara ordered retreat; while at an agreed sign the insurrection broke out inside Cosenza. Hence the republicans found themselves fighting on two fronts. Nonetheless, they still managed to take back the city and defend it for three days. Labonia and Vanni hurried to raise men in their lands. But when help came, Cosenza had already fallen. They were forced to perform valiant feats in order to defend Rossano. But Rossano, now isolated, fell too; as did Paola, one of the loveliest cities in Calabria, torched by the barbarous victor piqued by bravery which he ought to have admired. The reputation for success and terror he inspired put him in charge of all Calabria as far as Matera, where he joined up with the Corsican De Cesare, of whom we spoke in the sixteenth chapter.[5]

Ruffo's design was to force his way into Apulia. Altamura was an obstacle to this design. Ruffo attacked Altamura and it defended itself. To find examples of more obstinate defence, it would be necessary to go back to the times of ancient history. But Altamura did not have sufficient munitions to defend itself. Its inhabitants used the iron and stone of their own houses; even their coins were converted for use as machine guns; but eventually they had to surrender. Ruffo took Altamura by siege, as the inhabitants still refused to capitulate. While up to now, he had used apparent moderation in all his victories, in Altamura, secure on all other sides, and tired of winning over minds which by now he could simply conquer, he wanted to provide an example of terror. His soldiers had been promised that they would have a chance to lay siege to Altamura, and the city was abandoned to their fury. No quarter was given on account either of sex or age. The soldier's fury was increased by the inhabitants' noble

---

4 Gaspare De Chiara (d. 1800) had served in the royal army before 1799 before taking up the republican cause in 1799. He may have been an evil man, as Cuoco suggests, but it is not proven that he, as Cuoco notes, betrayed the republican cause by retreating.

5 News of the insurrection in the province of Lecce and the Corsicans' operations was given to me by my friend Giovanni Battista Gagliardo, who had a major part in all that happened in Taranto. The memoirs he wrote of the revolutionary episodes in his region are important. I have read many similar accounts. It is worth noting that the bells were always rung in all the uprisings in the kingdom, and that there was always a procession by the holy protector. (V.C.)

obstinacy, who, faced with a victorious enemy, knives at their throats, still exclaimed: "Long live the republic!" Altamura was no more than a pile of ash and corpses smeared with blood.

After Altamura had fallen, Sciarpa subdued the brave inhabitants of Avigliano, Potenza, Muro, Picerno, San Felè, Tito, etc., etc., who had joined forces for the common defence. The same lack of war provisions which had caused Altamura to be lost forced them to surrender to Sciarpa. But even in ceding to the victor, they retained the moral supremacy which bravery gives over numbers to the extent that their capitulation was honourable. This, with their acknowledging the king again, should have been sufficient to vouchsafe their persons and property. Few nations can glory in similar examples of bravery.

Meanwhile, Micheroux[6] had some Russian troops land on the Adriatic coast who then occupied Foggia. The occupation, whether by chance or on purpose, took place in the days when the inhabitants of the kingdom's other provinces were there, because of the fair. Hence news of the invasion spread rapidly, and brought terror to the other places even before the arms reached them.

Who, then, would not have rebelled against the republican government, following the grim example of those who had been victims of its party, seeing the enemy victorious everywhere and with no hope left of being defended by friends? It had already reached the stage where the republicans, reduced to a very small number, in fact appeared to be the insurgents. And yet love for the republic was so great that it caused the government still to be loved, and all the republicans died with it.

A small troop of French soldiers and patriots still in Campobasso was forced to abandon it. The county of Molise was lost too. No thought had been given to gaining the positions of Monteforte, Benevento, Cerreto, and Isernia, to prevent these insurrections from communicating with each other. The insurrection in Nola flared up, communicating with the one in Apulia; and Naples was now virtually under siege.

---

6 Antonio Micheroux (d. 1813) was a Neapolitan diplomat assigned to enlist the military aid of Russia and the Ottoman Empire on behalf of the king of Naples.

XLVI

The Minister of War

The full extent of the danger resulting from not taking sufficient notice of the insurrections had been explained to the [republican] minister of war[1] on thousands of occasions. But he believed, and had persuaded the government to believe, that these were merely rumours spread by alarmists. Spreading rumours reached a point where a very strict law was enacted against them;[2] but the law should have been made to prevent alarmists from misleading the people, not so that the government could be misled by flatterers.

On this point the government was ill served by its agents, both internal and external, for often their only qualifications for managing affairs of state was their enthusiasm. They feared not so much danger as the effort involved in having to anticipate it.

People were not believed. They asked the government for help to hold back the insurrection that had broken out in the Cilento.[3] They proposed to the minister that the French should be sent. "The French," he replied, "are not strong enough to hold back the insurrection"; and in this he was correct.[4] "Shall the patriots go instead, then?" "The patriots will fare even worse." But the worst option was to take no action at all; and the most fatal error was to believe that time would be of use and destroy the insurrection.

---

1 Gabriele Manthoné (1764–1799) was the war minister in the republic. Originally from Pescara, he had been a commissioned officer in the king's army before going over to the republican side. He became a member of the provisional government and was on its central committee in various capacities, including minister of war. Whatever mistakes he may have made as war minister, he paid for them with his life. He was hanged in 1799.

2 On 2 June 1799.

3 An area in the southern part of the province of Salerno.

4 For the reasons mentioned above, namely that an army is of little use against insurgents, which require rather small, permanent forces. (V.C.)

The war minister always told the government that he was drawing up a plan that would solve everything. But the first step in any plan should have been to act quickly.

The minister was told he should occupy Ariano, and he did not do so; he was told he should occupy Monteforte, and he did not do so. Manthoné believed the enemy was not to be feared. To the very last moments he deceived himself and the government: he believed that the Russians who had landed in Apulia were not really Russians but convicts, whom the king of Naples had sent there disguised as Russians. The insurgents had already reached Torre, Ruffo himself and the Calabrians were in Nola, Micheroux with the Russians had joined up with the cardinal, Aversa had risen up and broken all communications between Naples and Capua; and the minister of war, to whom all this was reported, replied that they were merely a handful of brigands, who would not dare to attack the capital. How odd! A huge capital city, exposed on all sides, whose people are hostile to you, who after one day are left with no water and after two days with no bread!

XLVII

Defeat at Marigliano[1]

But who could dissuade the minister of war from the idea of defending the republic in the capital? He wanted to defend it in his own way. He deployed only a few forces, which at one point would have sufficed to prevent the insurrection from arising, but now that it had started were insufficient to combat it.

He had led the government and the nation to believe that he could count on 8,000 line troops, but this column, which could have been deployed to set up a camp to defend Naples, was never seen in its entirety. Many believed that a large number of patriots could have been assembled if the country had been declared to be in danger. Whether out of fear or overconfidence, such frank language was never used by the government, which instead merely gave an order that at the designated sound of cannon fire, all the national militias were to take up their positions and the rest of the people to take refuge in their homes, and not leave them, on pain of death, until another signal was given. Such a measure was more alarming than any declaration of danger, for in not declaring the danger, free rein was given to people's minds to imagine that the danger was greater than it actually was: a measure which should have been used only in extreme cases and which, having been used imprudently the first time when there was no need, meant that it was used to virtually no avail when it was needed.[2]

---

1 Marigliano is a town in the province of Naples, and lies about nineteen kilometres from the city of Naples.

2 The first time a great many patriots assembled; the national guard took up its position. They were kept there in discomfort for one night; and the following morning were dismissed without so much as a thank you, and without even being allowed to understand the reason for the alarm. The second time they believed it to be as frivolous or false as the first occasion; and this caused many good patriots to be lost, who found themselves shut in their own homes when they could have been in the castles defending them. (V.C.)

The order of general mobilization was given on 2 June 1799, to become effective 13 June. What Cuoco refers to here took place on 3 June.

Meanwhile, the tiny columns sent by Manthoné were destroyed one by one. The column led by Spanò[3] was defeated at Monteforte; the other, led by Belpulsi, which ought to have consisted of at least 1,200 men, the vanguard of a more numerous corps, but which in fact found itself with no more than 250, was forced to retreat from Marigliano, where it was no longer able to stand in the face of all Ruffo's forces. Only the column led by Schipani could put up any resistance, at Torre dell'Annunziata, because it had more men, because it could be surrounded only if Marigliano was taken first, and because it was protected by the gunboats, which kept the enemy away from the road that goes along the coast. Our navy again proved itself worthy of the country, and as long as the smallest ship remained there, continued to keep the British at bay. Who was not worthy of the country, apart from those who did not belong to the country?

But eventually Ruffo, now in charge of Nola and Marigliano,[4] advanced from that route towards Portici, cutting off the possibility for Schipani's column to retreat, and removing all communication with Naples. Between Portici and Naples was the small fortress of Vigliena, defended by a handful of patriots, who, despite the infinitely superior forces of Ruffo, managed to hold the fortress beyond all belief. When eventually they were forced to cede it, they decided to blow it up. The author of this audacious resolution was Martelli.

Schipani's column did not display any less bravery. They opened a path between the enemy forces for ten kilometres, took some cannons, and reached Portici. The news from Naples, which was believed to have already been taken, led some cowards to proclaim "Long live the king!" and forced the others to surrender themselves as prisoners of war.

3 Agamennone Spanò (1756–1799), a one-time officer in the royal army, sided with the republicans and became commandant of the national guard of Naples. He fought without success against the forces of Ruffo, and was executed at Ischia on 19 July 1799.

4 Marigliano was occupied on 31 May, and Nola on 10 June.

XLVIII

Surrender

Naples had not yet been taken. Our men fought unsuccessfully on the day of 13 June at the Ponte della Maddalena, and were forced to retreat inside the garrisons (*castelli*). The government had already retreated into the Castello Nuovo. Only the Castello del Carmine,[1] which is no more than a coastal battery and cannot be defended by land, fell into the hands of the insurgents.

But what castle in Naples, apart from Sant'Elmo, can be defended? The best option would have been to abandon the city, form a column of patriots, which given the need might well have become numerous, and gain Capua via Aversa or Pozzuoli. This was the plan of Girardon,[2] who was head of the French forces in Capua, the few still in the Neapolitan republic. If this plan had been followed, Naples would not have become, as it did, the scene of slaughter, arson, evil, and cruelty; and we would not now be bemoaning the loss of so many citizens.

During the siege of the garrisons, the Neapolitan people joined with the insurgents in committing atrocities that make one shudder: cruelties were even perpetrated against women, pyres were erected in public squares where the limbs of the unfortunate victims were thrown, some still alive, some dying, and burnt. All these acts of wickedness were carried out before Ruffo's eyes with the British present.

Meanwhile, the two castles, Castello Nuovo and Castello dell'Ovo, defended by the patriots, for a few days managed to put up the most vigorous resistance.[3] With just a few more reinforcements the patriots

1 Which fell on 14 June.

2 Brigadier General Antoine-Alexandre Girardon had succeeded General Macdonald as head of the French army in Naples on 7 May 1799. He signed the surrender of Capua on 28 July, and that of Gaeta on 31 July. He managed to secure leave of the French as prisoners with the honours of war, but did little for the Neapolitan insurgents in the forts, who were handed over, as he must have known, to their executioners.

3 They resisted until 19 June.

could have won back Naples: but there were barely 500 men able to bear arms, and Mégeant,[4] commanding forces in Sant'Elmo, did not allow his French troops to join with ours.

The 300 Spartans of Thermopylae were so admired because they knew how to die. Our men did even more: they knew how to surrender to the enemy and save themselves; they knew how to ensure that the Neapolitan republic was recognized, on at least one occasion.

The surrender was signed at the end of June. An amnesty was promised. Each man was given the liberty to depart or remain, as he saw fit; and person and property were vouchsafed for both those who departed and those who remained. The surrender was signed by Ruffo, general viceroy of the king of Naples; Micheroux, the general of his armies; the Russian admiral; the commander of the Turkish forces; Foote,[5] commander of the British vessels in action; and Mégeant, who in the name of the French came in as guarantor of the Neapolitan republic. Ruffo gave hostages as security for the execution of the treaty, and these were handed over to Mégeant.[6]

To execute the treaty, an armistice was established, but treachery was prepared in the armistice. As soon as the queen heard that Naples had been taken, she sent Lady Hamilton from Palermo to join Nelson. "I

4 This name is usually written as Mejan, Joseph. As commanding officer, he was later accused by some his own officers of having sold out to the British, but it is not clear how much truth there was in this accusation.

5 Captain Edward James Foote (1767–1833). The publications of British documents relating to the suppression of the Neapolitan Revolution help to better understand the role that Foote played in the suppression. See Gutteridge (1903).

6 The text of the surrender reads as follows:

Article I. Castello Nuovo and Castello dell'Ovo shall revert to the hands of the commander of the troops of His Majesty the King of the Two Sicilies and his allies, the King of England, the Emperor of all the Russians and the Ottoman Porte, with all the war and food provisions, artillery and effects of every kind existing in the stores, of which an inventory will be drawn up by the respective commissioners once the present surrender has been signed.

II. The troops which compose the garrison shall hold their fortresses until the ships to transport the individuals wishing to go to Toulon (see below) are ready to set sail.

III. The garrisons will come out with the honours of war, arms, luggage, beating drums, flags unfurled, fuses lit, and each with two items of artillery; they shall lay down their arms on the shore.

IV. The persons and property, moveable and immoveable, of all the individuals who go to make up the garrisons will be respected and vouchsafed.

V. All the aforementioned individuals may elect to board the parliamentary ships which will be presented in order to convey them to Toulon, or to stay in Naples, without either them or their families being disturbed.

would sooner lose both kingdoms than humiliate myself in surrendering to the rebels," the queen had told her. That Hamilton should have offered herself to serve the queen is not unusual; ultimately only her own honour was at stake: but that Nelson, who found the surrender already signed, should prostitute his honour, the honour of his arms, the honour of his nation to Hamilton; this is what the world was not expecting, and what the British government and nation ought not to have allowed.[7]

Nelson arrived with the rest of his fleet in the harbor of Naples during the armistice, and declared that a treaty entered into without him, as admiral in chief, could not be valid; almost as though the honoured and brave Foote, who could legitimately receive the garrisons, could not legitimately observe the terms of the surrender; as though a surrender could be legitimate for one party and not for the other, and as though, in not wishing to honour the promises that had been made to the Neapolitan republic, it was not necessary to return to its representatives all that had already been delivered under such promises. Acton said, and had the king, who was on board the British ships, surrounded by Maria Carolina's lackeys, say that "a king never capitulates to those who rebelled against him."[8] He was indeed free not to enter into the agreement; but he could have asked himself if a king who has agreed should not at least keep his word!

Meanwhile the Neapolitan patriots had been arrested; the departure of those who had boarded the ships was delayed. Mégeant, who had the hostages in his hands, who still had the forces to resist, and who could

---

VI. The terms of this surrender apply equally to all persons of both sexes enclosed in the fortresses.

VII. The same terms shall apply to all prisoners from the republican troops made by the troops of His Majesty the King of the Two Sicilies and those of his allies in the various battles that preceded the blockade of the fortresses.

VIII. The Archbishop of Salerno, Micheroux, Dillon, and the Bishop of Avellino shall be remitted to the commander of the fortress of Sant'Elmo, where they shall remain hostages until the individuals being sent to Toulon have reached their destination.

IX. All the other hostages and prisoners of state held in the two fortresses shall be released immediately once this surrender has been signed.

X. All the articles hereof may not be executed until such time as they have been approved in full by the commander of the fortress of Sant'Elmo. (V.C.)

7 One of Nelson's secretaries wrote to one of his friends at Maone: "We commit the most horrendous atrocities to put the most stupid of kings back on his throne." I am disgusted at reporting these words, which I have read myself. Oh! How the British express compassion for their victims! (V.C.)

8 An expression used in a dispatch. (V.C.)

and should have been the guarantor of the surrender, slept. During the armistice he permitted the enemies to erect batteries under his fortress. He was attacked, and defeated. He did not attempt even a sortie, nor fire even a cannon. He was beaten and surrendered.

He recorded a quite shameful capitulation in the name of the French. If he was to remain alone only to cover himself in disgrace, why did he not surrender along with the other fortresses? He returned the hostages, even though he could see that the patriots had yet to depart, and even though resistance was still being put up by Capua, where the hostages could have been kept. He promised to hand over the patriots who were in Sant'Elmo, and he did so. He was seen scurrying through the ranks of his soldiers, recognizing and pointing out some unfortunate soul who had hidden from the searches, disguised among the good French soldiers with whom he had shed his blood. Not even Matera, an old French official,[9] was spared, despite the national honour that should have saved him and despite the law of nations. Mégeant boarded with his troops, departed with his troops alone, and did not even stop to enquire about the Neapolitans.

Is there anyone who even dares to question whether Mégeant is a traitor? Meanwhile, this man still "dishonours the French uniform" which is the uniform of glory and honour,[10] "by wearing it." You good, honoured soldiers who will judge him, note well: the sentence that you pronounce on him will be the sentence that 5 million men will pronounce on you!

9 Pasquale Matera (1766–1799) had gone into exile following the repression of the late 1780s and early 1790. Enlisted in the French army, he fought with the French and distinguished himself in the north Italian campaign and the occupation of Rome.

10 An expression used by the first consul under very similar circumstances. (V.C.)

XLIX

Persecution of the Republicans

Following Mégeant's departure, the full horror of the fate that threatened the republicans was unfurled.

One of the customary State Councils (*Giunte*) was set up in the capital. Two months earlier, a man named Speziale,[1] sent expressly from Sicily, had opened a slaughterhouse for human flesh in Procida, where a tailor was sentenced to death for having sewn republican clothes for the citizens, as was a notary, who had done nothing whatsoever throughout the entire duration of the republic, and had remained perfectly impartial. "He is a schemer," said Speziale; "it is right that he should die." By his order, Spanò, Schipani, and Battistessa[2] died. The latter did not die on the gallows: having hung there for twenty-four hours, when they took him to church to bury him they noticed he still showed some weak signs of life. Speziale was asked what they should do with him: "Slaughter him," came the reply.

But the *Giunta* [defined above] set up in Naples happened to be composed of upright men who loved justice and hated bloodshed. They dared to say to the king that it was right and reasonable that the terms of the surrender should be respected: right, because if prior to the surrender there had existed the possibility of not agreeing to it, once the surrender had been made the only course was for it to be executed; reasonable, because it is never helpful for peoples to become accustomed to mistrust the words of a king, and because in this way the cause of every

---

1 He was Vincenzo Speziale (1760–1813), a Palermo magistrate, originally from the town of Burgio in the present-day Agrigento province. The reputation he gained in Naples of being a magistrate applying martial law by the book – a tough and even cruel judge – seems justified, but it is not clear if he, as Cuoco claims, actually "opened a slaughterhouse for human flesh in Procida."

2 Pasquale Battistessa (1769–1799), the republican commissar for the Cilento area, fought valiantly against the anti-republican insurgents. At the time of surrender, he was the commanding officer at the castle in the Baia area of Naples.

other sovereign is damaged, and all means of calming revolutions are removed.

It was Acton who then said that if the surrender was not observed, the king could show mercy. But what mercy, what generosity could be hoped for from a man who does not abide by the terms of a treaty? The first trait of a coward is to show himself to be better than the just, and to seek to give of his own volition what he is bound to give by law. He thus hides cowardice beneath the appearance of a whim, and promises more than is due, so as not to have to respect what he has promised. Justice should be done to Paul I.[3] He knew how important it was for the peoples to have faith in their sovereigns' words, and his cabinet was in favour of the surrender. The majority of the British fleet's officers also realized how much infamy would be poured on their nation, as their admiral had been the one and only author of such a violation of the law of nations; and engaged in open sedition.

However, the *Giunta* reminded the government of the laws of justice; and, having been invited to draw up a classification of the 30,000 people who had been arrested (for no fewer than this number were in the kingdom's prisons), said that all those accused of no more than a deed that had occurred after the French arrived should be released as innocent. The revolution in Naples could not be called a "rebellion," the republicans were not rebels, and the king could not charge actions committed after he was no longer king of Naples as crimes. This is so, for the French had occupied his kingdom based on a right as legitimate as that of conquest, the same right which both he and his father had claimed. They said that even if the republicans had professed principles which appeared to be destructive of the monarchy, not even this could be held against them as a crime, for they were the victor's principles, which had to be obeyed. They had professed democracy because the victors professed democracy. If the victors had governed under monarchical orders, the defeated would have followed other ideas. Their opinions should therefore not be taken into consideration, because not only were they not voluntary, they were necessary and right, for it was right to obey the victor. To seek to prove the opposite, to demand that a people, following a legitimate conquest, should retain the old affections and ideas, is effectively to seek to promote insubordination and so perpetuate civil war, mutual distrust between governments and peoples, the destruction of public and private

3 The czar of Russia.

morality, the destruction of Europe. The minister of Naples did not like this, because he had been on the losing side in the war. But if he had won, if rather than losing a kingdom he had gained one, would he have liked his new subjects to retain their affection for the old principles and orders tenaciously and to the point of obstinacy? Would he not have punished as a rebel anyone who expressed an excessively manifest desire for the old sovereign? True morality of princes should seek to make victory easy, rather than to make defeat childishly spiteful.

The *Giunta*'s principles were those of reason, not those of the [royal] court. In the court the factions were divided. It is said that the queen did not want the surrender, but once it had been made, she wished it to be observed; it was pointless to allow oneself to be covered with scorn, merely in order to do away with 200 or 300 wretched individuals. Ruffo, the author of the surrender, wanted it in any case, which made him unpopular with both the queen, who had not wanted the surrender, and the others, who did not object to it having been made but did not want it to be observed. The instructions given to the *Giunta*, I am assured by reliable people, were written by Castelcicala. These established as a fundamental principle that all those who had followed the republic were to be put to death: all that was necessary was for them to have worn the national cockade. To have cause for vengeance, he was forced to admit that the king had departed; but to have a reason for it, he swore that despite the departure, the king had been in Naples the whole time. The kingdom was declared to be a conquered kingdom when it was a question of destroying all the city's and the kingdom's privileges (which are called "privileges" in virtually all of Europe when they should be rights, in the sense that they are founded on promises made by kings), but when it came to punishing the republicans, the kingdom had never been lost.[4] Such was the logic of Caligula, when those who wept at Drusilla's death and those who rejoiced at it were condemned equally.

Nelson, the sole author of the breach of the treaty, the same Nelson who had ferried the king to Sicily, brought him back again to Naples, still his prisoner. Neither in departing nor returning did he have the least concern for his [the king's] honour. In departing, he kept him on display to the people, as though he despised every sign of affection that they gave him; in returning, it was as though he was insulting the ills

4 Both edicts still exist: in the first, the kingdom is declared to be a conquered kingdom; in the second, it is declared that the king never lost it. (V.C.)

that they suffered. From his vessel, the king witnessed the massacres and looting that took place in the capital. Shortly afterwards, in his rescript[5] he informed the magistrates that he had forgiven the *lazzaroni* for sacking his palace, and hoped that his other subjects would follow his example and forgive the damages they too had suffered! All the unfortunate individuals whom the people arrested were taken and presented to him, beaten, smeared with dirt and blood, virtually to the point of breathing their last. Not a word of compassion was heard from him. Was this the time, the place, and the way for a king to show himself to his people? He was among ships full of wretched individuals who had been arrested, and were perishing before his eyes because of the lack of space, food and water, because of the insects, under the searing heat of the dog days in the burning Neapolitan climate. He even had the wretched individuals in chains on his own ship.

With principles such as these, the court was bound soon to tire of the care that the *Giunta* was taking over humane concerns, and indeed did so. The upright men who formed part of it were removed, leaving only Fiore, who from modest beginnings had reached the post of provincial auditor in Catanzaro, from where he fled during the time of the republic in fear of reprisals, only to return to Naples breathing slaughter and vengeance as Marius had done in Rome.[6] Guidobaldi[7] too returned, leading back the cohort of spies and informers who had fled with him in triumph. To these two were added Antonio La Rossa[8] and three Sicilians: Damiani,[9] Sambuti,[10] and the worst of all, Speziale.

Guidobaldi's first action was to come to an arrangement with the executioner. Given the huge number of people he wanted hanged, the reward of six ducats for each hanging which the executioner had demanded from the revenue authorities under the old establishment

5 A formal and authoritative royal declaration.

6 Gaius Marius (157–86 BC) during this consulship.

7 Baron Giuseppe Guidobaldi (d. 1815) had been police chief of the Neapolitan police.

8 Pietro Colletta, in his *History of the Kingdom of Naples* ([1838] 1858: 1, 372), refers to judge Antonio La Rossa as "a man who was notorious for his dealings with the police." La Rossa is also recognized as one of those magistrates who argued that punishment be applied with discrimination.

9 Felice Damiani, a magistrate who in time became president of the Commercial Tribunal.

10 Gaetano Sambuti, magistrate, had earlier served as judge of the high court of criminal affairs for Caltagirone in eastern Sicily.

appeared exorbitant to him. He felt he could obtain a substantial saving by replacing this reward with a monthly income. He believed that the executioner would be kept busy each day for at least ten or twelve months.

History shows us thousands of examples of kingdoms lost and then won back by arms; but in none of them are equal examples of stupid ferocity to be found. Sulla caused 100,000 Romans to perish for no other reason than his will; Augustus laid down his ferocity with his arms.

Another king of Naples, Ferdinand I of Aragon,[11] similarly came to terms with his subjects and then, under the guise of friendship, had them assassinated. But while he was committing the most horrible act of treachery known to history, he did at least show apparent respect for the sanctity of the treaties. His allies, who had vouchsafed them, did at least show that they were merely enforcing them. Our historian Camillo Porzio attributes the calamities which overtook and eventually destroyed the Aragonese dynasty in Naples soon afterwards to this wickedness.[12]

The true glory of a victor is to be merciful, as to seek to destroy enemies solely in order to be the strongest is easy, and contains nothing that the most cowardly of men cannot imitate. Swift, strong vengeance comes like lightning; but it does at least have a certain nobility. Delighting in blood, taking pleasure in sipping from the chalice of vengeance, prolonging it beyond the danger and anger of the moment that alone can render it excusable, if not praiseworthy, defeating the ferocity of the people and the terror of the vanquished, and doing all this by prostituting the most sacred formulas of justice: this is neither useful, right nor noble. Among the tyrants, history has assigned a distinct place to the dark, slowly cruel minds of Tiberius[13] and Philip II,[14] to whose deeds posterity will add the horrors perpetrated in Naples.

---

11 Cuoco may be referring here to Ferdinand I (1458–1494), who was an important figure in the Renaissance.

12 The Neapolitan lawyer and historian Camillo Porzio (1526–1580) is remembered for the pro-royalist account of the unsuccessful conspiracy of barons against Ferdinand I in 1485. The account was first published by Manutius in Rome in 1565 as *La congiura dei baroni*. Porzio also wrote a history of Italy, *Storia d'Italia*.

13 Tiberius (42 BC–AD 37) was the second emperor of Rome. A successful soldier, he acquired a reputation, which may or may not be true, for arrogance, cruelty, and debauchery.

14 Cuoco may have in mind here Philip II (1527–1598) who became king of Spain in 1556.

The law of *majestas* eventually became known, which was meant to guide the *Giunta* in its judgments: a terrible law, issued after the fact from which not even the innocent could save themselves. Here are the main articles of it, such as could be gleaned from the rumours most consistent with each other and with the sentences pronounced by the *Giunta*, for it should be noted that this law, under which almost 30,000 individuals were sentenced, was never actually published.

"All those who occupied prominent positions in the so-called republic are declared to be guilty of lese-majesty in the first degree (and are therefore to be put to death)." "Prominent positions" meant the posts of national representation, the executive directory, the generals, the high military commission, and the revolutionary tribunal.[15] Equally, "all those who had been conspirators before the French arrived" were guilty. This heading also included all those who had occupied Sant'Elmo and all those who had gone to meet the French in Capua and Caserta. All this despite several facts: that Capua had been ceded by legitimate authority; that the privileges of the city of Naples acknowledged by the king included the city of Naples being allowed, once the enemy had reached Capua, to take such measures as it saw fit, even welcoming the enemy, without being open to the charge of rebellion; that, with the cession of Capua and all the provinces of the kingdom to the north of the line of demarcation being legitimate, an infinite number of persons who resided in the capital but were citizens of those provinces had legitimately become French citizens; and, finally, that following the surrender of Capua, all legitimate authority in Naples had ceased: there was no king, no viceroy, no general, no public force; everything was in anarchy, and everyone in a situation of anarchy was allowed to save their lives as best they could.

Despite all this, however, the following groups were declared guilty: "all those who in the two anarchies fired on the people from their windows"; that is, all those who had not allowed the most evil dregs of the people to assassinate them amid the licentiousness of anarchy.

"All those who continued to fight in the face of the king's armies commanded by Cardinal Ruffo, or in the sight of the king aboard the British

15 Given that there had been no rebellion in Naples, there should no longer have been any difference between those who had held posts and those who had merely acknowledged the republic. All should have been equally guilty or equally innocent. (V.C.)

vessel." This article could have led at least 20,000 people to their deaths, including all those who had found shelter at Sant'Elmo, who could no longer separate themselves from the French even if they had wanted to.

"All those who assisted in planting the [liberty] tree in Piazza dello Spirito Santo (on which occasion the statue of Charles III was pulled down) or took part in the national celebration at which the royal and British flags taken by the insurgents were torn."

"All those who, during the time of the republic, offended the king or his august family, by preaching or in writing." Under the law of the kingdom, anyone who had done no more than speak was exempt from the death penalty. The law said: "If a person is moved by frivolity, we disregard him; if by madness, we feel sorry for him; if by reason, we are grateful to him; and if by malice, we forgive him, unless his words may give rise to more serious aggression." A law enacted subsequent to this condemned all those who had spoken or written in a time when possibly no one was able to give a reason for what they had done. It was clear that in order to be safe, it was not enough merely not to have offended the laws.

"Finally, all those who showed decisive empathy towards the so-called fallen republic." This last category included everyone.

Indeed, the unfortunate Luisa Sanfelice[16] was condemned to death by this article. She had committed no crime other than to have revealed the Baccher conspiracy[17] to the government when it was on the point of breaking out. She had no part in either the revolution or the government. She had been inspired to perform this deed out of the purest virtue. She could not bear the thought of the massacre, arson, and total ruin of Naples which the conspirators had planned. This generous act of humanity, free from every opinion of government and partisan spirit, cost her her life; and the ferocity was taken so far that she was made "to enter the chapel"[18] three times, despite the custom of the kingdom

16 Luisa Sanfelice de Molino (1764–1800), daughter of a Spanish officer at the service of the Neapolitan king.

17 Vincenzo Baccher is first mentioned in chapter XXXVI; see note 3 in that chapter.

18 It was the custom in Naples to take prisoners condemned to death "to enter" or stay in the prison chapel where they would wait for the execution to be carried out. If twenty-four hours elapsed without the execution being carried out, it was customary to set the condemned free. Cuoco is correct in recalling this customary practice, but he does not mention another fact which may have complicated matters: the execution was postponed repeatedly because Sanfelice claimed to be expecting a baby. Eleonora de Fonsesa Pimentel used the same stratagem without success.

which quite reasonably established that anyone who had been through the "chapel" once should be pardoned with their life. Indeed, has not the person who has seen their death as inevitable and imminent for twenty-four hours effectively suffered the death penalty already? Instead, against every law of compassion and every custom of the kingdom, poor Sanfelice was beheaded a year later, without having even committed a crime! "Of those who were enrolled in a patriotic salon, despite the fact that they had written their death sentences with their own hands (although it is not clear why: a patriotic assembly in a monarchy is a crime, because it is revolutionary; in a democratic government it is an action that makes no difference), His Majesty, out of his innate mercy, condemns those who swore oaths to a lifetime's exile with the loss of their property; those who did not are condemned to fifteen years' exile."

"Finally, those who had subaltern posts or did not commit crimes shall be reserved to such pardon as His Majesty chooses to grant." This pardon was conceived for two purposes. The first was to cause those who had committed no crime to languish in the prisons for a year. "My son is innocent," said an unfortunate mother to Speziale. "Well," he replied, "if he is innocent, he shall have the honour of being the last out." The second was to ensure that even those who should have been absolved on account of their innocence were condemned, in the public opinion at least, by their pardon.

Was the queen perhaps not right, if it is true what they say, that she was opposed to such a gross misrepresentation of judgments?

In my view the judgments of the *Giunta* and those who directed it should be examined based not on the principles of reason and natural justice, nor even on those of civil justice, for not even these could provide a reason why those who did no more than obey a legitimate superior force, to which even the king himself had to submit, should be condemned as rebels; but on the principle of the king's interest. I will not argue that justice is a king's primary interest; I admit, rather, that the king's interest is what guides justice. Even so, who could forgive so many (I say "many," but I am careful not to say "all": I am far from believing that all members of the *Giunta* were like Speziale, and perhaps some are guilty only of not having taken a strong enough stand against the times); I repeat, who could forgive so many not only for suppressing justice but also for betraying the king?

When Sulla had 6,000 Samnites slaughtered, he said to the senate, whose members were alarmed at the groans and cries of those unfortunate people: "Turn your attention to other matters: it is only a few rebels being corrected on my orders." Sulla was a greater man, and also less cruel.

If those who counselled the king had used the language of wisdom, and made him write an edict in which the peoples were addressed as follows:

> Now that the Republican Party has fallen, those who followed it felt that they needed a surrender to ensure their own safety. If they had known my heart, they would have realized that such surrender was superfluous. This was the cause of all their errors. I choose to forget everything. May all parties cease, and everyone be united to me for the true good of the country! May this act of generosity cause them to understand my heart and make me worthy of their love! May the many events and misfortunes they have suffered make them wiser! And if, despite all this, there are some among you who do not like the new order of things, they are free to leave. But whether they stay or go, their property, persons, families will not be touched, and in me they will find only a father.

At this point, a time of disillusionment, possibly a proclamation of this kind would have united all minds. The nation would not have been destroyed by a civil war; the people's love would have ensured the king's safety, and formed the strength of the kingdom.

If today the Kingdom of Naples is divided, desolate, full of internecine hatred, and virtually on the point of breaking up, why does the king not say to his ministers and counsellors: "You have all been traitors! You are to blame for my ruin!"?

Even the *Giunta*'s executioners baulked at enforcing this law. It was bound to cause the people to rebel, and its very cruelty meant moderation was indispensable. The notifications of exile came from Palermo; but the law remained, so that they could be charged with a crime.

The verdicts were delivered before the ruling. Those who were destined for death had to die, even if the crime of which they were accused was a lesser one.

All means were used to find the crime; none were admitted for use in defending the accused's innocence. The king's name was sufficient to dispense with all the formalities of trial, almost as though it were possible to dispense with formalities without dispensing with justice. The defence was granted twenty-four hours: witnesses were not admitted, they were removed, threatened, intimidated, sometimes even arrested. But the time passed, and the unfortunate individual remained defenceless.

No confrontation of witnesses was allowed, and suspicions [of guilt] were accepted; acknowledgment of deeds was not admitted; weakness of sex or senility could not save them from death. Young people aged sixteen were condemned to death; children aged twelve were sentenced and exiled. Not only were all means of defence removed, but all sense of humanity was extinguished as well.

If the *Giunta,* faced with incontrovertible proof of innocence, was forced on occasion and despite itself to absolve some unfortunate person, it was reproached from Palermo for such an act of justice, and whoever was so absolved or condemned to a much reduced punishment was sentenced discretionally. [Carlo] Muscari's trial revealed nothing to condemn him for, but our Muscari had showed too much zeal for the republic, and they wanted him dead.[19] The *Giunta,* it is said, had orders to suspend the sentence of absolution and not rule on the case until a cause for putting him to death had been found. After two months, it is easy to surmise that such a cause was found.[20] [Flavio] Pirelli, one of the country's finest men, one of the state's finest magistrates even in the time of the king, was absolved by the *Giunta*; it was as though the thirty tyrants of Athens blushed to condemn Phocion.[21] Pirelli, however, had been earmarked as one of the victims, and from Palermo was condemned to eternal exile. Michelangelo Novi[22] had been condemned to exile; the sentence had already been executed, he had already boarded the ship which was about to set sail, when an order arrived from Palermo, and he was sentenced to life imprisonment in the Favignana.[23] Gregorio Mancini[24] had already been sentenced, he had already been condemned to fifteen years' exile; he was already saying goodbye to his wife

19 Carlo Muscari was a republican official hanged on 6 March 1800.

20 Using a false accusation as pretext. But according to Visceglia (1970–1: 201–9), the *Giunta* found him not guilty on 15 January 1800, and this non-guilty sentence received royal assent on 12 February 1800.

21 Phocion (ca. 402 BC– ca. 318 BC), a disciple of Plato and an austere and wise Athenian politician who was accused of betrayal and forced to drink hemlock.

22 Michelangelo Novi (1766–?) had been the chief clerk of a country tribunal during the republic, the *Tribunale di campagna.*

23 A then prison island off the coast of Sicily.

24 Gregorio Mancini (1753–1799), a lawyer in Bari, who in the old regime had often defended members of the popular class against abuses from members of the upper class. During the time of the republic, he was active in debates and mobilizing public opinion in support of the new political order.

and children. An order from Speziale summoned him, and took him ... where? To his death. In other times it was said that the laws condemned and the kings issued pardons; in Naples absolutions were granted in the name of the law, condemnations in the name of the king.

Meanwhile Speziale, who was entrusted with the people whom they particularly wanted dead, spared no effort in terms of threats, intimidation, and deceit to serve in the court's vengeance. Niccolò Fiani[25] was an old friend of his; Niccolò Fiani was destined to die, but had not been convicted and had not confessed. Speziale remembered their old friendship, and had poor Fiani called out of the depths of the pit where he languished, in chains. He had him taken, unchained, not to the place where the *Giunta* used to meet, but to his own quarters. When he saw him, his tears flowed; he embraced him. "My poor friend! What have they done to you! I no longer want to act as executioner. I want to save you. You are not talking to your judge now; you are with your friend. But for me to save you, you will have to tell me what you did. These are the charges against you. You were wise to deny everything to the *Giunta*; but the *Giunta* will not even know what you tell me ..." Fiani believed these words of friendship; Fiani confessed. "It will all have to be put in writing; it will serve as a record." Fiani wrote it down. He was sent back to prison, and two days later was put to his death.

Speziale interrogated Conforti. After asking him his name and enquiring as to the post he had held in the republic, he had him sit down. He gave him cause to hope for the king's clemency. He told him that he had committed no other crime than the post he held,[26] that holding eminent posts was considered to be an indication of "patriotism," and hence a crime, for those who had been raised to such a position not by merit or reputation, but solely as a result of the revolutionary faction's

25 Niccolò Fiani (1757–1799) had been a cavalry officer in the royal army. In the early 1790s, he became associated with the covert spread of Jacobinism in Apulia; in 1799, he put his knowledge of military affairs to the service of the republic. He is remembered as a martyr for Italian liberty, and the town where he was born, Torremaggiore, Foggia, remembers him with a memorial plaque.

26 It is Gian Francesco Conforti (1743–1799) already identified in the preface and chapters XXV and XLIX. It may be worth remembering that he was ordained to the priesthood in 1766, and became professor of history at the University of Naples. He was also at one point a royal censor of foreign books. He turned against the monarchy when he was accused of taking part in some conspiracy yet unclear. He served the republic as minister of the interior.

favour. Conforti was the kind of man who would honour any government. Next Speziale spoke to him of the court's claims on the Roman state. "You know these interests in depth," he said. "The court has many reports of mine," replied Conforti. "Yes, but in the revolution they were all lost. Could you not concern yourself with them again?" In saying this, he more or less gave him cause to hope that his life would be spared as a reward. Conforti occupied himself with them; Speziale received the work of this respectable old man; and once he had achieved his intention, sent him off to his death.[27]

What kind of a monster was this Speziale! His evil soul knew no other pleasure than to insult the wretched. He delighted to spend almost every day in the prison tormenting them, oppressing by his presence those he was not yet able to kill. If he received a report of some unfortunate individual who had died as a result of disease or infection, inevitable in the horrendous prisons in which those arrested were basically piled together, for him such a report merely heralded "one less inconvenience." An insurrectionist soldier killed an old man who had briefly approached a window in his prison to breathe in some less infected air; the others in the *Giunta* wanted to bring him to account for this. "What are you doing?" Speziale asked; "All he has done is to relieve us of the inconvenience of having to issue a ruling." Baffi's[28] wife pleaded for her husband to him. "Your husband will not die," Speziale said to her. "Take heart: he will only be exiled." "But when?" "As soon as possible." But many days passed, and there was no news of Baffi's case. So his wife went back to see Speziale, who apologized for not having been able to deal with her husband's case earlier due to his other engagements. He bade her farewell, confirming the same hopes that he had given her previously. "But why do you insult this poor unhappy woman?" someone present during the interview asked him, for Baffi had already been condemned to death

---

27 This fact seems so incredible that I would not have recounted it, had I not been notified of it by a great number of very reliable people. But even if they were lying, good God! how much hatred must he have aroused in the public for them to be moved to imagine, peddle or believe such horrors! (V.C.)

28 Pasquale Baffi (1749–1799) from Calabria held the chair of Greek and Latin at the University of Salerno and had served as chief librarian of the Royal Library. For his linguistic expertise he was often consulted by the royal administration in support of its claims against the barons. After lending support to the republic, he served as representative of the government in the organization of public administration. The name of the wife is not clear.

though his wife was unaware of the sentence. Who can describe the desperation, laments, cries, reproaches of this unfortunate wife? With a cold smile, Speziale said to her: "What an affectionate wife! Ignorant even of the fate of her husband. This is exactly what I wanted to see. I understand: you are pretty, you are young, you are looking for another husband. Goodbye."

Under the leadership of such a man, the manner in which the prisoners were held is readily apparent. How often must those wretched individuals have desired and invoked death! But my mind does not want to concern itself with the ills of humanity any longer. Already my heart shudders![29]

---

29 Bravo (1975: 139n17) notes that in the months of July and August 1799 alone more than 1,500 accused languished in jail in Naples, and about 120 death sentences were carried out later. By contrast, Harold Acton in *The Bourbons of Naples (1734–1825)* notes the widespread tendency among historians "to subordinate facts to phrases, with the added resolve consistently to blacken the Bourbons. All the official records of the state trials were destroyed in 1803 to set a seal on the King's amnesty, so that it has been easy for propagandists to invent 'authentic details' and weave silk purses out of the sows' ears of 'popular tradition." Acton further notes that "of the 8,000 political prisoners, 1,056 were condemned to death, six of whom were reprieved, 222 were condemned to life imprisonment, 322 to shorter terms, 288 to deportation, and 67 to exile, from which many returned: a total of 1,004. The others were set at liberty." Acton also recalls that a minority did seize power, with the aid of the French, and that the so-called "royalist Reign of Terror [that followed] … pales into a provincial side-show beside quite recent and far more systematic pogroms. Granted that the Court's policy of revenge was cruel and unintelligent, but there is little to be said in favour of the rebels, whatever their individual talents." And then he calls up the views of Luigi Blanch, "the most balanced of Neapolitan historians," for support (Acton 1956: 409). For a list of all those hanged, see appendix II.

L

Some of the Patriots

After the fall of the republic, Naples presented only an image of squalour. Everything that was good, great, industrious there was destroyed. Moreover, barely a few of its illustrious men were left, having escaped almost miraculously from the shipwreck, wandering, without family or homeland, across the immense surface of the earth.

The loss to the nation in terms of industry may be estimated at more than 80,000 ducats: it lost almost the same amount in furniture, silver, and confiscated property; the product of four centuries was destroyed in moments. British monopolists were seen trading the masterpieces of Neapolitan painting, which in the looting had passed from their old owners into the hands of the populace, who knew neither their merit nor their price.

The ruin of the active part of the nation led to the ruin of the nation as a whole. People were left with no means of subsistence, because those who had maintained or inspired its industry had been either killed or exiled; and even the counter-revolutionaries now regret the loss of those whom they themselves drove to their deaths.

Added to these damages is the loss of all principles and the corruption of every custom: fatal, inevitable consequences of the events of a revolution; a Court which henceforth regards the nation as separate from it and believes that its misery and ignorance are the source of its own security; and the thinking man will see, sadly, a great nation driven back in its political development to the unhappy state it was in two centuries ago.

Let us salvage some examples of virtue from among such ruin: the memory of those we have lost is the thing of value we have left, and the only good (*bene*) that we can hand down to posterity. The noble souls of those whom Speziale tried in vain to destroy live on; and they will see that their names, handed down by us to the posterity which they loved, serve as a spur for others to emulate the virtue that was the sole object of their vows.

We have suffered terrible damage; but we have also provided great examples of virtue. Posterity will rightly forget the human errors committed by those men to whom the republic was entrusted; in vain, however, it will search for a coward or a traitor among them. This is what should be expected of a man, and this is what makes man's glory.

Faced with death, none of them showed any sign of cowardice. All of them looked on it with the same aspect they would adopt to condemn the judges of their destiny. Manthoné, interrogated by Speziale on what he did during the republic, merely replied: "I surrendered." At every interrogation, he gave no other response. He was told to prepare his defence: "If surrender is not sufficient, I would blush at any other."

Cirillo,[1] interrogated as to what his profession was in the time of the king, answered: "Doctor." "And in the republic?" "Representative of the people." "But who are you to me?" Speziale continued, trying to humiliate him.[2] "To you? A hero."

When Vitaliani's[3] sentence was announced to him, he was playing the guitar, and he continued to play it and sing until the time came for him to go to his fate. Leaving the prison, he said to his guard: "Look after my companions: they are men, and one day you too might be as unfortunate as they are."

Carlomagno[4] climbed the steps to the gallows, turned to the public and said to them: "Foolish people! now you gloat over my death. But a day will come when you will miss me. My blood is already being poured out on your heads, and if you are lucky enough not to be alive any longer, it will be poured on the heads of your children."

Granelais[5] from the same place surveyed the crowd watching him: "I recognize many friends of mine among you," he said: "Avenge me!"

---

1 Domenico Cirillo, see author's preface and chapter XXXIX.

2 It should be noted that Speziale spared no one the crudest or most vulgar epithets. (V.C.)

3 Andrea Vitaliani (1765–1799) was forced to go into exile in the early 1790s for his republican sympathies; he returned to Naples with the French troops. During the republic he was a member of the board overseeing the police in Naples, and was hanged on 20 July 1799.

4 Niccolò Carlomagno (1761–1799), lawyer from Naples, presided over the committee which oversaw the police in Naples during the republic.

5 Luigi de la Granelais (1753–1800). Originally an officer of the Neapolitan royal navy, he continued in that post in the republican regime.

Nicola Palomba[6] was already beneath the gallows: the tax officer told him he was still in time to reveal his accomplices. "You cowardly slave!" replied Palomba. "I never bought my life with infamy."

"I will send you to your death," Speziale said to Velasco.[7] "You? ... I will die, but it will not be you who sends me to my death." In saying this, he measured up the height of a window in the judge's quarters with his eye, and threw himself out of it before Speziale's own eyes, leaving the wicked man astonished at the sight of such courage, and angry at having lost his victim.

But if courage is required to kill oneself, no less is required not to do so when one is sure to die at the hands of others. Baffi,[8] who was already certain of his fate, was offered opium. He refused it; and in dying, he showed that he had not refused it out of cowardice. Like Socrates, he too was persuaded that man is placed in this world as a soldier for a cause, and that it is as much a crime to abandon one's life as it would be to abandon one's post.

This sangfroid, far superior to courage, found its fullest expression in the person of Grimaldi.[9] Sentenced to death, he was kept in chains for more than a month after the sentence. Eventually the fatal hour arrived. In the night, a company of Russians and another of Neapolitan soldiers transported him from custody to the place of execution. He was brave enough to elude the guards' grip; he defended himself against all the soldiers, gave them the slip and managed to escape. The troop pursued him in vain for almost two kilometres; and they would certainly not have caught him had he not, rather than fleeing, thought it better counsel to take shelter in a house, the door of which he found open. The night was dark and stormy; a flash of lightening gave him away, and revealed him to a soldier who had been following him from afar. They caught up with him. He disarmed two soldiers, defended himself, and they managed to take him only when he fell, barely alive as result of his many wounds.

---

6 See chapter XXII.

7 Antonio Velasco (d. 1799) covered important positions in the Neapolitan royal navy, before becoming a member of the republican military commission that condemned anti-republican conspirators to death.

8 Baffi was one of the most learned men, one of the leading Greek scholars in Italy. (V.C.)

9 Francesco Antonio Grimaldi (1759–1799). A one-time royal officer, he served as general in the republican army.

How many losses did our nation mourn, and for how long! I should like to do honour to the names of all those who merit it, and scatter on their ashes those flowers which who knows if they will ever have? But who could recall them all? I cannot do justice to all as they deserve, for I cannot know everything that took place in all the various parts of the kingdom, and also because in my exile I have had no other guide than my memory, which was unable to retain everything. For this reason, allow me to dwell for a moment on some of the better known.

Francesco Caracciolo[10] was without doubt one of the greatest geniuses in Europe. The nation esteemed him, the king loved him; but what could the king do? He was envied by Acton, hated by the queen, and therefore persecuted continuously. Acton did not spare him any kind of humiliation; he was constantly bypassed for promotion. Caracciolo was one of those rare men who combined the purest virtue with the greatest genius. Who loved the country more than he did? What would he not have done for it? He said that by nature the Neapolitan nation was made to have a great navy, which he could raise up in a very short space of time. He held our sailors in the greatest esteem. He died a victim of Thurn's[11] old jealousy and Nelson's cowardice. When his death was announced, he was walking the quarterdeck, reasoning on the construction of a British ship in front of him, and calmly went on with his reasoning. Meanwhile, a sailor had received the order to prepare a noose for him; compassion prevented him from doing so. He wept over the fate of this general, under whose orders he had fought so many times. "Hurry up," Caracciolo said to him: "it is a fine thing for you to be weeping while I have to die." Caracciolo was hanged like a criminal from the mast of the frigate *Minerva*, and his corpse was thrown into the sea. The king was in Ischia, and arrived the next day, setting up his residence on Admiral Nelson's vessel. Two days later Caracciolo's corpse appeared under the vessel, before the king's eyes. It was gathered up by the sailors who had loved him so much, and the last rites were administered to him in the church of Santa Lucia near to his home. These rites that were all the more splendid, being conducted without pomp and almost despite the one who could do everything at that time, for being accompanied by the sincere tears of all the poor inhabitants of this district, who looked on him as their friend and their father.

10 See chapter XXXVII.

11 For Thurn, see chapter XIV.

Similar to Caracciolo was Ettore Carafa.[12] This hero, along with his able assistant Ginevra, held Pescara even after Capua, Gaeta, and Sant'Elmo had surrendered. Having fallen into Speziale's hands, he showed him what true courage was, and went to his death without fear or trepidation.

Domenico Cirillo[13] was one of the foremost doctors in a city where medicine was well understood and cultivated; but medicine was the least part of his knowledge, and his knowledge was the least part of his merit. Who can praise his morality sufficiently? Blessed with a large estate and a reputation beyond all envy, a friend of calm and peace, without any ambition, Cirillo is one of the few men – few in all times and all places – who in the midst of a revolution seek only the public good. Is this not the most sublime praise a citizen and a man can receive? I was with him in prison. Hamilton and even Nelson, to whom he had given the benefit of his knowledge on several occasions, wanted him saved. He refused a pardon, the price of which would have been cowardice.

Francesco Conforti.[14] I have already spoken of the treachery that Speziale reserved for him. It should also be noted that throughout his life Conforti had provided the court with important services. He had defended its rights of sovereignty against the claims of Rome; he had established new principles for the ecclesiastical properties, principles which brought wealth to the state and prosperity to the nation. Many useful reforms stemmed from his counsel. Through his efforts the court had clawed back more than 50 million ducats in funds. Conforti was the Giannone, the Sarpi of our era; but in fact he did more than them, providing instruction from his university chair, and effectively forming a new generation. Few Neapolitans who can read have not had him as their teacher. And this man was sent to his death, without having committed a single crime! He combined all that goes to make up a man of letters and a statesman with consummate elegance.

The name of Francesco Mario Pagano[15] deserves an encomium. His book on *Criminal Process* has been translated into every language, and is still one of the best books there is on this subject.[16] In the sublime course

---

12 See chapter XXXII.

13 See author's preface and chapter XXXIX.

14 See author's preface and chapters XXV and XLIX.

15 See author's preface and chapters XVI, XXIV, XXV, and XXXVIII.

16 It is not clear that this book was indeed translated into every language. But Pagano's work on the criminal process is still cited, see Nissan (2001). For Pagano's other works, see Solari ([1934] 1993) and *Pensiero Politico* (1995).

of the eternal history of mankind, to serve as your guide to reach the heights achieved by Vico you will find only Pagano's footsteps.

Eleonora de Fonseca Pimentel.[17] "*Audet viris concurrere virgo.*"[18] But like Camilla in the war, she took part in the revolution only out of love for her country. While still young, this woman earned Metastasio's approval for her verse. But poetry was just a small part of the knowledge that adorned her. During the republican period she wrote the *Monitore napolitano,* a newspaper which radiated the purest, most ardent patriotic love. This paper cost her her life, and she faced death with an indifference that was equal to her courage. Before going to the gallows she wanted to finish her coffee, and her words were: "*Forsan haec olim meminisse iuvabit.*"[19]

Vincenzio Russo.[20] It is impossible to take love for one's country and for virtue further than he took it. His work on *Political Thoughts* is one of the strongest that can be read. He was preparing a second edition, which would have improved it, making it more moderate. His popular eloquence was sublime, extraordinary. He thundered and roared; nothing could withstand the force of his words. It would have been useful if the reports of his conduct in prison had been collected. He was a hero at all times. Having reached the place of torture, he spoke at length in a thundering voice and with warmth of feeling, which showed well that while death could destroy him, it could never humiliate him. Almost five months later, his speech was recounted to me by the officers who had been there, with that profound impression which the effect that sublime spirits make on us leaves forever, and the kind of spite with which cowardly spirits resent the irresistible impressions made by those who are too sublime ... Oh! if only your shadow could still be with those who were dear to you; look at me, your friend since the time of our tenderest youth, I do not weep for you (what use would that be?) but for the country, for which you died uselessly.

Francesco Federici.[21] He was a marshal in the time of the king, and a general in the time of the republic. The minister of war rendered him useless, when he could have been very useful. For the same reason he had been rendered useless during the king's time as well. He knew the

---

17 See chapter XXXVIII.

18 "A girl dares fight with men." Virgil, *Aeneid,* book I.

19 "Perhaps one day, remembering even these things will bring pleasure." Virgil, *Aneid,* book I.

20 See author's preface and chapters XXI, XXXI, and XL.

21 See chapter XLIV.

art of war very well; but he knew a thousand other things too, things of which those familiar with the art of war are generally ignorant. His courage on the point of death was surprising.

Marcello Scotti. It is hard to imagine a more Christian heart than his.[22] He was the author of the *Nautical Catechism*, a work intended for the instruction of sailors on the island of Procida, where he was from, which deserves to be known everywhere. On the dispute over the *chinea* he wrote, albeit anonymously, the *Papal Monarchy*, a work the like of which had not been seen since Sarpi and Giannone. In the republic he was a representative. He died a victim of the envy of some of his compatriots.

In speaking of Scotti, my mind recalls Vico's virtuous bishop, the respectable prelate Troise, and who would not? Sons and daughters of the homeland![23] Your memory is precious, for it is the memory of virtue. The day will come, I hope, when in the place ennobled by your martyrdom, posterity, which is more just, will be able to express that praise which at present I am forced to keep in the depths of my heart, and more fortunately, will be able to erect a more enduring monument for you than my feeble voice alone can.[24]

---

22 See chapter XXXIX. Scotti was a priest.

23 "*Figli della patria.*"

24 To bring together, at a single glance, all the ill which the counter-revolution produced in Naples, the following calculation may suffice: Ettore Carafa, Giovanni Riari, Giuliano Colonna, Serra, Torella, Caracciolo, Ferdinando and Mario Pignatelli of Strongoli, Pignatelli-Vaglio and Marsico Pignatelli are from the leading Italian nobility; and twenty other noble families of the same rank have been virtually wiped out. Of the others, there is not one which does not mourn a loss. The revolution counts among its number thirty to forty bishops, another twenty to thirty magistrates respectable for their rank and even more so for their merit, many leading lawyers and an infinite number of men of letters. To those we have named, among the dead we might add Falconieri, Logoteta, Albanese, De Filippis, Fiorentino, Ciaia, Bagni, Neri ... The medical profession appears to have been the target of counter-revolutionary persecution. One day the ardour which our doctors had developed for the good cause will be a source of admiration for posterity. The young doctors of the large *Ospedale degl'Incurabili* formed the "sacred battalion" of our republic. I am speaking only of the capital. Equal and perhaps even more ferocious was the destruction wrought by the *Giunta*'s emissaries, under the name of "inspectors," in the provinces. The number of those who died as a result of the insurgents' fury may be estimated at 4,000, such as the unfortunate Serao, bishop of Potenza, a man respectable for both his teachings and morals; young Spinelli di San Giorgio ... All the others, equally, were the nation's finest. After which, let the damage be calculated. The nation can replace the men, but not culture. Is it perhaps an exaggeration to say that we have been set back two centuries? (V.C.)

LI

Conclusion

The king, led astray by false counsel, brought ruin to the nation. His ministers either did not love the nation or did not care for it; hence it was bound to be lost, and it was. The republicans, with the purest of intentions, with the warmest of patriotic love, and with no shortage of courage, lost their lives and the republic. They fell, with the country, victims to that order of things which they sought to resist, but to which in the end they were forced to give in.

A delayed or failed revolution is a terrible thing from which mankind recovers only when its ideas realign themselves with those of its government. Then the government becomes more humane; because it is more secure, humankind becomes freer; because it is more at peace, more industrious and prosperous, and because its forces do not have to be consumed in fighting the government. But centuries may pass and barbarities can reign before such times return; and humankind can arrive at a new order of good only by passing through extreme ill.

What will be the destiny of Naples, Italy, Europe? I do not know. A deep night surrounds everything, casting an impenetrable shadow over it. It appears that fate does not yet favour Italian liberty; but on the other hand it seems that, with the new, improved order of things, all hope has not been lost. Destiny is ensuring that the kings strive to prepare the work attempted unsuccessfully by the republicans. Perhaps the Court of Naples, in its exaggerated desire to retain the kingdom, will take matters too far and lose it again; and we will give the court a second revolution, like the first but more successful because desired and effected by the nation as a whole, out of need, rather than simply as a gift received from others.

I wrote these things at the end of 1799, and events have since confirmed them. The Court of Naples has produced a change in policy, guided by different principles, which can bring about that prosperity in the kingdom that was hoped for to no avail from the first one.

From 1800 until 1806, the Court of Naples continued to follow the same principles that had caused so many problems. While France changed those orders from which no benefit, no lasting benefit, could be hoped for, as they never can be from irregular orders, it may be said that both the obstinacy of the Court of Naples and the changes that occurred in France contributed equally to the new prosperity that the great Napoleon has now given us.

As a result of the former, the same errors confirmed and increased the kingdom's weakness: in domestic policy, the same sluggish administration, the same negligence in the military, the same inconsequential planning, the lack of trust between government and nation, animosity, partisan spirit as opposed to reason; in foreign policy, the same weakness, the same audacity of hope and timidity of action, the same bad faith. Equally incapable of avoiding war and of waging it successfully, the court has invited war, and lost it.

As a result of the latter, the public orders in France have become more regular; the various powers are more in agreement with each other. The greatest powers are more stable, more secure; hence less intent on defeating the others than directing them all to the good of the country. Ideas have come into line with those in all the other European nations; hence the promises are less exaggerated, there is less animosity between the parties, it has proved easier, following a victory, to establish a new order of things among other peoples. Power is more concentrated, hence there is less disorder and greater coordination in the military commanders' operations, less abuse in the exercise of more minor powers, greater prudence because prudence is common to all, dependent on the common nature of orders rather than on the particular nature of individuals. The system of democratization has been replaced by federation, which ensures peace, always the greatest of benefits for peoples; and which, finally, has procured for Italy all the advantages it could not have had under the previous system. It was wanted as a friend but feared as a rival and accordingly, given that no strong and independent state was ever formed, it had to be destroyed entirely. Over and above all these benefits, the greatest gift of a king[1] whom all Europe venerated for his mind and heart.

1 Cuoco is referring to new king of Naples, Joseph Bonaparte, following the Napoleonic conquest of Naples that also allowed Cuoco to return from exile. See also "Principal Events in Vincenzo Cuoco's Life" in the beginning of this book.

I will be happy if reading this book convinces even one of my readers that the partisan spirit in a citizen is a crime, and in a government foolishness: that the destiny of states depends on certain, unchanging, eternal laws; that these laws require citizens to love their country, and governments to show justice and energy in domestic administration, and bravery, prudence, and good faith in international affairs; that institutions are more necessary than men for the prosperity of peoples. After successive events, we have now reached the stage where we have both good institutions and an excellent king. Let the memory of the past, for every man who does not hate his country and himself, be the strongest incentive to love the present.

Notice

With reference to the commission appointed to enforce collection of the tax levied by General Championnet (chapter XXVIII), it should be noted that there were in fact two of these. The second was made up of excellent men, who would have corrected the many mistakes of the first; but by this stage it was too late.

Appendix I
Fragments of Letters by Vincenzo Cuoco Addressed to Vincenzio Russo

Fragment 1[1]

... Do you think it a simple enterprise to pronounce an opinion on a work that may be judged only by the experience of centuries?

I have never thought it was easy to give laws to a people. Plato, who was invited to do so on several occasions, always believed such a trial to be beyond his capacities. Anyone who aspires to the glory of being a legislator must say to themselves: "I have to make 5 million men happy, decide on the destiny of two centuries. The nation entrusted to me contains audacious criminals who must be restrained, good but weak men whom I have to comfort, ignorant and misguided men whom I must enlighten and direct. I have to know the ideas and customs of a different age. I have to make the nation happy, and also – which is more difficult – make it feel and love its own happiness. What could I achieve on my own, if all the people do not understand or follow me? I would be left with the useless remorse of having removed the old law without having provided a new one, for a law which the people neither understand nor love is not deserving of the name. "What is the greatest difficulty in giving laws to a people?" Aristotle asked.[2] "To ensure that they last. And what is the only means to ensure that they last? To make sure that they are loved."

---

1 These letters were written upon the occasion of the plans for the Neapolitan constitution being drawn up by Francesco Mario Pagano, who, through the agency of our mutual friend Russo, had sent a copy to the author of these letters and invited him to give his opinion on it. I felt it would be useful to preserve some fragments of them, to make both Pagano's constitution and the nation for which it was devised better known. (V.C.)

2 In his *Politics* (1962: 1319b), Aristotle wrote: "Legislators and would-be founders of any constitution of this type [democracy] will find that the work of construction is not their only or principal business. The maintenance of a constitution is the thing which really matters" (Aristotle 1962: 267, the Barker translation).

Constitutions which are dictated by force fill me with little hope. Whether this force is that of a conqueror disposing of 100,000 bayonets, or of an assembly of philosophers who, helped by favourable prejudice, manage to wring from the people a consensus which they did not understand, matters little. In the first case one does violence to the will, in the second to the intellect. Durable constitutions are those which the people themselves form. "But this people," you say, "does not speak." Very true; but while they are silent, everything speaks for them: their ideas, prejudices, customs, and needs all speak for them. Why have a people ever risen up in revolution? Well, the object for which a people have risen up must be the only one to be reformed. If you touch the rest, you will only offend the people needlessly. You will recall the words of praise which Macchiavelli[3] devoted to the prudence shown by Brutus, who, having expelled the Tarquinians from Rome, saw fit to provide the people with a sacrificial king, for he saw that the Romans still thought it necessary for there to be a king in their sacrifices; and his wish was that, in the new order of things which he intended to institute, the people should have no good thing left to desire which they had had under the old order.

Constitutions are like clothes: each individual, each age in which each individual lives, must have its own, which will not fit another if you try to give it to them. There is no item of clothing that, however lacking in proportion in its parts it might be, cannot fit a man who is shaped differently; but if you want to make one item of clothing alone for all men, even if it is measured up from a model statue by Polykleitos, you will always find that the majority are taller, shorter, thinner, fatter, and you will never be able to use your garment.

"You are too corrupt to be able to have laws," Plato said to the inhabitants of Cyrene.[4] How many say today, with Platonic gravity: "This people is not yet ready for liberty!" But even if one wishes to believe that Plato, who, like all men and philosophers especially, answered at times out of inability, at times out of ignorance, and at times answered simply because he did not want to answer anything else, spoke wisely when he said what he did. Do you think that the Cyrenians would not have been entitled to

3 *The Discourses* (2003: bk. 1, chap. 25).

4 Cuoco is probably here recalling Plato from Rousseau's *The Social Contract* (1968: bk. II, chap. 8).

repeat back to him: "It is true, we are corrupt; but if this takes away our right to be entirely happy, we may at least demand to be less unhappy. Give us, then, laws that are befitting corrupt men."

Constitutions have to be made for men as they are, and as they for ever will be, full of vices, full of errors; for it is as likely that they will want to give up their customs, which I believe to be second nature, to follow our institutions, which I believe to be arbitrary and variable, as it is reasonable for a shoemaker to demand to shorten the foot of someone for whom he had made a shoe that was too small.[5] When a constitution is unsuccessful, I always blame the legislator, in exactly the same way as I blame the shoemaker when a shoe does not fit well.

To want to reform everything is tantamount to wanting to destroy everything. To seek to devise a constitution that is of use to wise men, is tantamount to seeking to devise a constitution for those who have no need of it, while not giving it to those who do have need of it. You know this is what I think about the French constitution of 1795.[6] Is this constitution good for all men? Well, this means it is good for no one, and indeed, after two republican constitutions another is still needed to form the republic's happiness.

Our philosophers, my dear friend, are often deceived by the idea of something excellent which is the worst enemy of the good. If their counsel were always to be followed, the world, in seeking always to do better, would end up doing nothing at all. Time, after a given period, always brings back the same ideas, the same truths, the same errors. We are like the Greek philosophers in the times of Plato and Aristotle, who, having tired of all the vices of all peoples and the disorders of all the governments known to them, concerned themselves with the quest for a constitution that was flawless, to serve a people without any vices. At the time it was the fashion, as it is now, that everyone who craved to be known as a thinker drew up their own draft constitution; and everyone pushed their own as the only one that could become established and endure. What happened? It was precisely at this point that Greece lost all its constitutions: before, it had been content with the best laws it could have, and

5 Echoing Machiavelli, *The Discourses* (2003: bk. 1, chap. 18).

6 This is the so-called constitution of the Year III, adopted in August and effective in October 1795. It established the Directory and lasted until the coup of 18 Brumaire (9 November 1799), which ended the revolution and signalled the ascendancy of Napoleon Bonaparte.

used them to restrain their arms; when it wanted excellent ones, the vices knew no restraint. The excellent is not made for man ...

Oh forgive me! I forgot that I was writing to one who follows in the footsteps of the fine memory of Condorcet, in believing that infinite perfectibility is possible in a finite being like man.[7] Forgive an ignorant, humble man still lost in the errors of his old ways: strive to make us angels, and then we shall found the republic of Saint-Just.[8] For now, let us content ourselves with a provisional one, which can make us less unhappy for three or four more centuries, for at least as many as this in my view will have to elapse before we reach a stage where your design can be executed. Let us speak of the constitution to be given to the idle *lazzaroni* in Naples, the fearsome inhabitants of Calabria, the fickle inhabitants of Lecce, the spurious Sannites, and the other, similar kinds who make up 9,999,999 10-millionths of that human race which you wish shortly to regenerate.

For this race of men, in my view, the draft constitution which Pagano has given to us is not the best. His is certainly better than the Ligurian, Roman, and Cisalpine constitutions: but like these it is too French and too un-Neapolitan. Pagano's edifice is constructed with the materials given to him by the French constitution: the architect may be great, but if his building is made out of plaster ...

If I were invited to participate in the enterprise of giving laws to a people, I should like first of all to know that people. There is no nation, however corrupt and wretched it may be, that does not have customs which it would be advisable to preserve; there is no government, however despotic it might be, that does not have many parts befitting a liberal government. Every people that is enslaved today was free at one time. Despotism has never arisen suddenly, but always gradually. The people's power has rarely been conquered, but on the majority of occasions has been usurped; and every time it has been usurped, the despots have always aimed to conceal their steps, and to preserve the external forms and old appearances, insofar as this was possible.

7 In his *Sketch for a Historical Picture of the Progress of the Human Mind* (1795).

8 Louis-Antoine de Saint-Just (1767–1794) was one of the most ardent leaders of the French Revolution. He served with Robespierre on the powerful Committee of Public Safety. Like Robespierre, Saint-Just died on the guillotine. Their deaths marked the end of the Reign of Terror.

The heavier the yoke of slavery a people bears, the dearer these vestiges from other times will be; for never are the memories of happy times so fond as in times of adversity. The more barbarous the government you wish to destroy, the more numerous the traces of old customs you will find; for in clashing too violently with its own people, that government has virtually forced them to become entrenched amid their old institutions, nor have they found reason in the new events to follow them and to abandon and forget the old ones. You will encounter at every step in our provinces, under the most arbitrary government, institutions which are evidently Sannite and Greek; the Neapolitans of today are the same as those of Petronius; go through Greece, and amid the barbarity you will still recognize the Greeks, and the most oppressed people will seem to you the most capable of liberty.

Such vestiges of customs and governments of other times are encountered in every nation, are precious to a wise legislator, and form the basis of his new ordinances. The people always retain a great deal of respect for everything that comes from their elders; respect which sometimes can produce problems, but which very often produces great benefits. Those who would destroy it, do they not realize that in so doing they would destroy every foundation of justice and principle of social order? We can no longer make the gods speak, in the same way that the ancient legislators used to: so let us at least allow the heroes to speak, who in the eyes of the people are still their elders. A people who change their constitution only out of love of novelty, could do no better than to give themselves a new constitution once every year. But fortunately, such a people exist only in the odd philosopher's imagination.

What can a legislator who loves the nation and follows nature rather than a system not achieve? He should despair of nothing: there is no nation that he cannot make happy. But all is lost, when a legislator measures the infinite extension of nature with the small dimensions of his head, and, knowing only his own ideas, goes around the land like an empiricist with his secret, with which he claims to be able to heal every ill. I cannot consider the fate of a nation which has removed its own constitution to give itself another, possibly better but entirely different one, to be painless. "You want us to be democrats," those peoples might say, "and we want to be democrats, too, but we are also virtuous, for we have a constitution and we love it. But you want to give us another, which we cannot love, and then we shall not be free but not good either; for liberty does not consist of having one constitution rather than another, but in having the one that the people want; and virtue is merely loving the constitution which one has ..."

In our nation, we have the best basis for a republican government; an old basis, well known and dear to the people, and by building on the same edifice of the sovereignty of the people, it might even be better organized than others elsewhere are.

Fragment 2: Sovereignty of the People

The exercise of sovereignty has two parts: legislation and election. In a truly democratic government, the legislator should be the people themselves; but, since such a system is believed to be, and indeed is, impractical in a nation which has 5 million inhabitants and which occupies such a vast expanse of terrain, representation has replaced assemblies. "A people which has representatives ceases to be represented," says Rousseau, and Rousseau is right.[9] The English constitution has merely the division of powers; this is the first step towards liberty, but is not liberty itself. Since, then, it is necessary to use representatives, let us make sure that they do in fact represent the people, and that their will is as closely linked to that of the people as is possible. Let us make them responsible for their votes; let us ensure that the people may ask for an account from them, that they may at least know them; let us at least put them in the position where they have to consult the people.

"The Dutch members of parliament," wrote Sidney, "must give an account to their populations, for they are deputed to represent provinces; the British ones do not, for they are representatives of boroughs."[10] Respectable Sidney! Forgive me if I confess to you that I do not understand what you mean.

---

9 Cuoco paraphrased Rousseau who observed the following: "Sovereignty, for the same reason as makes it inalienable, cannot be represented; it lies essentially in the general will, and will does not admit of representation." *Social Contract* (1968: bk. III, 78).

10 Algernon Sidney (1623–1683) was an English republican theorist and popular hero who had a tendency to get into trouble for his democratic and unpopular views. He was executed for treason. The reference is to Sidney's well-known *Discourses Concerning Government* ([1698] 1996: chap. 3, sect. 38). Most likely Cuoco paraphrased Sidney from Montesquieu's *The Spirit of the Laws,* bk. XI, chap. 6: "Mr Sidney says properly that when the deputies represent a body of people, as in Holland, they should be accountable to those who have commissioned them; it is another thing when they are deputed by boroughs, as in England" (Montesquieu [1748] 1989: 159–60). See also section 44 of Sidney ([1698] 1996: 563–4).

"Each representative," says Pagano, "represents not the department that elected them but the Neapolitan nation as a whole."[11] This, though, is a step further; at least with the British, the representatives represent the city and the borough from which they are elected, and while they might not receive orders, they do at least receive instructions. But in Naples no representative is responsible for any opinion,[12] even if this opinion has become law and brought about the unhappiness of an entire nation. This is the rational consequence of the first principle. So will the Neapolitan nation not be right, then, if it complains that sovereignty has been transferred from Ferdinand to an assembly of 200 persons? It certainly will not have regained its own sovereignty.

Robespierre's constitution gave greater authority to the nation. However, it was not practical to have the people come together every day in primary assemblies, which were often tumultuous and always terrifying. Robespierre's was a constitution of neither wisdom nor peace.

The Neapolitan nation offers a simpler method. It has its own assemblies, which are those parliaments that all our populations have; vestiges of ancient sovereignties, which our nation has always defended against the encroachment of the barons and tax authorities. It is a delight for me to attend some of these parliaments, and to find an entire people gathered there to discuss their interests, defend their rights, and choose the persons to whom to entrust their affairs. This is how the peace-loving inhabitants of the Swiss mountains exercise sovereignty; in this way the greatest of all peoples, the Roman people, chose their consuls and decided on the fate of the universe. Do you want a sovereign people in Naples too? Then without proclamations, without pompous revolutionary rhetoric, without even giving the people cause to suspect anything different might be afoot, say to them all: "A new order of affairs is coming to restore your rights to you. From today onwards, each community [*popolazione*] may provide for its own interests without the barons being able to override your resolutions, without the revenue authorities being able to delay or distort their effects. How many struggles have you had to endure, merely to defend your rights against the revenue authorities and the barons? Well, from now on there will be neither one nor the other; your interests will be governed and decided by yourselves."

---

11 This is said in article 47 of the projected constitution of the Neapolitan republic.

12 Article 108 of the constitution of the Neapolitan republic.

The populations thus assembled will begin by choosing their own municipal councillors, who in a republic must be the leading magistrates, for they must, at the same time, be both the principal executors of the government's orders and the only formal convenors of the national assemblies. With the French constitution of 1795, everything was reversed. In France, the municipal councillors are not elected by the people, and give an account of their operations to the government, that is, to the party which can most easily – and often wants to be – deceived.

I can forgive the French for their system of municipality. They had never had one before, nor did they know anything better; perhaps it was neither safe nor a good idea to pass to our system in one leap and without preparation. But nature itself, which does not tolerate discontinuities, does not tolerate the possibility of going back either; and when our legislators seek to give us the same system as France has, do you not think that our nation is entitled to complain of an institution that deprives it of its oldest and most attractive rights?

What a horrible mess that electoral assembly is! How much scope is left open for intrigue and oppression by a college of persons with only temporary authority, the use of which is so hard to distinguish from its abuse! In not being able to prolong it, their main interest will be to sell it before losing it. As the electoral college is neither the people nor the government, it will easily be oppressed by the latter without ever being defended by the former, which never defends the will of others as zealously as it defends its own. Have we not seen the electoral assemblies of France being corrupted and violated the whole time? The government raged against the electors; the electors complained about the government; the people, who should have been the judges, wavered between the government and the electorate. And what on earth could the people do? Either they had to remain indolent spectators, or, if they wanted to take part in the struggle, civil war would inevitably have broken out, for the law had thought neither to prevent an operation by the people, nor to manage it. Civil war is avoided by ordering things so that neither fraud nor violence can be perpetrated against the law; popular movements are directed to ensure that the law is at least clear and precise, that every act of fraud or violence that is sought to be perpetrated is recognized immediately, hence whoever seeks to oppose violence has the law on their side. When all is uncertain, undetermined, the popular movements may still be just, but they will always be illegal, and what is illegal will sooner or later become unjust.

It is very hard to commit violence against a people that elect themselves. "But," you will say, "the people can also deceive themselves, and be deceived." Machiavelli, who knew the people better than any politician ever did, believes that they are rarely deceived in the detail. But let them be deceived: a significant part of liberty will always consist of being able to do oneself harm.[13]

Each community (*populazione*), then, called to parliament (I prefer this term to that of "assembly," for it is ancient, national and noble; the people understand and use it: so many reasons, then, for keeping it!) will elect its own councillors (*municipi*). They will have the community's executive power, they will be the government's chief agents, and they will have to give an account of their conduct to both government and population. Their term of office shall last one year. You will doubtless see that to this point I would be doing no more than renewing the people's former laws for them.

One of the duties of the municipal council's chairman will be to convene the parliaments of his population, preside over them and set the agenda. These parliaments must take place in locations and at times and with all the formalities required by the law. Under a separate law I would order all parliaments to be called within a non-deferrable term of fifteen days.

For someone to be admitted to vote, I would require that they:

1. be older than thirty years of age. Wise counsel is for the most part the fruit of years: those who are too young are better off in the fields than in the court;
2. be either married or widowed. My intention is not for this condition to be requested only for certain positions, those believed to be more illustrious. For what position could be more illustrious than that of citizen? Few aspire to representation, even fewer aspire to be ministers or executive commissioners: should we restrict a law that is so useful to the republic to just a few, and precisely those few who least need it? Believe me, the danger is that there will be a shortage of citizens useful to support a state; directors and ministers who want to dominate it will never be in short supply.

13 Machiavelli says this in *The Discourses* (2003: bk. I, chap. 34): "wounds and other ills which are inflicted on one's own accord and choice, grieve you much less than those that are inflicted on you by others."

You will readily understand that I also want them to:

3. be able to read and write;
4. have served in the national guard;
5. have neither been bankrupt nor accused of crimes which involved the loss of natural or civil life or of honour; the law shall determine which these crimes shall be;
6. own assets, or have a business, or exercise a trade that is not servile. I do not like a man to be called a "citizen" and have the right to vote merely because he lives in a given territory and pays a poll tax; sooner or later the assemblies will be filled with seditious elements who will disturb the public order.[14] If in Britain public spirit sometimes drives many to donate the necessary funds to their fellow party members for them to be elected representatives, despite the fact that the funds required by law for such purpose are not inconsiderable, how many factious individuals will dominate an assembly where it costs but six francs to buy a vote?

Up to this point everyone, or almost everyone, is in agreement. But shall I tell you that I wish also that all were fathers of their own households? I use this term in the sense that our jurisprudence uses it: "*cui res tutelaque rei suae.*"[15] The young will forgive me for the respect I still have for the old, most precious and sacred of authorities, which in a free government I should prefer to strengthen rather than destroy. I do not believe that it is possible to have customs in any other way. Am I not perhaps also young myself? Well, I see that if I am a fool, if I experience all the passion and feel all the tempestuous agitations of my age, my voice in the assembly could be lethal. But if I am wise, if my ideas are those of prudence and common utility, I will be superfluous there, for I will be listened to by my father, and my father will speak for me. There would not, however, be any restriction on children accepting positions of any kind which the people or government were to offer them: in this case, such a child would be tacitly emancipated by the law, which removes him from

14 A criticism of article 6 on what it means to be a citizen in the constitutional design of the Neapolitan republic.

15 This seems to be a shortened version of a longer phrase but I have not been able to find the longer version in Roman law and in the Twelve Tables as reported by different authors. We take the shortened version to mean something like "to his man his estate, and the guardianship of his estate." We are grateful to Professor Michael Fronda, a classicist, for his help in the search.

the place where he could be most dangerous, and uses him where he could be most useful. This was the practice among the Romans as well; and when a son, having been tested in various minor posts, reached the point of having merited others that required greater trust, at this point he was believed to be above all suspicion and was emancipated forever. What a difference between us and the Romans! We believe all men to be wise and virtuous;[16] they wanted to train them to be so, and were not happy; they wanted also to test them.

I have spoken to you on this subject, for I see that it is unduly neglected in modern constitutions. The Americans were reproached for this. I do not want to give the elderly as much scope as they were given by Rome, Sparta, and all the other ancient legislators, who were more attentive than we are to customs and virtue; but it is clear to me that today we are going to the opposite extreme, and that too much is being given to the young.

Having organized the municipalities in this way, and determined the rights of the citizens, they should then have the incentives to act. My first constitutional law would be that "any community (*popolazione)* of the republic gathered in solemn parliament may take, for its particular needs, those decisions that it believes to be the best; and those determinations shall have the force of law in its territory, provided they are not contrary to the general laws, or to the interests of the other populations."

This right cannot be taken away from our populations, since they had it even under the old order of things, so far as the will of whoever reigned over them allowed it; and it must not be taken away, for it is just and useful to the nation as a whole.

The law is the general will; but, while the nation has its law, each individual has their particular will, and freedom is no more than these two wills being in agreement. A man who is alone is always free, for his law is merely the same as his own individual will. But when several men are joined together in a nation, the general will remains one, but the number of individual wills increases as the number of individuals increases; with number, the disparities between two wills increase, and with the disparities, the number of unhappy and oppressed people increases, too.

16 This principle – that the people were wise and virtuous – was accepted by William Penn in the framing of the government of Pennsylvania in 1682. It was reiterated during the French Revolution by Robespierre and the Montagnards.

This is the reason why large republics cannot last, for as it is impossible that so many individual wills may all agree with the general one, hence it is inevitable that either each will give expression to their own individual will, and the state will fall into anarchy; or that there will be some force that will compel man to obey in spite of himself. This force will necessarily be different from that of the people, and so man will no longer be free; he will be either licentious, or a slave.

But observe, by contrast, the order of nature, and it will be seen how she has suggested the remedies for all those ills that the philosophers fear. Observe how laws are formed. The first men who were joined in society, in small numbers, with simple and almost uniform customs, had few laws. Each one of them was virtually self-sufficient; there were few public needs, few public ills; their laws were no more than the practices of their elders. But these laws, albeit few in number, were not strict; this means that they embraced all objects: property, marriage, religion, customs, clothes, food, even the very chords of Timothy's lyre ...; everything was covered by the law, for everyone wanted the same thing. Hence in Sparta, even under the strictest of governments, man continued to be free.

The populations grew, their ideas extended, their needs multiplied, private will no longer conformed to the public will, ancient custom lost its sanctity, fraud began to be committed against the laws, fraud was soon followed by scorn, scorn by insult. To destroy the law, war was waged against its defenders: anarchy came, and after anarchy, despotism. But do you know why the usurper was accepted? Because he relaxed the former laws; because he concerned himself with merely a few objects, which he subjected to his will, which then took on the name of the "general will," and left the remainder to the individual will of each man. Do you recall the speech which Livy put in the mouths of Brutus's children?[17] Well, every man who follows a usurper, every nation which tolerates him,

17 Livy, bk. II, chap. 3. See Machiavelli, *The Discourses* (2003: bk. I, chap. 16): "The government of a state which is free and has been newly formed, will evoke hostile factions but not friendly factions. If then one desires to remedy these difficulties and to cure the disorders which the aforesaid difficulties bring about, there is no way more efficient, more sure, more safe or more necessary, than to kill the sons of Brutus who, as history shows, would not together with other Roman youths have been induced to conspire against their country if it had not been that, under consuls, they could not attain to an outstanding position, as they could under the kings" (155). See also *The Discourses* (2003: bk. III, chap. 3).

adopts the same language. "*Idque apud imperitos 'humanitas' vocabatur, cum pars servitutis esset.*"[18]

I do not know what these ideas of mine will seem like to you; they are not the ideas of today's constitutionalists; perhaps they are not anyone's ideas.[19] What does it matter? They are mine, and I believe they are borne out by the experience of centuries.

The more nations grow, and the more they are cultivated, the more the objects of the general will must be restricted, and the more extensive those of the individual will must be. But, to ensure that so many particular wills do not become entirely singular, and to prevent the state from falling into dissolution in this way, we should ensure that such objects are taken into consideration by those who are most affected by them, and affected by them most closely. There is a greater difference between one land and another than there is between one man and another from the same land. If the foundation of liberty is that each man is not allowed to do what is harmful to another, why should the same not be allowed of a population? Why, if a population requires a bridge, a road, a doctor, and if all this requires a fresh contribution from its citizens, will it have to apply to the legislative assembly, as previously it had to come before the chamber? How can we hope that those populations which were impatient of the chamber's yoke will today tolerate the yoke of others, who under new names bring together the old ignorance of places and affairs, the old negligence?

Today we have excellent governors; but will we always? Now, a good constitution is not one which only brings the excellent to government. If that were so, the nation would prosper, whatever its form of government. But since it is inevitable that we will sometimes have mediocre rulers, and sometimes even awful ones, a good constitution will be one which even under such conditions, and virtually in spite of the men concerned, manages to bring about the state's happiness [prosperity].[20] When Scipio is consul, it is Scipio who conquers Carthage; but when Varro is consul, after the defeat of Cannae, only the constitution can save the republic. But in order to achieve this objective, as little confidence as possible must be placed in men and as much as possible in things.

---

18 "It is this which ignorant people called 'humanity,' whereas it was merely an aspect of servility." Tacitus, *Agricola*, XXI.

19 Certainly not Rousseau's *Social Contract*.

20 Machiavelli, *The Discourses* (2003: bk. I, chap. 11).

How many good public works would we have, if the populations had been left freer in the exercise of their will? I have travelled part of the Adriatic coast; there is virtually no population that does not have a fund earmarked for the construction of a port, indispensable in a stormy sea. There is virtually no population that either did not have it one day, or at least started it. But since a brake has been applied to the municipalities, the public spirit has cooled, too; the government has taken care of everything; but the government, in seeking to do everything on its own, has either done nothing, or has done everything badly.

Italy, before the fourth century of Rome, and Greece in its heyday, showed how much can be achieved by national activity being developed in all of its points; until the fifteenth century, upper Italy replicated the example of Greece. A traveller who has read Pausanius, if he crosses the Alps and descends into Lombardy, will, says Chastellux,[21] believe himself to have been transported to Greece. Change the destiny of a nation, entrust everything to just one man (be it a king, or an assembly); and see whether, over such a small expanse of land, you see Venice, Padua, Verona, Brescia, Milan, Bologna, Turin, Florence, Genoa arise ... You will see one or two very large, densely populated cities, oppressed by luxury and riches, while the remainder will be merely a desert.

Those nations which were later joined into one sole body are the ones which have the greatest number of large cities: France, which until Louis XIV was divided, has many; Spain, which was divided until the time of Ferdinand the catholic, still has many; Germany, which was divided until our own times, has a great deal; the kingdoms of Naples and England, which were unified before the others, have only immense capitals without even one city in the provinces.

"So you want a federal republic, then?"[22] Not at all. I know the problems that federation brings with it; but since, on the other hand, it also brings us infinite advantages, I should like to find a way to avoid the former without losing the latter. I should like to retain individual activity to the extent that this is possible. Then the republic will be what it should

21 François Jean Marquis de Chastellux (1734–1788) was a French aristocrat and soldier whose book *De la félicité publique ou Considérations sur le sort des hommes dans le différentes époques de l'histoire* (1772) was praised by Enlightenment figures, including Voltaire and Malesherbes. Probably Cuoco may have been familiar with the abridged version of the book that was translated and published in Naples.

22 According to Cortese (1926: 374n4), the possibility of a federation of cities was discussed among patriots during the Neapolitan republic.

be: the development of all national activity towards the greater good of the nation, which is none other than the sum of the good of its private individuals. National activity is developed across all points of the land. If you restrict everything to the government, you will ensure that a single eye and a single arm, from a single point, have to do everything that a thousand eyes and a thousand arms would see and do from a thousand different points. This single eye will not see well, and its arm will be slow to act. It will have to rely on other eyes and arms, which often will not know and often will not want to see or to act. Everything in the government will be embezzlement, everything in the nation will be torpor. The government will have to see everything, direct everything.

The more I reflect on these subjects, the more reasons I find to believe that establishing the Neapolitan republic is no more than a question of restoring matters to their former state, and removing the obstacles that the events of time and the barbarianism of men have put in the way of the natural liberty of peoples. If the re-establishment of the municipal system procures infinite advantages, it also preserves against an infinite number of ills. The objects of legislation must be general, while nature produces only individuals. The government, for example, requires certain taxes to be paid at given times; while the products of the nation from which such tributes must be collected are varied and uncertain. One community (*popolazione*) has only foodstuffs, another only manufactured products: among those communities (*popolazioni*) which have only the riches of their territories, how much variety of produce is there, and how much variety in the times of production! A population from Messapia[23] has no other product than oil, and has to wait for it to be harvested in the month of November; the inhabitants of the plains of Daunia,[24] which have sheep farming and agriculture, have their harvest as early as the month of July; the inhabitants of the cold mountains of Abruzzo, which have sheep farming and agriculture, have to wait until September; the farmer harvests in a day the fruits of a year's labour; the manufacturer reaps it every day; the merchant must wait for the time of the fairs. It would be a very harsh collector that forced all to pay at the same time and in the same way; and what would this harshness be, if not injustice? When the need arises, it is never possible to devise a law which has as many exceptions, as many amendments, as there are inhabitants of your

23 The modern area of Salento in the south-eastern area of Apulia.
24 Coincident with the modern province of Foggia, also in Apulia.

republic. All that remains for you is to impose the sum of taxation and divide it among every population, leaving the choice of how to satisfy it up to them. In this way the general will of the nation shall determine the imposition, the particular will shall determine the method. The latter could not do the former task well, the former could not do the latter.

How many irritations the people are spared by this system! How much expense the government is spared! A population called to parliament is always less unjust and less harsh than a tax collector; the agents which it elects are always less so than a collector appointed by the government. The French, who under their kings did not even have an inkling of the municipal system, at the same time had the harshest system of finances it is possible to imagine. The people, divided up by parishes, were at the mercy of a collector to whom they consigned themselves, numbered like a flock, and to whom the life of men was contracted. This disorder rendered France's finances more of a burden than the entire deficit and all the taxes. Vauban,[25] who in devising his tithe, founded a school within the science of finances of which he himself was not part, had realized that the whole problem stemmed from the poor system of collection; but the remedy he proposed could not be enforced, nor was anyone after him able to propose a more effective one. If I had had to reform France's finances, I would have reformed the method of tax collection, and in this way all the horror would have been removed. Indeed, I see that the *corvée* that weighed so heavily on the French was tolerated in Rome, in the happiest times of the republic, by a people who were more intolerant of tributes than any other.

We have an example of the effect that those laws whose execution is entrusted to the communities (*popolazioni*) can produce. You well know how much was spent so we could have roads in our region, and yet none were built; the tax agents and architects swallowed everything up. We wanted the Sora road.[26] Parisi, to whom this operation was entrusted, having made a design, invited each population to construct that part of it

25 Sébastian Le Prestre de Vauban (1633–1707) was a celebrated French military engineer and a prolific writer on many topics, including monetary policies. In his *Projet d'une dixme royale* (designed in 1698 and published in 1707), he proposed a reform of the taxation system and the imposition of a single 10 per cent tax on all agricultural outputs and on income from trade and manufacturers.

26 The Sora road was an interprovincial road linking the town of Cajaniello, in the province of Caserta, to Tagliacozzo, a town in the province of L'Aquila.

which fell within their territory. The road was built in a year; and despite the embezzlement, which did take place, it cost basically one-third of what the construction of the other roads cost.

You see that I have immersed myself in a discussion of finances; but what subject is extraneous to a constitution? I do not believe that a constitution consists of a declaration of the rights of man and the citizen. Who does not have rights? But the majority of men cede them out of fear; even more sell them out of interest. The constitution is the way to ensure that man is always in a position not to be induced to sell them or forced to cede them, or driven to abuse them. The majority of the revolutions that have shaken the earth to date, including Luther's religious revolution, have been either caused or incited by financial disorder.

I know the objections that could be raised to my principles. The first is born of the fear which some might have that the government's operations might be delayed by the excessive authority thus granted to the municipal assemblies. Vain fear! Since the municipal parliaments cannot make general law, you will see they can do nothing but good; for what is bad, is bad everywhere, and sooner or later will become the object of the general law. Fear of tardiness in the execution of the law is similarly vain. Did we not also see the communities (*popolazioni*) have the same authority under the abolished government as I am proposing to give to them under the new constitution, with everything still in order nonetheless? Do we not see the same order in Austria, Hungary, and the other countries of Europe, where the states exist to divide up and exact that imposition which the courts so like to impose? These states provided the first idea of the French administration, which our Pagano has imitated without adapting it in the slightest. But, once the municipal system has been changed, you will clearly see that the departmental administration must be reformed as well.

Another difficulty ... How to prevent disputes in the parliaments, and to ensure that the will of the people is neither extorted nor forced? The first safeguard against this problem is to ensure that the best men in the nation enter the parliament. The best of governments, says Aristotle,[27] is the one in which the excellent have greatest influence. Now, excellent men are not sought individually but by classes: the precautions I have suggested above, along with others that could be taken, produce

27 *Politics* (1962: 1287a).

precisely this effect of giving the class of optimates the greatest influence. Another remedy: any resolution taken by a population would have legal force only after one month. Within a month, it could be revoked at two other subsequent parliaments; within a month, each member of the people could have recourse to the ephorate,[28] which would be responsible for recognizing the validity of the resolution taken (or the lack of it). Do we not see the royal chamber[29] in the old government having this power? But in a monarchic constitution, the regal chamber took on the spirit of government, and pronounced judgment on not only the validity but also the experience, that is, the reasonableness and justice of the will of others. Out of a desire to do too much, it often made itself unjust and always ridiculous. The general will is always just. The ephorate can do no more than see if some resolution, against which a complaint has been made, is or is not the general will. The functions of the ephorate would be more or less those that the Areopagus exercised in publishing the laws and criminal sentences among the Athenian people.[30]

The final difficulty, lastly, comes from those who are seeking uniformity in all things, the kind of uniformity which so resembles the precision of men and differs so much from that of nature. The only uniformity I want is in the love of our country. What does it matter to me if everyone goes about their business differently, if the operations of each, all different, tend nonetheless towards the general good? So much the better, if the utmost liberty of the country is achieved while retaining the utmost liberty of the individual! Then social love will be the same as love of self.

Often our philosophers fear all possibilities, like the mathematicians fear the island of Lilliput.[31] If I had time, I should be able to predict precisely what use our populations would make of their municipal sovereignty. "But some would say, would do ... ?" Well: the force of all the others, the force of the government would call them back to their duty. "But

28 Originally the ephorate was a body of five elected magistrates exercising supervisory power over the kings of Sparta. Cuoco has an extended discussion of the ephorate in *Fragment* V.

29 The *Real Camera di S. Chiara*, created in 1735, inherited many of the powers of the earlier Collaterale Council which had served as the highest legislative body, the court of justice in the last resort, and the head of the executive government. Colletta ([1838] 1858: 1, 4–5).

30 The Areopagus functioned in classical times as the high court of appeal for criminal and civil cases in Athens.

31 In *Gulliver's Travels* by Jonathan Swift, originally published in 1726.

what if all, what if the majority ... ?" Well then, my dear philosopher, you shake the dust from your feet and abandon a city that will not welcome you. It is stronger than you are, and consequently also more just; for if it is stronger, it must also be more numerous, and as justice is no more than the maximum prosperity divided among the maximum number of persons, so you, who have made this majority unhappy, must necessarily be in the wrong.

The people love the government as much as the government loves the people. And how would they not love a good government, says Gordon,[32] when they show so much affection for those sovereigns who least deserve it? The people are often right, are always powerful; yet they are always the last to assert their rights. Such is the effect which respect for the sanctity of the laws and love of order can have on their mind!

Are you now convinced that the article which I should like to be fundamental in our constitution is reasonable? Then you will concede me this second article as well: "If two or three different communities (*popolazioni)* have common interests, they may meet them equally; and each time their resolutions are uniform, they shall have the force of a binding law for all the populations involved."

For as long as communities are able to meet, representation is superfluous. But as soon as interests start to expand unduly, and it becomes impossible to assemble populations, representation becomes necessary. The general objects are precisely those for which the people are unsuited, and which are better entrusted to a congress of wise men.

We will therefore have an assembly of representatives, the number of which shall be proportionate to our population. Pagano has followed the division of departments made by Zannoni[33] and, giving each department ten representatives, has formed a legislative body of 170 individuals. I should like the number of representatives to be equal to the number of cantons, so that each representative would belong to one canton in particular, and that to elect them there should be no need to convene

32 Cortese (1926: 380n1) suggests that Cuoco here is referring to Thomas Gordon (ca. 1691–1750), author of *An Essay on Government* (1747). See also Villani ([1966] 2004: 338n14).

33 Giovanni Antonio Rizzi Zannoni (1763–1814) was the Neapolitan geographer and cartographer who divided the territory of the republic into 17 departments, with each department divided into cantons and communes.

an entire department (such meetings cannot be convened without riots, which is why they have been replaced by an electoral assembly); but the populations of a canton, gathered in a moderate assembly, would choose their representative in the same way that the population of each land, gathered in parliament, would today choose their own lawyer or attorney, who must reside in the capital. The office of representative and that of attorney should differ from each other less than is thought.

The French constitution confuses municipality with canton, so that each canton may have more than one population, while it will never have more than one municipality. I draw a distinction between two parliaments: one municipal, for each community in a canton; the other cantonal, for all the various communities which make up the canton itself. For, given that every community has some particular interests in certain other municipalities, it is right that sometimes it should take joint decisions, and on other occasions individual ones. But the cantonal unions ought to concern themselves only with those elections which the law has entrusted to them: it would be pointless, inconvenient, dangerous to entrust them with objects that require their communities to meet together too frequently. The cantons, by following these principles, could be slightly larger than those in France.

I also do not like the way Pagano has imitated the French constitution in the method by which the legislative body is reappointed.[34] That one-third must be reappointed each year results in too violent an imbalance of opinions, whereas republics should be founded on continuity of principle. The sovereignty of the people would become too inconsistent in this way. The effects of such changes would be too considerable for conspirators and, in particular, the executive power, which always tends to encroach, not to seek to profit from it; and as soon as this hope comes to be entertained, it will become impossible to resist in practice. You know what the Directory is like in the French elections. But if, instead of having the elections held by the departments, they were to be held by the cantons; if the renewal took place gradually, one, two, three, four cantons in different places in the republic would peacefully elect their representatives, and eventually the whole legislative body would be reappointed, without any disruption to the state's opinions and principles and without too much intrigue. For to engage in intrigue to change just

34 Article 48 of the constitutional design of the Neapolitan republic.

one person in a numerous assembly would be pointless; to do so for all elections would be no easy matter, nor would it produce any hope, or at least not until a good time in the future, that is, when the person entertaining such hopes would generally have left office already. There are two types of intrigue: some agitate in order to gain a position; others to ensure that those who abuse their positions dispense favours to them. The intrigues among established authorities are mostly of this second kind; and they are always more lethal to the freedom of the peoples than the former are. But such problems would be entirely removed by following our system, for the hope of deriving profit from them would also be removed, which is what inspires and incites them.

Will this number of 170 representatives be divided into two chambers, or combined into just one? Pagano believed that division was useful and necessary; he merely altered the functions of each chamber. In France, the Great Council proposes and that of the seniors approves, whereas Pagano believed it was more appropriate for the latter to propose and the former to approve. If I were persuaded of the usefulness of the division, I should agree perfectly with Pagano regarding the functions of each chamber.

But what use is this division of chambers, where there is no division of interests? In Britain it makes sense, for men are not equal. It makes sense in America too, for although the Americans declared all men to be equal by law, even so (and in this their thinking was like that of the ancients), they did not allow themselves to be deluded by their declarations, and realized that effectively a perpetual inequality continued to exist between men, which, while it must not affect the enforcement of the law, does irreparably affect its formation. The Americans sought in wealth the same difference which the British sought in rank. The French constitution adopted the American establishment needlessly.

Much has been made of "initiative in legislation"; a word which de Lolme[35] made fashionable, and which is useless outside of Britain. Where there is no conflict of interests, where the reasons for bribery (since it

35 Jean-Louis de Lolme (1741–1806) wrote *The Constitution of England* which first appeared in French in 1771. The book ranked among the most influential and celebrated treatments of English political liberty produced in the eighteenth century; it has been justifiably reissued by Liberty Fund Inc., Indianapolis, in 2007. Villani ([1966] 2004: 341n17) recalls that Cuoco had already cited de Lolme in the 1801 edition of his *Historical Essay*.

cannot be hoped that these will be removed in any government) are equal in all men, there you can give the initiative to whomever you want. What use is it to retain and pay an assembly of 500 planners?

It is fine to say that division of the councils obstructs the natural speed of the legislature. You will subject the two councils, as you prefer, to two, three, four readings: you will establish the interval you want between one reading and another; but will you ensure provision is made for urgent cases, in which it is necessary to dispense with such formality? Now, who will be the judge of this urgency? The legislative body itself. And so farewell to formality, farewell to institutions! Everything will be turned on its head. Among 100 laws enacted by the French legislative power, you can count ninety-nine marked as being urgent beforehand, but barely one that genuinely is.

I am persuaded of the truth of Pagano's principle, that the few and the wise are better able to propose, and the many are better able to discuss and approve. Like him, I find the institution of senates in the ancient republics to be laudable. But in modern ones, it is not the case that those who propose are few in number, nor that many resolve; and by virtue of a secret syllogism, the gap between those who propose and those who resolve has been reduced to the point where it is now virtually imperceptible. There was a huge difference between the senate and the people of Athens. But imagine that the whole Athenian people consisted of just 170 individuals; and moreover, that they were wise, intelligent, well mannered, as our representatives should be (or as it is assumed they should be), and far removed from those vices which render the people unsuited to making good laws; then imagine a legislator saying to fifty of them: "You are the people." I very much fear that the pleasure-loving Athenians would have laughed at their Solon. As many principles work on a small but not a large scale, so, by contrast, many others are of use and wise on a large scale, but superfluous and thus puerile on a small one.

(Here the organization of the Neapolitan nation is spoken of at length; the initiatives handed to a small council; the discussion entrusted to all representatives gathered in one chamber, obliged to receive their instructions from the cantons to which they belong. A formal method is established whereby all draft laws should be proposed, published, and submitted to review by the populations, before they pass to the resolutions by the representatives ... But all of this is omitted for the fact that it concerns the Neapolitan nation only. The author of the letter moves on to resolve a problem submitted to him regarding the urgency of certain matters, which in many cases would appear to compel the formalities required by the constitution to be dispensed with.)[36]

Urgency! A grim word, which destroys all republics! When the Romans were lords of the earth, when they discussed the world's gravest interests in their assemblies, the Roman sages were never seen altering their constitution to serve the urgency of their affairs.

What on earth are urgent cases? I laugh every time I see criminal laws or civil laws announced with this name: laws that must decide the fate of two centuries, and which should require at least a year of discussion and review. The only true urgency is when the country is in danger, threatened and attacked by an enemy or traitor; and the nature of truly urgent ills is such that once the danger has passed, only their memory remains. It would be madness, once the danger has passed, to want to maintain those laws which danger alone dictates.

The new diplomacy in Europe has caused new types of urgency to arise in wars and in treaties; but such urgencies arise, on due reflection, from the unjust principles of ambition which all powers entertain, and from the poor state in which the warring forces are retained in all nations. When will the time finally come, when the kings and republics renounce their plans for conquest, whatever the title they give themselves and the pretext with which they colour themselves, and renounce also their political dominations, more lethal still and no less unjust than the conquests themselves? What a noble spectacle a nation would give of itself, if it were to declare its rights of war and peace to the world; and in listing the cases in which it would withstand every aggressor and defend its own security and honour, for all other cases give all mankind the word of peace! Such a nation would put justice as its constitutional article; it would restore the fine days of Numa[37] to the desolate earth, or at least the less illustrious, but also less marvellous, days of Penn.[38] Such a nation, always ready to wage war when justice requires it, would almost never need a new law to declare war, but would rush to accept the government's invitation where the well-being of the nation required it, and the edict ordering war would be merely the execution of the most sacred of its constitutional laws.

36 This paragraph was in italics.

37 The legendary king of Rome, successor to Romulus, to whom are ascribed the origins of Roman ceremonial law and religious rite.

38 William Penn (1644–1718), founder of Pennsylvania who established liberal government in the colony. He also laid out Philadelphia in 1682.

Perhaps sweet delirium deceives me, but it will always be true nonetheless, that urgent cases, even where they do exist, are still rarer than is thought. They have multiplied as a result of the mania to restrict executive power unduly; and to want to give to legislative power that which should not belong to it. This has meant that legislative power has become excessive. Urgency, moreover, requires facts, not law, as a remedy; in any case, it is better in an emergency to suspend rather than alter the constitution. A dictator may be created or a dictator's powers given to the government for reasons of urgency; the power which the senate had in Rome can be given to the legislative assembly; a thousand other expedients can be devised, all of which ultimately come back to dictatorship. But the dictator, who momentarily is above the law, must be able to do everything bar actually make laws ...

Fragment 3: Executive Power

Pagano's executive power is the same as the French executive power. That this in Naples is called "the Archontate"[39] rather than "the Directory," that it should last two years rather than five, are differences that merit no attention.

Some have thought, as Rousseau did,[40] that the dictators did not abuse the power that was entrusted to them, for the simple reason that they held it for only six months; that if they had held it for two years, they would have been tempted to try to retain it for longer. But such a short term of office also implies a lack of instruction in affairs, and too abrupt a change of ideals and principles, which I believe is fatal to any republic.

The Neapolitan nation does not offer a national form for executive power. This power is the hardest of all to tame, and organizing it has always been felt to be the hardest part of a constitution. But I will tell you, without intending to underestimate this difficulty, that the problem has become greater since constitutions have started to be thrashed out around negotiating tables, and men have been forgotten in the process; hence the true knowledge of affairs and their importance has been lost.

---

39 From the constitutional design of the Neapolitan republic, article 130. The office was taken from the archontate, the group of often nine chief magistrates of Athens in classical times.

40 Rousseau, *The Social Contract* (1968: bk. IV, chap. 6).

Things have been separated which ought not to have been, and the difficulties of ordering the executive power properly have increased, since the other powers, of which executive power is but a consequence, have been neglected. Perhaps we have never been further from a true science of legislation than we are now, when we believe that we have learnt its sublimest principles.

Do you want proof of what I am saying? Take any one of the many constitutions that men have had until now, and show me even one of them that our philosophers say is not poor. And yet the nations which had them prospered, and were happy and great because of those very constitutions of which we are so critical. I very much fear that if we seek to make a constitution the philosophers approve of, it will bring about the peoples' desolation.

In every form of government, I draw a distinction between rights themselves and the exercise of them. The object of the right is public happiness, but this is obtained only by the exercising of the rights themselves. The fairest constitution is the one in which each person retains their own rights; but only the constitution in which the exercising of such rights produces happiness deserves to be called normal [*una costituzione regolare*].

It is easy to go back to the origins, to analyse the nature of the social contract, make a declaration of the rights of men and citizens; but to ensure that man, who is not always wise and is rarely just, does not abuse his rights, or that he uses them only when common welfare requires it, *hoc opus, hic labor.*[41] Hence I repeat, all the research carried out to discover which is the fairest form of government is basically useless. We will not find any, so let us content ourselves with knowing which is the most normal. We often lose normal government because we are seeking fair government.

Democratic government (you will see, of course, that ours is not so) may be the fairest, but it cannot be normal where the people are not wise; monarchic government may not be fair, but each time the monarch is wise, it is always normal. A wise sovereign on the throne, though, is less of a rarity than a wise people in their assemblies.

The most normal of governments, says Aristotle, are those in which the best men govern;[42] I would add, the ones where those who govern are best. Now, since the corrupting principle of each government is the

41 "That is the work, that is the task." Virgil, *Aeneid* VI, 129.

42 Aristotle, *Politics* (1962: 1286a).

love of self, which has greater power over man than love of his country, if you manage to extinguish this love of self, you will ensure that the best men govern; and if, not being able to extinguish it, you manage to limit its effects, you will ensure those who govern are best. One should not hope for the best from man because he desires to do good so much as because he is unable to do evil. Each time that man can make a law to his own advantage, and can have it enforced, be assured that he will do so, despite all considerations of the public good.

What will you do to make amends for this inconvenience? Will you divide up the powers? It will not be sufficient. Of these powers, one will always be stronger than the others, and sooner or later will always end up oppressing the weakest. If you do not divide the forces as well, you will achieve nothing. When Dionysius aspired to tyranny and, pretending to fear for his life, asked the people of Syracuse for a guard, the inhabitants of that city wasted no time making useless distinctions of powers, but instead answered: "We will grant you a guard to defend you from the people, and shall retain another, to defend the people from you."[43] Do you not think that the people of Syracuse understood the principles of liberty better than we do?

The English constitution was much concerned with the division of forces, and was more scrupulous on this subject than it was on the division of powers; the Swedish and American constitutions concerned themselves more with this matter than the English one did; and in France itself, the first constitution was more attentive to this issue than the other ones were. But this division of forces depends on a nation's political circumstances; and very often, the state of affairs and the course of events overcome man's prudence: with the result that, in wanting to divide the armed force unduly, the risk is run, rather, of weakening it excessively, and in so doing sacrificing the nation's independence for the constitution's liberty.

Every nation has need of a particular size of forces, and a degree of energy in its forces, if it is to maintain internal peace and external security. This need is greater or smaller, depending on the political state of the nation. In Britain, for example, you may diminish the executive power's influence over the land troops, and in so doing diminish this force's energy, for the nation has little need of it; while the executive power's

43 Aristotle, *Politics* (1962: 1286b).

influence over the maritime force is enormous, as is this force's energy, because the need which an island society has of it is enormous as well. If you order the ground troops in France in the same way they are ordered in Britain, what will happen? You will ruin France, as you would ruin Britain if you sought to extend those orders which it has for its ground troops to the maritime forces as well.

What an odd thing it is, to believe it possible to diminish the force of a state! If a state requires few forces, its forces will be small; but do not delude yourself that you can diminish with impunity the force which the nation needs. For if you wish to divide it, I will ask you: what part of the force which you remove from the executive power and commit to another will remain idle, and which part will be active? In the former case, you come to lack the force required to preserve the state; in the latter, you do no more than engage in a play on words, for any power that has force is a power which I call "executive."

This is the difference between the ancient and modern legislators. The former never thought to weaken powers, for they realized that such weakening could only be an obstacle to what is good; the powers would always retain sufficient force to do evil. If the executive power does not have sufficient force to defend the nation's borders, it will still have sufficient force to surround and oppress an electoral college. So instead of weakening powers, they made them more energetic, and so, as all were equally energetic, they came to balance each other out.

But if a nation's armed force must absolutely depend on the executive power, there are other, less dangerous forces, but forces which are no less resilient for this reason, that may be deployed to guard against the other powers; and this division of force and opinion was the source of all that was wonderful about the great legislators. The customs of the elders, respect for religion, the prejudices of the peoples themselves serve at times to restrain the whims of the most terrible despots, even when the legislative power is combined with the executive power. What advantages might we hope for, then, if the powers are divided?

I do not know if you have ever compared the despotism of a sultan with that of a Roman emperor. I have concerned myself with this comparison on several occasions. I will not say, as Linguet did,[44] that there

44 Simon-Nicholas Linguet (1736–1794), French journalist, advocate, and author of many pamphlets. He was guillotined in Paris in 1794 for his one-time defence of King Louis XVI and for his positive description of the Austrian and British rulers.

was greater liberty in Constantinople than there was in Paris under Louis XV, but I would be so bold as to say to you that, if I had to choose, I would rather have lived in Constantinople than in Rome. Turkish despotism is fiercer, but less cruel, more terrible to the Greeks than to the Turks; if your riches do not try the rapacity of a pasha, if your rank does not offend the jealousy of a vizier, you will live peacefully, as little bushes are at peace in the eye of a storm that shatters and strikes down ageless oak trees and proud mountain pines. Your opinion, your wife, the security of your person are always safe. You will see a despot stop and suspend his exploits a thousand times in the face of a public custom, religion, your habits, which are so dear to the people that the despot could not offend them without bringing upon himself the wrath of an entire people, who are even more powerful than his janissaries. It appears that Osman's[45] descendants negotiated well with their followers, and while they reserved the right to do a great deal, there was also much more which they said they could not do. But in Rome, what remained safe from the Caesars' fury? Caesar was everything: censor, pontifex, augur, judge, consul; public opinion, religion, custom, rites, rights; everything was in his hands, and nothing remained entrusted to the people.[46] I do not think that due attention is paid to this difference between the various types of despotism. The first type is that of a nation still barbarian, the second, that of corrupt nations; the former is the despotism of force, the latter that of the law.

This latter form of despotism is resorted to when, out of an excessive love of normality, attempts are made to remove from a people all its customs, all its opinions, all its uses, which I would call the "base of a constitution." This base must rest on the character of the nation, must come before the constitution itself; and while the method by which a nation is bound to exercise its sovereignty must be determined by the constitution, there must also be many things more sacred than it is, which the sovereign, however constituted, must not be able to alter. From barbarian despotism (which, using Aristotle's language, we might call "heroic"), in which the despot has much power, for the only restraint on

45 Osman I (1259–1326), founder of the Ottoman dynasty.

46 In *The Discourses* (2003: bk. 1, chap. 10), Machiavelli noted critically that none "should be deceived by Caesar's renown when he finds writers extolling him before others, for those who praise him have either been corrupted by his fortune or overawed by the long continuance of the empire which, since it was ruled under their name, did not permit writers to speak freely of him" (135–6).

him is the national character, that is, only the base of the constitution, peoples pass to a state of normal government, in which there are laws to restrain the excessive discretion that the customs on their own would allow. But if a despot takes charge of the laws, or, which amounts to the same thing, assumes the appearance of doing so, then you fall back into the despotism of corrupt peoples, which Aristotle would call "*panbasilios*" [*pambasileus*, or "universal king"].[47]

It is dangerous to extend the dominion of the laws themselves too far, for then they remain without defence. The laws in themselves are mute; it is the people who have to defend them. But the people do not understand the laws, and defend only their opinions and customs. This is the danger which I fear, when I see constitutions that are too philosophical, and hence without base, for they are too far removed from the people's senses and customs.

Everything in a nation must therefore form part of the constitution. This is the reason why it is so difficult to make a new one, and so dangerous to change an old one. I could not condemn the excessive severity of Zaleucus:[48] how often do we believe that something new is useful, when in fact it is only dangerous!

After its opinions and customs, the people have nothing dearer than the appearance of normality and order. The laws which strike the senses with the greatest external solemnity are the ones which are most respected by the people. Do you want the people to be attached to the law? Then you must ensure that they can never be deceived as to its nature, that they may never fall into error between the government's operations and the sovereign's resolutions. In this way the attachment to the solemnity of the law will defend its constitution.

This solemnity of the law may become so prevalent that it may even make insurrection against the government's orders legitimate and free from danger. Indeed, it produced no difficulties among the Cretans, whose laws served as a model for Lycurgus. Montesquieu, in seeking the reasons for this phenomenon, missed the ones that were obviously true while pursuing those which were abstruse and frivolous. How on earth could Montesquieu forget that the English constitution had virtually the same model that was so admired in the Cretan one? But many times in

47 In Aristotle, *Politics* (1962: 1285b).

48 The celebrated lawgiver of Locri in South Italy or Magna Grecia.

seeking to explain a phenomenon, we start from the premise that it is a miracle.[49]

In France they wanted to establish insurrection as a constitutional principle. But without the circumstances that accompanied and directed this principle in Crete, it could produce only civil war. It is fortunate for France that this principle was guillotined along with Robespierre. The French founded their constitution on principles that were too abstruse, from which the people were unable to arrive at material things save by means of a syllogism; and when we reach the point where a syllogism is required, there is no longer uniformity of opinions, and it is no longer possible to hope for any normality of operation. The people see the facts, and abuse the principles. Filangieri[50] accuses the Romans of an excessive love of particulars, which they displayed in all their laws; and does not realize that their liberty was founded on this same love. The Roman constitution was tangible, living, speaking. A Roman citizen noticed every infringement of his rights, in the same way that an Englishman notes every infringement of the Magna Carta. Imagine if, rather than this, the English had the Declaration of the Rights of Man and the Citizen: they would not then have had the compass which served to guide them in all revolutions. The Romans did overstep the mark in their desire to detail everything, hence in later times they made their laws into a burden for many beasts. But, while we know their errors, we should also avoid the opposite excesses, and depart as little as possible from the senses. If the multiplicity of details forms a thicket that is too dense, in which the path may be lost, principles which are too sublime and too universal resemble the lofty heights of mountains, from which the objects below them are no longer visible.

After you have divided up the powers, rendered the base of the constitution solid, and fortified the law with opinion and external solemnities, in order to restrain force you still have to divide up interests. Ensure that one man's power cannot extend so far that it offends the power of another; do not allow all powers to be obtained and preserved in the same way; some perpetual magistratures, some random elections, some

49 Montesquieu, *The Spirit of the Laws* ([1748] 1989: bk. 4, chap. 6). Cortese (1926: 396n2) suggests comparing what Machiavelli said in *The Discourses* (2003: bk. 1, chap. 4) that discord between the plebeians and the senate of Rome made the republic both free and powerful.

50 Filangieri in *La scienza della legislazione* (2004: II, part I, chap. 9).

promotions by law, so that a man who has conducted himself well in one post is sure to obtain a better one without needing anyone's favour; all these varieties, far from destroying liberty, are rather its surest support, because in this way all the landowners, and those who hope for some favour from them, fear an overthrow of the constitution; which would be contrary to their interests. For this reason the senates and politicians during the final years of the Roman republic were always in favour of the constitution.

Sometimes, in multiplying the methods of election, some are found which are more reasonable and lead to better elections. It is right, for example, that the people should elect their own judges; but once they have chosen the departmental judges, I should like them to choose one person from their number, to sit in the supreme court of cassation. The people are the judge of the good, but only the good can be the judge of who is best (*ottimi*).[51]

Many times those parts of a constitution which appear to be defective when looked at individually together produce an effect which is excellent. In the same way, many times two poisons combined with each other cease to be harmful. In Rome, the power that the courts had was too extensive, for they could oppose not only those of the senate's deeds that were anticonstitutional, but also those which they believed to be contrary to the public welfare: in this way, on many occasions they did not merely restrain the executive power but destroyed it. But the senate, on the other hand, also had immense power, which was comparable to that of the courts; and these powers, which were both possibly excessive, in continuing to be well matched with each other, never resulted in destruction, only competition, which was converted to the nation's advantage. Each of the parties, in order to defeat the other, had to attract the people to it, and was able to do so only by offering greater advantages than the other.[52]

Many principles, which we believe to be axioms of the political sciences, appear to be imprecise; hence they are not always found to be true in practice. For example, we have calculated the power that can

51 By contrast the constitutional design of the Neapolitan republic gave voters the choice of judges of districts and of Cassation.

52 The view that the Senate and the creation of the tribunes of the plebs made the Roman republic "even more perfect" is shared by Machiavelli in *The Discourses* (2003: bk. 1, chaps. 2–4). For a modern discussion of the office of the Roman Tribune discussed by Machiavelli, see McCormick (2011).

be entrusted to one person, while no attention has been paid to the security of this power; indeed, the security decreases (and here the term "security" also of course includes its duration) the more that the power increases. But no thought has been given to the fact that excessive power, when it is more secure, is also humane, and that in order to make it fearsome it is necessary merely to render it insecure and give it grounds for suspicion. Without the necessary restraints, we have chosen to combine excessive power with short terms of office and elections; ambition and suspicion have thus been incited, and rather than liberty, civil war has been obtained.

It has been felt that executive power diminishes as the number of persons to which it is entrusted grows; so the whole work of our philosophers has been to determine the number of individuals that should make up the government of a given nation, to ensure that it is neither too passive nor too active. Numbers thus prevent the executive power from usurping those of others, which is what happens when this power becomes active in the extreme; while unity prevents the power from being weak, which ultimately brings about a nation's dissolution and political death. And the Romans, in devising a senate whose minister was a consul, instituted a power which combined number and unity, which showed full maturity in its deliberations, and great dynamism in its execution: The consul's specific interest revitalized the senate's lethargy, whereas the senate's interest directed the consul's dynamism, and the people, between the consul and the senate, enjoyed the benefits of the government's dynamism without having to fear for their safety.

When attempts were being made to keep the number of persons and their dynamism in proportion with each other, it went unnoticed that executive power in fact has two parts which are quite distinct from each other. Once the course of action has been determined and before it is executed, it is advisable to discuss how it should be executed. The first activity is the responsibility of the legislative power; the other two of the executive power. But of these activities, writers have forgotten the former; either they have confused it with the functions of legislative power, and so destroyed the executive power; or they have confused it with execution itself, and disorganized it.

It is difficult to judge constitutions; what we believe to be an ill can often produce good. When, out of excessive desire for normality, you remove all force from opinion, when you make all elections uniform, when you limit each magistrature's term of office to the same duration; then you will deprive the people of every defence; the constitution will no longer have any [material] base. Instead of dividing up private interests, you will combine them, because all will have only one interest, which is that of extending their terms of office for as long as possible, and will be able to achieve this objective only by going down the same route: everyone will be in agreement on the need to oppress the people. A hereditary king, says Mably,[53] in speaking of the Swedish constitution, even if he serves no other purpose, serves to remove the ambition from others to be such; and I believe that tempered monarchy is less of an enemy to free society than is believed to be the case.[54] In the silence of your cabinet you will applaud yourself; but the wise men will laugh at your vanity, and your constitution, thrown out after three years, will be a torch reduced to ashes, the object of ridicule of those same children, who to begin with applauded its passing splendour ...

Fragment 4: Judicial Power

Pagano has made some reasonable reforms of the organization of this power. I am pleased he removed those correctional courts, which had no judicial power but still had despotic power. Whether a punishment is heavy or light, it must still be handed down in the name of the law by means of a sentence. It is also a good thing, because it is more convenient to the populations, that the court of one department should not be able to appeal to the court of another, and that appeals should be allowed between different sections of the same court.

But why did Pagano stop at this point? Why did he not attempt greater reforms? It was easy to imagine, for example, that the Court of Cassation,[55] as it came to be organized among us, rather than reducing the number of disputes would in fact multiply them and, in calling them all

53 Gabriel Bonnot Abbé de Mably (1709–1785), French philosopher and politician of republican sympathies who thought that the state should redistribute wealth on grounds of equality. We have been unable to locate the text paraphrased by Cuoco here.

54 Cortese (1926) suggests that this view was also shared by Giuseppe Maria Galanti in his *Testamento forense* (1806: I, 4).

55 Located in Naples, the Court of Cassation had the authority to annul government decrees that did not follow proper procedure but did not have the authority to review the substance of cases or court rulings (unlike the Cassation in France).

back to the capital city rather than raise up the provinces, would in fact oppress them. The Court of Cassation in France was the successor to the Parisian parliament, which rightly or wrongly wanted to be the first parliament in the kingdom, and often reviewed and threw out the sentences passed by the other parliaments.

Those government commissioners who form such a large part of the republican tribunals have taken the place of the former king's agents, but the functions which they assign to themselves are very odd and obscure. At times they act as prosecutor for the parties, at other times as prosecutor for the court, at other times again as presiding officers. Sometimes they have too much power, sometimes not enough; the constitution is always at the mercy of men.

I like executive power to play a role in the courts, but it should be that which the praetor had in Rome, and virtually the same as the president had in our now defunct constitution. If you look at a ruling, you will find it involves many acts that lie outside the judicial power's responsibility. Such, for example, is the judge's appointment, which illogically is entrusted to fate. I say "illogically," in part because fate does not distribute cases equally, and could therefore burden one of the judges unduly while another remains idle; and in part because fate has no regard for a judge's merit, which is sometimes greater, other times lesser, sometimes better suited to one case than to another. In Rome it was the praetor who appointed the judges; the parties, however, had the right of choice by either consenting to or rejecting a given number of them. This method appears to me better than fate.

In this connection, I will also say that I do not care much for those rapporteurs who are always the same for all trials. I prefer the old system of our commissioners; a system in which there are as many rapporteurs as there are judges, and where cases tend to be dealt with more quickly as a result.

The praetor in Rome not only appointed the judge, but also brought the *actio*, which is not, strictly speaking, even part of the *iudicium*, merely an invitation for the judge to see whether a given law can be applied to a given fact, while the *iudicium* itself consists of the actual application. The presidents of our own courts are for the most part entitled to vote in judgments, whereas they ought not to be; and do not bring the *actio*, for in Naples there is neither action nor normality of judgment. Rather, the petition which the president has to make comes at the end of the procedure, meaning it no longer has the advantage of making the procedure normal; and as there are no solemn *formulae* for the action, the right to make such a petition serves no more purpose than to give the executive power a pointless or even harmful influence over the judicial power.

Not even the deed with which the appeal is made and granted forms part of the *iudicium*, for the party making the appeal is merely saying: "The law grants me this ancillary right to appeal against the initial conviction; I intend to avail myself of it; you, therefore, must find the means." You will well understand that such a matter can be only the government's responsibility.

The same executive power, finally, is responsible for publishing and enforcing the verdict issued by the judges, and also for ensuring that the rulings cannot be avoided, that the guilty do not escape punishment, that those arrested remain in custody ...

Will the police be joined together with, or separated from, the administration of justice? You will recall that this question was discussed in the Cisalpine republic,[56] and as is usually the case, many things were said on one side and the other, from which very little was concluded; very many things were concluded badly, and an infinite number of others were concluded completely differently from how they ought to have been.

It was said that justice punished different objects, and that the police prevented crimes. This would be like saying that the doctor who prevents diseases should be different from the one who cures them.

At the time there was discussion in the Cisalpine republic as to whether there should be two separate ministries, police and justice, or just the one. This question should have been decided by observing if one person might have sufficed for the affairs, or if two were needed. It would have been better to have counted the labour force than to examine the nature of things. The French, tired of a police force which was called "active" only because it had letters of seal, arbitrary detentions, and the Bastille, at the start of their revolution, when the memories of the ills suffered were at their keenest, combined the police force with the ministry of justice. In the early times of the directorial constitution, when new ills were arising and only the ancient remedies were known, justice was again separated from the police force.

But where, as perhaps in France, the number of cases does not warrant separation, I would prefer them to remain united. I am no admirer of lax

56 This was discussed in the Great Council of the Cisalpine republic on 26 November 1797. The Cisalpine republic extended over territories centred in the Po River Valley of North Italy and was created by Napoleon in 1797 by uniting the Transpadane and Cispadane republics. The republic lasted until 1802.

justice; nor do I tolerate a police force that is unjust. Our political character affects our moral character. The man who is accustomed to bring the circumspect attention of a judge to affairs will also bring it to bear on people; and if it is the case that in order to be slightly more energetic, the police sometimes need to be corrected by justice, this correction will be so much quicker and easier when the person to whom the police are entrusted belongs to the same college of judges who have to correct it. Men are such that they more willingly correct themselves than allow themselves to be corrected by others.

The police are the active part of justice, and must naturally be joined with the executive power of the courts. What use are so many commissioners and clerks, multiplied infinitely across our territory? And does it seem to you but a minor ill that useless posts should proliferate to such a degree, causing expense to the state, distracting citizens from useful occupations, and subjecting them to the temptation of using the part of their activity which they are unable to employ to the advantage of their position to the detriment of the country?

I do not know if I am mistaken, but it seems to me that the civil and political branch of the 1795 constitution[57] absorbs too much expenditure; and in wishing to avoid the inconvenience that a nation suffers when its affairs exceed the forces of its public functionaries, we have gone to the opposite extreme, which is no less dangerous, whereby public functionaries are multiplied to the point where they infinitely exceed our affairs.

Much of the police work could be entrusted to honest citizens. In Peru, the wisest and most virtuous man was chosen from ten families, to monitor the conduct of others; a centurion was chosen from among these decurions; others chosen from among the centurions; then others still, if necessary, until the unit was reached that constituted the government ... An admirable law, says Genovesi,[58] which entrusted security to

57 In France.

58 A leading Neapolitan political economist of his time, Antonio Genovesi (1713–1769) drew repeatedly on the work of Garcilaso de la Vega (1535–1568) to present the political and military organization of the Incas in his lessons of commerce and civil economy, *Delle lezioni di commercio o sia di economia civile* ([1765–67] 2005). Unfortunately, we have not been able to locate what Cuoco here attributes to Genovesi (see also Sabetti 2012).

the safe-keeping of virtue! We had a very similar institution in our *capodieci*;[59] an institution that had become corrupt, but which, if reformed, could have become excellent ...

Thus far I have spoken only of the judicial power's organization. Eventually, however, this machine will have to act. Shall I also speak to you of the laws themselves, of the order of judgments, the formulae, the actions and so many other things that have largely been ignored by our political writers? Many have concerned themselves with jurisprudence that regards persons; very few, so far as I know, have dealt with jurisprudence that regards things. Perhaps, of all the nations known to us, the Romans were the ones who best understood its importance, and it was only among the Romans that civil legislation formed an integral part of the constitution. From the precision of their civil law, which we deride as being unduly scrupulous, from the normality of their judgments, from the sanctity of their formulae, derived the pre-eminent position that the Romans accorded to men of the law; and in this way they were able to balance the influence which the men of arms had, which is so dangerous in a warring republic. The Romans had equal need of the wise man and the hero. The French, in the early days of their revolution, were too afraid of the military's influence, and rather than balancing its power, sought to remove from the people all the needs that could have kept them dependent. While they feared the men of arms as oppressors, they feared the men of the law as imposters. But even when you have taken all the people's needs away from them, you will not be able to take away all their fears. Physical force will continue to exist, and will no longer be counterbalanced by the force of opinion. To succeed in your project, all the people will have to be good; the emergence of even one bad citizen will ruin everything. The Romans' devotion to the sanctity of the formulae and their respect for the laws of property saved the state a thousand times over. When your friend, the virtuous but unwise Gracchi, seduced the people with those agrarian laws which threatened the republic's

59 Cuoco is referring here to the ten consultors chosen through successive rounds of election by the family heads of each of the twenty-nine districts (*ottine*) of the city of Naples. These consultors aided the single People's Representative (Sedile del Popolo) in the running of the city with the Nobles' *Seggi*. Between 1642 and 1734, when Naples acquired its own Bourbon king, viceregal authority was compelled to come to terms with the *Seggi*, which functioned as a kind of new Neapolitan parliament, as the old parliament had fallen in desuetude by 1642. See Marino (2011), and editors' introduction to this volume.

survival, the most virtuous of the Scipios, despite the interest of the moment which exerted such a powerful sway over the people's minds, used reasoning based on jurisprudence to keep them to order and duty.

Disorders in jurisprudence produce effects which are possibly more lethal in southern Italy than elsewhere in Europe. Petronius's Neapolitans, Monsignor Della Casa's Neapolitans, today's Neapolitans have always been, and still are, too enamoured of litigation. Naturally smart, they quickly take advantage of any oversight on the part of the legislator. This national character renders them argumentative, when the legislator fails to address it; fraudulent, when there is no legislator such as Pietro of Toledo[60] to use it to his own advantage. A wise legislator, however, who loves his country and knows the nation, will easily turn it into love for normality of judgment and respect for property and for the laws. A wise legislator could cause the Romans to be reborn ...

Fragment 5: The Ephorate

The institution of the ephorate is the best part of Pagano's project. This part, this senate responsible for safeguarding the people's sovereignty, was entirely lacking in the 1795 constitution, and you well know how easy it was for the Directory to destroy it, especially on that fateful day of 18 Fructidore.[61] A magistrate to watch over and guard the constitution, to observe the conduct of all without having any of their powers, is even more necessary, given the current state of the European peoples, given how easy it has become to usurp executive power with the system of permanent militias, which render the smallest part of a nation stronger than its larger part. Nor is this problem remedied by the system of national militias, whose form may be national but always to no avail; nor by any other solution that I could imagine.

But when Pagano restricts the ephorate's sessions to fifteen days per year, does he not realize that in this way the ephors will be able to concern themselves only with those violent, noisy infringements [*usurpazioni*] of power which are always few in number and from which there is little to fear? I fear rather the small, daily infringements, most of which

60 Toledo was viceroy of Naples between 1532 and 1553.

61 4 September 1797, when troops invaded the houses where the councils were meeting.

are made under the appearance of good, and which go either unnoticed or to which little attention is paid, until abuse becomes customary and the ill is revealed only when, having become enormous, it mocks those tardy, useless memories. Never will a usurper with any sense seek to start from large infringements.

Does Pagano not realize that, in having the ephors remain in office for just twelve months, while all the other magistrates have more than a year, the former would have to be either supremely virtuous or supremely stupid to take on those who, but one minute later, might take their revenge on a man sentenced by law to remain as a private individual? What philosophy is it that always seeks to set the will against the law, to set virtue against interest?

Pagano is afraid that this magistrature might become too powerful. Rousseau[62] believed it could never be weak enough. The examples of Rome and Sparta, which were overthrown by the tribunes and ephors, are recalled, but it is forgotten that these same tribunes and ephors supported Sparta and Rome for five centuries. And which human institution can flatter itself as being eternal?

The power of the ephors is restrained sufficiently by increasing their number, and Pagano has wisely provided that there should be as many of them as there are departments in the republic, and that if matters cannot be resolved by an absolute majority, then they should be approved by a majority of at least two-thirds.

The ephorate is feared excessively, for it has been given more power than it should have been. The ephors, it is said, should watch over the conduct and prevent the usurpations of all powers. All of them? One of the powers in any case never usurps anything, for even when it takes from the other powers, all it is doing is taking back what it has given. Ephors are not needed against the legislative power, or against the sovereign, for sovereignty is inalienable. The Roman tribune opposed the senate; but as soon as the people had decided, the tribune fell silent. The tribunes did not corrupt the Roman republic by confusing powers, but by corrupting the people, often to pernicious ends; hence the people abused their own powers without usurping anyone else's. But this danger is diminished considerably when faced with an assembly of wise men, who are under no illusions and are not easily distracted the way the always inconstant and fickle people are.

---

62 *The Social Contract* (1968: bk. IV, chap. 5).

The idea of entitling the ephorate to watch over the legislative power arose when sovereignty ceased to belong to the people and was given to the people's representatives instead. If the people cannot usurp, its attorneys certainly can, who are able to usurp those powers which the people have not granted them. But then I ask: where is the sovereignty? The people no longer have it, for they have transferred it to their representatives; the representatives do not have it, for sovereignty cannot be divided; and they are subject to the ephors. Who, then, will be sovereign? Either it will be the ephors, which is how the Spartan nation fell; or there will be no sovereign, which is how all nations fall.

Organize sovereignty in the same way that France chose to do in 1795, but in a way that is also suited to the Neapolitan nation; and the people, always vigilant over their own interests, and never meeting in tumultuous assemblies, will never be robbed by their representatives, nor seduced by their tribunes. Then the ephors would return to their primary institution, more sublime and at the same time less dangerous than the institution which is proposed for them. Then they would become the custodians of the people's sovereignty, without ever being able to impede or obstruct the exercise of it; then, rather than correcting infringements, which is never unaccompanied by violence, they would be able to prevent them.

Among all the various institutions of the ephorate, the one which seems best suited to a representative constitution is that of the *avvogadori* in the republic of Venice. Contarini[63] describes them well, when he says that they are the tribunes of Venice, but tribunes of the law; whereas those of Rome were tribunes of the people. In any case, though, I would not like to imitate such an institution without changing some parts of it, which the Venetians themselves would have changed at other times and in other circumstances ...

"How, then, would you do so? What rights would you give to your ephors?" Since you want to know, I shall tell you.

1. The ephorate should recognize the legality of all municipal parliaments. The way to achieve this has already been mentioned: I have been speaking to you of the functions of the ephors for some time now, without once having mentioned the ephorate.

---

63 Gasparo Contarini (1483–1542) in his *De magistratibus et Republica Venetorum* (1543: bk. III). It was translated by Lewes Lewkenor as *The Commonwealth and Government of Venice* (1559). For a recent biography of Contarini, see Gleason (1993).

2. Recognize the legality of the cantonal parliaments, and direct the elections which would be held in them. In the French constitution, elections are under the sway of the executive power, and you well know the number of abuses that have arisen from this. The English constitution is freer in this sense than the French constitution is. I am amazed that Pagano has not noticed such an error, and not entrusted the election of the electoral assemblies to a magistrate who, having no other political influence, would not be tempted into some form of abuse that would be fruitless for him.

3. Recognize anyone to whom citizenship has been given as a citizen. Why? Because citizenship is part of sovereignty; hence it must be entrusted to the same magistrate to whom custody of sovereignty has been committed.

In this connection, I would say that I find it very odd that the right to grant citizenship is entrusted to the assembly of representatives, rather than to the municipality and the government, as was the case in all the ancient republics, and also in our now defunct constitution. I repeat: I am very much afraid that the Neapolitan people will lose rather than gain in seeking to follow the institutions of other peoples. I am no admirer of that illusory kind of citizenship whereby a man belongs to an entire nation, while in fact belonging to no part of it: I would prefer each man to have a country [*patria*] before he has a nation. When a population has formally said to a man: "Remain with us; you are worthy of being called one of us," then he will present himself to the ephorate, through which he will announce to the entire nation that he is a citizen and that he already has a country.

4. Recognize, at the same time, the legal capacity of all other public functionaries, so that none may start to exercise their post if their commission has not first been approved by the ephorate. Wherever there is found to be a constitutional impediment, either in the elected person or in the method of election, the ephorate shall withhold its approval.

5. As the ephorate is responsible for safeguarding the people's sovereignty, so too a law will not have public authority if the formalities required by the constitution do not appear to have been observed through it in the making of this law. The ephorate must not examine whether or not the general will is fair or unfair, only whether or not it is the general will; and in order to do this, it may recognize only those external formalities which the constitution requires as signs of the general will.

In Venice, at least one of the *avvogadori* had to take part in the Great Council to see if the formalities required by the constitutions were being observed. The *avvogadori* were in Venice what the *nomophilagi* were in Athens, custodians of the original copies of the laws, so there was no dispute over their authenticity at any time.

6. The ephorate may suspend any representative accused and convicted of having transgressed the instructions of their canton. But such an accusation may not be produced by anyone but the canton itself, and can be proven only by comparison with the letter of the instructions given to the representative or their own vow as recorded in the minutes of the legislative assembly meeting.

7. It may annul any deeds approved by the executive power that are contrary to an article of the constitution. "Anticonstitutional deeds by the executive power" are those which have no reference to any law or which are in breach of the law thus referred to. The English constitution gives a very clear idea of what represents an unconstitutional deed.

I would not give the ephorate any influence over the judiciary, partly because this power can never be free enough; partly because the ills which abuse of this power can produce never affect society as a whole, nor are its effects so rapid that they cannot be remedied in normal fashion. One of the abuses perpetrated by the Roman *tribunatus* was possibly that of opposing the praetors too often.

8. It may lay charges against any constituted authority, but only when the latter seeks to transgress the constitutionally imposed limits of action. But to be able to exercise these last three functions, I would require a majority of at least two-thirds of the votes cast to be in favour.

I shall stop talking to you about the ephorate. Though you were the one who wanted me to. How hard it is to be a legislator, and how we must fear being ridiculous, when we choose to speak up! …

Fragment 6: The Censor's Office

The ephorate is the guardian of the constitution, the censor's office the guardian of customs. Pagano has replaced this office with the correctional tribunals, and while a censor could be useful, I find nothing wanting in Pagano's institution, apart from the fact that I would rather the censors did not reside in the main centres of the cantons but in each individual community [*terra*]. A censor cannot observe things on his own, but has to depend on an accuser; however, only a judge can listen to an accuser with impunity. A judgment is concerned with facts, whereas censorship is concerned with customs (*costumi*); facts are proven, but customs are felt.[64]

How to prove, for example, that a man lives undemocratically, that he behaves with excessive arrogance, that he is a spendthrift or miser, intemperate, or imprudent? ... You will reopen those trials which deafened our courts in cases between husbands and wives; trials in which, after the parties had revealed their weaknesses to those who did not know them and who had no desire to do so, nothing was concluded apart from the fact that both parties displayed exceptional talent for revealing the weaknesses of others and no desire whatsoever to correct their own.

But what is there to hope for from censorship in a corrupt nation? When public opinion has been lost, says Rousseau,[65] the censor's office either ceases or becomes harmful.

Censorship may conserve the customs of a nation which has them; but it can never give customs to one which does not have any. In a corrupt nation, you must begin by rekindling a love of virtue. Instead of giving such a nation censors, I would give it judges to publicly reward merit and virtue; I would establish festivals, prizes, or, rather than promising prizes, I would concern myself with directing the nation's esteem and the government's approval: I would bring man back to the right path not so much by seeking to remove him from evil, as by reacquainting him with good. Love of virtue must become a passion before it becomes a requirement, but before becoming a passion, it must be in the people's interest.[66]

Freedom! virtue! this is what has to be the goal of every legislator; this is what forms all the happiness of the peoples. But nature has established

---

64 Cuoco seems to be using the term *costumi* with the same meaning as Tocqueville in *Democracy in America* ([1835] 2010: I, part 2, chap. 9, 287) attached to mores [*moeurs*] in its original Latin meaning: the whole moral and intellectual state of a people: the habits of the heart but also "the different notions possessed by men, the various opinions current among them, and the sum of ideas that shape mental habits."

65 *The Social Contract* (1968: bk. IV, chap. 8).

66 Cortese (1926: 412n2) suggests that what Cuoco says here was amply discussed by Genovesi in his *Lezioni di economia civile,* and that Pagano followed Montesqueiu in *The Spirit of the Laws* ([1748] 1989: bk. 5, chaps. 7 and 19) when he noted that censors were necessary to the well-being of a republic.

an unavoidable path by which to not only arrive at virtue but also achieve freedom; and what we are seeking to follow is not the way of nature.

What fatal law is it which decrees that this same enthusiasm for virtue, when taken to excess, can prove lethal to mankind! We are deceived by the examples of peoples who are no longer, whose vices and weaknesses time has caused to be forgotten. Through the veil of the centuries, they appear to our eyes as perfect models of a virtue that is no longer human; and by seeking to be excellent citizens of Sparta or Rome, we cease to be good inhabitants of Naples and Milan.

I shall tell you another time of my ideas regarding the study of mores (*morale*), the reasons why this has been so neglected among us, the reasons for the contradictions that continue to exist between different precepts, between books and men; and perhaps you will agree with me that the principles that could render this science, which is so important to mankind, both profitable and truthful are still unknown.

Virtue is one of those ideas that has yet to be well defined, which presents itself to our minds under a variety of aspects; it is a name which is capable of referring to an infinite number of things. There is the virtue of man, of the nations, of the citizen: virtue may be considered by its principles, or by its effects.

The virtue of citizens is merely the conformity of their mores to those of the nation. The old nations feared excessive good and ill to an equal extent. When the Ephesians expelled Hermodorus,[67] they did not say to him: "Go, because you are evil"; but said to him: "Go, for you are better than we are." Since we no longer have public mores, virtue for us has become the most abstrusely metaphysical concept, and morality has become the subject of endless scholastic disputes. We have many learned books to teach us what man's duties are, and very few men who actually observe them.

A nation will be said to be virtuous when its mores are such that they do not make its citizens unhappy; and if all nations could be wise enough to seek to help and be of profit to one another, rather than pursue mutual warfare and destruction, this would be the virtue of mankind. The end of virtue is happiness, and happiness is the meeting of needs, that is, the achievement of a balance between wants and resources. But since these two quantities always vary, happiness may be achieved, that is, the balance obtained, only by either reducing wants or increasing resources.

67 Cicero, *Tusculanes desputations* (1957: bk. V, chap. 6).

A man who has what he wants will never be unjust; for that sentiment of compassion which causes us to feel others' discomfort to the same degree as our own is natural and almost physical in us. This sentiment alone is sufficient to restrain our injustice, always provided we consider such injustice to be fruitless. The savage man does not care for his peers, for they are of no use to him: he has only to satisfy his own needs, which are few. His needs must increase if he is to realize that another person might be useful to him, at which point he becomes human. For a time in the political progress of the nations, man's resources will exceed his needs; at this point he will also be generous. But this period lasts only a short time; the needs return to exceeding the resources; man comes to believe that other men are not only useful but necessary, hence he is no longer content to have them as his friends, but will also want them to be his slaves.

In which period of history do we find ourselves? Our needs greatly exceed our resources; and our needs cannot be diminished, for our ideas cannot go backwards. What do you hope for, in preaching ancient precepts and simple customs to us, which are not our own? In vain you will eloquently rage against our luxury, our whims, and our love for riches; we will admire you, and will leave you alone. But if you show us how to meet our needs; if you cause our resources to grow, you will inspire a love for hard work in us, you will unlock the treasures which a fertile soil conceals in its breast, you will exempt us from the taxes which we currently pay for the foreigner's useless trifles, you will make us great and happy: and without being either Spartans or Romans, we will be able to match them for virtue, for like them we shall have resources that are equal to our wants.

The love of hard work, it seems to me, must be the sole foundation for the only virtue which our century can have. The government's concern must be to destroy the professions which produce nothing, as well as those which consume more than they produce; and it will succeed in doing so if it establishes that order whereby such riches may never be hoped for from those professions as can be achieved by means of the useful arts. When a citizen no longer looks to earn his living from holding positions, when serving one's country ceases to be equated with making one's fortune, as is currently believed, you will have destroyed three-quarters of dangerous ambition. The love of hard work will remove a thousand of the whims and weaknesses which currently dishonour us, for it will change our effeminate upbringing. A love of the countryside, which will replace our current obsession with the capital, will release us from our passion for fashionable trifles, for those luxuries which are all the more wasteful the more frivolous the objects involved are; and man will use his surplus in a luxury of arts, which is longer lasting, more glorious to the individual, and more profitable to the nation. The fine arts were enjoyed and promoted by the wealthy in Naples in other times, when their wives did not consume in hats, veils, ribbons, and clothes all the surplus, and at times also all that was necessary to live on for an entire year; when the wealthy class was not a class of ignorant people as it is today, nor was it yet widely held that doctrine and taste had to be a profession by which the poor could make a living, rather than a fine entertainment to divert those who, by some favour of fortune, were entitled to remain idle. Work will give us the arts we are lacking, it will make us independent of the nations on which we currently depend; and so, in increasing the use of our own resources, esteem for them will also increase, and with esteem for our resources, the love of our country will increase, too. Patriotic love, self-esteem, taste for the fine arts, and the glory inseparably associated with them, more virile education, more noble ambition, honest ease of subsistence which, by increasing emulation in men, at the same time reduces envy between them, all the other virtues which depend on and accompany these ... If virtue and happiness are more than a vain name, what else could there be left to desire?

But, philosophers! if you want to bring us to this point, follow the course of nature. Do not come to insult us, as Diogenes came to Athens. If you do, you will cause us to laugh at the new virtue you want to give us, and you will cause us to lose what little of the old virtue we still have. Our speeches do not destroy our needs, nor increase our forces; and we will remain without that balance which alone can produce virtue, and without those principles which can restrain, at least in part, the vices which we have. Your new principles, having destroyed the old ones, will be despised by us as being unrealizable.

In order to revive some virtue in us in our present state, rather than diminishing greed I would actually prefer to increase it among the lower classes, offering them the prospect of a more comfortable way of life. In this way, they would be sure to become freer and more active. To use mathematical terminology for a moment, I could say that liberty, which is always proportionate to equality, is inversely related to the pressure which the upper classes exert, and that such pressure is always directly related to the surplus that the lower classes have. Oppression is therefore at its highest either where nature grants so much surplus that all of man's greed cannot absorb it or where man is so humiliated, so brutalized, that he has only very few needs. In the most liberal governments, the lower classes are better off and more active; and the desire to be better off, which is believed to be the effect of liberty, has in fact often proved to be its cause.

I do not know what course would have been taken by those ideas, too lofty, which at times became mixed up with each other, and which interrupted and disturbed the course of the French Revolution, but I fear that the effect would have been to reduce France to a forest, where men feed themselves with acorns, but the rivers do not flow with milk and honey as they did in the golden age. Along with barbarism, violence would have returned, and the rivers would have flowed with men's blood. Such opinions fell from the throne, despite the force with which they were argued. But their nature is such that, even if they remain among the shadows of the schools, even if they are not accompanied by force and terror, and fail to produce civil war as they did in France, they are still, however, either causes of or precursors to the corruption of customs (mores, *costumi*). For many years the Greeks were virtuous in their actions. Socrates was the first to form a theory out of practice and transport virtue from the level of actions to that of ideas. But once Antisthenes and Diogenes exalted these ideas to their highest point, Greece ceased to have mores (*costumi*).[68]

Listen to me. You know my adolescence and my youth. You know that I love virtue, and whether or not I know how to prefer it to life itself ... But when, in speaking to men, we forget all that is human; when, in seeking to teach virtue, we are unable to cause it to be loved; when, in following our ideas, we seek to reverse the order of nature, I fear that rather than virtue we will teach fanaticism, and instead of ordering nations we will found sects.

I am very sad not to have kept the letter which Mario Pagano wrote to me after Russo had informed him of my ideas. I would be proud of the approval of a man whose death, if it is fatal to our country and a source of mourning to all good men, is most bitter to me, for in his passing I mourn not just the loss of a fine citizen and great man, but also that of an excellent teacher and friend.

---

68 Cortese (1926: 417n1) and Villani ([1966] 2004: 369n2) elaborate what Cuoco meant this way: For Socrates virtue is a perfection of human life as when a virtuous man engages in a computational analysis of the different pleasures and then chooses the one that brings him most pleasure; for the Antithenes and Diogenes virtue is something sufficient in itself, suppressing human preferences and limiting those preferences only to essential needs. This way pleasures and life goods tend to be viewed as bads, or distractions from the practice of an abstract notion of virtue.

Appendix II
List of Patriots Who Died on the Scaffold[1]

Albanese, Giuseppe, born in Noci (Bari), 30 January 1759; jurisconsult. Put to death in Naples, 28 November 1799.

Albano, Cesare, born in Spaccone, about twenty-five years old; peasant. Put to death in Procida, 1 June 1799.

Alberino, Bernardo, about twenty-eight years old. Put to death in Procida, 1 June 1799.

Andreassi, Colombo, born in Villa Sant'Angelo (Aquila), 19 October 1770; lawyer. Put to death in Naples, 31 October 1799.

Arcucci, Gennaro Felice, born in Capri, 5 January 1738; doctor. Put to death in Naples, 18 March 1800.

Assante, Vincenzo, born in Procida, about fifty-five years old; surgeon. Put to death in Procida, 1 June 1799.

Assisi, Pasquale, born in Cosenza, 5 January 1750; marine. Put to death in Naples, 14 October 1799.

Astore, Francesco Antonio, born in Casarano (Lecce), 28 August 1742; lawyer. Put to death in Naples, 30 September 1799.

Baffi, Pasquale, born in Santa Sofia di Calabria, 11 July 1749; university professor of Greek language and literature, librarian at the Herculaneum Academy. Put to death in Naples, 11 November 1799.

Bagno, Francesco, born in Cesa (Caserta), 26 June 1774; professor of medicine at the Incurabili hospital. Date of death uncertain, possibly 1799.

Battistessa, Pasquale, born in Centurano (Caserta), possibly in 1769. Put to death in Ischia, 23 July 1799.

Belloni, Giuseppe Carlo, born in Vicenza, 4 February 1754; friar of the Minore Osservante Order of Santa Maria la Nova. Put to death in Naples, 13 July 1799.

1 List adapted from Villani ([1966] 2004: 371–9).

Bisceglia, Domenico, born in Dominici (Cosenza), 3 January 1756; lawyer. Put to death in Naples, 28 November 1799.

Bozzaotra, Luigi, born in Massa Lubrense, 20 August 1763; notary. Put to death in Naples, 22 October 1799.

Buonocore, Francesco, born in Ischia, 30 November 1769; artillery commander for the castle of Ischia. Put to death in Procida, 1 June 1799.

Cacace, Giuseppe, about twenty-one years old. Put to death in Procida, 1 June 1799.

Calise, Giacomo, born in Procida, about thirty-six years old; sailor. Put to death in Procida, 1 June 1799.

Cammarota, Giuseppe, born in Atripalda (Avellino), 27 July 1764; clerk. Put to death in Naples, 4 January 1800.

Caputo, Severo, born in Naples 1757; marquise of Petrella; part of the Olivetan Monastic Order of Lombardi di Sant'Anna; theology professor. Put to death in Naples, 31 October 1799.

Caracciolo, Francesco, born in Naples, 18 January 1752; admiral. Put to death in Naples, 29 June 1799.

Carafa, Ettore, born in Andria, 10 August 1763; count of Ruvo. Put to death in Naples, 4 September 1799.

Carlomagno, Niccolò, born in Lauria (Basilicata), 1762; lawyer. Put to death in Naples, 13 July 1799.

Ciaia, Ignazio, born in Fasano (Bari), 24 October 1762; scholar. Put to death in Naples, 29 October 1799.

Ciampriamo, Michele, born in Naples, about forty-one years old. Put to death in Procida, 1 June 1799.

Ciccone, Michelangelo, born in Moro Teramano, 17 January 1751; clergyman of Pietrasanta. Put to death in Naples, 18 January 1799.

Cirillo, Domenico Leone, born in Grumo Nevano, 10 April 1739; doctor, university professor. Put to death in Naples, 29 October 1799.

Colonna, Giuliano, born in Naples, 3 October 1769; prince of Aliano. Put to death in Naples, 20 August 1799.

Conforti, Gian Francesco, born in Calvanico (Salerno), 7 January 1743; priest, university professor of history. Put to death in Naples, 7 December 1799.

Costagliola, Michele, born in Procida, about twenty-three years old. Put to death in Procida, 1 June 1799.

Cotitta, Giuseppe, born in Naples, 1761; hotelier. Put to death in Naples, 8 July 1799.

D'Agnese, Ercole, born in Piedmonte d'Alife, 3 May 1745; literature professor. Put to death in Naples, 1 October 1799.

D'Alessandro, Leopoldo, born in Ischia, about twenty-four years old. Put to death in Procida, 1 June 1799.

D'Avella, Antonio (Pagliuchella), born in Naples,1739; oil merchant. Put to death in Naples, 29 August 1799.

De Colaci, Onofrio, born in Parghelia (Catanzaro), 25 April 1746; magistrate. Put to death in Naples, 22 October 1799.

De Filippis, Vincenzo, born in Tiriolo (Catanzaro), 4 April 1749; mathematics professor at the University of Bologna. Put to death in Naples, 28 November 1799.

De Fonseca, Pimentel Eleonora, born in Rome, 13 January 1752; director of the *Monitore Repubblicano.* Put to death in Naples, 20 August 1799.

De La Grenelais, Luigi, born in Naples, 1766. Put to death in Naples, 8 February 1800.

De Luca, Antonio, born in Ischia, about sixty-two years old; priest. Put to death in Procida, 1 June 1799.

De Marco, Gaetano, born in Naples, 1759; fencing teacher. Put to death in Naples, 29 August 1799.

De Marini, Filippo, born in Naples, 2 May 1778; marquise of Genzano. Put to death in Naples, 1 October 1799.

De Meo, Niccola, born in Naples, 1749; of the Padri Crociferi order. Put to death in Naples, 30 September 1799.

De Renzis, Leopoldo, born in Naples, 1749; baron of Montanaro; infantry colonel. Put to death in Naples, 12 December 1799.

De Simone, Giambattista, born in Naples, 1771. Put to death in Naples, 8 February 1799.

D'Ischia, Vincenzo, born in Gaeta, 6 April 1779; clerk. Put to death in Naples, 7 December 1799.

Doria, Anton Raffaello, native of Genova, born in Cotrone di Calabria, 11 June 1766; lieutenant. Put to death in Naples, 7 December 1799.

Falconieri, Ignazio, born in Lecce, 16 February 1755; priest, oratory/rhetoric professor. Put to death in Naples, 31 October 1799.

Fasulo, Niccola, born in Naples, 11 November 1768; lawyer. Put to death in Naples, 29 August 1799.

Federici, Francesco, born in Naples, 1735; marquise of Pietrastornina; cavalry general. Put to death in Naples, 23 October 1799.

Feola, Francesco, born in Procida, about forty years old; artisan. Put to death in Procida, 1 June 1799.

Fiani, Niccolò, born in Torremaggiore (Foggia), 23 September 1757; bodyguard. Put to death in Naples, 29 August 1799.

Fiorentino, Doctor Andrea, born in Vocariello, about forty-one years old; proprietor. Put to death in Procida, 1 June 1799.

Fiorentino, Niccola, born in Pomarico di Basilicata, 3 April 1755; lawyer, mathematics professor. Put to death in Naples , 12 December 1799.

Granata, Michele, born in Rionero di Basilicata, 25 November 1748; provinciale dei carmelitani, professor in the military academy. Put to death in Naples, 12 December 1799.

Grimaldi, Francesco Antonio, born in Seminara (Reggio Calabria), 1743; cavalier gerosolimitano, infantry colonel. Put to death in Naples, 22 October 1799.

Grossi, Cristoforo, born in Lagonegro (Basilicata), 19 May 1771; medical student. Put to death in Naples, 1 February 1800.

Gualzetti, Giacomo Antonio, born in Naples, 1772; poet. Put to death in Naples, 4 January 1800.

Guardati, Giuseppe, born in Sorrento, 27 February 1765; Benedictine monk of the San Severino order, university professor. Put to death in Naples, 13 November 1799.

Iossa, Raffaele, born in Naples, 1780. Put to death in Naples, 31 October 1799.

Logoteta, Giuseppe, born in Reggio Calabria, 12 October 1758; lawyer. Put to death in Naples, 28 November 1799.

Lubrano, Niccolò, born in Martino, about sixty-six years old; permanent vicar in the parish of Procida. Put to death in Procida, 15 June 1799.

Lupo, Vincenzo, born in Caggiano (Salerno), 15 August 1755; lawyer. Put to death in Naples, 20 August 1799.

Maffei, Melchiorre, born in Naples, 1729; clerk. Put to death in Naples, 23 November 1799.

Magliano, Niccola, born in Naples, 1739; lawyer. Put to death in Naples, 19 November 1799.

Mancini, Gregorio, born in Naples, 1762; lawyer. Put to death in Naples, 3 December 1799.

Manthoné, Gabriele, born in Pescara, 23 October 1764; artillery captain. Put to death in Naples, 24 September 1799.

Marino, Michele (Il Pazzo), born in Naples, 1753; wine merchant. Put to death in Naples, 29 August 1799.

Massa, Oronzio, born in Lecce, 18 August 1760; duke of Galugnano; artillery major. Put to death in Naples, 14 August 1799.

Mastrangelo, Felice, born in Montalbano Ionico, 6 April 1773; medical doctor. Put to death in Naples, 14 October 1799.

Matera, Pasquale, born in Syracuse, 28 September 1768; infantry general. Put to death in Naples, 10 October 1799.

Mattei, Gregorio, born in Montepaone (Catanzaro), 7 June 1761; magistrate. Put to death in Naples, 28 November 1799.

Mauri, Carlo, born in Naples, 1772; marquise of Polvica. Put to death in Naples, 14 December 1799.

Mazzitelli, Andrea, born in Parghelia (Catanzaro), 26 July 1753. Put to death in Naples, 8 February 1800.

Mazzola, Niccola, born in Durazzano (Benevento), 16 February 1742; notary. Put to death in Naples, 18 January 1800.

Montemayor, Raffaele, born in Naples, 1765. Put to death in Naples, 8 February 1800.

Morgera, Gaetano, born in Forio d'Ischia, 4 January 1770; priest. Put to death in Naples, 22 October 1799.

Muscari, Carlo, born in S. Eufemia d'Aspromonte (Reggio Calabria), 18 March 1770; lawyer. Put to death in Naples, 16 March 1800.

Natale, Michele, born in Casapulla (Caserta), 13 August 1751; bishop of Vico Equense. Put to death in Naples, 20 August 1799.

Neri, Nicola, born in Acquaviva Colle Croce, 28 November 1761; doctor. Put to death in Naples, 3 December 1799.

Nicoletti, Pietro, born in Rogliano(Cosenza), 22 January 1769; clerk. Put to death in Naples, 3 December 1799.

Pacifico, Niccola, born in Naples, 22 June 1734; priest, botany professor. Put to death in Naples, 20 August 1799.

Pagano, Domenico Antonio, born in Naples, 1763; lawyer. Put to death in Naples, 8 October 1799.

Pagano, Francesco Mario, born in Brienza (Basilicata), 8 December 1748; lawyer, university professor. Put to death in Naples, 29 October 1799.

Palomba, Niccola, born in Avigliano di Basilicata, 23 October 1746; priest. Put to death in Naples, 14 October 1799.

Palombo, Gian Leonardo, born in Campobasso, 23 July 1749; lawyer. Put to death in Naples, 9 November 1799.

Perla, Domenico, native of Lusciano (Aversa), born in Palermo, 1765; clerk. Put to death in Naples, 6 July 1799.

Piatti, Antonio, born in Trieste, 7 April 1771. Put to death in Naples, 20 August 1799.

Piatti, Domenico, born in Trieste, (?) 1746; banker. Put to death in Naples, 20 August 1799.

Pigliacelli, Giorgio, born in Tossicia (Teramo), February 1751; lawyer. Put to death in Naples, 29 October 1799.

Pignatelli, Ferdinando, born in Naples, 21 September 1769; prince of Strongoli. Put to death in Naples, 30 September 1799.

Pignatelli, Mario, born in Naples, 1773. Put to death in Naples, 30 September 1799.

Pucci, Gaspare, born in Sambuca Zabut (Agrigento), 6 September 1774; clergyman, medical student. Put to death in Naples, 1 February 1800.

Riario, Sforza Giuseppe, born in Naples, 5 May 1778; marquise of Corleto. Put to death in Naples, 22 October 1799.

Ricciardi, Niccola, born in Caserta, 4 April 1776; army official. Put to death in Naples, 4 January 1800.

Romeo, Carlo, born in Guardialfiera (Campobasso), 1755; lawyer. Put to death in Naples, 12 December 1799.

Roselli, Clino, born in Esperia (Caserta), 14 March 1754; engineering professor at the military academy. Put to death in Naples, 28 November 1799.

Rossi, Luigi, born in Montepaone (Catanzaro), 20 January 1773; lawyer. Put to death in Naples, 28 November 1799.

Rossi, Niccola Maria, born in Laurino (Salerno), 6 December 1733; university professor. Put to death in Naples, 8 October 1799.

Rotondo, Prosdocimo, born in Gambatesa (Molise), 14 April 1757; lawyer. Put to death in Naples, 30 September 1799.

Ruggi, Antonio, born in Salerno, 22 April 1755; lawyer. Put to death in Naples, 23 November 1799.

Ruggi, Ferdinando, born in Salerno, 13 May 1760; lieutenant. Put to death in Naples, 7 December 1799.

Ruggiero, Eleuterio, born in Capua, 11 December 1772; infantry captain. Put to death in Naples, 20 January 1800.

Russo, Gaetano, born in Naples 1759; infantry regiment colonel. Put to death in Naples, 3 August 1799.

Russo, Vincenzio, born in Palma Nolana, 16 June 1770; lawyer. Put to death in Naples, 19 November 1799.

Sanfelice de Molino, Luisa, born in Naples, 6 January 1763. Put to death in Naples, 11 September 1800.

Sardelli, Antonio, born in San Vito de' Normanni (Lecce), 18 April 1776; lawyer. Put to death in Naples, 7 December 1799.

Schiano, Onofrio, born in Procida, about sixty-four years old; pharmacist. Put to death in Procida, 1 June 1799.

Schiano, Salvatore, born in Procida, about fifty-three years old; notary. Put to death in Procida, 1 June 1799.

Schipani, Giuseppe; general. Put to death in Ischia, 19 July 1799.

Scialoia, Antonio, born in Procida, about fifty-one years old; priest. Put to death in Procida, 15 June 1799.

Scotti, Marcello Eusebio, born in Naples, 9 July 1742; priest. Put to death in Naples, 4 January 1799.

Serra, Gennaro, born in Portici (Naples), 30 October 1772; duke of Cassano. Put to death in Naples, 20 August 1799.

Sieyes, Giuseppe, born in Naples, 1763; shopkeeper, vice-consul of France. Put to death in Naples, 24 September 1799.

Spanò, Agamennone; general. Put to death in Ischia, 19 July 1799.

Tocco, Antonio, born in Naples, 1772; lawyer. Put to death in Naples, 14 October 1799.

Tramaglia, Antonio, born in Naples, 1771; lawyer. Put to death in Naples, 7 July 1799.

Troisi, Domenico Vincenzo, born in Rocca Gorga (Frosinone), 23 December 1749; priest of the Vergini di Napoli, university professor. Put to death in Naples, 24 October 1799.

Varanese, Giovanni, born in Monacilioni (Campobasso), 13 July 1777; medical student. Put to death in Naples, 22 October 1799.

Vernaud, Luigi, son of Francesco, lord of Ponza. Put to death in Ponza, 15 June 1799.

Vitaliani, Giovanni Andrea, born in Portolongone (Toscana), 23 July 1761; watchmaker. Put to death in Naples, 20 July 1799.

Added to this list is Captain Antonio Velasco, who threw himself out of the window of the inquiring magistrate's office.

Bibliography

Primary Sources

Most of the papers of Vincenzo Cuoco are in the Biblioteca Nazionale Vittorio Emanuele III in Naples. Filippo Sabetti consulted them in the summer of 2012; most papers of interest to this project are also available in the various editions listed here.

Biscardi, Luigi, and Rosella Folino Gallo, eds. 2012. *Scritti sulla Istruzione Pubblica*, by Vincenzo Cuoco. Bari: Laterza.

Bravo, Anna, ed. 1975. *Saggio Storico sulla Rivoluzione Napoletana*, by Vincenzo Cuoco, 2nd ed. (1806). Turin: Unione Tipografica Editrice.

Conte, Domenico, and Maurizio Martirano, eds. 2007. *Epistolario (1790–1817)*, by Vincenzo Cuoco. Bari: Laterza.

Cortese, Nino, ed. 1926. *Saggio Storico sulla Rivoluzione Napoletana del 1799*, by Vincenzo Cuoco, 2nd ed. (1806). Florence: Vallecchi Editore.

Cortese, Nino, and F. Nicolini, eds. 1924. *Scritti vari*, by Vincenzo Cuoco. 2 vols. Bari: Laterza.

De Francesco, Antonino, ed. 1998. *Saggio Storico sulla Rivoluzione di Napoli*, by Vincenzo Cuoco, 1st ed. (1801). Manduria: Lacaita Editore.

De Francesco, Antonino, and Annalisa Andreoni, eds. 2006. *Platone in Italia*, by Vincenzo Cuoco. Bari: Laterza.

De Francesco, Antonino, and Luigi Biscardi, eds. 2009. *Scritti di Statistica e di Pubblica Amministrazione*, by Vincenzo Cuoco. Bari: Laterza.

Di Maso, Nunzia, ed. 2007. *Scritti Politico-Giuridici*, by Vincenzo Cuoco. Bari: Laterza.

Nicolini, Fausto, ed. 1913. *Saggio Storico sulla Rivoluzione di Napoli*, by Vincenzo Cuoco. 2nd ed. (1806). Bari: Laterza.

—, ed. 1924. *Platone in Italia*, by Vincenzo Cuoco. Bari: Laterza.

Rao, Anna Maria, and Maïté Bouyssy, eds. 2001. *Histoire de la Révolution de Naples*, by Vincenzo Cuoco. Translated by Bertrand Barère (1807). Naples: Vivarium.

Tessitore, Fulvio, ed. 1988.*Saggio Storico sulla Rivoluzione di Napoli,* by Vincenzo Cuoco. Reprint of 1801 edition. Naples: Itinerario.

—, ed. 2011. *Pagine Giornalistiche,* by Vincenzo Cuoco. Bari: Laterza.

Villani, Pasquale, ed. 1976. *Saggio Storico sulla rivoluzioine napoletana del 1799,* by Vincenzo Cuoco. 2nd ed. (1806). Bari: Laterza.

—, ed. [1966] 2004. *Saggio Storico sulla rivoluzione napoletana del 1799,* by Vincenzo Cuoco, 2nd ed. (1806). Milan: BUR classici.

Secondary Sources

Acton, Harold. 1956. *The Bourbons of Naples (1734–1825).* London: Methuen.

Ajello, Aurelio, and Mario D'Addio, eds. 1986. *Bernardo Tanucci. Statista Letterato Giurista.* Atti del convegno internazionale di studi per il secondo centenario 1783–1983. 2 vols. Naples: Jovene Editore.

Albert, Mathias, David Jacobson, and Yosef Lapid, eds. 2001. *Identities, Borders, Orders: Rethinking International Relations Theory.* Minneapolis: University of Minnesota Press.

Alianelli, Niccola. 1873. *Delle consuetudini e degli Statuti municipali delle provincie napoletane.* Naples: Stabilimento Tipografico Rocco.

Aligica, Paul Dragos, and Peter J. Boettke. 2009. *Challenging Institutional Analysis and Development: The Bloomington School.* New York: Routledge.

Anderson, Benedict. 2006. *Imagined Communities.* 2nd ed. London: Verso.

Aristotle. 1962. *Politics.* Edited and translated by Ernest Barker. New York: Oxford University Press.

Astarita, Tommaso. 1992. *The Continuity of Feudal Power: The Caracciolo of Brienza in Spanish Naples.* New York: Cambridge University Press.

—. 1999. *Village Justice, Community, Family and Popular Culture in Early Modern Italy.* Baltimore: The Johns Hopkins University Press.

—, ed. 2013. *A Companion to Early Modern Naples.* Boston: Brill.

Balbi, Giovanna Petti, and Giovanni Vitolo, eds. 2007. *Linguaggi e Pratiche del Potere.* Salerno: Laveglia Editore.

Bardazzi, Giovanni. 2003. "Sineddoche. Strutture del pensiero in Manzoni analista della Rivoluzione." In Giovanni Bardazzi and Alain Grosrichard, eds., *Dénouement des lumières et invention romantique,* 87–113. Geneva: Droz.

Baretti, Joseph. 1760. *A Dictionary of the English and Italian Languages.* London: Richardson.

Battaglia, Felice. 1925. *L'Opera di Vincenzo Cuoco e la formazione dello spirito nazionale in Italia.* Florence: R. Bemporad and Figlio.

Battaglini, Mario. 1994. *Mario Pagano e il progetto di Costituzione della Repubblica napoletana.* Rome: Archivio Guido Izzi.

Benedetti, Anna. 1974. *Le traduzioni italiane da Walter Scott e i loro anglicismi.* Florence: Olschki.

Bianchini, Lodovico. [1839] 1983. *Della storia delle finanze del Regno di Napoli.* Bologna: Arnaldo Forni Editore.

Biscardi, Luigi. 1962. "Manzoni e Cuoco." In Atti del V Congresso nazionale di studi manzoniani. Lecco, 7/10 ottobre 1961, 47–51. Lecco: Annoni, 1962.

Biscardi, Luigi, and Antonino De Francesco, eds. 2002. *Vincenzo Cuoco nella cultura di due secoli.* Bari: Laterza.

Bronzini, Giovanni B. 2002. "L'albero della libertá e l'albero della fecondità." In Antonio Cestaro, ed., *La rivoluzione napoletana del 1799 nelle province in relazione alle vicende storiche dell'Italia giacobina e napoleonica (1799–1815),* 21–34. Atti del convegno di Maratea 15–17 novembre 1999. Venosa: Edizioni Osanna.

Bulgarelli Lukacs, Alessandra. 2011. "La gestione delle risorse collettive nel regno di Napoli in età moderna: un percorso comparativo." In Guido Alfani and Riccardo Rao, eds., *La gestione delle risorse collettive. Italia settentrionale secoli XII–XVIII,* 227–245. Milan: FrancoAngeli Editore.

Burke, Edmund. 1967. *Reflections on the Revolution in France.* Edited by A.J. Grieve. London: Dent.

Caesar, Michael, and Franco D'Intino, eds. *Zibaldone* by Giacomo Leopardi. New York: Farrar, Straus and Giroux, 2013.

Calabria, Antonio. 1991. *The Cost of Empire: The Finances of the Kingdom of Naples in the Time of Spanish Rule.* New York: Cambridge University Press.

Cantimori, Delio. 1956. *Giacobini Italiani.* 2 vols. Bari: Laterza.

Carpi, Umberto. 1992. "Appunti su Ideologia postrivoluzionaria e riflessione storiografica dopo il triennio giacobino." *Rivista italiana di Studi Napoleonici* 39, nos. 1–2: 41–128.

Castiglione, Caroline. 2005. *Patrons and Adversaries: Nobles and Villagers in Italian Politics 1640–1760.* New York: Cambridge University Press.

Cerere, Domenico. 2011. "Suppliche, resistenze, protesta popolare. Le forme della lotta politica nella Calabria del Settecento." *Quaderni Storici* 46, no. 138: 765–96.

Cestaro, Antonio, ed., 2002. *La rivoluzione napoletana del 1799 nelle provincie in relazione alla vicende storiche dell'Italia giacobina e napoleonica (1799–1815).* Atti del convegno di Maratea (Proceedings of the Conference of the Centennial of the Revolution), Maratea, 15–17 November 1999. Venosa: Edizioni Osanna.

Cicero, Marcus Tullius. 1957. *Tusculanes desputations.* Stuttgart: Teubner.

Colletta, Pietro. [1838] 1858. *History of the Kingdom of Naples 1734–1825*. Vol. 1. London: Hamilton Adams.

Contarini, Gasparo. 1543. *De magistratibus et republica Venetorum.* Translation, 1559, *The Commonwealth and Government of Venice.* Translated by Lewes Lewkenor. London: John Windet.

Corona, Gabriella. 2004. "Declino dei Commons ed equilibri ambientali. Il caso italiano tra otto e novecento." *Societá e storia* 104: 357–83.

Corona, Gabriella. 2010. "The Decline of the Commons and the Environmental Balance in Early Modern Italy." In Marco Armiero and Marcus Hall, eds., *Nature and History in Modern Italy*, 89–107. Athens: Ohio University Press.

Cospito, Giuseppe. 1999. "Il giovane Manzoni, Vico e la Milano napoleonica (1799–1805)." *Annali Manzoniani*, n.s., 3: 21–50.

Craiutu, Aurelian. 2012. *A Virtue for Courageous Minds: Moderation in French Political Thought, 1748–1830*. Princeton: Princeton University Press.

Croce, Benedetto. [1896] 1961. *La Rivoluzione napoletana del 1799*. Bari: Laterza.

—. 1912. *La rivoluzione napoletana del 1799. Biografie, Racconti, Ricerche.* 3rd ed. Bari: Laterza.

—. [1925] 1970. *History of the Kingdom of Naples.* Chicago: University of Chicago Press.

—. [1943] 1989. "La vita di un rivoluzionario. Carlo Lauberg." In *Vite di Avventure di Fede e di Passione*, 365–437. Edited by G. Galasso. Milan: Adelphi Edizioni.

D'Alessio, Carlo. 1960. *Un giudizio di Vincenzo Cuoco sul Monti.* Florence: Sansoni.

Dainotto, Roberto M. 2011. "With '*Plato in Italy*': The Value of Literary Fiction in Napoleonic Italy." *Modern Language Quarterly* 73: 399–418.

Dandalet, Thomas J., and John A. Marino, eds. 2007. *Spain in Italy: Politics, Society and Religion 1500–1700*. Boston: Brill.

Dardi, Andrea. 1995. "La forza delle parole." In *Margine a un libro recente su lingua e rivoluzione.* Florence: Stabilimento Grafico Commerciale.

Davis, John A. 1991. "1799. The 'Santafede' and the Crisis of the ancien régime in Southern Italy." In J.A. Davis and Paul Ginsborg, eds., *Society and Politics in the Age of the Risorgimento: Essays in Honor of Denis Mack Smith*, 1–25. New York: Cambridge University Press.

—. 2006. *Naples and Napoleon: Southern Italy and the European Revolutions.* Oxford: Oxford University Press.

— 2009. Introduction to *The History of the Kingdom of Naples*, by Pietro Colletta, vol.1, ix–xxxiv. London: I.B. Tauris.

De Felice, Renzo. 1990. *Il Triennio Giacobino in Italia (1796–1799)*. Rome: Bonacci.

De Francesco, Antonino. 2000. "How Not to Finish a Revolution." In G. Imbruglia, ed., *Naples in the Eighteenth Century: The Birth and Death of a Nation State*, 167–82. New York: Cambridge University Press.

—. 2011. *L'Italia di Bonaparte. Politica, statualità e nazione della penisola tra due rivoluzioni, 1796–1821*. Turin: UTET.

—. 2013. *The Antiquity of the Italian Nation: The Cultural Origins of a Political Myth in Modern Italy, 1796–1943*. Oxford: Oxford University Press.

De Lolme, Jean Louis. [1771] 2007. *The Constitution of England*. Edited by David Lieberman. Indianapolis: Liberty Fund.

De Maistre, Joseph. 1974. *Considerations on France*. Translated by Richard A. Lebrun. Montreal: McGill-Queen's University Press.

Di Maso, Nunzia. 2005. *Il repubblicanesimo di Vincenzo Cuoco. A partire da Machiavelli*. Florence: Centro Editoriale Toscano.

Eco, Umberto.2003. *Mouse or Rat: Translation as Negotiation*. London: Weidenfeld and Nicolson.

Ellero, Diego. 2010. *Manzoni. La politica le parole*. Milan: Casa del Manzoni.

Elliott, J.H. 2012. *History in the Making*. New Haven: Yale University Press.

Felice, Domenico. 1995. "Immagini dell'Italia politica moderna nell'*Esprit des Lois* di Montesquieu." *Pensiero Politico* 28, no. 2: 270–82.

Ferrone, Vincenzo. 2012. *The Politics of Enlightenment: Constitutionalism, Republicanism, and the Rights of Man in Gaetano Filangieri*. Translated by Sophus A. Reinert. New York: Anthem Press.

Filangieri, Gaetano. 2004. *La scienza della legislazione*. 7 vols. Edited by Vincenzo Ferrone et al. Venice: Marsilio.

Forgacs, David, and Matthew Reynolds, eds. 1997. *The Betrothed and History of the Column of Infamy*. London: Dent, Everyman.

Gallarti Scotti, Tommaso. 1959. "Due maestri del Manzoni." *Corriere della Sera*, 27 May.

Galasso, Giuseppe. 1989. *La filosofia in soccorso de' governi. La cultura napoletana dei Settecento*. Naples: Guida Editore.

Galanti, Giuseppe Maria. 1806. *Testamento forense*. Venice: Presso Antonio Graziosi.

Genuardi, Luigi. 1911. *Terre comuni ed Usi civici in Sicilia prima dell'abolizione della Fedualitá*. Palermo: Tip. Boccone del Povero.

Genovesi, Antonio [1765–67] 2005. *Delle lezioni di commercio o sia di Economia Civile con Elementi del Commercio*. Edited by Maria Luisa Perna. Naples: Istituto Italiano per gli Studi Filosofici.

Gentilcore, David. 2013. "Tempi si calamitosi: Epidemic Disease and Public Health." In T. Astarita, ed., *A Companion to Early Modern Naples*, 281–307. Boston: Brill.

Germino, Dante. 1972. *Modern Western Political Thought: Machiavelli to Marx.* Chicago: Rand and McNally.

Giannone, Pietro. 1978. *Istoria civile del regno di Napoli.* Edited by Sergio Bertelli. Turin: Einaudi.

Giarrizzo, Giuseppe. 1981. "La storiografia meridionale del Settecento." In *Vico, la politica e la storia,* 176–239. Naples: Guida Editori.

—. 1994. *Massoneria e Illuminismo nell'Europa del Settecento.* Padua: Marsilio.

Gibbons, David. 2011. "Conceding the Point: Leopardi's Use of Concession in the *Zibaldone.*" *Rivista Internazionale di Studi Leopardiani* 7: 109–28.

—. Forthcoming. "'Mob, Multitude or Populace?' Le voci dell'insurrezione nelle prime traduzioni anglofone dei *Promessi sposi.*" In *Milano, capitale culturale 1796–1898, Atti del convegno, Università degli studi di Milano / casa del Manzoni* (Proceedings of the conference held at Manzoni House, University of Milan), 16–17 November 2011.

Gil-Bardaji, Anna, Pilar Orero, and Sara Rovira-Esteva. 2012. *Translation Peripheries: Paratextual Elements in Translation.* Bern: Peter Lang.

Gleason, Elisabeth. 1993. *Gasparo Contarini, Venice, Rome and Reform.* Berkeley: University of California Press.

Goldstone, Jack. 2008. "Revolution." In Todd Landman and Nick Robinson, eds., *The Sage Handbook of Comparative Politics,* 319–47. Los Angeles: Sage.

Grafton, Anthony. 1997. *The Footnote: A Curious History.* London: Faber and Faber.

Gramsci, Antonio. 1966. *Il Risorgimento.* Turin: Einaudi.

Grossi, Paolo. 1981. *An Alternative to Private Property: Collective Property in the Juridical Consciousness of the Nineteenth Century.* Translated by Lydia Cochrane. Chicago: University of Chicago Press.

Gutteridge, H.C., ed. 1903. *Nelson and the Neapolitan Jacobins: Documents Relating to the Suppression of the Jacobin Revolution at Naples June 1799.* London: Navy Records Society.

Habermas, Jürgen. 1989. *The Structural Transformation of the Public Sphere: An Inquiry into a Category of Bourgeois Society.* Translated by Thomas Burger with the assistance of Frederick Lawrence. Cambridge: Polity.

Haddock, Bruce. 1986. *Vico's Political Thought.* Swansea: Mortlake Press.

—. 1996. "Michael Oakeshott: Rationalism in Politics." In Murray Forsyth and Maurice Keens-Soper, eds., *The Political Classics: Green to Dworkin,* 100–20. Oxford: Oxford University Press.

—. 2000. "State, Nation and Risorgimento." In Gino Bedani and Bruce Haddock, eds., *The Politics of Italian National Identity,* 11–49. Cardiff: University of Wales Press.

—. 2005. *A History of Political Thought: 1789 to the Present.* Cambridge: Polity.

Hamilton, Alexander, John Jay, and James Madison. [1788] n.d. *The Federalist.* Edited by Edward M. Earle. New York: Modern Library.

Headley, Thomas. 1997. *Tommaso Campanella and the Transformation of the World.* Princeton: Princeton University Press.

Hoffman, Philip T. 1996. *Growth in a Traditional Society: The French Countryside 1450–1815.* Princeton: Princeton University Press.

Imbruglia, Girolamo, ed. 2000. *Naples in the Eighteenth Century.* New York: Cambridge University Press.

Klosko, George. 2003. *Jacobins and Utopians: The Political Theory of Fundamental Moral Reforms.* Notre Dame, IN: University of Notre Dame Press.

Knight, Jack, and James Johnson. 2011. *The Priority of Democracy: Political Consequences of Pragmatism.* Princeton: Princeton University Press.

Kukathas, Chandran. [1989] 1990. *Hayek and Modern Liberalism.* Oxford: Clarendon.

Laura, Anna, and Giulio Lepschy. 2008. "Punteggiatura e linguaggio." In Bice Mortara Garavelli, ed., *Storia della punteggiatura in Europa,* 3–24. Rome-Bari: Laterza.

Lennard, John. [1991] 2003. *But I Digress: The Exploitation of Parentheses in English Printed Verse.* Oxford: Clarendon.

Leri, Clara. 2002. "Manzoni e Scott." In *Manzoni e la "littérature universelle,"* 59–79. Milan: Centro Nazionale Studi Manzoniani.

Leso, Erasmo. 1991. *Lingua e rivoluzione. Ricerche sul vocabolario politico italiano del triennio rivoluzionario 1796–1799.* Venice: Istituto veneto di scienze lettere ed arti.

Machiavelli, Niccolò. 1960. *Il Principe e Discorsi.* Edited by Sergio Bertelli. Milan: Feltrinelli.

—. 1961. *The Prince.* Edited by George Bull. Harmondsworth: Penguin.

—. 1965. "The Art of War." In *Machiavelli. The Chief Works and Others.* Translated by Allan Gilbert, 561–725. Durham, NC: Duke University Press.

—. 1965. "The History of Florence." In *Machiavelli: The Chief Works and Others.* Translated by Allan Gilbert, 1025–435. Durham, NC: Duke University Press.

—. 1979. "The Art of War." In *The Portable Machiavelli.* Translated and edited by Peter Bondanella and Mark Musa. New York: Penguin.

—. 1995. *The Prince.* Edited and translated by David Wootton. Indianapolis: Hackett.

—. 2003. *The Discourses.* Edited by Bernard R. Crick. Translated by Leslie J. Walker. New York: Penguin.

Manzoni, Alessandro. 1995. *I promessi sposi; Storia della colonna infame.* Edited by Angelo Stella and Cesare Ripossi. Turin: Einaudi-Gallimard.

Marino, John A. 2007. "The Rural World in Italy under Spanish Rule." In T. Dandelet and J.A. Marino, eds., *Spain in Italy: Politics, Society and Religion 1500–1700,* 405–31. Boston: Brill.

—. 2011. *Becoming Neapolitan: Citizen Culture in Baroque Naples*. Baltimore: The Johns Hopkins University Press.

Marshall, David L. 2010. *Vico and the Transformation of Rhetoric in Early Modern Europe*. New York: Cambridge University Press.

McAdam, Doug, Sidney Tarrow, and Charles Tilly. 2001. *Dynamics of Contention*. New York: Cambridge University Press.

McCormick, John P. 2011. *Machiavellian Democracy*. New York: Cambridge University Press.

Muir, Edward. 2000. "'Was There Republicanism in the Renaissance Republics?' Venice after Agnadello." In John Martin and Dennis Romano, eds., *Venice Reconsidered: The History and Civilization of an Italian City State, 1297–1797*, 137–67. Baltimore: The Johns Hopkins University Press.

Musella, Silvana Guida. 2012. "The Business Organization of the Bourbon Factories: Matercraftsmen, Crafts and Families in the Capidimonte Porcelain Works and the Royal Factory at San Leucio." *California Italian Studies* 3, no. 1: 1–31.

Musi, Aurelio. 2007a. "The Kingdom of Naples in the Spanish Imperial System." In T. J. Dandelet and J. Marino, eds., *Spain in Italy. Politics, Society and Religion 500–1700*, 73–97. Boston: Brill.

—. 2007b. "Italy." In Peter Bickle, ed., *Resistance, Representation and Community*, 219–319. Oxford: Clarendon Press.

Montesquieu, Charles Louis de Secondast. [1748] 1989. *The Spirit of the Laws*. Edited by Anne M. Choler, B. C. Miller, and H.S. Stone. New York: Cambridge University Press.

Naddeo, Barbara Ann. 2011. *Vico and Naples: The Urban Origins of Modern Social Theory*. Ithaca, NY: Cornell University Press.

Nissan, Ephraim. 2001. "Can You Measure Circumstantial Evidence? The Background of Probative Formalism of Law." *Information & Communications Technology Law* 10, no. 2: 231–45.

Oakeshott, Michael. 1962. *Rationalism in Politics and Other Essays*. London: Methuen.

Ostrom, Elinor. 1990. *Governing the Commons: The Evolution of Institutions for Collective Action*. New York: Cambridge University Press.

Ostrom, Vincent. 2007. *The Political Theory of a Compound Republic: Designing the American Experiment*. 3rd ed. with Barbara Allen. Lanham: Lexington Books.

Pagden, Anthony. 1994. "Francesco Mario Pagano's 'Republic of Virtue': Naples 1799." In Biancamaria Fontana, ed., *The Invention of the Modern Republic*, 139–53. London: Cambridge University Press.

Palmieri, S. 1998. "'Le abominevoli carte formate in tempo dell'abattuta anarchia.' La tradizione documentaria della Repubblica napoletana." *Archivio storico per le province napoletane* 116: 155–73.

Parigi, Maristella. 1977. "Per una rilettura del 'Saggio Storico sulla rivoluzione Napoletana del 1799' di Vincenzo Cuoco." *Archivio Storico Italiano* 135, nos. 491–492: 217–56.

Placanica, Augusto. 1970. *La Cassa Sacra e i beni della Chiesa nella Calabria del Settecento.* Naples: Biblioteca degli Annali di storia economica e sociale.

Pensiero Politico. 1995. "Symposium on the Work of Francesco Mario Pagano." 28 January–April. With essays by Eluggero Pii, Laura Salvetti Firpo, Raffaele Ajello, Arturo Colombo, and Fernanda Mazzanti Pepe.

Petraccone, Claudio. 1984."Il giacobinismo napoletano." In M.L. Salvadori and N. Tranfaglia, eds., *Il Modello politico giacobinismo e le rivoluzioni,* 132–53. Florence: La Nuova Italia.

Pincus, Steve. 2009. *1688: The First Modern Revolution.* New Haven: Yale University Press.

Pocock, J.G.A. 1982. "The Political Economy of Burke's Analysis of the French Revolution." *The Historical Journal* 25, no. 2: 331–49.

Possumato, Tommasino. 1999. *Vincenzo Cuoco e il giovane Manzoni. Saggio storico-letterario.* Campobasso: Enne.

Prendergast, Christopher. 2003 *For the People by the People? Eugène Sue's "Les Mystères de Paris": A Hypothesis in the Sociology of Literature.* Oxford: Legenda.

Rahe, Paul A. 2009. *Soft Despotism, Democracy's Drift: Montesquieu, Rousseau, Tocqueville and the Modern Prospect.* New Haven: Yale University Press.

—. 2012. "Review of Alexis de Tocqueville's *The Ancien Regime and the French Revolution* ed. Jon Elster." *H-France Review* 12, no. 53: 1–5.

Rao, Anna Maria. 1986. "La repubblica napoletana del 1799." In G. Galasso and R. Romeo, eds., *Storia del Mezzogiorno.* Vol. 4: *Il regno dagli Angioini ai Borboni,* 470–539. Naples: Edizioni del Sole.

—. 1999. "The Neapolitan Revolution of 1799." *Journal of Modern Italian Studies* 4, no. 3: 358–69.

—. 2002. "La rivoluzione napoletana del 1799 nel quadro del triennio repubblicano italiano." In Antonio Cestaro, ed., *La rivoluzione napoletana del 1799 nelle province in relazione alle vicende storiche dell'Italia giacobina e napoleonica (1799–1815),* 35–64. Venosa: Edizioni Osanna.

Rao, Anna Maria. 2012a. "The Neapolitan Revolution of 1799." *Journal of Modern Italian Studies* 4, no. 3: 358–69.

Rao, Anna Maria. 2012b. "The Feudal Question in the Kingdom of Naples." In Micheal Broers, Peter Hicks, and Augustin Guimera, eds., *The Napoleonic Empire and the New European Political Culture,* 227–40. London: Palgrave Macmillan.

Rao, Anna Maria, and Pasquale Villani, eds. 1995. *Napoli 1799–1815. Dalla Repubblica alla Monarchia amministrativa.* Naples: Edizioni del Sole.

Renan, Ernest. 1882. *Qu'est-ce qu'une nation? Conférence faite en Sorbonne, le 11 mars 1882*. 2nd ed. Paris: Calmann Levy.

Robertson, John. 2005. *The Case for the Enlightenment: Scotland and Naples 1680–1760*. New York: Cambridge University Press.

Romano, Michele. 1904. *Ricerche su Vincenzo Cuoco*. Isernia: L. Colitti and Figli.

Rousseau, Jean-Jacques. 1968. *The Social Contract*. Translated by Maurice Cranston. Harmondsworh: Penguin Books.

Rudé, Georges. 1964. *The Crowd in History, 1730–1848*. New York: Wiley.

Sabetti, Filippo. 2011a. "Italian Political Thought." In George T. Kurian, ed., *International Encyclopedia of Political Science*, 1–8. Washington, DC: CQ Press.

–. 2011b. Review of Paul Rahe, *Montesquieu and the Logic of Liberty* and *Soft Despotism, Democracy's Drift. Perspectives on Politics* 9 (December): 946–9.

–. 2012. "Public Happiness as the Wealth of Nations: The Rise of Political Economy in Naples in a Comparative Perspective." *California Italian Studies* 3, no. 1: 1–31.

Salvadori, M.L., and N. Tranfaglia. 1984. *Il modello politico giacobino e le rivoluzioni*. Florence: La Nuova Italia.

Salvioli, Giuseppe. 1909. "L'origine degli usi civici in Sicilia." *Rivista Italiana di Sociologia* 13: 154–79.

Skocpol, Theda. 1979. *States and Social Revolutions*. New York: Cambridge University Press.

Sidney, Algernon. [1698] 1996. *Discourses Concerning Government*. Edited by Thomas G. West. Indianapolis: Liberty Fund.

Solari, Giole. [1934] 1963. *Studi su Francesco Mario Pagano*. Edited by Luigi Firpo. Turin: Edizioni Giappichelli.

Spagnoletti, Angeloantonio. 1994. "Le istituzioni statali e il potere locale nel regno di Napli (1730-1780)." *Archivio storico per le province napoletane* 84: 7–28.

Spriano, Enzo. [1986] 2013. *Il Resto del Niente*. Milan: Oscar Mondadori.

Stella, Angelo. 1999. "La parola della rivoluzione." In *Il piano di Lucia. Manzoni e altre voci lombarde*, 91–107. Florence: Cesati.

Torquato Tasso. [1580] 1624. *Jerusalem Delivered / Gerusalemme Liberata*. Translated by Edward Fairfax. London: Printed by Iohn Bill; first published in 1580 in Parma, Italy.

Tessitore, Fulvio. [1970] 1995. "Cuoco tra Illuminismo e Storicismo." In *Contributi alla Storia e alla Teoria dello Storicismo*, 247–89. Rome: Edizioni di Storia e Letteratura.

—. 1982. "Cuoco e Galanti." *Archivio storico per le province napoletane* 21 (3rd series): 257–80.

—. 1988. "Introduzione: Il 'Saggio Storico' di V. Cuoco dalla prima alla seconda edizione." In *Saggio storico sulla rivoluzione di Napoli (1801)*, by Vincenzo Cuoco, vii–xxxiv. Naples: Itinerario.

—. 2008."Il 'ritorno di Cuoco." *Archivio della Storia della Cultura* 21: 227–32.

Themelly, Mario. 1990. "Letteratura e politica nell'etá napoleonica. Il 'Platone in Italia'di Vincenzo Cuoco." *Belfagor* 45: 125–56.

Tocqueville, Alexis de. [1835] 2010. *Democracy in America.* 2 vols. Edited by Edoardo Nolla. Translated by James Schleifer. Indianapolis: Liberty Fund.

—. [1856] 2008. *The Ancien Regime and the French Revolution.* Translated by Gerald Bevan. London: Penguin Books.

Tournier, Maurice. 1975. "Le mot 'peuple' en 1848: désignant social ou instrument politique?" *Romantisme* 9: 6–20.

Trifone, Romualdo. 1974. "Sintesi storica degli usi civici nell'Italia meridionale e nelle Isole." *Rivista di Economia Agraria* 2: 287–316.

Ventura, Pietro. 2007. "Il linguaggio della cittadinanza a Napoli tra ritualità civica, amministrazione e pratica politica (secoli XV–XVII)." In Giovanna P. Balbi and Giovanni Vitolo, eds., *Linguaggi e pratiche del Potere.Genova e il Regno di Napoli tra Medioevo ed Eta Moderna,* 347–75. Salerno: Laveglia Editore.

Venturi, Franco. 1962. "Francesco Mario Pagano. Progetto di costituzione della Repubblica Napoletana presentato al governo provvisorio dal Comitato di Legislazione." *Riformatori Napoletani.* Milan: R. Ricciardi Editore.

Venuti, Lawrence. 1995. *The Translator's Invisibility: A History of Translation.* New York: Routledge.

Vico, Giambattista. 1971. *Opere filosofiche.* Edited by Nicola Badaloni. Florence: Sansoni.

Villani, Pasquale. [1966] 2004. Introduction to *Saggio Storico sulla Rivoluzione di Napoli,* by Vincenzo Cuoco (1806), 5–36. Milan: BUR Rizzoli.

—. 1976. Introduction to *Saggio Storico sulla Rivoluzione Napoletana del 1979,* by Vincenzo Cuoco, v–xlix. Bari: Laterza.

Villari, Rosario. 2012. *Un sogno di libertà. Napoli nel declino di un impero.* Milan: Mondadori.

Visceglia, Maria Antonietta. 1970–71. "Genesi e fortuna di una interpretazione storiografica: la Rivoluzione Napoletana del 1799 come 'Rivoluzione passiva.'" *Annali Facolta di Magistero,* Università di Lecce 1: 163–209.

Vocabolario degli Accademici della Crusca. 1729–38. 6 vols. 4th ed. Florence: Accademia della Crusca.

Wastl-Walter, Doris, ed. 2011. *The Ashgate Research Companion to Border Studies.* Farnham, UK: Ashgate.

Zapperi, Roberto. 1965. "Edmund Burke in Italia." *Cahiers Vilfredo Pareto* 3, no. 7/8: 5–62.

Index

THE LORENZO DA PONTE ITALIAN LIBRARY

General Editors: Luigi Ballerini and Massimo Ciavolella

Pellegrino Artusi, *Science in the Kitchen and the Art of Eating Well* (2003). Edited and translated by Luigi Ballerini and Murtha Baca

Lauro Martines, *An Italian Renaissance Sextet: Six Tales in Historical Context* (2004). Translated by Murtha Baca

Aretino's Dialogues (2005). Translated by Margaret Rosenthal and Raymond Rosenthal

Aldo Palazzeschi, *A Tournament of Misfits: Tall Tales and Short* (2005). Translated by Nicolas J. Perella

Carlo Cattaneo, *Civilization and Democracy: The Salvemini Anthology of Cattaneo's Writings* (2006). Edited and introduced by Carlo G. Lacaita and Filippo Sabetti. Translated by David Gibbons

Benedetto Croce, *Breviary of Aesthetics: Four Lectures* (2007). Translated by Hiroko Fudemoto; Introduction by Remo Bodei

Antonio Pigafetta, *First Voyage around the World (1519–1522): An Account of Magellan's Expedition* (2007). Edited and translated by Theodore J. Cachey Jr.

Raffaello Borghini, *Il Riposo* (2008). Translated by Lloyd H. Ellis Jr.

Paolo Mantegazza, *Physiology of Love and Other Writings* (2008). Edited and translated by Nicoletta Pireddu

Renaissance Comedy: The Italian Masters (2008). Edited and translated by Donald Beecher

Cesare Beccaria, *On Crimes and Punishments and Other Writings* (2008). Edited by Aaron Thomas; Translated by Aaron Thomas and Jeremy Parzen; Foreword by Bryan Stevenson; Introduction by Alberto Burgio

Leone Ebreo, *Dialogues of Love* (2009). Edited and translated by Cosmos Damian Bacich and Rossella Pescatori

Boccaccio's Expositions on Dante's Comedy (2009). Translated by Michael Papio

My Muse Will Have a Story to Paint: Selected Prose of Ludovico Ariosto (2010). Translated with an Introduction by Dennis Looney

The Opera of Bartolomeo Scappi (1570): L'arte et prudenza d'un maestro Cuoco (The Art and Craft of a Master Cook) (2011). Translated with commentary by Terence Scully

Pirandello's Theatre of Living Masks: New Translations of Six Major Plays (2011). Translated by Umberto Mariani and Alice Gladstone Mariani

From Kant to Croce: Modern Philosophy in Italy, 1800–1950 (2012). Edited and translated with an introduction by Brian P. Copenhaver and Rebecca Copenhaver

Giovan Francesco Straparola, *The Pleasant Nights*, Volume 2 (2012). Edited with an Introduction by Donald Beecher

Giovan Francesco Straparola, *The Pleasant Nights*, Volume 1 (2012). Edited with an Introduction by Donald Beecher

Giovanni Botero, *On the Causes of the Greatness and Magnificence of Cities* (2012). Translated and with an introduction by Geoffrey W. Symcox

John Florio, *A Worlde of Wordes* (2013). A Critical Edition with an Introduction by Hermann W. Haller

Giordano Bruno, *On the Heroic Frenzies* (2013). A Translation of *De gli eroici furori* by Ingrid D. Rowland; Text edited by Eugenio Canone

Alvise Cornaro, *Writings on the Sober Life: The Art and Grace of Living Long* (2014). Translated by Hiroko Fudemoto; Introduction by Marisa Milani; Foreword by Greg Critser

Dante Aligheri, *Dante's Lyric Poetry: Poems of Youth and of the Vita Nuova* (1283–1292) (2014). Edited, with a general introduction and introductory essays, by Teodolinda Barolini. With new verse translations by Richard Lansing. Commentary translated into English by Andrew Frisardi

Vincenzo Cuoco, *Historical Essay on the Neapolitan Revolution of 1799* (2014). Edited and Introduced by Bruce Haddock and Filippo Sabetti. Translated by David Gibbons

www.ingramcontent.com/pod-product-compliance
Lightning Source LLC
LaVergne TN
LVHW041112090826
844660LV00061B/717/J
* 9 7 8 1 4 4 2 6 4 9 4 5 3 *